THE

NEW YORK

SOCIAL SCIENCE REVIEW:

DEVOTED TO

POLITICAL ECONOMY AND STATISTICS.

EDITED BY

ALEX. DELMAR, AND SIMON STERN.

VOLUME I.—COMPLETE

FOR THE YEAR 1865.

NEW YORK:
PUBLISHED FOR THE PROPRIETORS,
At No. 84 Nassau Street.
LONDON: TRÜBNER & CO.
1866.

ERRATA TO VOL. I.

Page 41, line 17—Words, "from whose works we have just quoted" should be expunged.
" 48, " 1—Word, "desirable" should read "derivable."
" 99, " 18—Insert "to" in place of "and."
" 103, " 30—Insert "career" in place of "history."
" 109, " 21—After "Islander" insert "is a physical monstrosity."
" 131—For table on this page insert the following, which differs from it in calculating the "reserve" at 15 instead of 25 per cent., and in recognizing the limit of capital to be $50,000 instead of $10,000—the National Banking law having been changed :—

Purchase of U.S. bonds at par.	Issues of *quasi* Legal-tender Paper.	Reserve required by law of 15 per ct. in "lawful money."
$500,000	$450,000	$67,500
382,500	344,250	51,637
292,613	263,352	39,502
223,850	201,465	30,219
171,246	154,122	23,118
131,004	117,904	17,685
100,219	90,198	13,528
76,670	69,003	10,350
58,653	52,788	7,917
$1,936,755	$1,743,082	$261,456

Page 137, line 34—After word "government" insert "when it has assumed a practically democratic form."
" 144 " 8—After "times" introduce "persons within."
" 144 " 12—Strike out "physiological."
" 161 " 29—Insert "hard" in place of "loud."
" 275 " 2—Insert "Yes" in place of "Yet."
" 334 " 9, 12, and 19—For "Guttemberg" read "Gutenberg."
" 357 " 10—In place of "an almost priceless monopoly!" insert "a single monopoly."
" 357 " 37—In place of "110" insert "10."
" 363 " 14—After word "interest" insert "in Venice."
" 366 " 31—For "remaining" substitute "remained."
" 370 " 38—For "upon" substitute "at."
" 373 " 29—For "Euclid" substitute "Ænead."
" 422 " 7—For "in that form" read "of that form."
" 427 " 7—For "this comes on" read "this comes of."
" 427 " 31—For "function" read "functions."

INDEX TO VOLUME I.

NEW YORK SOCIAL SCIENCE REVIEW, 1865.

PAGE.

PAGE.

THE

SOCIAL SCIENCE REVIEW:

A JOURNAL OF

POLITICAL ECONOMY AND STATISTICS.

JANUARY, 1865.

GOVERNMENT.

PART I.

THE fearful trials through which the people of the United States are now passing, and the important consequences they are sure to entail on the present and future generations, ought to convince every thinking man that the science of Government, *i. e.*, the knowledge of the natural laws that control human governments, has not been sufficiently studied and analyzed. We therefore propose to examine the subject of Government, from a purely scientific point of view, divesting ourselves as far as possible from all party biases or prejudices, and from preconceived opinions. We seek truth on this, as on every other subject, for its own sake, ready to follow it wherever it may lead, and willing to accept any logical conclusion it may establish, religiously believing that a knowledge of truth and of natural laws, will destroy error and evil, and lead to the general well-being and progress of all.

We approach this vast and important subject almost with awe, for to do it justice requires not only the successful elimination of truth from error—alone not an easy task—but also the examination and explanation of the wondrous, the perfect, the all-wise and beneficent natural laws of the Creator; laws which not only constantly and efficiently control and direct all things, but which also reveal to us a glimpse of the Divine Idea in regard to man—the most interesting, as well as the most sublime, subject that can occupy the mind. No talents can do full justice to such a theme; and if we make the attempt, it is only because others seem disposed to examine Government solely as subject to short-sighted, fallible, human control, instead of examining it as subject to the control of natural or divine laws. Any one who will study and analyze these laws cannot fail to acquire an intense faith in the innumerable benefits that will accrue to humanity, whenever Governments shall be conducted in strict accordance with natural laws—with that which is the omniscience of God himself.

At present, wherever we turn our eyes, we find proofs that the science of Government—the knowledge of the natural laws that control the actions of man in regard to Government—are very imperfectly known and understood. Even in this country, where the greater part of the evil consequences of feudalism, and other errors of the past, never found a footing, we yet see on all sides the disastrous effects of misgovernment. Our municipal, our State, our Federal affairs, all share in the fatal consequences of our ignorance of the true principles of Government.

When we look to other ages, and to other countries, similar sad evidences of the general ignorance of the true principles of Government crowd upon us. Without going further back than the present century, have we not seen in France, the country which has long claimed to lead the vanguard of civilization, a Napoleon attain an undying page in history, and the most prominent niche in the Temple of Fame, by the immolation of hundreds of thousands of men, and by the destruction of untold millions of the useful results of patient toil, which should have contributed to the well-being and progress of humanity? Think of the harrowed feelings—of the bitter tears—of the broken hearts of parents who saw the sons whom they had tenderly nursed and educated to be the stay and solace of their old age, torn from their embraces to be sent to fertilize with their heart's blood the fields of carnage that gave Napoleon the name of the great Captain of the age; —or to leave their bones, unshrined by the hand of love and affection, to bleach amid the snows and ice of Russia;—or to return to their homes broken in health or maimed for life! Think of the brothers and sisters rudely separated from the loved companions of their childhood—of the maidens who, with breaking hearts, saw depart, probably never to return, those to whom they had pledged the most intense feeling of life—the ardent affection that was to make them helpmates and sharers in the future joys and sorrows of this checkered life! All these lacerated feelings; all this agony; all these terrible sufferings; all this wanton and useless destruction of life and property—was produced by Government in the name of the law—of that which was instituted for the common protection and good of all! And all this was done merely to gratify the insatiable ambition of one man! But strangest of all, despite all this, that same France, a few years later, still so worshipped and adored the name of Napoleon, that an almost unknown adventurer, merely because he bore the charmed name, was elevated to an Imperial Throne, and thus placed in a position to renew the scenes that should have made the name the terror and abhorrence of humanity.

Surely so long as we see these things occur, it is but too evident that the science and object of Government have been but little examined, and still less understood.

Governments are invariably instituted or organized under the pretence of benefiting humanity. Since, therefore, its ostensible, as well as its true object, is the well-being of humanity, before Government can be properly understood, man himself must be carefully analyzed and examined.

The more closely we study Nature, the more thoroughly we analyze the wonderful natural laws or forces that control every existing thing, the more we become convinced that everything is perfect for the purpose for which it was created. Nothing but profound ignorance can permit a doubt of this to enter the mind, or suggest a change for the better in anything. All knowledge leads to the conclusion that those things which appear imperfect to us, are those whose purpose, or mode of action, or final effects, we have not fully discovered. Our present knowledge is already sufficient to warrant us in asserting, deductively, not only that nothing in Nature is useless,—that nothing is superfluous,—that nothing is imperfect,—but also that all things contribute more or less to man's well-being and progress,* and that everything that exists is constantly, efficiently, and beneficially governed or controlled by natural laws or forces.

Nature seems to govern all things by the antagonism of opposing forces, whose effect is the maintenance of constant and perfect harmony everywhere.

Man, like everything else, is subject to this system of opposing forces. He is constantly impelled by his wants, his desires, his passions. These are ever kept in check by his susceptibility to pain or suffering, and by his love of ease, of enjoyment, of happiness.

Man appears to have been placed on the earth in perfect ignorance of the uses and nature of things, as well as of the effects of his own actions. He acquires this knowledge by his own experience, and by the experience of others. Everything that produces pain or suffering to himself, he avoids. Everything that produces enjoyment and happiness, he seeks.† Prompted by these opposing impulses, man constantly seeks with avidity that which, though it at first gratifies some desire or passion, finally produces consequences fatal to his well-being. But man soon discovers this error, and needs no supervising control, other than the consequences of his acts, to correct every error of the kind he may commit.‡

Man is so organized that he is susceptible of innumerable and constantly increasing wants. In a state of nature, which is the state of almost total ignorance, he depended entirely on

---

* If, then, Nature makes nothing imperfectly, and nothing in vain, she must of necessity have made all these things for the sake of man.—(Aristotle, Politics, l. i., c. 8.)

† Happiness is the centre to which all the duties of a man and a people tend; and this is the great end of the law of Nature. The desire of happiness is the powerful spring that puts all men in motion; felicity is the end they all have in view, and it ought to be the grand object of the public desire.—(Vattel, The Law of Nations, p. 47. London, 1760.)

‡ The same passions that must be looked upon as the germ of an infinity of errors, are also the source of our intelligence. If they mislead us, they alone give us the necessary force to advance; they alone can release us from the inertia and the indolence which are always ready to seize all the faculties of the mind.—(Helvetius on the Mind, vol. 1, p. 77.)

the unaided productions of Nature for the supply of his wants, which then, though undeveloped, and, therefore, quite limited, were yet very imperfectly and irregularly supplied. But man soon learned by experience that, by labor and forethought, he could greatly increase his means of supplying his wants.

The object of all labor, mental as well as physical, is the supply of some want or desire of humanity; and the effect is an increase of man's enjoyments. But no sooner is one want satisfied, than another arises; so that labor, physical or mental, never lacks an object. And to insure constant efforts to supply new wants, man has been so organized, that the pursuit of an object is a source of greater enjoyment to himself than its possession.

This constant increase of the wants of man renders necessary a corresponding increase in the variety of his occupations and pursuits. That man was intended to pursue an infinite variety of occupations, is evident from the fact that hardly any two men are precisely alike in their tastes, inclinations, and dispositions. This infinite variety in Nature greatly adds to man's enjoyments. The greater the diversity of tastes, inclinations, and dispositions in men, the greater the number of their wants, the greater their means of supplying these wants, and the greater their enjoyment when these wants are satisfied. Every man has a natural tendency to turn his attention to the supplying of the want which is most imperious to his own nature.

But in antagonism to this constant impulse to new efforts, is the fact that every effort is fatiguing to man. He loves his ease, in spite of all the gratification he derives from his pursuit of an object. Man, consequently, rarely makes an effort unless forced to it by some strong impulse. This love of ease induces him to seek and to use the powerful natural forces, which, apparently, were intended to free him from physical labor, and enable him ultimately to devote his time and energy, almost exclusively, to mental efforts—that fertile source of man's highest enjoyments.

Political Economists of the most advanced school, after long and careful analysis of the natural laws or impulses that control man in the social condition, have arrived at the conviction that man's self-interest, so long as he is left entirely free from governmental interference, will lead him to do that which, for the time being, is most beneficial to himself and to his fellow-beings. They are convinced that ignorance, indolence, waste, vice, crime, can nowhere exist without inflicting injury and deprivation of enjoyment on every member of the human family; and, therefore, that, without any interference from Government, all men will unite to eradicate these sources of evil. And they believe that intelligence, industry, economy, virtue, wherever they exist, confer such important benefits on humanity, that these virtues will everywhere be encouraged and protected, without the intervention of Government. Most persons will doubt these conclusions because they only look at the first effects, and not at the final results, of men's actions. They see, for example, a man disregard justice and virtue, and yet acquire wealth and position. They think this a proof that dishonesty and deceit may be profitable and advantageous. They see, in this, evidence that Providence does not invariably punish crime and reward virtue in this world. But is not this a very short-sighted view of man's interests? Is it not taking for granted that money and power are the only objects man seeks or enjoys? It is true that it is a great blessing to possess sufficient wealth to drive want and care from our dwellings and our minds. But thanks to the progress already achieved by humanity, mere necessaries and comforts are now easily secured; and, beyond these, what are the enjoyments that wealth and power confer, compared to the sweet joys of a happy home, that true centre of all that makes life dear; compared to the unfailing enjoyments of a cultivated mind, that communes not only with the celebrated living, but also with the illustrious dead; compared with the esteem, the respect, and even reverence, universally paid to truth, to justice, and to rectitude, even by those who disregard these glorious principles in their own actions? No! if we could look into the hearts of those who allow wealth and power to tempt them from the path of duty, we should find ample proof that they sacrificed the truest, the keenest, and the most enduring enjoyments of life, in exchange for mere cares and vexations. In the attempt to grasp a glittering prize, they miss all that makes life truly happy and desirable. How consoling, how encouraging to humanity, are these conclusions! How greatly do they elevate the Beneficent Creator above the position accorded to Him in the old theory that there exists a radical antagonism between self-interest and duty—between all men—all classes—all communities—all nations!

Let us now examine the principles of Government, keeping constantly in mind the natural laws that control man.

Government has, evidently, heretofore been based entirely on the idea of the radical antagonism between nations, communities, classes, and men;* and between self-interest and moral duty; on the idea that war is the normal condition of man; whereas, in truth, there is perfect harmony between the interests of all humanity; and were it not for Governments, and the power conferred on them by human laws, wars would have ceased long ago: for it is a long time since men have waged war of their own free will, for their own account. It is invariably at the bidding, and for the supposed benefit of the governing classes alone, that the wars, which devastate the world and impede the well-being and progress of humanity, are commenced and carried on. In fact, war only accords with the nature and condition of a savage. A civilized man depends on industry and commerce for his well-being and happiness, and war is inconsistent with both industry and commerce. War, by destroying life and the results of labor, diminishes the well-being and progress of humanity more than any other act of man.† War has been condemned as

---

* The merchant cannot manage his business but by corrupting of youth; the husbandman does his by the dearness of corn; the builder by pulling down of houses; the officers of Justice by lawsuits and quarrels; the grandeur and calling of the clergy by men's deaths and vices; no physician is much pleased with the health of his friends, as an ancient Greek comedian says; nor a soldier with the peace of his country; and so of the rest. And, what is worse, if every one would search himself, he would find his inward wishes are, for the most part, raised and supported at the expense of others; which being considered, it arises into my mind that Nature does not in this swerve at all from her general course; for physicians hold that the original growth and increase of everything is the alteration and corruption of another; for, as Lucretius says (lib. ii., ver. 752, 753):—

Nam quodcunque suis mutatem finibus exit,
Continuò hoc mors est illius, quod fuit ante.

—(Montague's Essays, l. i., ch. 20.)

† Favonius said: "A civil war is worse than any tyranny;" and Cicero: "Any peace is preferable to a civil war."—(Grotius, book i., ch. iv., p. 207.)

injurious for centuries upon centuries, and yet it is still of constant occurrence. Why is this so? Simply because powerful nations still suppose they can profit by war, whatever be its effects on other nations; because the governing classes suppose they are rather benefited than injured by a war, whatever be its effects on the other classes of the community; because men constantly excuse the means for the sake of the end.*

The sole proper object of Government and human laws is, undoubtedly, the well-being of the governed.† To that end Government and human laws should especially protect the weak and the ignorant, and dispense strict and even-handed justice to all. The strong and the intelligent can easily protect themselves. But has any Government, at any time, anywhere, efficiently protected the weak and the ignorant against the strong and the intelligent? Let history answer. Slavery, oppression, class privileges and class legislation, are entirely due to human laws and Governments. How long would slavery have existed in this world, had not human laws legalized and perpetuated that most ini-

---

* Prudence will never advise the use of unlawful means towards a just and praiseworthy end. * * * The very safety of the people, the common safety of nations, interdicts the use of means contrary to justice and probity. Why are certain means unlawful? If we closely answer the point, if we trace it to its first principles, we shall see that it is purely because the introduction of them would be pernicious to human society, and of ill consequences to all nations. * * * It is, therefore, for the interest and even safety of nations to account it a sacred maxim that the end does not legitimate the means.—(Vattel, Law of Nations, book iii., p. 16.)

Who will dare to maintain that good can be attained through evil? That it is possible to deny a law of God for some miserable idea, the creation of our brain?—(Jules Simon, *Le Devoir*, p. 364.)

In the pursuit of some useful end, what constitutes a violation of the law of God? It is the substitution of our judgment, possibly our passion, for the eternal oracle of Divine Wisdom. What man will dare thus to replace the Law by his own ideas—to substitute his own ideas in the place of the law of God? —(*Ibid.*, p. 362.)

† Vattel very correctly says, "that Government is established only for the sake of the nation, with a view to its safety and happiness. That the end of civil society is procuring for the citizens whatever their necessities require, the conveniences and accommodations of life; and, in general, whatever constitutes happiness, with the peaceful possession of property, a method of obtaining justice with security; and, in short, a mutual defence against all violence from without.—(Law of Nations, p. 12.) Government is established only for the sake of the nation, with a view to its safety and happiness.—(P. 17.) It is evident that men form a political society and submit to laws solely for their own advantage and safety. The sovereign authority is, then, established only for the common good of all the citizens."—(P. 19.)

quitous and unnatural institution? Would not the brute force which established slavery have been overcome by brute force, as soon as the slaves became more numerous than the masters, had not the latter been protected by human Governments and human laws? Would not man, from natural impulses, have attempted to overcome every evil as soon as seriously felt, had he not been constantly prevented by human laws, and by Governments, whose powers were obtained under the plea of benefiting the masses, whilst they have generally been used to oppress and injure them? The fact is, there is not a single proper object or result that is sought to be attained through Government or human laws, that is not better, more fully, and more certainly attained by the mere action of the natural laws, forces, or impulses that control man. And, on the contrary, there is not a single improper object now attained by means of human laws and Governments, that could be obtained were natural laws not interfered with by human laws and Governments. This must be so; for is it not the natural laws and impulses alone that induce man to overcome, not only his own evil or erroneous impulses and actions, but also all the evil effects of Governments and human laws?

Power attained by individuals as individuals, by the voluntary but revocable assent of the community, is invariably beneficial; for, whenever it ceases to be beneficial, it is withdrawn; whereas power obtained by Governments through human laws, is invariably retained and exercised long after it has ceased to be beneficial to the community. In fact, such power is never relinquished or destroyed except by a more or less violent struggle, after its injurious effects become unendurable.

The *beau ideal* of the possible results of governmental action is well expressed in that axiom of the pure, high-minded and honest Jeremy Bentham—"The greatest good of the greatest number." This is really the utmost result that can be obtained from human laws and Governments. But does not this axiom acknowledge that the State can only protect a majority; and that, to do this, it may oppress and injure the minority? Does not this axiom give an apparent sanction even to slavery, as long as the slaves are in the minority?

How much more beneficial, how far more desirable, are the results produced by the action of natural laws, which, when uninterfered with by man, protect minorities as well as majorities. For, under their unimpeded sway, each man will find means to protect himself, by some means or other, for, as men become more intelligent, they perceive more and more clearly that to permit the attack of the weakest, soon leads to the attack of others; that to sanction the attack of unimportant rights, soon leads to the attack of the most important. The same principle that permits the attack of one, permits the attack of all.

Governments are created by the delegation or absorption of some of the rights of the individuals, which, it is supposed, can be better or more economically exercised by the few than by each and every member of the community. The Government or State thus represents and administers certain interests of the individuals who compose the community or nation. It therefore follows that the Government, deriving its authority from the individual, can only properly do, should only do, under any and every circumstance, what an individual could properly do under similar circumstances. No other rule can be found by which to judge the actions of Governments, than to examine the propriety and the effect of similar actions, under like circumstances, on the part of individuals. Whatever is wrong or injurious when done by an individual, must be wrong and injurious when done by a Government, although sanctioned by law. But how different the general practice from this undoubtedly correct principle! It is generally supposed, and all Governments act more or less on the supposition, that what is wrong, improper, or injurious, when done by an individual, may be proper and beneficial when done by a Government.* Hence, a different code of action, as well as of morals,

* Euphemius, in Thucydides (book vi.), says: "To a king or city imperial nothing is unjust that is profitable."

Grotius says, in the Preface to "The Rights of Peace and War:" "It is a saying that no Commonwealth can be governed without injustice (p. 8). One thing may be just in respect of those who live together on an equal footing, and another so in respect of the governor and the governed."—(P. 40, London Ed., 1715.)

Seneca complains that we can punish homicides, and yet smile at the destruction of a whole nation: ambition and tyranny have no limits; by the authority of Senate and people barbarities are acted, and what is condemned in private persons, is enjoined by the public."—(Grotius, book ii., ch. i., p. 3.)

is established for Governments and for individuals. Thus individuals are prohibited from being judges and redressers of their own wrongs; but Governments, it is held, are the only proper judges and redressers of national wrongs. Hence, wars have ever been rather the rule than the exception. Why this difference in cases perfectly analogous? Why cannot, why should not, nations leave their wrongs to the judgment of tribunals as advantageously as individuals do theirs? Is there not the same danger of an unjust or an erroneous decision in the case of an individual, as in the case of a nation? and are not the consequences of the decisions relatively as important, nay, most frequently, more important, to an individual than to a nation? Can it be right, even for a nation, to redress a wrong by committing infinitely greater wrongs against innocent parties? And what is war but the destruction of the property of innocent individuals, and the infliction of death on parties in no way properly responsible for the wrongs attempted to be redressed by these ruthless means? Suppose, for example, that the Trent affair had involved this country and Great Britain in a war, who would have been the sufferers by the attempt of Great Britain to maintain the honor of her flag? Certainly not the Queen of Great Britain and the President of the United States; nor the members of the Governments of both countries; but innocent men, of both nations, who had nothing to do with the transaction which caused the war, and who yet would have been made to lose their lives or their property that the honor of the countries might be unsullied! But can the wanton spilling of innocent blood, and the destruction of property, reflect honor on any flag? Is it not a crying shame, a disgrace to the civilization, to the intelligence, to the spirit of justice, of the 19th century, that such gross wrongs are still permitted to be perpetrated in the sacred name of justice and equity, and that, on the plea of benefiting humanity!

Every human law must be based on one of the following hypotheses:—

First. That there exists something not governed by natural laws, which, therefore, requires to be governed by man; or,

Second. That human laws can improve on, or supersede, or control, natural laws.

The mere statement of these hypotheses should be a sufficient refutation of them to every man at all acquainted with any department of science, for all science bears conclusive testimony that everything is governed, amply and perfectly, by natural laws. Men have no confidence in natural laws, simply because their existence, as well as their effects, are unknown to them. They believe natural laws entirely insufficient to govern humanity, unless aided by laws of their own making.* As if the fallible could be necessary to the efficient action of the Infallible! Nothing can exceed the vanity of ignorance!

If man, like everything else, is fully and perfectly governed by natural laws or forces, it follows, that no human law can be beneficial, unless it be in perfect accordance with natural laws; and then it becomes a work of supererogation. But human laws and Governments are only necessary, and therefore only resorted to, when it is desired to insure actions which men are disinclined to make. Now, why are men disinclined to any particular action required of them? Is it not invariably because they think the required action either injurious or not beneficial to themselves? And are they not the best judges of what is really beneficial or necessary to themselves; and ought they not to be allowed to control freely, not only their own actions and those of their children, but also all property legitimately acquired by them, so long as they do not by these means infringe the equal rights of their fellow-beings? †

But it is constantly asserted that it is natural for the individual to steal, to commit murder, to invade the rights of others, etc. Yes, these are natural impulses, but only of the ignorant, of the inexperienced. Each of these actions produces, as its natural consequences, such terrible evils, such severe penalties, that it requires but little experience to induce men to cease to resort to them as means of obtaining the ob-

---

* Man appears to believe that matter alone is governed by immutable laws that regulate its movements and its conservation, as if the Creator had left his works imperfect, and had less occupied himself with the stability of the moral than of the physical world. (Quetelet, *Système Social,* p. 103.)

† Every proprietor has a right to make what use he pleases of his own substance, and to dispose of it in such a manner as he pleases, when the property of a third person is not injured by it.—(Vattel, Law of Nations, § 254, p. 104.)

ject of their desires—enjoyment, happiness, and well-being.* Governments have at all times far more aided theft and the invasion of the rights of individuals, than repressed them; for Governments have been, from time immemorial, mainly occupied in robbing the industrious classes of a portion of the results of their labor, and in carrying on war, that gigantic source of theft, devastation, and murder.† Human laws and Governments have perpetuated every evil from which humanity has suffered, far beyond the time during which it would have existed, had men been left entirely free to follow their natural impulses; for human laws and Governments annul or overpower man's natural means of resisting the aggressions of those favored by Governments.

But is there any truth in the idea that men, if left to their natural impulses, would produce anarchy and destroy society?‡ Evidently not. And even if it were true that the natural impulses of man are destructive to his own happiness and well-being, how could it be possible to secure these desired results by the action of Government, which can only be carried on by men endowed with the same impulses, subject to the same errors and passions, as those whom they are placed to control? Are men made better or more perfect by the possession and exercise of power? On the contrary, does not the possession or exercise of power, invariably increase

---

* The duties of humanity are based on the nature of man himself. * * Nature rewards the observation of her laws, and severely punishes their infractions. Happiness, abundance, the tranquillity of society and of each of its members, are the consequences of submission to the laws of Nature; misfortune, distress, discord, vice, crime, destruction, are the terrible punishments inflicted on those who refuse to conform to them.—(*La Politique Naturelle*, by Baron d'Holbach, vol. i., p. 15.)

† Philo speaks of men "who commit great robberies, and under the venerable name of Government conceal what is, more truly and in fact, theft and roguery."—(Grotius, book ii., ch. i., p. 4.)

‡ The law of Nature every way obliges nations to seek and cultivate peace. This divine law has no other end than the welfare of mankind. To this all its rules and all its precepts tend; they are all deducible from this principle —that men should seek their own felicity, morality being no more than the science of acquiring happiness. As this is true of individuals, it is equally so of nations.—(Vattel, Law of Nations, book iv., p. 114.)

No people can be happy unless governed according to the laws of Nature, which always lead to virtue.—(*La Politique Naturelle*, by Baron d'Holbach, Preface, p. 7.)

the evil passions and impulses of men?* If men cannot beneficially govern themselves, they certainly cannot beneficially govern others. Many persons, however, suppose that the interests of the individual and those of the community are different, but it has never been demonstrated how national interests can be other than the aggregate interests of the individuals who compose the nation. The only individuals whose interests may be different from those of the community, are the Government officials, to whom individual interests are so confidingly, though so mistakenly, intrusted, and those who, through class legislation and Government favoritism, obtain special privileges at the expense of the other members of the community.

The State is constantly appealed to, because it is supposed to be a disinterested party. But is this so? Are not the Government functionaries more or less interested in nearly every action of Government? Do they not profit by each increase of governmental power, and by each increase of governmental expenditures? and, being a party in interest—in fact, the only party having an interest adverse to that of the community, can it be beneficial and proper to delegate to them, authority which can be exercised by the individual?

Government, even when administered by the pure and the

---

* Why should our passions have greater command of us (in a state of nature than in society)? If the fear of laws keeps the people to their duty, it will make a like impression upon the great ones and persons of quality, but they easily find out means to evade the laws; for those on whom the passions reign with the greatest fury, and in a manner most prejudicial to society, are, beyond contradiction, those persons in authority of which we cannot find any example in a state of nature; nor can there be any in a condition of doing so much mischief.—(Barbeyrac, Note to Puffendorf, of the Law of Nature and Nations, book ii., ch. ii, § 2, p. 105; London Ed., 1729.)

"No frame of civil constitution can be so exactly modelled and so well guarded by laws but that, either through the negligence or the wickedness of those who bear rule, the same Government which was instituted for the security of the subjects, may turn to their prejudice and mischief. The reason of which is, because Government was first established as a defence against those evils which men were capable of bringing on each other. But, at the same time, they who were to be invested with the Government, were likewise men, and, consequently, not free from those vices which are the spurs to mutual injury.—(Puffendorf, book vii., ch. vi., § 22, p. 686.)

For he that thinks absolute power purifies men's blood and corrects the baseness of human nature, need read but the history of this or any other age, to be convinced of the contrary. He that would have been insolent and injurious in the woods of America, would not probably be much better on a throne —(Locke, vol. v., p. 391.)

intelligent—those free from all selfish objects and passions—is but an attempt to govern man by the experience, the opinions, and the convictions of others, instead of by his own. Is not this slavery, to a more or less limited extent?* The general excuse for slavery is, that the slave is ignorant, indolent, incapable of directing or controlling beneficially his own actions. The excuse for Government is precisely the same—that the governed are ignorant, indolent, incapable of directing or controlling beneficially their own actions. It is claimed, in both cases, that it is necessary for the benefit of all, that the slave and the governed should be deprived of the right of controlling their own actions; of acquiring knowledge by their own experience, and enjoyment by their own efforts. Slavery and Government are not only based on precisely the same theory, and defended on precisely the same grounds, but they both act through the same means—force and compulsion—and both produce the same results. They both make men less active, less intelligent, less self-reliant, less progressive; whereas Liberty, and the non-intervention of Government, make them more active, more intelligent, more self-reliant, more progressive. Both slavery and Government diminish man's happiness, well-being, and progress, whilst liberty and the non-interference of Government increase these universally-sought objects. The only difference between the results of slavery and of Government is in degree; and this difference is in exact proportion to the extent of the interference with man's freedom of action. This is the only possible explanation of the superiority of Republican institutions over a despotism.

All Governments, whether despotic, limited, or democratic, are based on the supposition that the Government officials are better judges of the interests of the community than the individuals who compose it; that the governing classes are more pure, more intelligent, more active than the governed.†

---

* It would be better for man to have been entirely deprived of the faculty of reasoning, than to be obliged to regulate this faculty by the caprices of others.—(*La Politique Naturelle*, by Baron d'Holbach, vol. ii., p. 80.)

† The men who enact laws, and those who compose books, are not of a different nature from those for whom the laws and the books are made. It would be absurd to believe that the governors or the legislators of a nation, by their

Is this true? All Governments are carried on by men who act as the agents of the community, to insure the happiness and well-being of individuals. And it is supposed, by men claiming to be intelligent, that these agents will better attend to the interests of the individuals, than the individuals could or would do themselves. Now, what does experience and common sense teach us? Do we find that men, in general, act more efficiently and more beneficially for others than for themselves? Who must be the best judge of what is most conducive, most imperatively necessary, to happiness and welfare, at any given moment—the individual who has to bear the immediate, as well as the ultimate consequences of his actions? or the Government functionaries, who are only indirectly and slightly affected by the consequences of their official acts, and who, besides, can generally fully indemnify themselves, at the expense of others, against these indirect effects? Man's self-interest generally controls him, and controls him beneficially, so long as he is not aided by human laws. He is, therefore, ever more mindful of anything that affects himself directly and promptly, than of those things that affect him indirectly or at some future time. We therefore rarely find, by practical experience, that an agent performs any task or duty better than a principal; and, even in those cases where an agent attends to the interest of his principal, better than the latter could have done himself, it is very doubtful whether, on the long run, it is a real service rendered to the principal; for the errors we commit, and their natural consequences, are certain and sure means of making us active and intelligent; and it is far better that all the members of a community should possess these beneficial qualities, than that they should be possessed by only a few, to whom all the interests of the others would then have to be intrusted.

---

nature, have a tendency towards good, and the people towards evil.—(Chs. Comte, *Traité de Législation*, vol i., p. 149.)

When legislators and the people are spoken of, it would seem as if they were beings so totally distinct that they do not belong to the same nature. The ones are spoken of as a species of gods, who give to all that are placed below them, motion and life. The others, on the contrary, appear to be beings deprived of the power of action, or possessed of only an irregular or disorderly action. But if we refuse to be deceived by words, we shall find that legislators and the people, are beings endowed with the same nature, subject to the same wants, the same passions, the same prejudices.—(*Ibid.*, pp. 149, 159.)

A few can never secure the same beneficial results, as the many who co-operate voluntarily towards one common object. Acting through agents has been attempted in all ages, and under nearly every conceivable circumstance, with one invariable result,—that we can never secure the same benefits from the action of others, as from our own. It is evidently not in accordance with Nature, that we should derive the same benefits from the acts of others, as from our own; and Nature, as ever, is perfectly right; for could we, by acting through agents, attain the same results as when acting for ourselves, would it not tend to increase idleness and indolence, and cause many men of the highest capacity, to withdraw in the prime of life, from the sphere of their present efforts, which benefit others far more than themselves? And would it not permit the creation of gigantic monopolies, which Nature prevents, by rendering it impossible to act properly and beneficially, through agents? What could prevent large companies from grasping the control of our most important interests, if capitalists could act as efficiently through agents as when acting directly for themselves? The more we examine the effects of delegating duties, functions, and powers, the more clearly will it be seen, that it is perfectly impossible to delegate them, if our own well-being and the general good of all, are the objects to be desired. Functions delegated to others, and particularly to Governments, are either not performed at all, or very imperfectly performed; and, having delegated them to others, we cease to exercise them ourselves, and, consequently, we are deprived of the enjoyment these functions would have produced, had we retained and exercised them ourselves.*

Governments, even when administered by honest men, in the attempt to protect the present interests of man, constantly prevent or impede the advent of that which is to be of vast future benefit to him. Governments only know, and can only attempt to maintain or develop, existing interests; the future interests of humanity cannot be foreseen by them, for man has no knowledge of what the future has in store for him. Therefore, we constantly see Governments and human laws,

* See Herbert Spencer's Essay on Over-Legislation.

from ignorance as well as from dishonesty, attempt to crush the rising interests that are to replace, advantageously, existing interests, which are thus attempted to be perpetuated beyond their natural existence, after they have ceased to be useful. It is an attempt to prolong, artificially, the existence of a useless pigmy, by crushing at his birth, the infant giant that is to confer untold blessings on humanity! No truly beneficial action requires governmental protection or assistance to insure its continuance. It is only an injurious or useless action that requires the intervention of Government to insure its perpetuation. But, thanks to the All-wise, All-powerful Creator, who has so perfectly ordered all things, the effects of Governments and human laws are invariably overcome by the natural laws, which alone control all things. Human laws invariably end by being annulled, either by being disregarded and thus becoming a dead letter, or by being repealed because felt to be injurious and unendurable.*

Monopolies are generally admitted to be injurious, but what constant efforts have not Governments made to establish and maintain monopolies! and these efforts have not ceased yet, notwithstanding the general condemnation of monopolies, and the experience of the past as to the evils they produce. If monopolies are not universal to-day, it is entirely due to the fact that every natural law is opposed to them, and that man has never yet been able to overcome natural laws, although he has constantly and persistently attempted it. Now monopoly is only another word for the possession of centralized power, and it yet remains to be shown that any monopoly has proved beneficial. And if the centralization of power and monopolies are identical in their nature, as they undoubtedly are, is not the decentralization of power absolutely indispensable to man's well-being and progress? Is not the centralization of power,—the delegation of power to a distant agent,—a great injury and a source of wrong to all—of benefit to none? For even the very Government functionaries themselves, it can be easily demonstrated, could obtain in industrial and other bene-

---

*No human laws can last forever; the eternal laws of Nature alone are fitted to control us perpetually.—(*La Politique Naturelle*, by Baron d'Holbach, vol. i., p. 69.)

ficial occupations, much greater results than they obtain at their present injurious occupations. The proof of this is the well-known fact that, everywhere, office-holders under Governments receive less remuneration, and attain fewer great prizes, than the same order of intelligence in any other career. The possession of power invariably leads, sooner or later, to its abuse. Centralization of power alone has permitted wars to be carried on in modern times, since industry and commerce have become the great sources of the well-being of all. Power is centralized on the plea that it is necessary for the defence of the country and the rights of the individual; but it is no sooner secured, than it is used for aggression on other countries, and on the just rights of the individual. The career of Louis Napoleon is a recent example of this universal principle. Were Governments limited everywhere to mere local Government, wars would become impossible. European wars have generally for object or excuse, the maintenance of the balance of power between the present States or nations. Reduce Governments entirely to local Government, say of counties, and the balance of power becomes perfect, and war is, forever after, without this excuse. The boundaries of nationalities are the landmarks that divide the possessions of the governors; of those who live at the expense, and to the great injury, of the governed. The maintenance of these landmarks may be of interest to the governors, but certainly not to the governed; and the people, as soon as they correctly comprehend their true interests, will cause these landmarks to disappear forever. The whole of humanity forms one great family, over which our Father in Heaven rules with paternal tenderness, by means of his immutable, beneficent, laws. It is perfectly immaterial to all of us, who it is that supplies our wants, so long as they are regularly provided for; or who it is that consumes the results of our own efforts, so long as there is a regular demand for them. A bushel of wheat raised in Canada, is just as beneficial to a laborer, as a bushel of wheat raised in Illinois, Ohio, or New-York. The great point to the laborer, and to all, is, who will supply the greatest amount of anything in exchange for the smallest possible amount of our labor, or of the results of our labor.

If the Canadian can supply wheat cheaper than the

farmer of Ohio or Illinois, the latter should cease to produce wheat, and turn his attention to something else. Why does machinery by superseding manual labor, benefit all classes? Is it not because it leaves the labor formerly occupied in satisfying one want, free to direct itself to the supplying of other wants, without depriving us of any satisfaction previously enjoyed? Is not man happier with two wants supplied than with one, particularly when the supplying of the two wants only requires the same effort formerly made to supply the one? Governmental interference with labor and industry, is always urged on the plea that without governmental protection, labor would have insufficient occupation. Now the truth is, that there are no limits to man's wants but his ability to supply them; and, therefore, whenever any one will supply any want we formerly provided for ourselves, it leaves us free to address ourselves to the supplying of some want previously ungratified. Labor can never be without ample occupation so long as machinery and the natural forces do not supply, spontaneously, all our wants; and should such a miracle ever occur, it would, evidently, not be the laborers who would suffer from its effects. There is, in fact, no valid excuse for the slightest interference by Governments with industry and commerce; and these once left entirely unrestricted, how greatly would the functions and expenditures, as well as the evils, of Governments be diminished!

The greater the interference of Government in the actions of the individual, the greater becomes the cost of Government, and the greater the opportunities to abuse the power delegated to its functionaries; the greater, also, become the number of the non-producing members of the community, and the lesser become the results of individual efforts, for these are diminished by every interference on the part of Government. The freer men are in all their actions, the greater will be the beneficial results of these actions—for, thanks to the natural laws which so wisely and beneficially control man's actions, a man can only benefit himself permanently, when left to his own resources, by conferring benefits on his fellow-men,* who gen-

*** God has disposed the nature and constitution of rational creatures after such a manner, that they cannot advance their private, without contributing something to the public interest. Community does not exclude the pursuit of private advantage.—(*Arian, Phil. Epictetеæ*, lib. i., ch. xix.)**

erally remunerate him for his efforts in proportion to the necessity they feel for the results of these efforts. Can any other motive be as powerful, as constant, and as certain of inducing beneficial efforts, as this admirable provision of Nature?

Governments and human laws, by limiting or prohibiting individual action, invariably tend to maintain uniformity in men and in things; whereas the true interests of humanity require the greatest possible diversity of occupations, of opinions, of tastes, of actions; and to secure this diversity, entire liberty of individual action is requisite.* Nothing else can produce it. When Governments attempt to control the education, the occupations, and the opinions and morals of the individual, they produce and maintain an unnatural uniformity of character, occupation, and mind, which prevents, not only the development and supply of new wants, but also the proper supply of existing wants.

Another reason for the non-interference of Government in the actions of the individual is, that man's wants vary in accordance with his position, his wealth, his intelligence, his habits, &c., &c. How can any one but himself judge which of his various wants is most imperious at any given moment? No one should, therefore, ever be forced to do any act against his own inclinations, no matter how advantageous or how necessary it may appear to others, except it be to prevent him from infringing the just rights of others.

Man either is, or is not, organized to govern and control his own actions beneficially to himself. If he is so organized, all

---

* Now, as individuals differ greatly from each other, in intelligence, sagacity, energy, perseverance, skill, habits of industry and economy, physical power, position and opportunity,—the necessary effect of leaving all free to exert themselves to better their condition, must be a corresponding inequality between those who may possess these qualities and advantages in a high degree, and those who may be deficient in them. The only means by which this result can be prevented are, either to impose such restrictions on the exertions of those who may possess them in a high degree, as will place them on a level with those who do not, or to deprive them of the fruits of their exertions. But to impose such restrictions on them, would be destructive of liberty,—while, to deprive them of the fruits of their exertions, would be to destroy the desire of bettering their condition. This inequality of condition between the front and rear ranks, in the march of progress, gives to progress its greatest impulse. To force the front rank back to the rear, or attempt to push forward the rear into line with the front, by the interposition of the Government, would put an end to the impulse, and effectually arrest the march of progress. —(John C. Calhoun, *on Government*, p. 57.)

governmental interference with his actions must be injurious and improper; if he is not, every governmental interference is beneficial, and Government should control every one of his actions. There can be no limit to a natural law, except the limitation produced by an opposing natural law.

Let us now, by the light of these principles, examine some of the leading systems of Government. By doing this, we shall find that all Governments that have ever existed have proved failures, if we consider the well-being of the governed the true and proper object of Government; and it is very apparent that their failure can be traced to the ignorance or disregard of natural laws, and to the non-recognition and protection of the rights of humanity. And we shall also find, that the nearer a Government has been based on the full recognition of the rights of humanity, the less injurious, or the more advantageous, has it proved.

The Jewish Theocracy was based on the idea that the Jews were the favored children of God, who would deliver their enemies into their hand; sconsequently the Jews lived in constant warfare with nearly all the nations with whom they came in contact, and their nationality ended by the sword. They fulfilled the prediction, that those who draw the sword shall die by the sword.

The Grecian Republics were all based on the interests of a class in the city which formed the nucleus of each Republic. Their Governments recognized and protected only the rights of this class, whilst they ignored and disregarded those of all the rest of humanity. The Greeks divided humanity into two classes—the Greeks and the barbarians, the latter comprising all the other races. Their philosophers held that the citizen must be a man of leisure, except when occupied with arms or in the Council of the State. Xenophon, it is true, admitted agriculture to be an occupation that formed obedient citizens and robust soldiers. But Aristotle was unwilling that any labor should degrade and bend the noble form of a freeman. Aristotle maintained that the barbarians were born to be slaves, and were incapable of being anything else; that as slaves they were better off than as freemen; that they possessed only sufficient mind to comprehend the orders of their masters; that they were incapable of virtue, and therefore not capable of enjoying happiness; that they had no natural rights, and that it was as legitimate to hunt them for the purpose of reducing them to slavery, as to hunt and kill the wild beasts of the forest.

Every colony and dependency of the Greek Republics, was governed despotically, and solely for the benefit of the governing class of the parent city. Aristophanes states that more than one thousand cities were subject to the Hellenic sway. Contributions were levied within and without the State: in one place, in the form of confiscations and penalties; in another, by means of war contributions; in another, by monopolies. No one thought of the resources produced by labor. More than three-fourths of the population of Athens were slaves. The State maintained public physicians, professors, and artists to decorate the public buildings. Notaries and attorneys were paid by the State. Education was gratuitous. It was to these erroneous economic habits of living mostly at the expense of the State, that are attributable the loss of the liberties of Greece, as well as the little development which her industry attained. We shall find everywhere, that liberty is the child of labor and economy. The public distributions of the State having become periodic, all persons desirous of popularity, purchased the good-will of the multitude by largesses, which exhausted the State, without enriching the receivers, merely inducing them to disregard, more and more, the important fact that labor is the main source of the well-being of all. Plato remarked, that this fatal system had rendered the Athenians indolent, grasping, intriguing, and fickle. The people were flattered by enormous contributions levied on the wealthy, or by confiscations. An Athenian orator said openly, that the distributions of money were the cement of democracy. Thus based on slavery, and on the interests of a single class of each parent city, the Governments of Greece rested on no permanent basis. Constant wars between the different Grecian States, as well as with foreign nations, became their normal condition, and they soon fell a prey to foreign invaders.

Rome rested on a broader basis, in consequence of the policy pursued of incorporating into the State every conquered city and province. This prolonged her existence as a nation long beyond that of the Grecian States. But slavery also became the basis of her internal and social polity, and war and plunder that of her foreign policy. Under these circumstances industry and commerce could not be developed, and without these man cannot progress. Rome, like Greece, attacked the rights of humanity, instead of protecting them; and therefore, eventually, shared the fate of Greece, by becoming also the prey of foreign invaders.

As to the feudal States of Mediæval Europe, they all rested on brute force, on class interests, and on serfdom. Like Rome, war and rapine were their foreign policy, and serfdom the basis of their industrial and social polity. Under such a system of Government, industry and commerce were crushed, and human well-being and progress were impossible. Even England, always claimed as being the home and refuge of liberty, protected few or none of the rights of the masses. Her vaunted Magna Charta is merely the recognition by King John of the rights of the nobles and the clergy. Those of the people are almost ignored in that instrument.

Probably the most remarkable Government that has ever existed is the Chinese. Based on the recognition and protection of the rights of industry, of intelligence, and of capacity, that country was long far in advance of all other nations, both in industry and in the arts and sciences. But it is the most gigantic example of the centralization of power that has ever existed. France is as nothing in this respect compared to China. The area of France is about 200,000 square miles, that of China 1,300,000. The population of France is about 36,000,000; that of China 400,000,000. Everything in China is regulated by the Government, and, apparently, on a just and beneficial basis. There are no castes there. Talent and capacity are said to be the only passports to office and power. The most capable scholars, after a proper examination, are appointed to local offices. The most capable local functionaries, after a due examination, are promoted to district offices; and the most capable of the district officers are promoted to provincial offices, and so on to the counsellors and ministers of the Emperor. What system could be more just, equitable, or proper? It is the system the English are now attempting to introduce, partially, into their administrations; particularly that of India. But the Upas-Tree does not seem more fatal in its blighting effects, than the interference of Government with individual efforts and actions. Even justice in the distribution of office and power cannot prevent this. The reason evidently is, that a Government official, encountering no competition, and having no especial interest in the consequences of his actions, which fall upon others and not on himself, never initiates a progress; and the minimum amount of effort that will satisfy the requirement of the superior officials, is generally the maximum amount of effort made by their subordinates. It is undoubtedly this intervention of Government in all things, and the non-intercourse with foreign nations, that are the true causes of the extraordinary fact that the inhabitants of China—that great bee-hive of industry—notwithstanding their industry and thrift, make no progress, merely repeating, like the bees, year after year, what their predecessors have done before them. The Chinese appear to have become so thoroughly dependent on Government, that their minds seem to have ceased to act, and, consequently, for a long time, no progress has been realized by them.

The first people of Europe that attained liberty through industry, were the Flemings. Agriculture, manufactures, commerce and navigation, were each made to contribute to enrich them; and the assistance they were thus enabled to afford to their princes, secured from the latter important political privileges, which established the independence of the citizens. There was a great tendency to distinct individuality in the different provinces of the Low Countries. Peopled by different races, speaking different languages, Charles V. found it impossible to consolidate them into a monarchy. He had to take, against his wishes, the position of the head of a republic, or rather of a confederacy of republics. Each province had its own courts of justice, with an appeal to a Supreme Court at Mechlin. Each State had its own Legislative Assembly. The States-General were vested with no legislative authority, possessing only the right of consultation, and of petitioning the sovereign. No subsidy could be voted by the States-General without the express sanction of each of the provincial legislatures. It was a Government not suited for military enterprises, but well suited to the genius of the inhabitants and to their circumstances, which demanded peace. They had no ambition for foreign conquest. Industry never has, for it is by the arts of peace that it attains prosperity, and by them alone that it can hope to maintain it. The Low Countries were as thickly studded with large towns as other countries were with villages. In the middle of the 16th century it was computed to contain 350 cities, and more than 6,300 towns of smaller size. These towns were not the resort of monks and mendicants, as in other parts of the continent, but swarmed with a busy, laborious population. No man ate the bread of idleness in the Netherlands. Antwerp had a population of 100,000 when London contained only 150,000; 250 vessels at a time were to be seen in the harbor of Antwerp, and that city, in the 16th century, was what London is now, the great banking centre of Europe. The merchants of Antwerp rivalled the nobles of other lands in their dress and domestic establishments. Something of the same sort showed itself even in the middle classes. The humbler classes, in so abject a condition in other parts of Europe, felt the good effects of this general progress in comfort and civilization. It was rare to find one so illiterate as not to be acquainted with the rudiments of grammar, and there was scarcely a peasant who could not both read and write, at a time when these accomplishments were not possessed in other countries by those in even the higher classes of life.*

This prosperity and happiness was brought to an end by that cruel bigot and hypocrite, Philip the II., whose true character has been well revealed by the archives of Simancas and the talents of our Prescott and Motley. By his edicts against the Protestants, and by his suppression of the rights of the people, enforced by foreign mercenaries, he spread sorrow and dismay throughout the whole country. The more timid or prudent emigrated to Protestant States, and particularly to England, where no less than 30,000 took shelter, carrying with them the manufactures of the Netherlands. Government and human laws thus destroyed in a deluge of blood, what industry and commerce had patiently and laboriously created. Here again it was the brutal passions of the governing classes,

* Prescott's Philip II.

and not those of the people, that produced the violence and anarchy that destroyed society.

The rights of humanity were, however, never fully recognized and advocated until it was done by the French Philosophers, towards the middle of the 19th century. Louis the XIV. had established in France an iron-handed despotism and an unheard-of corruption. About the middle of the reign of Louis the XV., an unprecedented impetus given to the cultivation of the physical sciences, stimulated the intellect of thinking men, who began to appreciate the sad results of despotism and corruption. A sudden craving after knowledge seemed to seize all ranks. The curiosity of even the more thoughtless parts of society was aroused, and women of fashion listened with eagerness to discussions on scientific subjects. About 1751, Quesnay and Gournay examined the leading principles of Political Economy, and the spirit of France became so democratic, that it seemed impossible to delay a revolution. Principles were investigated and the foundation of power questioned on all sides. All classes began to examine and discuss the rights of man. This great revolution in public opinion carried Turgot, the eminent financial minister of Louis the XVI. into power in 1774. His appointment was an official recognition of the truth of the doctrines enunciated by the Philosophers and the Economists. Turgot was an ardent and sincere disciple of the Economists, and, during his whole career as minister, was apparently solely prompted by a desire to benefit his country, by restoring liberty to commerce and industry, and by relieving the lower classes of the unequal share of taxation imposed on them. With the assent of the king, he liberated the wine trade and the corn trade from the restrictions and monopolies that encumbered them. He repealed the prohibition of the export of corn, and abolished the trade corporations, which had made each mechanical and industrial occupation a monopoly in the hands of a few. His last and most important reform, was to equalize taxation among all the classes of society, and to reduce it to one single tax on land, in accordance with the doctrine of the Physiocrates; but, before he could accomplish this, all the vested interests, whose unjust privileges he had attacked by his reforms—nobles, clergy, magistrates, financiers—the aristocracies of trade—all banded together and urged the king to dismiss Turgot, on the ground that his economical views would throw France into commotion. On the twelfth of May, 1776, Turgot was dismissed by the weak king, who, only four months previously, had said to him, "You and I are the only persons who love the people."

This dismissal of Turgot undoubtedly caused the destruction of the French monarchy. Neckar, who succeeded Turgot, after trying every expediency in his celebrated *compte rendu*, confessed the necessity of returning to the measures proposed by Turgot—the equalization of taxation, and economy in the expenditures of the State. His advice, like that of Turgot, was disregarded. The courtiers, under the administrations of Calonne and Brienne, attempted to weather the storm without doing justice to the people; but rights once acknowledged must be conceded when claimed by the masses, and the ruins of the Bastile and the death of Louis the XVI. on the scaffold, soon proved the wisdom of Turgot, who, through reforms, sought to prevent the Revolution. Had he remained in power, there is every probability that the French Revolution would never have taken place; and humanity would, today, be a century in advance of its present social condition, had that terrible event, and the long and bloody wars that followed, been prevented. The dreadful scenes of the French Revolution, produced by the refusal of the nobles and the Government to concede rights that were generally and publicly acknowledged, were ascribed, by the conservatives and the governing classes of Europe, to the recognition and acknowledgment of the rights of man by the French Philosophers; and, for fifty years thereafter, that subject was thrown aside, as one destructive of society. The old idea that man is incompetent to govern himself was revived; despotism and bigotry were everywhere strengthened; and in France, under the sway of Napoleon, and, subsequently, of the Bourbons, the spirit of inquiry and the love of liberty which preceded the French Revolution, were gradually crushed out. We have in this a striking proof that all real progress is the result of peace and industry. No matter how noble or pure may be the motive that leads to it, war or violence invariably brutalizes man, leads to despotism, and arrests progress. In the attempt to remove an evil by war or violence, tenfold evils are generated, and the good is completely overpowered by the evil. All true progress is achieved by the victory of the mind over power or brute force, and no revolution can take place until after this victory has been achieved; but, then, the revolution is unnecessary, for a right once acknowledged must soon be conceded to those to whom it belongs.

MR. FESSENDEN'S REPORT.

THE task of analyzing a cotemporaneous State paper, and submitting it to the ordeal of a critical temperature, is always one of peculiar delicacy, particularly in times of civil commotion; for no matter how the analysis ends, one party or the other is sure to maintain that your crucible was not a scientific one; that it was a partisan affair;—in short, that it was good for nothing. The other party, if they happen to be satisfied with the crucible, will probably complain that the fire was not hot enough. To avoid both Charybdis and Scylla, the unlucky critic steers his subject into such a tempest of commonplaces, that it is odds if either party ever care to read his review. Happily for our case, the canons of criticism we shall use, are to be found in the acts of Congress. Our crucible bears the stamp of authority. With this talisman in our hands, we are proof to the assaults of either party. The tree stands before us, the law has given us the tools, and with a steady aim, and a blow that fears no recoil, we shall lay it bare to the public. If the timber proves to be sound, so much the better.

An act of Congress, bearing date the 10th of May, 1800, provides "that it shall be the duty of the Secretary of the Treasury to digest, prepare, and lay before Congress, at the commencement of every session, a report on the subject of Finance, containing estimates of the public revenue and public expenditures, and plans for improving or increasing the revenues, from time to time, for the purpose of giving information to Congress in adopting modes of raising the money requisite to direct the public expenditures."

Under this law, which is still in force, Mr. FESSENDEN makes his first report to Congress. From the great importance of this document in times of war or financial commotion, its advent is always looked for with great interest and anxiety. It comprises the balance-sheet of the country. Upon its pages are inscribed those figures of cruel precision which point to prosperity or adversity, to wealth or poverty, to strength or weakness, to resources or debt. When its great columns of numerals are traced down to their final consummation, we then know how far it is safe to tempt further fortune, or to brave calamity. Here lies the grand residuum into which filters the whole history of a nation. There is no brevity so portentous as that which adds up the capabilities and resources of an entire people in a sum of dollars and cents. The preparation of this great synopsis of accounts requires more consideration, more care, more exactness, and more experience than any other public document. It is the only one that absolutely requires a technical knowledge of details. The Message, and the Reports of the other departments of the Administration, may be written by politicians, and very creditably, too; but the Report of the Finances of the Nation demands for its proper preparation, very comprehensive faculties, and a long familiarity with accounts. The law requires that the Secretary of the Treasury shall first "digest" and then "lay before Congress, a report," &c.

Such a Report properly divides itself into five heads:

1st. A Statement of Expenditures.
2d. A Statement of Income.
3d. The Overplus, or the Deficit.
4th. "Plans for improving or increasing the Revenues."
5th. A Statement of the Public Debt.

As all figures are but terms of comparison, it is important that the Report should be arranged in tabular form; that it should be brief, exact, and, above all, perfectly clear.

Measured by such a standard—and this is certainly the standard which the law prescribes—we are compelled to say in all candor, that Mr. FESSENDEN's Report falls far short of the mark. Few of the statements called for are made up to a later date than last July, a date which in the present mad speed of events makes the statements contained in the Report almost too old to be of interest; while its rambling form, its want of precision, we had almost said of truth, and its incomprehensible obscurity, renders it unsatisfactory in every aspect, both to the suffering debtors and the expectant creditors of the Nation whose financial condition it is its professed object to clearly exhibit. As for the measures it proposes, "to improve or increase the revenues," we shall speak of these hereafter. We are now more particularly alluding to its statements and estimates of expenditures and income; and its marked omissions of important data for computing the present condition of the finances.

Whatever consequences may flow from the unsatisfactory nature of this Report, the Secretary of the Treasury cannot with fairness be called upon to father them. The circumstances of his appointment to office should not be forgotten. At a critical moment, Mr. Chase, his predecessor in office, suddenly resigned. Mr. Todd was immediately nominated by the President, but the Senate failed to appoint him. Such was the confidence of that body in the financial capacity of Mr. FESSENDEN, that it was clear no other prominent person could be appointed without much delay; and as time pressed, Mr. FESSENDEN was at once named and confirmed. Immediately afterwards Congress adjourned.

Not to speak of the impolicy of appointing an officer to succeed Mr. Chase, who, while Mr. Chase's course had become deservedly unpopular, had never exhibited any dissent from his doctrines, the Senate could not have forgotten what Mr. FESSENDEN himself said during the debate upon the bill authorizing the issue of legal-tender notes:

"I am entirely inexperienced in these things, as we all are more or less, and I must say, that after all the study I have tried to give this subject, and in all the advice I have tried to get from experienced men, I have come to the conclusion, at last, upon the whole, that owing to the peculiar condition of things in this country for so many years, nobody knows much upon the question of Finance—not even those most familiar with it." After citing in support of this extraordinary assertion, an instance of disagreement between two leading financiers upon the legal-tender question, he continued: "Now, sir, with all this it is rather a difficult thing for lawyers and farmers and men not accustomed to all these things, like financial gentlemen, to tell precisely what to do; and I am obliged after all to draw upon the very shallow fountain of my own intelligence and my own study to endeavor to come to right conclusions, although I acknowledge myself very much indebted to many gentlemen for the aid they have afforded me, of which, perhaps, I am making a very poor exhibition." And again: "I would say further, that with reference to all these matters of detail merely, I am very much more inclined to trust the judgment of the Secretary of the Treasury than my own. It is a matter that he has studied."

Here is a Senator who has confessed himself inexperienced in the details of Finance, and more inclined to trust Mr. Chase's judgment than his own, chosen to succeed Mr. Chase in office, under the singular hallucination that the substitution would prove beneficial. Was it not folly to expect that the National Finances would be properly managed by a man known to be favorable to the very measures which had just proven inadequate to the state of affairs, and who had publicly admitted that he possessed less financial ability than his predecessor in office?

And here we at once come upon a crying source of evil and bad administration—the appointment to offices of a *technical* nature, of men not qualified by previcus training to fill them. Here is an amiable gentleman, a person of undoubted talent, a distinguished lawyer, an eminent Senator, a man who in many ways had rendered his name famous, and who, because in all previous positions he had acted well his part, is suddenly transplanted from his sphere of usefulness to one of an entirely different nature, filled with difficulties which the very character of his previous occupations make it impossible for him to overcome. Because a man has been a successful merchant, is no good reason why he should be apapointed an Admiral in the Navy. Because another has been distinguished as a physician, is no reason why he should be assigned to the office of Secretary of War. And because a third has become illustrious at the bar is equally no better reason why he should be entrusted with the care of the National Finances. Leave these persons to themselves to win their own way to preferment, in their own professions, by their own efforts, and all would be right; but let Government interfere, and upon the score of availability or popularity, appoint a shop-keeper to sail a ship, a doctor to lead armies, or a lawyer to conduct Finances, and whatever may be the merits of these persons in their own proper spheres, no good can be expected to result from it.

Expenditures.—On the 1st of July, 1864, the public debt was $1,740,690,489; on the 1st of July, 1865, it is placed at $2,223,064,677; on the 1st of July, 1866, it will be $2,645,-320,682. This is equal to estimating the Deficit of this year at $482,374,188, and that of next year at $422,256,005. How the Secretary arrives at these conclusions defies the scrutiny of any one but an expert. No sooner does one commence to apply the rules of common arithmetic to the sums in the Report than he is met by Certificates of Indebtedness classed among resources, or by other amounts prefixed by some such phrase as "allowances for unexpended balances from above," which are not at all to be found "above" or in any other proper place in the Report, but are arbitrarily set down here and there seemingly for no other purpose than to make the Report utterly unintelligible.

The actual expenditures of the Government for the fiscal year ending June 30th, 1864, are stated to have been $865,234,088, as follows:

Civil Service,	$27,505,599
Pensions and Indians,	7,517,931
War Department,	690,791,843
Navy Department,	85,733,293
Interest on Debt,	53,685,422
Total,	$865,234,088

The actual expenditures for the first quarter of the fiscal year 1865, are stated to have been as follows:

Civil Service,	$8,712,423
Pensions and Indians,	4,935,179
War Department,	286,200,289
Navy Department,	33,292,916
Interest on Public Debt,	19,921,054
Total, exclusive of principal of public debt,	$353,061,861

For the estimated expenditures of the three remaining quarters of 1865, we have:

War Department,	$677,479,384
Navy Department,	109,929,644
Civil Service,	26,852,489
Pensions and Indians,	6,516,595
Interest on Public Debt,	71,889,160
	$892,667,274
Add first quarter,	353,061,861
	$1,245,729,135
Less, probable unexpended appropriations,	350,000,000
Total, exclusive of principal of public debt,	$895,729,135

As the Secretary deducts $350,000,000 for "probable unexpended appropriations" from the total estimate for the year (of $1,245,729,135), without informing us what portions of the deduction are applicable to each separate Department, we are actually without definite estimates for the year 1865.

For the year ending June 30, 1866, the estimated expenditures are given as follows:

Civil Service,	$33,082,097
Pensions and Indians,	14,196,050
War Department,	531,758,191
Navy Department,	112,219,667
Interest on Public Debt,	127,000,000
Total,	$818,256,005

Let us now arrange the estimates of expenditures in tabular form, and compare them with former years:

Year.	*Civil.*	*Pen. & Ind.*	*War.*	*Navy.*	*Interest.*	*Total.*
1862.	$21,408,491	$3,102,985	$394,368,407	$42,674,569	$13,190,324	$474,744,778
1863.	23,253,922	4,216,520	599,298,600	63,211,105	24,729,846	714,709,995
1864.	27,505,599	7,517,931	690,791,843	85,733,293	53,685,422	865,234,087
1865.	No definite particulars of expenditures are estimated for this year.					895,729,135
1866.	33,082,097	14,196,050	531,758,191	112,219,667	127,000,000	818,256,005

A glance at these figures is sufficient to reveal the fact that the estimates for 1865, whatever the particulars may be, are much too low. An increase of thirty millions over the expenditures of 1864 does not fairly represent the increase of interest and the advanced prices of war supplies arising from a depreciated and fluctuating currency. And if 1865 is underestimated, what must we think of 1866, which is made to sum up much less? Here, from being possessed of the particular estimates, we are enabled to see where the error lies. Manifestly in the War Department, which appears to be estimated some three hundred millions under the mark. This almost leads to the conclusion that the Secretary looks to an early cessation of hostilities; but, besides distinctly avowing his intention in the Report to estimate upon the existing state of affairs, the estimates of 1866 for the other departments of Government are plainly based upon the expectation of a continuation of the war.*

Having now finished with the Creditor side of the national balance-sheet, let us turn to the Debtor side.

Receipts.—The actual receipts of the Government for the fiscal year ending June 2, 1864, are stated to have been $265,961,761, as follows:

Customs,	$102,316,153
Lands,	588,333

* No better proof exists that the Secretary's estimates of expenditures are too low, than is furnished by the statement of debt issued by the department on the 31st of October last. At that date the public debt was $2,054,615,415; and yet Mr. Fessenden estimates it in his Report as only destined to be $2,223,004,667 on the 1st of July next, which amounts to an allowance of $168,389,252 for the Deficit of eight months! Another cause for believing the estimates of expenditures to be too low is, that there are doubtless large sums hanging over unpaid at the close of the fiscal year. These sums are not mentioned; but they must of course be met.

Miscellaneous,*	47,511,448
Direct Tax,	475,649
Internal Revenue,	109,741,134
	$260,632,717
Add balance on hand July 1, 1863,	5,329,044
	$265,961,761

The actual receipts for the first quarter of the fiscal year 1865 are stated to have been as follows:

Customs,	$19,271,092
Lands,	342,186
Direct Tax,	16,080
Internal Revenue,	46,562,860
Miscellaneous,	9,020,171
	$75,212,389

Taking these actual receipts of the first quarter as a basis of calculation, the estimated receipts for the three remaining quarters are:

Customs,	$ 51,000,000
Internal Revenue,	203,000,000
Lands,	300,000
Miscellaneous,	15,000,000
	$269,300,000
Add for first quarter,	75,212,389
	$344,512,389
Balance in Treasury July 1, 1864,	18,842,558
	$363,354,947

* Captured and abandoned property,	$ 2,146,715
Premium on gold shipped from San Francisco to London,	2,799,921
Sales of prizes due to captors,	4,088,111
Internal and coastwise intercourse fees,	5,809,287
Premium on sales of gold coin,	16,498,975
Commutation money,	12,451,898
All other sources,	3,716,542
	$47,511,448

For the year ending June 30, 1866, the estimated receipts are given as follows:

Customs,	$ 70,000,000
Internal Duties,	300,000,000
Lands,	1,000,000
Miscellaneous,	25,000,000
	$396,000,000

Let us now compare these sums in tabular form with the receipts of former years.

Year.	*Customs.*	*Lands.*	*Direct Tax.*	*Int'l Rev.*	*Miscellaneous.*	*Total.*
1862.	$ 49,056,397	$ 152,203	$1,795,331	none.	$ 931,787	$ 51,935,720
1863.	69,059,642	167,617	1,485,103	$ 37,640,787	3,046,615	111,399,764
1864.	102,316,153	588,333	475,649	109,741,134	47,511,448	260,632,717
1865.	70,271,091	642,185	16,079	249,562,859	24,020,171	344,512,389
1866.	70,000,000	1,000,000	none.	300,000,000	25,000,000	396,000,000

There is nothing in this comparison to indicate that the Secretary is not correct in his estimate of receipts for the future. An instructive lesson is gained, though, from observing how, by gradual means, colossal sums are year after year extracted from the industry of the nation to support the public burthens.

The receipts from Public Lands do not appear to amount to much, while those from Direct Tax are dwindling down to nothing.

Of course there is no Overplus to deal with in the Report. We have now to consider Mr. Fessenden's estimates of Deficit.

DEFICIT.—As we have already stated, the Secretary assumes, whether right or wrong, we have had some previous opportunity of judging, that the Deficit for this year will amount to $482,374,188.

This is reached in the following way:

Difference between Expenditures and Receipts,	$551,216,746
Less Cash in Treasury, July 1, 1864,	18,842,558
Making the Actual Deficit,	$532,374,188

But the Secretary does not stop here. He actually goes beyond his own previous estimates of Receipts, and subtracts from the above sum, "an additional sum of fifty millions, *if* it should be realized, as proposed by the Commissioner, from internal duties (revenue), &c."

In this extraordinary manner the Deficit for 1865 is reduced to $482,374,188, which tallies with the future annual increase of debt assumed in the Report, and mentioned above on page 33.

The amount to be raised during the current fiscal year by loans, would therefore be $645,727,508, as follows:

Assumed Deficit,	$482,374,188
Add to this the following portion of the public debt matured and maturing during the year, viz.:	
Certificates of Indebtedness,	$160,729,000
Texas Debt,	2,149,000
Loan of 1842,	196,808
Treasury Notes under Act of March 2, 1861, and prior thereto,	278,511
Total, to be raised by loans during the fiscal year ending June 30, 1865,	$645,727,507

This is all plain sailing; but turn to the Report, and after a bewildering maze of figures dashed in here and there, without much regard to relevancy, if the reader catches at anything but the final sum, we are much mistaken.

Through this want of methodical arrangement, the important document which forms the subject of this review, is found to be almost unintelligible. Add to this, an equal lack of precision,—and a Report which ought to form the most inflexible of all national guides, at a moment like this, becomes a sealed book to the majority of the nation, and a riddle to the rest.

We now turn with pleasure from a division of the subject, the details of which, with its figures and estimates, must have taxed the patience of the reader, to that which comes under the head of "Plans for Improving or Increasing the Revenue."

Expressed in the briefest manner, the following are the most noticeable measures recommended by Mr. FESSENDEN:

First. The various suggestions of the Commissioner of the Internal Revenue; to whose report on the subject the Secretary of the Treasury makes reference. These are chiefly suggestions concerning the taxes on cigars, tobacco, coals, matches, spirits, petroleum, assays, publications, iron, and rents.

Secondly. A uniform tax upon sales.

Thirdly. A "pledge of the proceeds" of the public lands, other than mineral lands, should the Homestead Law be repealed.

Fourthly. A revenue from mineral lands owned by the nation.

Fifthly. A system for deriving revenue from the purchase of "any products of States declared in insurrection."

Sixthly. Loans.

Those of less importance are concerning the National Banking system, abandonment of the Sinking-fund system, provisions for more effectually preventing evasions of the Revenue Laws, etc.; but the limits of this review compel us to pass these measures over without comment.

Before proceeding to investigate in detail these numerous recommendations of the Secretary of the Treasury, a few remarks upon the general subject of taxation, may not be amiss to the better understanding of the questions involved.

In the first place: Is an increase of the revenue desirable? Obviously: Yes. For terrible and lasting as are both the direct and indirect consequences of taxation, the people have manifested, in the most unmistakeable manner, their desire to shoulder them. A minority, it is true, have said—No. But our system of government has no respect for the rights of minorities; and the majority having said Yes, there is no appeal. It may be argued that the majority, when it said Yes, said it without understanding its consequences: that it was said in a moment of political excitement; that it was said by the interested, the ignorant, the indolent; and, even in many cases, not said at all, but made to appear so by the raising of false issues and other simulated means. But this is not proved; and furthermore, we are met by precisely the same answer as before: Our system of Government—a Government which we fondly term "the best one on earth"—provides no remedy for these mistakes, if mistakes they are.

The people having decided in the affirmative, it obviously became requisite to point out the best means for raising the increased revenue rendered necessary by the action of the people. To tax is one thing; to tax judiciously, another. It was a matter of no very great difficulty to bleed a nation which had never been bled before; but to bleed it so that neither its life should be endangered, nor its health impaired, was a task of a very different nature—and to call upon it for further sacrifices, after it had already suffered during a period of three or four years of active warfare, was a duty requiring no ordinary amount of tact and discrimination.

This arduous task Mr. FESSENDEN was called upon to perform. It had been partially anticipated by his predecessor in office, who left him a system of fiscal measures more or less complete.

For the most part, therefore, Mr. FESSENDEN's duty was to observe the workings of these laws, and make such suggestions for improvement as might be deemed expedient; and if it was thought they would fail, even with those improvements, to yield sufficient revenue, then, to recommend such additional legislation as would effect the desired result.

The question now is: Has he done this properly? To perform this task, required that he should not only keep in view the system which the "combined wisdom" of the nation had already established, and, if it seemed best to change it beyond an ordinary amount of modification, only to change it as a whole, for tax systems must be consistent in their parts, and will not bear patching; but to be careful that the taxes imposed did not defeat the very end in view, by driving away or suppressing any of the industries which constituted sources of revenue—in other words, killing the goose that laid the golden eggs. In addition to this, he was required to remember that (as all taxes are more or less unjust, and inconsistent with the spirit of liberty and free government,) it became his solemn duty to omit no means that could lighten the self-imposed burdens upon freedom, decentralization, and individual enterprise. These were the main conditions; but the labors of Political Economists had furnished detailed rules which might have proved an easy guide to Mr. FESSENDEN'S inexperience, had he chosen to avail himself of them. Some of these rules, or maxims, like those of Adam Smith, from general concurrence, may be said to have become classical.

But we find, upon referring to his Report, that the Secretary has ignored many of these now well-recognized rules. He has turned aside from the paths of experience, and plunged into a wilderness of ancient errors—a wilderness through which all the nations of Europe have passed, but in which only a few of the least progressive are still involved.

The changes proposed in the administrative provisions of the present laws are most of them highly commendable, and conform to the advice of the great Economists from whose works we have just quoted. But beyond this we find little to praise. The very first thing we come upon is a proposal that the Government should monopolize the business of assaying gold and silver, as though Governments were made to usurp private rights.

We next come upon an old and worn-out Continental measure in Mr. FESSENDEN'S Report—a project to exempt the national securities from taxation and seizure for debt. And still another, for making the public lands a basis of credit.

But we look in vain for anything new and striking—anything adapted to these times, and to present circumstances. Even the tax upon sales, which the Secretary recommends, commendable as it is in many respects, is an ancient device, which can be made to sit too easily upon the shoulders of a nation, to be consistent with the exercise of a free form of government.

All we perceive is a system of taxation, imperfect at the best, but rendered still more so by the hideous old clothes raked up from mediæval times which the Secretary has thrown over it, and recommends it to wear. We do not believe that the Secretary has cased our system in these rags from any deliberate desire to add to its repulsiveness; but, like the renowned Don Quixote, who, when he considered himself summoned to vindicate before the world his claims to knighthood, crowned his rusty and ill-fitting suit of armor, by clapping a paste-board helmet upon his head—Mr. FESSENDEN, when driven by the duties of his office to give an account of it to the nation, appears to have flung on anything to give his Report an air of completeness, and boldly adopted it without being aware of its incongruity or unadaptiveness.

Witness the general feeling of unnecessary despondency which pervades the Report—the despair of expecting to discover any better means to increase the revenue than those pointed out by the Commissioner of Internal Revenue—the fear of not being able to meet the future gold interest on the public debt—the plaintive moan which closes the Report about the embarrassing and onerous duties of his office—and the hopelessness of expecting Congress to be intelligent enough to assist him in them, unless it consents to be guided by a Commisson.

The latter is too singular an episode to be passed over. Either from a natural repugnance to personally serve as the executioner who shall wield the axe of taxation upon the willing neck of the nation; or from the honest conviction that neither himself, nor the advisers who surround him; nor the two houses of Congress, together, possess that knowledge of Political Economy which is adequate to the occasion—Mr. FESSENDEN urges in his Report the institution of "a Commission, properly constituted, for the purpose of inquiring as to profitable sources of revenue, and devising improvements in the modes of its collection." This, if not owing to the repugnance we have hinted at, is tantamount to that virtual confession of inability to manage his own affairs which a bankrupt makes when he transfers his business to an assignee for the benefit of his creditors. Congress, after all, it seems, requires a Commission, to "assist its deliberations, lighten its labors," and make it "effective." After this, we should not be surprised to see a proposition to abolish Congress altogether.

Upon a par with the hopelessness, implied by the Secretary, of expecting Congress to discharge its duties effectively, without the aid of a Commission, is the evident dejection with which he confesses his inability to perceive any "other re-

"source for raising the additional revenue, so necessary to "the national credit, than those pointed out by the Commis-"sioner" (of Internal Revenue). From this it is plain, that the simple, effective, and important measure, of returning to specie payments, by repealing the Legal Tender law, has never occurred to Mr. Fessenden. Can this be true? Is it possible that, not even a thought has been bestowed upon a measure, which, not only would insure incalculable advantages to the Treasury, but save the nation from the greatest curse which legislation has ever laid upon it?

But, more of this, hereafter.

We now proceed to notice the suggestions contained in the Commissioner's Report, and to make a few remarks upon each, in turn. As we go along, we shall sort them into such groups as the lessons to be gathered from them admit; and, after labeling them with their appropriate deductions, put them away into imaginary pigeon-holes, until such time as it may be necessary to draw them forth again. By this means, we hope to avoid confusion, and to attain that clearness and order of arrangement which is so important in a review embracing so many subjects.

The Cigar Trade.—An effective method of taxing manufactured tobacco appears to be so difficult of attainment, that the Commissioner advocates, in lieu of it, taxing the whole tobacco product in the leaf.* Should it, however, be decided to continue the tax upon the manufacture, he suggests that an ad valorem scale be adopted, the present plan of specific duties being too complex and unfair. Statistics are adduced in the Report, to show that, while the exports of unmanufactured tobacco to Canada have largely increased, the exports of manufactured tobacco have as largely decreased. This is only one of the natural results of injudicious legislation.

Exports of Leaf Tobacco to Canada.

1855	Value	$ 69,779
1860	"	124,115
1863	"	1,237,840

* "The law furnishes no rule by which the taxable value of cigars shall be assessed, yet the assistant assessor must assess them. * * * Another result of this mode of taxation is, that it is more profitable for a manufacturer to sell his cigars at $11 per thousand than at $15, at $25 than at $31, at $69 than at $85, and at $84 than at $98."—*Report of Commissioner of Int. Rev.*

Exports of Manufactured Tobacco to Canada.

1859–60	Value	$1,205,684
1860–61	"	683,875
1862–63	"	76,026

The Coal Trade.—The statistics of the coal trade exhibit the same principle at work. By the Excise Act of 1862, a duty of three cents and one-half per ton was laid on mineral coals. "This was not a large tax, and, of itself, could pro-"duce but little effect on the course of trade," says the Commissioner. But the Commissioner is wrong; for, when an industry is unprotected, it will be found, on examination, that it is prosecuted for the lowest possible profits, and, upon this minimum gain, it is difficult to conceive of a tax so small that it will have "but little effect."

While it requires extraordinary means to turn aside a river walled in by granite cliffs, the least impediment suffices to alter the course of one whose waters flow unrestricted and unencompassed. The consequence is, that, to some considerable extent, our coal trade has gone where our tobacco trade has—to the British Provinces. "In 1860–61, the amount of coal imported "from Nova Scotia was but 204,420 tons, valued at $702,165 "[$3.43 per ton?]; while, in 1862–63, it had risen to 282,767 "tons, valued at $757,048 [$2.67 per ton, paper money?]; and, "in 1863–64, to about 500,000 tons, worth more than "$2,500,000 [$5 per ton, paper money?]. *The present tax "(Act of June 30, 1864) of five cents, will operate somewhat "more decidedly in the same direction.*" While we suspect the exactness of the Commissioner's figures (for the amounts of tons do not appear to agree very well with the gross valuations accompanying them, and which we have reduced to the price per ton), we find, in the exhibition of the fact they are adduced to support, another confirmation of the universal principle, that progress, like force, moves in the direction of the least resistance.

The Match Trade.—The result has been the same with the trade in friction matches, as with that in tobacco and coal. According to the Commissioner's Report, even this darling heir-loom of New-England industry has, to a considerable extent, departed from the land, and gone over to our neighbors in Canada and New-Brunswick.*

THE LIQUOR TRADE.—The statistics of the corn trade establish the same condition of affairs in regard to spirits. The export of Indian corn to Canada, during the last three years, according to the tables of exports of foreign and domestic commerce, communicated by the Secretary of the Treasury to Congress, under the Act of March 12, 1864, appear to have been as follows:—

YEAR.	BUSHELS.	AGGREGATE VALUE.	PRICE PER BUSHEL.
1860–61	1,891,740	$ 810,346	43 cents.
1861–62	3,218,438	1,010,243	31 "
1862–63	4,211,897	1,622,825	38 "

Repeating the suspicion we have already had occasion to express, concerning the accuracy of the Commissioner's figures, we proceed to quote, in the words of his Report, the corollary established by these statistics:—

"This large amount, it is certain, was not needed for consumption in Canada, *but for manufacture*, for that country produces grain abundantly; and, during the last year, while it exported the great quantity of corn already stated, we imported thence 806,153 barrels of flour. *The corn was, it is presumed, for the most part, converted into spirits.* It is difficult to conjecture what else became of it. and the business of distilling is known to be prosecuted there with much activity. The Provincial excise duties being lower than ours, and the opportunities for illicit traffic being great, it can hardly be doubted, that no inconsiderable portion of Canadian distillation, the material for which was the growth of our own soil, crossed the line without paying duty, and was sold in

* Speaking of the Excise Act of June 30, 1864, the Commissioner says: "In order to relieve importers of the articles described in Schedule C, from the necessity of affixing stamps to the bottles, boxes, or parcels contained in each package, in which they were exported before disposing of them by wholesale, it was provided, in the 169th section, that, when any such imported articles shall be sold in the original or unbroken packages, in which the bottles or other inclosures were packed by the manufacturer, the person so selling said article shall be subject to any penalty, for want of the proper stamps. But for this provision, every importer would have been obliged to break each original package, and stamp every particular parcel contained in it, before he could have legally sold it, even to a wholesale dealer. Manufacturers of friction matches in Canada and New Brunswick have abused the privilege thus allowed them, and have made up packages of their wares in convenient sizes, for sale by retail, and they are sold, unbroken, to the consumer. The impost duty on friction matches is too inconsiderable to protect the domestic manufacture, which is threatened with destruction by this sharp device. * * * Lest, however, the manufacturers of other articles named in the schedule may follow the example of the foreign friction match makers, and thus pervert the liberality of the law to fraudulent purposes, *the repeal of the proviso* is recommended."—*Report of the Commisioner of Int. Rev.*, *p.* 14.

our markets. *Now that the excise on spirits in the United States is ten times greater than that imposed in the adjoining Provinces, the stimulus to this manufacture, beyond the border, and to contraband importation, will act with increased power.* The information we receive from private sources gives point to this suggestion."

The remedy suggested by the Commissioner is alike for all the cases;—a recision of the Reciprocity Treaty with Canada, and increase of the customs and revenues, so as to make profitable importations of these manufactures from the Provinces impossible. In other words, around the pack-horse whose burden has been so great that he has been obliged to shake part of it off, and lie down for momentary rest, a wall is to be built, which will not only keep his pack in its place, but prevent him from ever again indulging his ease. Can any one doubt, that if it be, as is commonly averred, England's desire to humble this country, she now possesses a more effectual means of doing so, by gradually, through her Canadian Provinces, usurping our manufacturing industries, and absorbing our productive population, by reason of the laws we have ourselves set up, than she ever did by hostile diplomacy, or armed intimidation? Speaking the same language, owning a common ancestry, and separated by no greater barrier than a bridged stream, it only remains for England to strike off the light bonds that now fetter the progress of her American Provinces, to see large portions of our industrial population, emigrate to them, banished from the land of their nativity and adoption, by the workings of unequal and oppressive tax laws.

We have now done with the taxes on cigars, tobacco, coals, friction matches, and spirits. We bundle them up together, tie a piece of red tape around them, labelled, "Industries which have partly emigrated to Canada, and are now sought to be brought back," and put them away in a pigeon hole. We next take up the balance of the principal suggestions made by the Commissioner, and which are not repeated at length in Mr. Fessenden's Report proper. Those which are, we reserve for more especial consideration.

The Petroleum Trade.—The operation of the tax upon this industry, is sufficiently exhibited in the words of the Commissioner:—

"I had the honor last year to suggest a duty on Petroleum. A duty of twenty cents per gallon is now imposed on the refined product. Representations have been made, which I deem worthy of consideration, that it would be eligible to tax the oil in its crude state as well as when refined; and I have no doubt the revenue would be benefited by the measure, even if attendod with a reduction of the present duty. I am persuaded that Petroleum will bear a tax of two or even three cents per gallon, without benefit of drawback, and no sensible injury accrue to our export trade; and that the tax on the refined being reduced to fourteen or fifteen cents, the yield of the crude and refined together, would considerably exceed the sum now realized from the refined alone. The revenue would gain by the increased home consumption of the refined article, as well as by the duty on the crude; *and the tendency of the present tax to destroy small distilleries, and to throw the business into the hands of large operators would be modified.*"

We have only to remark in regard to this matter what will apply to every species of indirect taxation: when industries are thrown exclusively into the hands of large capitalists by the action of revenue laws, the poorer classes, instead of being able to pursue, as before, the most profitable employments, are compelled to eke out a scanty subsistence in those pursuits which are the most risky, the most distasteful, and the least remunerative. It is the same whether certain occupations are made monopolies by revenue laws, slave laws, patent laws, or any other species of human injustice. It debars the poor man from being, to the extent of his means, a cotton factor, a maker of sewing machines, of India-rubber goods, of wood screws, of what not; from turning banker, if he pleases, or from reaping the large rewards which accrue to underwriters of insurance policies. It is all of a piece. It is class legislation, and some day or other its true character will be recognized by the people. We file the Petroleum tax away, and label it: "Type of a class of manufactures from which in the future the comparatively poor are debarred from participating."

THE ASSAYING TRADE.—We now come to an extraordinary recommendation contained in the Commissioner's Report, viz.: "that it be enacted, that the business of assaying gold and silver shall be done in offices established by the Government whenever needed, and by officers appointed for the purpose." This is a clear departure from all true principles of Free Government. Under what clause of the Constitution is the power to transact this business granted? The trifling advantages desirable from this exercise of unlawful power, such as, that it would influence the the miner "to make the Government his depository," or induce him to "convert his unassayed product into negotiable securities," (Government bonds), we reject with contempt. To avoid the delay incidental to all labors performed by Government, the miner, impatient to exchange his yet unassayed product for some kind of money, would frequently permit his claim to be forestalled by accepting Certificates of Indebtedness or other depreciated securities for his gold. It is in this manner that many Government creditors are now paid off; and to extend the advantages thus secured by the Government to the extensive business of mining which exists in the Pacific States and Territories, is what the Commissioner probably desires, and the Secretary appoves of. But is this a laudable object of ambition to a great and wise Government;—a Government professing the most complete respect for private rights? We are sure that no honest-minded American, no true lover of his country, would wish to see her at the mean work of entrapping some gold miner, perhaps an emigrant Chinaman, or aboriginal Digger Indian, into buying a few Treasury bonds against his wishes, for the poor proceeds of his uninviting toil; not to say anything of the higher principle of non-interference with private enterprise, which this recommendation dooms to renewed infractions. What greater right has Congress to monopolize the assaying business than the business of boiling soap or pickling herrings? Is it because it is more profitable? This, though proved, which it is not, would establish a principle that would involve the business of making reaping machines, patent hammers, revolving pistols, and T rails, into serious difficulties; for *they* are confessedly very profitable pursuits, and in the hands of Government, and under the pressure of routine delay, might be currently swapped off for unlimited quantities of Debt Certificates and greenbacks. This plan for improving the revenues, we file away with the rest, and label it, "Industry sought to be monopolized by the Government."

THE PUBLISHING TRADE.—The Commissioner recommends an alteration in the present law taxing printed books, magazines, reviews, and similar publications, on which a tax of five per cent. *ad valorem* is imposed; "to be paid by the manufacturer or producer." The present law gives no rule for determining who the manufacturer or producer is, and here is where reform is demanded. We file this subject away with the label, "Industry which the present Tax Bill does not reach, but which is sought to be reached by a very proper verbal amendment to the law."

THE IRON TRADE.—It is plain that the Commissioner, and the Secretary who adopts his recommendations, both belong to the school of monopoly and protection. They both appear to think that nothing can stand of itself; nothing can be productive; nothing can prosper; unless it is duly bolstered up and "protected" by acts of Congress. Asking for further "protection" to the iron trade, Mr. Commissioner LEWIS says: "In order to maintain the revenue derived from manufactures, it is necessary that their permanence should be secured, and, whenever endangered, *protected*."

Notwithstanding the fact that it costs 75 per cent. advance on its original value to import railroad iron, the statistics prove that in the year ending June, 1864, no less than 120,000 tons, valued at $4,800,000, were imported. This is equal to about half the entire quantity made in the United States, which is approximately stated at 280,000 tons. It is to foster a trade which already has 75 per cent. advantage, that the Commissioner risks the assertion, that "there are other and urgent considerations which now induce the Government to cherish every branch of domestic industry and sustain it against foreign competition." We file this away with the label, "Type of a class of industries which, to make them yield revenue, it is thought necessary to straight-lace them with the corsets of protection."

TAX ON RENTS.—The Commissioner says:

"The best test of the yearly income derived from real estate is its rental value. A rule requiring such income to be assessed on that value would be conveniently practicable, and would obviate the necessity of the vexatious inquisition now required in ascertaining the comparative value of live stock at different periods of the year, the amount of butter, beef, mutton, pork, cheese, wool, hay, grain, and other products sold or on hand. Estimates of these must needs be very unequal, and returns incomplete, so that the burden of the tax is unequally distributed. I am unable to see why a man who consumes his income should not be taxed for it as well as one who saves it; nor why one who lives in his own home should not be taxed on its rental value, as much as if he let it to another and put the rent in his purse. If it be deemed right to allow an occupant of his own homestead such a portion of its rental value unassessed as would suffice to pay the rent of a moderate dwelling, the excess of the annual value of such homestead above that sum might, with justice, be taxed. An allowance of three hundred, or perhaps of four hundred, dollars, might not be unreasonable; and, to the same amount, the deduction to be allowed to a lessee of real estate, for rent actually paid, ought to be fixed, so that owners and renters should enjoy equal privileges under the law."

We hail this suggestion of the Commissioner with great satisfaction, for we regard it as the entering-wedge of correct principles into the present bad system of indirect taxation introduced by Congress. "A tax on rent falls wholly on the landlord. There are no means by which he can shift the burden upon any one else. It does not affect the value or price of agricultural produce, for this is determined by the cost of production in the most unfavorable circumstances, and in those circumstances no rent is paid. A tax on rent, therefore, has no effect other than its obvious one. It merely takes so much from the landlord, and transfers it to the State."* It is, consequently, a direct tax, and as such, viewed from a social stand-point, is deserving of the highest approbation; for direct taxes being immediately felt and fully understood by those who have to pay them, afford, at such times, when taxes of some sort or other are considered indispensable, the best possible check upon the wasteful expenditures of Government agents, and the continuance of measures inimical to decentralization of power and the liberty of the people. We file away this important and excellent suggestion with the endorsement: "Only Plan of Direct Taxation."

This completes the principal measure embraced in the Commissioner's Report.

Now, drawing forth our deductions, and grouping them together, what lessons do they yield? That the well-known and philosophical maxims of acknowledged authorities in Political Economy have been confirmed in so startling and emphatic a manner by our recent experience, that we can no longer afford to disdain them in preparing future fiscal measures for the needs of this country.

They teach us in the case of the Cigar, the Coal, the

* John Stuart Mill, Polit. Econ., vol. 2, ch. iii.

Match, and the Liquor trades, that, as progress always moves in the direction of the least resistance, so industries, when taxed disproportionately, will either be destroyed, or diverted into less profitable channels; or, as in the present case, induced to escape the oppression of onerous laws, by removing to more favored countries.

They teach us in the case of the Petroleum trade, that when a revenue law so acts as to necessitate the investment of large capitals for the prosecution of enterprises that might before have been conducted with less means, it works a double injury to the poorer classes: by confining them to a choice of occupations which not only pay badly, but which involve personal risk and social degradation.

They teach us in the case of the Assaying trade, that as necessity knows no law, so Governments, when armed with unchecked power, and impelled to invent new schemes of revenue, are not to be expected to be at all scrupulous whether the measure involves an unlawful increase of their political power or not.

Finally, they teach us in the case of the Iron trade, that the most effectual way to ruin an industry, is to afford it the most absolute protection.

Surely, after all this, we ought to be able to turn these valuable and dearly-bought lessons to account.

We now return to Mr. FESSENDEN'S Report proper.

THE TAX ON SALES.—This is an *ad valorem* tax upon all sales of commodities not already so taxed; the tax to be paid by the seller. The subject is introduced by Mr. FESSENDEN in the following words, which occur in his Report:—

> "He believes, also, that, although a *tax on sales* would probably fail of collection to some extent, yet, by applying to it stringent rules, requiring frequent periodical returns, verified by oath, coupled with the power to compel an exhibit of books of account, it might become a very large and important item of revenue."

The principal arguments in opposition to this measure, are as follows:

1st. That it is a device of by-gone times."* It is the old

* "This tax was instituted in 1341, by King Don Alonzo XI." *Geronymo de Uztariz, Teorica y practica de Comercio y de Marina. Madrid:* 1742. "It was originally designed more than a century before, to furnish funds for the Moorish war," write Gomez and Quintanilla, speaking of Ximenes' reforms in the fifteenth century.

Spanish alcavala, the tax to which has been attributed the decadence of Spanish manufacturing industry.* It is an old Neapolitan measure, too; and, the fact that the Neapolitans preferred to pay commutation, in lieu of it, is a striking evidence of its odious nature.† It was also attempted to be enforced in Holland; but here, again, it proved unpopular.‡ Ruinous in its effects in one country, avoided by com-

* "In consequence of the notion, that duties upon consumable goods were taxed upon the profits of merchants, those duties have, in some countries, been repeated upon every successive sale of the goods. If the profits of the merchant, importer, or merchant-manufacturer, were taxed, equality seemed to require that those of all the middle buyers, who intervened between either of them and the consumer, should likewise be taxed. The famous alcavala of Spain seems to have been established upon this principle. It was at first a tax of ten per cent., afterwards of fourteen per cent., and it is at present only six per cent. upon the sale of every sort of property, whether movable or immovable; and it is repeated every time the property is sold." (*Mémoires concernant les Droits*, &c., tom. I., p. 455.) "The levying of this tax requires a multitude of revenue officers, sufficient to guard the transportation of goods, not only from one province to another, but from one shop to another. It subjects, not only the dealers in some sorts of goods, but those in all sorts, every farmer, every manufacturer, every merchant and shop-keeper, to the continual visit and examination of the tax-gatherers. Through the greater part of the country in which a tax of this kind is established, nothing can be produced for distant sale. The produce of every part of the country must be proportioned to the consumption of the neighborhood. It is to the alcavala, accordingly, that Ustaritz imputes the ruin of the manufactures of Spain. He might have imputed to it, likewise, the declension of agriculture, it being imposed not only upon manufactures, but upon the crude produce of land." —*Adam Smith, Wealth of Nations*, p. 600. *Aberdeen:* 1848.

† "In the kingdom of Naples, there is a similar tax of three per cent. upon the value of all contracts, and consequently upon that of all contracts of sale. It is both lighter than the Spanish tax, and the greater part of towns and parishes are allowed to pay a composition in lieu of it. They levy this composition in what manner they please, generally in a way that gives no interruption to the interior commerce of the place. The Neapolitan tax, therefore, is not near so ruinous as the Spanish one."—*Ibid.*, p. 601.

‡ The imposition of this tax in Spain and Naples could not have been so burdensome as it proved in Holland, for the latter was a country supported by intense commercial activity, where the national prosperity depended upon the freedom of its internal and foreign intercourse. It is in such countries, and the United States is such a country, that a tax of this nature proves most unbearable. The rigor with which it bore upon the Dutch is proved from the fact that, while they were patient under Alva's revengeful cruelties and religious persecutions, the moment he laid the alcavala, or, as it was called in Holland, the tenth denier, upon them, they revolted, and their revolt finally secured the independence of the Dutch Provinces, and led to the establishment of the greatest Republic which had ever existed since the days of Rome. It is related that, at the siege of Haarlem, the Dutch insurgents, enraged at the cruelty of the besiegers, beheaded eleven of their Spanish prisoners, and with grim facetiousness threw their heads over the walls into the camp of the Spaniards, with this note: "Duke of Alva, thou hast demanded a tenth from the town of Haarlem. Here is the sum, with an extra head for the interest!" Motley, in his Rise of the Dutch Republic, characterized this tax as "monstrous," "fatal to all trade and manufactures," "productive of an entire prostration of industry," &c., &c. See vol. ii., pp. 285, 289, 328, 347, 376 and 500 of Motley's work, and the authorities therein quoted, concerning the operation of this tax.

mutation in another, and violently opposed in a third, it would seem that this measure had been on trial often and long enough to be condemned.*

2. That, in a commercial country like the United States (and this distinction cannot be made too pointedly†), the tax would be especially infelicitous. Commerce, by employing a series of middle-men—such as jobbers, brokers, and the like—undoubtedly effects a great economy; but, if this tax measure were enforced, the economy which would ensue from avoiding it, would prove to be a consideration of superior moment; for the tax would, of course, apply to every repeated sale, from the producer to the final consumer, and thus would militate largely against the continued employment of middle-men or go-betweens. And, as these classes form no inconsiderable portion of the population, and would find it inconvenient, nay, even impossible, to discover other employments at once, they would suffer, at least for some considerable period of time, great loss, aud greater inconvenience.‡

3. That such as could afford to buy in large quantities, direct from the producer, would possess an unjust advantage over those who were compelled to buy at retail; for, in the

---

Bor says, boek vi., bl. 261, that when the Duke of Alva imposed this tax, which might attach itself twenty times a day to the same article, and each time enhance its value, "the shops were shut, the brewers refused to brew, the bakers to bake, the tapsters to tap."—(Consult Bor, boek v., bl. 279; Viglii, Comm. Dec. Denarii, s. 6; Grattan, Hist. Holland, p. 121, Phila., 1835, and the authorities therein quoted; Prescott's Ferdinand and Isabella, vol. iii., p. 438, Phila. Ed.; Meteren, boek iv., fol. 69; and Davies' Hist. Holland, vol. i., p. 569; London, 1841.)

* "Of taxes on contracts, the most important are those on the transfer of property; chiefly on purchases and sales. Taxes on the sale of consumable commodities are simply taxes on those commodities. If they affect only some particular commodities, they raise the price of those commodities, and are paid by the consumer. If the attempt were made to tax all purchases and sales, which, *however absurd*, was for centuries the law of Spain, the tax, *if it could be enforced*, would be equivalent to a tax on all commodities, and would not affect relative prices: if levied from the sellers, it would be a tax on profits; if from buyers, a tax on consumption; and neither class could throw the burden upon the other."—(*John Stuart Mill, Polit. Econ., b. v., ch.* 5.)

† "Alva could not understand why the alcavala, which produced 50,000 ducats annually in his native town of Alva, in Spain, should encounter such fierce opposition in the Netherlands."—Motley, *Dutch Republic*, vol. 2, pp. 287, 332.

‡ The recent distress of the Lancashire operatives is a striking instance of the difficulty and suffering attending the loss of accustomed occupations. The keen competition of trade forces men into special occupations, which, to be successful in their pursuit, require undivided attention and constant practice. When this normal condition of commercial and manufacturing countries is disturbed, the results of whole lifetimes are thrown away in a moment, and the world has to be begun over again.

latter case, the goods will have passed through intermediate hands, and, consequently, be burdened with extra taxes.*

4. That an unfair advantage would be created for those manufacturers whose goods were capable of being put up at once in packages suitable for retailing, for they would reach the consumer unburdened by the taxes of intermediate sales.†

5. That it would damage the employment of speculative capital, always an important encouragement to production, and confine commercial dealings within the limits of the immediate wants of consumers.‡

6. That, in a vast majority of cases, the tax would be impossible to collect, and would thus bear unequally upon those industries which could not escape it. For instance, a small farmer would carry a dozen chickens, or a basket of eggs, or a few pails of milk, or bunches of radishes to market, and sell them. This man cannot keep accounts; and, if he could, would it not be unfair to compel him to devote a half of each day to a record of the many little trifles he had disposed of during the other half? Can we expect a Western trapper, for instance, to keep an account of the furs he sells? Yet, these small industries make up an important aggregate. Take another instance, where the difficulty of collection consists less in the trouble of recording the sales, in order to comply with the assessor's requirements, than in that of determining what a sale is. Is filling a decayed tooth a sale? Is splicing a broken tooth a sale? If not, then why should putting in a whole set of false teeth be a sale? At what number of teeth does the surgeon's labor end, and the merchant's operations begin? Is the selling of medicine a sale? If so,

* A familiar exemplification of this is found in the case of hotel-keepers, and other large house-keepers, who buy their food, furniture, &c., in wholesale quantities.

† Uztariz (ch. xcvi., p. 320) notices this, and such other objectionable features of this tax, enumerated in the text, as were applicable to his times and the peculiar condition of his country, and says that it encouraged importations to the detriment of native manufactures, for the foreign article came to the consumer unburdened with the oft-repeated alcavala.

‡ This is one of the objections raised by Adam Smith. If a thousand barrels of flour were purchased on speculation, in Chicago, for instance, and before the flour came to be consumed in New-York, several fluctuations in its price were followed as they now most frequently are, by as many different sales, it is easily perceived the tax would soon get the better of the speculator, and drive him, and the employment of his capital, away.

then, does a physician make a sale, when he furnishes you with a homœopathic dose of iodine? Does a journalist make a sale, when he finds a market for his lucubrations?

7. That, as the tax is laid in money and not in kind, it would encourage bartering, and correspondingly discourage the more convenient use of lawful money; for, in the large number of cases where bartering might become the common method of transfer, the tax could not be conveniently collected.*

8. That those who produced all they needed to consume, as the farmer, who raises his own food and wears homespun clothes, would be exempted from the operation of the tax. This, besides being an injustice to all other classes, would encourage unprofitable production.

Thus, this tax would variously attack the interests of middle-men—certain buyers, certain sellers, speculators, and certain producers—and all these classes would conspire, in different ways, to evade its imposition.

But, the advocates of the measure may justly reply, that, because it is an old expedient, is no reason why it should not be a good one—the tax may be scientifically correct after all. As for the alcavala, it was collected at the time each sale was made; hence, its vexatious character, and the sacrifices made to avoid it. Besides, the alcavala was a tax of not less than five per cent., in Holland; six, in Spain; and, in the latter country, often, of ten, and even fourteen; hence, its disastrous effects. And, as to its having ruined Spain, the reply is, that there were other causes at work, which contributed to reduce that country to its unhappy condition. This appears to dispose of objection No. 1. Nos. 2, 3, 4 and 5 are met very plausibly by answering, that they apply as well to many other methods of taxation as to the tax upon sales. The circumstances of the producer, the middle-man, and the consumer are changed by the operation of all tax laws, which, in the present condition of society, are capable of being practically enforced; and, as a natural consequence, those persons suffer

* The Commissioner supplies instances in his Report where bartering is already the ordinary mode of exchanging commodities. One-fourth of the entire productions of the country, he estimates, "do not enter the market," and may, consequently, be supposed to be bartered, or personally consumed.

therefrom. But the statesman should be anxious less about particular interests than that the required yield of taxes be gathered with the least amount of disturbance to the interests and occupations of the whole people.

Objections Nos. 6, 7 and 8 would appear to be insuperable; but, it is contended, that, as this tax is not designed to supplant all others, but rather to be supplementary to those already in operation, except where a tax upon sales is already laid by existing laws—such as the sales by wholesale and retail dealers, by wholesale dealers in liquors, and by stock, money, and commercial brokers—those cases wherein the imposition of the tax would be either particularly oppressive to the tax-payer, or difficult to be collected by the revenue officer, could be covered by other modes of taxation—as upon production, income, real estate, etc.* This answer we must consider well founded.

In addition to the above, it is said to work well in the cases where it is already imposed; and that, if adopted as a general measure—taxing the sales of all "merchandise, produce, and other articles of traffic"—it would involve less expense in its collection than any other mode of taxation. These arguments, however, do not appear to be so convincing as the preceding ones; for, where the tax is already imposed, is just where it is most easily imposed, and easily collected, namely, —among the commercial classes; and this, of course, affords no criterion for the most numerous and important cases, of agriculturists, manufacturers, and small consumers. And again, as to its involving less expense, this could not be true while the tax was only supplementary to an extensive mixed system of taxation, already employing countless officers, and subject to an enormous expenditure.

The main argument in favor of this tax is, after all, the belief that it rests upon a principle, contained in those words of

---

* We have not included among what are termed the principal objections to this tax, its oppressive nature in the case of sales at auction, because we considered it subordinate to the more important ones enumerated, and not deserving to be classed among them; but its force is by no means insignificant when we consider the extent of this important branch of industry. The objection consists in the fact that the tax is extracted from necessitous sellers in the very crises of their difficulties. Nor is a sale at auction the only instance of this kind. Many sales are made without profit, and many at a positive loss to the seller.

the Commissioner of Internal Revenue, who, in commending this tax in his Report, says, in substance, that, the nearer a tax is laid to the consumer, the better; for, then he has to pay neither profits nor interest upon it. This principle is, undoubtedly, correct; and, did the proposed tax on sales agree with it, the tax would undoubtedly stand upon a sound, scientific basis. But, in order to agree with it, all consumers would have to be brought within the same degree of proximity to the producers; and the incidental consequences of such a state of affairs would be the tendency to destroy all intermediate traffic—in other words, commerce.

But, above all these considerations, is the higher and more important one—that the ease with which an oppressive augmentation of such a tax can be decreed by Government would form a constant temptation to its abuse. A nation which permitted the use of such a measure would (like Dr. Guillotine, who met his death by an instrument of his own invention) furnish to the enemies of its liberties a weapon, with which to strike at its very existence.* And, as statesmen are often unconsciously oblivious to the true interests of their country, such a power, in the hands of ignorance, might prove as fatal as though wielded by design. Other forms of taxation attack particular interests, and are kept within bounds by the opposition of the classes whose interests are jeopardized by them; but this, insidiously, strikes at all, and could only be opposed as it was opposed in Holland, where its odious nature became so patent to all, that universal indignation was evoked, and the whole nation arose to strike at it a blow which eventually shattered something more than the tax itself.†

Revenue from Public Lands.—Says the Secretary's Report:—

"In connection with the subject of increased taxation and the necessity of providing additional revenue from ordinary sources, the Secretary cannot but call the attention of Congress to our public domain, and more especially to

* "Whatever be thought of its legality, there can be no doubt it was one of the most successful means ever devised by a Government for shackling the industry and enterprise of its subjects."—(Note to Prescott's Ferd. and Isab., iii., 488.)

† "The seizure of the town of Brill, by the insurgent Hollanders, was the *Deus ex machina* which unexpectedly solved the inextricable knot of the situation."—(Strada, lib. vii., 357.)

that portion of it abounding in the precious and other metals, which, by the Policy of the Government, has been reserved to the nation. He can add little, however, on these points, to what has been so ably set forth by his predecessor.

"The agricultural region has, through the operation of the Homestead Law, almost ceased to afford a direct revenue. Whatever might be the opinions of the Secretary, as to the good effects of this law, either in a State or national point of view, it is not probable that any expression of those opinions would tend to effect any material change or modification. Possibly, had the struggle in which the nation is now engaged been foreseen, or even apprehended, Congress might have deemed it prudent not to adopt a system which renders so large a portion of the public domain unavailable as a basis of credit, either by way of pledge of its proceeds, or an appropriation of those proceeds, permanently, to the creation of a sinking fund for the ultimate redemption of the debt."

It is surprising that the history of the Homestead Law should be forgotten so soon. This important measure became a law May 20, 1862. The final vote in the House of Representatives, February 28, 1862, stood—107 to 16; and, in the Senate, May 6, 1862—33 to 7. It devotes the public lands to all citizens, or intended citizens; and to all persons, white or black, young or old, who have served fourteen days in the army or navy of the United States, and who may choose to actually settle upon them. It had been the subject of many a long contention in Congress, though the opponents of it found fault less with its general intent than its special provisions, and, when finally passed, was an act of the most deliberate kind.* Congress not only "foresaw and apprehended the struggle in which the nation is now engaged," but had passed through over a year of it.

The venerable Mr. Crittenden, of Kentucky, one of the few opposers of the measure, founded his opposition upon the very point on which Mr. Fessenden now bases his hypothesis. Said Mr. Crittenden, in Congress, December 18, 1861:—"While we agree with you as to the general policy of a "Homestead Bill, we think it wiser to defer its passage to a "more fitting period. We are making loans and imposing "taxes, to an extent hitherto unparalleled in the history of "the world. We may want these lands to assist our financial measures. Be just, before you are generous. Pay "your debts, before you give. This is not a time for us to "press these general measures of policy, which, in time of

*** See *Congressional Globe*, 2d Session, 37th Congress, 1862.**

"peace, may be wise and proper. I am for its postponement "until a time beyond this session."

But, not only in regard to the facts of this case does the Secretary appear to have bathed in the waters of Lethe. The same oblivious waves must have hidden from him the true theory of national resources. Science had long ago demonstrated that unimproved lands form no basis of either credit or taxation, and experience has since frequently confirmed this law of Political Economy. Neither a pledge nor an appropriation of their proceeds will, therefore, be likely to prove of any appreciable consequence, so long as the necessities of the Government tend to keep the rate of interest above the level of net profits derived from the cultivation of unimproved lands; and, when that ceases, if it ceases in time, their actual settlement, and the resources which labor will evolve, will prove to be the true basis of credit, for which the Secretary is seeking.

Revenue from Mineral Lands.—Says the Secretary:—

"With regard to the mineral lands, the question is freed from this embarrassment. These are still the property of the nation, and may be disposed of as Congress shall determine. That they shall yield a revenue to the owner, independent of the collateral advantages derived from individual enterprise, in extracting the precious metals, would seem to admit of no dispute. On the one hand, it may be said, that, to sell them absolutely, is to part with an unequaled and inexhaustible source of wealth and power," etc.

The scientific principles just adduced apply as well to mineral as to agricultural lands. By the unceasing operation of natural laws, the tendency of profits is always towards equalization; and, taking the extra risk of success and the increased personal exposure incidental to mining operations into consideration, mineral lands will be found on the average to yield no better profit than those brought under cultivation for their superficial products. The "inexhaustible source of wealth and power" which the lively imagination of Mr. Fessenden conjures up from the silent canons and artemesia bushes of the Salt Lake Valley, is simply a remnant of that old Mercantile Theory which considered all value to reside in the precious metals.

Revenue from Products of certain States.—This is a subject embarrassed by so many considerations, both direct and contingent, that, without a greater knowledge of the facts in relation to it than has been made public, and a prescience of the future influence which the progress of the war may have upon it, to measure it by any standard of scientific criticism is impossible. We therefore, though with some reluctance, pass it over at once. Time will doubtless develop many a curious feature in the management of this new and extensive department of Treasury jurisdiction.

LOANS.—By far the most important part of the Secretary's Report is that relating to loans; and herein is most strikingly observed that want of originality and fertility of resource to which we have already adverted. Upon this subject the Secretary does not venture a suggestion for improvement, save the ill-advised and pernicious one of exempting Government bonds from taxation and seizure for debt.* This, again, is a European measure, in this instance copied from France, where the Government *rentes* are so exempted.† Like the alcavala of Spain, it is a measure of doubtful adaptedness. Suitable enough, perhaps, to the form of government and the redundant wealth existing in the French Empire, we regard it as utterly unfitted to the situation and genius of this country. Europe, until late the scene of every possible phase of financial ignorance and mismanagement, is still asked to impart to us, not the lessons which a bitter, but wholesome, experience has taught her; but the schemes which, written on the dark pages of her past history, she would fain blot out from her own remembrance. Beyond this the Secretary is silent—silent upon a subject involving the withdrawal of six hundred millions a year from the working capital of the country!

"If the capital taken in Government loans is abstracted "from funds either engaged in production, or destined to be "employed in it, their diversion from that purpose is equiva-"lent to taking the amount from the wages of the laboring "classes. Borrowing, in this case, is not a substitute for rais-"ing the supplies within the year. A Government which "borrows does actually take the amount within the year, and "that, too, by a tax exclusively on the laboring classes: than

* See p. 22 of the Report. This suggestion is elaborated into more precise terms in the President's Message.

† See article *Saisies de Rent*, in the *Encyclopedie du XIX. Sièle*, Paris, 1846; and article 592 of the French *Code de Procédure Civile*.

"which it could have done nothing worse, if it had supplied "its wants by avowed taxation; and in that case the transaction and its evils would have ended with the emergency; "while by the circuitous mode adopted the value extracted "from the laborers is gained, not by the State, but by the employers of labor, the State remaining charged with the debt "besides, and with its interest in perpetuity. The system of "public loans, in such circumstances, may be pronounced the "very worst which, in the present state of civilization, is still "included in the catalogue of financial expedients."*

But how shall we determine if the money now being borrowed by the Government is extracted from productive capital? Most easily: by the rise in the rate of interest occasioned by Government loans. We need go no farther. No gauge can be more certain.

Bad as this is, the evil is aggravated in our case by the employment of irredeemable paper money, and this is the feature in which we might reasonably have expected Mr. FESSENDEN to attempt some "improvement." Not only does the Government pay extravagant prices for loans, and for all it buys with the money thus borrowed; not only does the ease with which it is procured, promote official corruption, and encourage that paucity of resource and that indolence which invariably accompanies facility of accomplishment; but incidental disadvantages arise from its use which are daily assuming more potent influences upon the fate of the people. Let us take one of these incidental disadvantages, for example: the inducement which a currency, hourly fluctuating in value, furnishes to speculative dealings, not in the currency itself, but in those endless departments of industry whose products rise in price with its fall, and fall in price with its rise; though not at the same time and not to the same extent. Let it not, however, be understood that we are opposed to the freest possible exercise of speculation. Speculators often perform very useful functions in the economy of civilization. We would only remove by natural means those unusual temptations to abandon ordinary productive occupations for the purpose of speculating which an irredeemable paper currency creates—temptations which arise from an unnecessarily artificial condition of affairs.

* John Stuart Mill, Polit. Econ., book v., ch. vii.

The value of a currency such as we now have, depends upon public opinion,* first as to its redundancy, and when redundant, as to its ultimate redemption. This, of course, depends upon the course of political events. As the proportion of redundant currency fluctuates every moment with the shifting requirements of commerce, and as the standard by which its value is measured is peculiar for its inherent qualities of indestructibility, divisibility, mobility, and tangibility; so merchandise, real estate, and labor, which possess these qualities to a greater or less degree than the precious metals, are affected by the fluctuating value of the currency *in unequal proportions*, and refuse to keep pace with its fluctuations at the same time, or to the same degree. This of course leads to constant speculation in these things, and the uneducated and inexperienced must lose by them.

In due time, of course, the prices of merchandise, real estate, and labor, will attain the level of the price of specie; and so does the troubled ocean eventually find its level; but not until destructive storms have damaged the shipping that floated on its bosom. Even so has every department of industry been tossed about and much of it completely wrecked by the working of this fluctuating currency; and even so are they still hove-to, at mercy of this fitful blast, unable either to proceed or to return to a safe anchorage.

It is not proposed to put a premium upon either ignorance or indiscretion; but it is certainly unjust that the great body of the nation, unused as it is to a state of war, should be exposed to the arts of that handful of sharpers who travel from country to country, and settle in none, extracting lessons from the extremities of one nation to reap from them golden harvests during the sore trials of another. It is true that we all ought to be familiar with the effects of war and irredeemable paper money upon prices; and so ought we to know the statute laws of the country and the laws of personal health. But who among us can dispense with the services of a lawyer or a physician, upon critical occasions?

* The Secretary (p. 22 of the Report) appears to have been almost on the eve of making this discovery for himself; but, after a casual examination of the extraordinary fluctuations in the currency which occurred last Fall, he gives it up, satisfied that "a solution of the problem may be found in the unpatriotic and criminal efforts of speculators, and, probably, of secret enemies, to raise the price of coin!"

It is this sort of speculation which it is desirable to no longer afford encouragement to; and remembering that it is the fluctuation of the currency which prompts speculation, and not speculation which causes the fluctuation, but the fact that its redundancy cannot discharge itself, nor its insufficiency supply itself concomitantly with the wants of commerce, we are now to inquire what is the most effectual means of bringing about this desirable consummation.

The Secretary, had he bestowed the least reflection upon the subject, could scarcely have failed to reply as we now reply: by coming at once to specie payments.* And how is this to be effected? By an immediate repeal of the Paper Legal-Tender Law. "But this would be repudiation," cries a nervous holder of Government securities. Not at all. The Treasury note will be worth as much when it is no longer a legal tender as it is to-day—so many cents in gold, so many pounds of flour, so many yards of cloth—just as in California, where it is neither practically a legal tender, nor is it repudiated. But who would take it? The Government, at its market price, for gold-interest-bearing bonds. And if the Government took it, everybody would take it. All present money contracts to be, of course, dischargeable in paper.

This great measure would at once confine speculation within rightful limits—speculations upon the chances of war, the influence of the seasons upon harvests, and other contingencies which affect prices, and which are proper subjects for the competition of individual judgment and foresight. Then everybody could speculate who wished to, and that state of things would be ended which furnishes an exclusive monopoly to the wandering adventurers whose talents for speculation are acquired in successive scenes of warfare and civil commotion.

Besides this incidental advantage, its direct ones would be very great. First of all, the Government would be able to borrow at any time. Whatever credit it possesses to-day,

* In the Report (p. 4), the Secretary reverts, with singular confidence, to what he designates the "unanswerable demonstrations" of Mr. Chase, in his Report of December, 1862, concerning the necessity of resorting to paper currency. Are these reasons of a narrow expediency, applied to a moment of great emergency, to be kept alive, like the alcavala tax of Alonzo XI., long after the occasion, which offered them even a plausible excuse, has passed away?

with the present discreditable system, would be vastly increased upon a return to specie payments. Then by the fall in prices and profits, and the economy which would follow the establishment of a sound currency, the present frightful expenditures of the Government would be reduced to comparatively moderate proportions; official corruption would be sensibly reduced; and requisite financial originality eliminated and called into play. The savings in interest alone would be enormous. Hitherto the Government, by means of periodically flooding the currency, and taking advantage of that moment of overflowing, which eventually settles down to a new level of exact fullness,* has succeeded in having allits loans taken at or over par. This result was inevitable, and might be effected over and over again ad libitum. But such loans are, in substance, forced loans, and are succeeded by all the consequences of such vicious measures, the most obvious of which is the withdrawal and absorption of large portions of first the investment, and then the working capital of the country, and the conversion of other portions of both into speculative capital.† It is the latter species of capital which it is desirable to borrow or to turn into more productive channels, and neither of these ends can be effected by any other means than a return to specie payments.

The consequence of borrowing money by these forced means has been the necessity of offering ruinous rates of interest—rates which can only be seen in the depreciation of the currency. United States Sixes are to-day offered at a rate

---

* The Secretary says (p. 19 of his Report), that: "It is observable, notwithstanding the apparently large circulation of paper money issued under the authority of Congress, *its scarcity in the market* has occasioned no slight embarrassment in the negotiation of loans," and attributes it to popular hoarding! It is really mortifying to meet with crudities like this, in a State-paper of such gravity as the Report of the Secretary of the Treasury. The fact is—a fact familiar to all students of Political Economy, that, of an inconvertible legal tender paper currency, none of it is unemployed.—See Tooke's Hist. Prices, iv., 222–23.

† By "investment capital" is meant, that which, being unaccompanied by the personal labor of the original owner, is first tempted from its regular employment by higher rates of interest, when added to security—the latter being its main desideratum. By "working capital" is meant, that with which the owner runs some risk, for the sake of larger profit. This yields next in order to the allurements of higher interest and Government security. By "speculative capital" is meant, that which is employed in enterprises involving considerable risk of security, for the compensation of those large profits or quick returns which distinguish such employment.

equal to fifteen per cent. interest per annum, and a few months ago were offered at eighteen. The primary cause which set such a system in operation was that inexcusable error which consists in refusing to believe that what the Government wants is not money, but supplies. After all, these ruinous rates of interest tell the whole story of financial mismanagement which we have been and still are suffering from. This is the quadrant which fixes the financial prospect, of which prosperity is the zenith and ruin the horizon. Fifteen per cent. per annum! Does it not make the Secretary blush, that he should resign himself to a policy which involves such extortion? We all know that in all probability the capital of this debt will never be paid. The time has passed when any hopes of redeeming it were entertained.* It is the payment of the interest to which we now look. To meet this promptly is all that the Government is expected to do; and to reduce the rate of interest as much as possible is the only means by which we can hope to decrease the debt. But this depends upon the savings of capital; and this again upon tranquillity, security, and prosperity. All these are affected by the war, but their interruption is unnecessarily aggravated by a fluctuating currency. Remove this pregnant cause of half our financial troubles, and not only will the credit of the Government be enhanced, and its capacity for borrowing concomitantly increased, but commerce will feel renewed encouragement, and the arts of peace will exert themselves to bind up the wounds which war is inflicting upon us. Then, instead of lying like a leaf in an eddy by the shore, while the mighty stream of civilization and development sweeps the rest of the world along, this people will once more join in the grand march of progress, and redeem its lost place among the nations.

We here close our review of Mr. FESSENDEN's Report. Neither to the nation of tax-payers to whom it is addressed, nor to the Government creditor either at home or abroad, can its contents afford any degree of satisfaction. Inaccurate in its figures, confused in its arrangement, entirely obsolete in its statements of the Public Debt, and infelicitous in its suggestions for improving the revenue, it has been a task of no little difficulty to impart to this review of it that required clearness

* Even the absurd Sinking-Fund law now extant has been abandoned.—See Report.

and method which was necessary to the proper elucidation of its contents. Engaged with the task of keeping a multiplicity of important topics in proper subjection to one another, many minor points of interest have necessarily been overlooked, such as the National Banks, Foreign Loans, future emissions of Gold-Interest-Bearing Bonds, &c. But enough has been said to show that Mr. Fessenden has not succeeded in laying foundations for repute as a financial minister. Nowhere has he risen above that level which is indicated by his recommendation for a law to punish speculation in gold, and which is to be found on page 23 of the Report. A reputation in public finance, as in literature, is to be gained only by sowing acorns which future generations will enjoy in sturdy and enduring oaks, and not by planting those early vegetables, which, like the measure alluded to above, may meet with sufficiently quick returns, but whose momentary existence serves but a transient purpose.

Nothing but a sense of public duty could have induced us to so severely criticise the official measures of a public officer distinguished for so many eminent personal endowments as is the present Secretary of the Treasury; and especially in a time when criticism sounds to the patriotic ear like the carpings of discontent or inimicality. But, like the surgeon whose scalpel lays bare the seat of disease with cruel insolicitude, we have probed the unhealthy parts of our financial system, only that it might derive those true restoratives which are to be found alone in the wise and well-considered lessons of Political Economy.

HERBERT SPENCER.*

In Literature and Philosophy, as a general rule, long after the achievement which earned, follows the popular verdict that bestows, the laurel wreath. Schopenhauer was compelled to wait forty years after the publication of his work on The Will, before Germany consented to recognize his merit. Confident of the truths of his philosophy, and their ultimate recognition, he awaited, calmly and serenely, the fruition of his fame, seemingly regardless of the slurs and sneers of hireling critics and jealous contemporaries.

The case of Byron, who awoke one morning and found himself famous, is an anomalous one in the history of literature. The deeper the philosophy, the more profound the thinker; the higher, intellectually, the benefits that he renders to society, the slower the pace of his fame, and the less is the world disposed to acknowledge the merits of the man whose life is dedicated to its service.

A brawling demagogue, whose few ideas are derived from weak solutions of some one of the world's teachers, rides rapidly to honor and distinction, while he who supplied him with his stock in trade lives and dies in obscurity and poverty. Nay, more: the same rule holds true as to those to whom the world has given the name of Statesmen, and with common accord agrees to believe in their wisdom and originality. Sir Robert Peel was reluctantly compelled to accept the teachings of men who had written upon and solved the question of International Commerce, seventy-five years before Peel came to power; yet, hundreds and thousands know of him who are ignorant even of the names, much more the writings, of Adam Smith, Turgot, and Quesnay. By the far greater majority of the law reforms which have been made within the

* *Social Statics:* London; John Chapman, 1851.
Education: New-York; D. Appleton & Co., 1865.
Illustrations of Universal Progress: New-York: D. Appleton & Co., 1864.
Essays: Moral, Political, and Æsthetic: New-York: D. Appleton & Co., 1865.

past century are due to Jeremy Bentham; yet the multitude will ever regard Lords Brougham and Grey as the authors of the great judicial reforms of the age. The difference between the thinker who sows the seed, and the practical man who reaps the harvest, is, that the former is ahead of, the latter even with, his age.

It would be a debatable question, so far as the happiness of the individual is concerned, whether it is not as bad to be ahead, as behind, the age, in which it is his lot to be born, were it not for the fact that he who is in advance of his contemporaries, experiences an inward satisfaction, an elevation of spirit, which places him above the desire for applause, and soon renders him callous to the neglect of his fellow-beings. A thinker, who, during long years of undeserved obscurity, remains true to principles; who refuses to enter that rut of routine in which men far below him in capacity earn honors and distinction; who submits to social ostracism rather than be false to his convictions of right; who spurns the rich food and certain sustenance society offers if he but consent to become its pack-horse; and who prefers to run his own career according to his own understanding of his mission in life—trusting to find sympathy and maintenance as best he can—presents a picture of moral heroism of which every age can boast but few examples.

To this class of men belongs HERBERT SPENCER. Not only that he ever remained true to his convictions of right, but he never lost faith in that society which neglected him. He constantly and steadily labored, and still labors, for the great cause of human progress and the liberty of man, notwithstanding the fact that society left him in poverty, and saw his distress with careless unconcern. When, years ago, SPENCER's first work appeared, it fell still-born from the press. Learned societies vied not with each other for the honor of making him an associate member. Well-fed and comfortably-positioned professors did not hasten to lay the results of his reflections before their classes. In the *curriculum* of universities his works were not catalogued. "Social Statics" could not boast of two hundred readers. His contributions to the periodical literature of England did not create a sensation. His profound work on Psychology was almost totally unknown even by philosophers. Here and there some mention in a periodical or foreign quarterly, of his name, and dead silence again enshrouded the obscurity of his existence. All the charms of style, the most powerful thoughts, expressed in the tersest Saxon English, availed not to catch the ear of the populace.

It is not surprising that the world refuses to read and pay heed to an author who has neglected to learn the rounding of a period, or the easy flow of a sentence; who chooses to surround the light of his ideas by an almost impenetrable wall of verbiage; and such a one cannot complain if the public will not undertake the task of deriving pleasure from his labors. But it may well be asked, with some degree of astonishment: From whence this neglect of one who had every element of success in the highest walks of literature; who unites the erudition of a Bentham with all the terseness and force of a Macaulay? The answer need not be long sought for. SPENCER is what the world persists in calling an *impracticable* man. He attacked, with vigor, every illegitimate vested in. terest in turn. His criticisms were directed against the existing evils of society:—evils upon which great classes feed, subsist, and prosper—and they became his mortal foes.

He attacked the evils of legislation, and every politician became his sworn enemy. He attacked the fetishisms of theology, and churchmen felt insecure in their livings. He showed the corruptions in moneyed institutions and railway companies; and directors, presidents and secretaries regarded him with fear and disfavor. He threw down the glove to the landed aristocracy of England, and they recognized in him a dangerous adversary. He wrote a stinging, biting criticism of the antiquated *curriculum* of the universities; and Deans of Faculties, and Professors, Fellows and Ushers were filled with fear lest his words be heard, and they be forced to change the incrusted habits of years of routine duties.

The methods adopted by these vested interests to silence this redoubtable champion of the rights of man, and adversary of every one who made capital upon bigotry, hallucinations, corruptions or fraud, were wonderfully alike;—they determined to silence him by silence. No pamphlet appeared attacking his positions; no work was written in opposition to his stand-point. Nothing was done which might ride SPEN-

CER into notoriety, if not secure his lasting reputation; and the same policy was adopted as to him that was pursued by the representatives of improper and illegitimate interests against a kindred spirit of SPENCER in France, Frederic Bastiat, and which induced the latter to write to his friend Fontenay, "they will smother me with silence."

But, at last, despite neglect and misinterpretation, the genius of SPENCER has a vista opened for it; and the rays of its light break through the mist which, for twenty-odd years, has prevented the world from enjoying its beneficent rays. Thanks to a few progressive thinkers of Europe—thanks to a few enlightened men of this country (more especially Prof. Youmans), SPENCER'S name is now known, his talents are recognized, his merits are being acknowledged, and his works are being read and studied. It is, perhaps, idle to hope that SPENCER will ever become a popular author, but he is fast becoming a well-understood and appreciated thinker. His direct influence will, in all probability, be restricted to a circle composed of a few thinking men in the community; but that suffices; as, from that circle, will be reflected—frequently discolored, perhaps, and scarcely recognizable—still, to a greater or less degree, reflected, upon the outside world the light of his ideas. From the Philosopher, who weaves SPENCER'S ideas and forms of thought into the web of his philosophy, down to the mere scribbler in some obscure journal—who will use his arguments in an editorial, without knowing from whence they came or to whom he is indebted for his ideas; Spencerean philosophy will permeate and penetrate the world of thought; and, eventually, to the extent of the truths which he has taught, will influence human conduct.

SPENCER'S Social Statics was written to illustrate the conditions essential to human happiness. We do not think that we are asserting too much when we say, that, from this Work, will date modern Social Science; as it holds the same relation to the indefinite speculations that were called Social Science anterior to its publication, that Adam Smith's "Wealth of Nations" holds to that which was called Political Economy, prior to 1776.

In the Introduction to the Work, SPENCER successfully refutes some of the current maxims relating to Government.

The doctrine that "whatever is expedient, is right," is disposed of by him, by the following line of argument: that expediency, as a rule of conduct, cannot safely be relied upon, is evidenced by the fact, that no two persons will agree upon the expediency of any measure, if they differ in culture and education. The higher our civilization, the more we discover that expediency and right are almost convertible terms. It would, therefore, be much nearer the truth to say that "whatever is right, is expedient." That the doctrine of the greatest good to the greatest number—a doctrine lying at the foundation of the political speculations of Bentham—is no safe guide, or, in other words, no guide at all, is evidenced by the fact that it gives rise to an almost interminable question of what *is* the greatest good to the greatest number. A Tory, of England, will argue that it is for the greatest good of the greatest number that they be without the elective franchise, and that the people should intrust the affairs of Government to the hands of the nobility and gentry; whereas a Democrat will have a radically different conception of what will contribute to the greatest happiness of the greatest number. That which constitutes the greatest happiness of an Esquimaux Indian differs widely from that which forms the happiness of a civilized European. The military plans and schemes in which the genius of a Napoleon would delight, would prove no source of pleasure to a Quaker. Therefore, the rule of the greatest happiness of the greatest number means nothing at all, because an agreement upon the subject cannot be arrived at. The question, therefore, of a rule of conduct lies deeper than any of the utilitarian school of philosophers conceived it to be—it lies within the nature and essence of things themselves. Once admitting that man in society is governed by natural laws—clearly, conformity to these laws is the only rule of conduct, and must lead to the greatest happiness of the individual and the greatest well-being of society. Universal conformity to these laws implies an ideal society. When we say that man is simple, weak, frail, we mean that he does not habitually fulfill the appointed law. Imperfection is another word for disobedience.

"And yet," says SPENCER, "unable as the imperfect man "may be to fulfill the perfect law, there is no other law for "him. One right course only is open, and he must either "follow that, or take the consequences. The conditions of his "existence will not bend before his perversity, nor relax in "consideration of his weakness. Neither, when they are "broken, can any exceptions from penalties be hoped for. "'Obey, or Suffer,' are the ever-repeated alternatives. Dis-"obedience is sure to be convicted, and there are no reprieves."

The fundamental law of equal freedom he deduces from the fact, that man's mission on earth is his happiness; that happiness is only attainable through the faculties; that the faculties yield those sensations, of which happiness consists only when they are exercised; for their fullest development and their exercise, it is essential that they be left free from external control or interference. Man, therefore, has a *right* to liberty. By the steps traced, he arrives at the formula of this law, which he puts in the following words: that, "Every "man has freedom to do all that he wills, provided that he "infringes not the equal freedom of any other man." The application of this principle to the social organism forms the subject-matter of the Work under review.

In some respects, SPENCER'S application of this first principle seems to us faulty. For instance, in the ninth chapter, on the Right to the Use of the Earth, he denies the right of ownership in land. He says: "Equity does not permit property "in land; for, if one portion of the Earth's surface may justly "become the possession of an individual, and may be held by "law for his sole use and benefit, as a thing to which he has "an exclusive right; the other portion of the Earth's surface "may be so held, and our planet may thus lapse altogether "into private hands.

"Observe, now, the dilemma to which this leads. Suppos-"ing the entire habitable globe to be so inclosed, it follows "that, if the land-owners have a valid right to its surface, all "who are not land-owners have no right at all to its surface; "hence, such can exist on the Earth by sufferance only."

SPENCER seems to forget, that the power of a person to hold land in the existing state of society for his own use and benefit, is limited by his power profitably to use it. He can only use land profitably to a very limited extent. The argument against the absolute possession of land, being of a similar character to the argument against the legitimacy of interest —the anti-interest advocates claiming that, within a definite period, a small capital, invested at compound interest, would eventually absorb the whole wealth of the world—forgetting that, while their calculations may be correct, there are always natural tendencies in operation, which counteract the too great influence and preponderance of capital in individual hands; and that, as with the possession of land, the growth of capital in the hands of individuals is limited by the power profitably to employ it—a power which, it becomes more and more difficult to exercise, the larger the capital to be employed.

To remedy what he believes to be an injury to society, SPENCER proposes that society should own the land and lease it to individual competitors, employing the rent, thus obtained, for the general purposes of society at large. Here SPENCER falls into several inconsistencies. In the first place, the letting of the land and application of the funds, thus obtained, would have to be done through agents, *i. e.*, Government. He has admirably shown, not only in this work, but also in his Essay on Over-Legislation, that trust should not be reposed in Government; that we should never intrust into the hands of agents that which, by any possibility, can be done by ourselves. And, it is certainly clear to the mind of any one familiar with that bungling, ill-contrived, and badly worked machine, called Government, that the moneys reaped from the rent of land by society, through the instrumentality of its agent—Government—would not be so well applied nor so faithfully and surely reinvested for the benefit of society, as it is now done by the individual landlords of the Earth's surface. But, there is another objection to HERBERT SPENCER's idea, quite conclusive of the question, and that is: that the adoption of his plan would not at all remedy the evils of which he complains. He says: "Put up the land at public auction, to be leased to the highest bidders." As there are by far more people in the world than desirable farms, it is clear that the great majority would have to leave this auction disappointed; and could they not be treated as trespassers by the successful of the competitors? Clearly so; and this injustice would last just so long as the leases would have to run, and a new set of leaseholders occupy the land, when like acts of injustice would be repeated, and so on *ad infinitum*. From a Politico-Economical standpoint, SPENCER's idea is not only not defensible, but must be unhesitatingly condemned. Private property in land is essential to society, because then only is the necessary inducement held out to use the land to the best advantage.

The man who is not secure in the possession of the land, who holds it only for the term of a few short years, will not cultivate it as profitably to society as he would who has the right to transmit it to his heirs, and who reap the benefits of any judicious outlays or improvements made upon it; and, as it is of more importance to society that they should be abundantly supplied with the products of the soil, than to quarrel about the right to supply the food, it is clear that anything which tends to produce the first-mentioned result is of higher importance; and the universal experience of mankind has proved that that result can only be obtained by the recognition on the part of society, and increasing, as much as possible, the security of ownership in land. SPENCER himself says, in a subsequent chapter, that "he who in any way increases the "power of production is seen by all, save a few insane Lud-"dites, to be a general benefactor, who gives rather than he "takes." If, therefore, the proprietors of land confer upon society, by virtue of proprietorship, greater benefits than society is deprived of by reason of the sole ownership, then, both upon the principle of abstract right and relative expediency, proprietorship in land is just and proper. If "those "that do not know that they shall reap, will not sow," how can Mr. SPENCER expect that the leaseholders of land will bestow upon it that proper attention and cultivation which will result not only in immediate gain, but future profit? The result of such a system as Mr. SPENCER proposes, would inevitably be, that the men, who take property on short leases, would exhaust the land by not returning to it in the shape of manure what it had lost in strength by the crop, as they would calculate that the increased value of the land, by reason of their expenditure, would probably inure to the benefit of some subsequent holder of it.

The ordinary system of polemical warfare against liberal ideas has ever been to force the advocates of liberty to accept either the utmost logical conclusion of their theories, or to abandon them altogether. Those who pin their faith to Governments, claim that, unless we apply our doctrine of Liberty of Man, to Women and Children, we are illogical, and destroy the very basis of our doctrine by our own limitations. If it is said that children should not be free, but on the contrary, should be placed under the absolute guardianship of parents, because their faculties are yet undeveloped, the answer to us is, "Then those whose faculties are limited, who "are admittedly below the average in intellect and culture, "should be placed under guardianship,—should have masters "appointed for them, and should be compelled to do the bid-"ding and obey the wishes of these masters;" then, to justify negro slavery, all that would be necessary to show, is, that upon an average, negroes are not equal to whites in intellect, and that certainly would prove an easy task. From this dilemma there appears to be no other escape than to accept the full logical conclusions of our theory; and however monstrous or inexpedient these conclusions may seem to be, if we are sure that our processes of arriving at them are correct, we cannot but accept them.

Spencer does not hesitate to apply his doctrine of equal liberty to Children and Women. Three-fourths of the conservatives who shall read Social Statics, will pronounce the man mad who claims that children and adults have equal rights, and who denies any *right* of coercion in the parent as against the child.

That there is an apparent incongruity between the lessons of experience and Spencer's doctrine, must be admitted; but whatever of Utopianism may seem to be in these doctrines, is due to ourselves, and not to any error in the doctrines.

It must not be forgotten that we are not in the purely moral state; that both from hereditary predisposition and the still existing barbarism of society, the natural law must appear incongruous and impracticable; but for all that, it is none the less the law, and the only law of conduct.

If it be urged that children cannot be governed by example and precept, without an admixture of coercion, we can reply that the objection, under the existing state of society, may be well founded, and yet it does not invalidate the principle for which Spencer contends. "Rods and ferules, equally "with the staff and handcuffs of the constable; the jailer's "key; the swords, bayonets and cannon, with which nations "restrain each other, are the offspring of iniquity—can exist "only whilst supported by it, and necessarily share in the "badness of their parentage."

That SPENCER himself does not believe the principle he inculcates—of the equal rights of children—to be immediately practicable, is evidenced by what he says upon the subject in his work on Education: "The truth is, that the difficul-"ties of moral education are necessarily of dual origin—neces-"sarily result from the combined faults of parents and chil-"dren. If hereditary transmission is a law of Nature, as "every Naturalist knows it to be, and as our daily remarks "and current proverbs admit it to be; then, on the average "of cases, the defects of children mirror the defects of their "parents: on the average of cases, we say; because compli-"cated as the results are by the transmitted traits of remoter "ancestors, the correspondence is not special, but only general. "And if, on the average of cases, this inheritance of defects "exists, then the evil passions which parents have to check in "their children imply like evil passions in themselves: hid-"den it may be from the public eye, or perhaps obscured by "other feelings, yet still there. Evidently, therefore, the gen-"eral practice of any ideal system of discipline is hopeless: "parents are not good enough.

"Moreover, even were the method by which the desired end "could be at once effected; and even had fathers and mothers "sufficient insight, sympathy, and self-command, to employ "these methods consistently, *it might still be contended that "it would be of no use to reform family discipline faster than "other things are reformed*," &c., &c.

The objects of SPENCER's Essays on Education are, to inculcate the necessity of substituting in the education of children sympathy for force—education for training;—to substitute for the worn-out *curriculum* of classical studies in our schools and universities, a knowledge of the sciences, and their practical application. In short, that children should be fitted, from infancy up, for the life of to-day, instead of the life of two thousand years ago.

In his inquiry of "What knowledge is of most worth?" he shows how beyond all comparison a scientific education is superior to a classical one. Accomplishments, the fine arts, *belles-lettres*, and all those things which, as we say, constitute the efflorescence of civilization, should be wholly subordinate to that knowledge and discipline in which civilization rests. "As they occupy the leisure part of life, so should they oc-"cupy the leisure part of education." The remainder of his book is taken up with an examination of the subject of Education in its three great subdivisions,—Intellectual, Moral and Physical.

There are two classes of books from which culling is difficult. The one class is too poor to afford a single blossom; the other so rich, that the critic suffers of an *embaras des richess.* We are in the latter position in the case of SPENCER's work on Education.

SPENCER's Education should be in the hands of every mother in the land. It should be conned and conned again by every person having in charge the education of the young; and should hold the place of honor in the family library. In one respect alone do we differ from SPENCER's opinions upon Education. We think that he underrates the value of a knowledge of modern languages. A knowledge of modern languages is necessary, and the time expended upon their acquirement must be deemed profitably employed for entirely different reasons, and upon different grounds than the acquisition of Latin or Greek. The present state of intellectual activity; the great progress made, contemporaneously, throughout the civilized world in every department of science, makes it a matter of necessity for almost all who desire to be up with their age, to be able to read the continental languages of Europe. It is idle to urge that good translations of every important work, in any language, will soon abound in every other. In the first place, this is not true. In the science of Political Economy alone, we know of a number of important works which have never been translated into English. Chas. Comte's Traité de Legislation, and Traité de la Propriété; Dunoyer's De la Liberté du Travail, are books which have exercised a very great influence upon the progress of Political Economy in France. Of these works Bastiat said, that if he were imprisoned for a number of years, and he could select but three works for meditation and reflection during his imprisonment, he would select the three works above mentioned.

Why should a man of science, or any one who may be desirous to be *au courant* with the literature of the world, be compelled to wait until some third person translates the work for him? It is a well-known fact that translators are, as a general rule, not of the first order of minds; and booksellers, with but few exceptions, are composed of a very inferior class of beings; and a person unfamiliar with the modern languages would, perhaps, have to wait years before some translator takes the trouble, or believes that it will pay to translate, and some publisher believes that it will pay to publish, some important foreign work; whereas a slight knowledge of a foreign tongue might have enabled him to study, within a few months after their issue, the speculations of some kindred spirit. Some of the most important works in the German language, upon the same subject—such as the writings of Rau, Moser, Rosher, and Dankwart—are not yet to be found in an English dress; and how great a treat and opportunity for intellectual profit is lost to the French or German philosopher who is unable to read our language; for we are quite certain that there is no translation whatever of HERBERT SPENCER's works in either of these two languages. Therefore, a familiarity with the leading languages of modern Europe is necessary, aye, almost indispensable, to complete living. The constant tendency on the part of the nations of the world, is towards greater and greater freedom of commerce and mutual exchange. This necessitates us to study the wants, tastes, and aptitudes of other nations; and we can only thoroughly do so by studying their languages.

The Essays of SPENCER, published in this country, under the titles indicated at the head of our article, are contributions to the periodical literature of England, gathered together and published in book form, originally in England, and subsequently here. Had SPENCER written nothing but the Essays on Progress, its Law and Cause, Over-Legislation, Railway Morals and Railway Policy, and Representative Goverernments, he would have been entitled to be ranked among the most gifted men of the the age.

The talents required for a succesful essayist are of a higher order than those requisite to write a treatise. It is necessary to condense and prune; to say the most in the fewest possible words; to give a *résumé* of a subject within a certain number of pages of a Review; and yet leave no essential point unsaid or unargued. This quality is eminently displayed in SPENCER's Essays. In his Essay on Representative Government, the secret of the bad working of all representative institutions is unfolded and laid bare. He shows that for all the *non-essentials* of Government, an absolute monarchy, by reason of its simplicity, is the best: that the bad working of representative institutions arises from the fact that we encumber them with the performance of non-essential functions: that they will be badly attended to, because of the peculiar fitness of this form of Government for its special functions,—that of the administration of Justice between man and man, and of police duty: that every machine as it becomes more and more improved, its function becomes more specialized, it becomes less and less fit for any other purpose than its ordained one. "An instrument that is intended both "to shave and to carve, will not shave as well as a razor, nor "carve as well as a carving-knife." The peculiar fitness of Representative Government for its special duties, peculiarly unfit it for any other duties.

The administration of Justice, and the maintenance of Order, are simple functions, in which legislators, executive, and people, are alike interested. But the moment we delegate to Government duties outside of these simple ones, from that moment we create an antagonism of interests which secures to us evils, instead of benefits; curses, instead of blessings. If a Representative Government is to administer charity, and educate the young; carry mails, and protect home industry,—frauds and corruptions will inevitably creep in, and every department will be maladministered.

The limits of a review article do not enable us closely to follow the author's reasoning. We can but state the conclusions at which he arrives.

The Essay on Over-Legislation is a sermon on the text, "Put not thy faith in Governments;" and he illustrates the soundness of the text by hundreds of examples.

The Essay on "Railway Morals, and Railway Policy," unfolds the secret workings of corporations, and reveals to us the mysteries of their management. We no longer, after the reading of this Essay, wonder at the unpopularity of this uncomfortable truth-teller. No wonder that many would like to see an author at the bottom of the Thames, who deals mercilessly with evils upon which they feed and prosper. Had SPENCER been the president of a railway board the greater part of his life, he could not have given us a better insight of the internal polity of large corporations; he could not have better or more happily illustrated the fact that all the evils of Government are represented in miniature in the workings of every incorporated body; and that the same blind faith which induces people to trust their representatives, under the delusive idea that their interests are identical with their own, induces shareholders to trust their directors, and with a like result:—misapplications of moneys, usurpations of power, and regardlessness of the interests of shareholders.

The Essay on Progress, its Law and Cause, is the most scientific of SPENCER's Essays on social subjects. In that Essay he shows how progress results, in the greater and greater differentiation of functions, and specialization of aptitudes: that the same rules which hold good in physical phenomena, hold true in the social organism: that "every active "force produces more than one change; every cause produces "more than one effect." Simple as this law appears, it is a comprehensive truth of the greatest magnitude, and one which is almost universally ignored.

There are a number of other Essays in these volumes, all of which are suggestive and valuable contributions to the philosophy of science; but as they, as well as his works on Psychology, and First Principles, treat of subjects but remotely connected with the objects of this Journal, we cannot properly examine them.

When we consider SPENCER's few defects and many merits, we are compelled to acknowledge that he is one of the most influential thinkers of the world. He belongs to those men of the age who stand as much above the average of the old school of scientists and theologians, as their science is broader and their theological opinions loftier. His influence upon the science of Political Economy is, and will hereafter be, to a still greater extent, a most powerful one. He is the first Political Economist who has that encyclopædic knowledge which qualifies him to step beyond, far beyond, the limits of schools; and the loftiness of his stand-point enables him to see truths and perceive harmonies which are beyond the ken of mere *doctrinaires.*

We cannot commend Mr. Youmans too highly for introducing this philosopher and publicist to American readers; and, fitly to conclude this bird's-eye view of SPENCER'S works, we quote from Mr. Youmans' introduction to the last published volume of our author's Essays: "The nature of "our political institutions implies, and their success demands, "on the part of the people, an acquaintance with those funda-"mental principles which determine the reason, the scope, and "authority of all civil rule. Repudiating, as we did, at the "outset of our National career, the ancient and prevailing "forms of Government; casting loose, to a considerable ex-"tent, from the traditions and precedents of the past, and "organizing a new system, professedly founded upon self-"evident truths, and aiming at the establishment of natural "rights, it is obvious that our citizens have a vital and "peculiar interest in the elucidation of those foundation "truths which should guide the course of legislation, and con-"trol the policy of Government. And now, when our politi-"cal system is convulsed to its centre, and we are passing into "a new order of things, this duty is pressed upon us with "critical urgency, and we are summoned with solemn and "startling emphasis to the task of moulding our civil policy "into complete harmony with those principles which advanc-"ing knowledge and a riper experience have combined to "establish.

"Mr. SPENCER has given these subjects profound and pro-"tracted study, and the views he advances are entitled to "grave consideration. A devoted student of science in its "comprehensive bearings upon the welfare and improvement "of society, he has labored to unfold and illustrate those laws "of human nature and human action, of social organization "and social growth, which rest at the foundation of all intel-"ligent administration of public affairs. Without, by any "means, assuming that his views are final, it may be claimed, "that they mark an immense advance in political philosophy, "and they indicate the inevitable direction of future progress, "and throw important light upon numerous questions of im- "mediate and practical concern."

MR. ABOUT'S PROGRÈS.

Our readers probably recollect that a few months since, a French author of considerable talent and notoriety, Mr. Edmond About, published a work, which, under the title of *Le Progrès*,* produced a certain sensation in Paris. Whether the success of the book—for every sensation now is a success —was due to its intrinsic merit, a demand for lucubrations of this character, or to the contrast exhibited when placed side by side with the racy novels, dull comedies, and pungent satires, which have rendered the name of the author familiar enough to all readers of light literature, is a question which we do not pretend to decide. Nor do we intend to examine the motives which may have prompted the publication of a work so different from what the French public had been led to expect at the hands of a writer who had exhibited political proclivities of a very dubious character, and who suddenly scorns his former associates, assumes the garb of a Social Reformer, and parades the most liberal opinions. Suffice it to say, that the *Progrès* having been republished and largely circulated in this country, it behooves a periodical like the Social Science Review, to devote a few pages to a cursory outline of its scope and purport.

The idea involved in the title to the work before us, is a very inviting one, and one which has not failed to engross the attention of many great thinkers. It implies a science based upon the development of humanity, a kind of social palingenesy, which offers a vast field, not only to the vagaries of reformers, but to the serious investigations of Economists and

---

* Paris, 8vo, 1864; New-York, 12mo, 1864.

historians. Moralists may likewise devote their attention to an exposition of its ultimate results, for it involves an absolute belief in the doctrine of perfectibility. Assuming that history is only the reflection of immutable principles, we may well claim that the theory of progress is positive, and, necessarily, scientific; and that the facts urged in favor of such a pretension do constitute a science, exact as to its source, and universal, if we consider its scope and consequences. The votaries to this pursuit assume, if they do not always demonstrate, that individualities exist only in a relative sense, and that all things, whatever may be their origin or apparent diversity, are closely connected with, and absolutely dependent upon, each other. This connection has been shown in almost everything pertaining to the physical world.

We take Mr. About's work to be a familiar exposition of the efforts already made, and of the objects attained, by the present generation; at least in France, with a sprinkling of hopeful suggestions as to the immense benefits still in store for mankind. No excessive perspicacity is required to see at a glance that a work of this description is highly moral, and susceptible of producing much good, taking it for granted that the reader has not already experienced in the flesh the benefits to a consciousness, of which he is expected to awake by means of Mr. About's volume. It may be, however, that the notion antecedently entertained by the reader is dim and incomplete, whilst the facts and figures agreeably displayed in the book tend to make him feel and appreciate fully the importance of the conquests achieved by himself and his ancestors. This possible result is likewise of some moment, and here, again, Mr. About's work fully deserves the thanks and approbation of all well-meaning critics.

As to the work itself, it is certainly written with method and perspicuity. The author considers the subject-matter, as lawyers are wont to say, of nearly all human cogitations: To be or not to be? Does it pay? How shall I make both ends meet? Is it as bad as it looks? &c., &c. These questions naturally lead to a searching discourse concerning the exact characteristics and ultimate nature of what translators now call "The Good." Existence and Life, we are told, constitute its intrinsic nature. So far as existence is concerned, we must be permitted to say, that modern science predicates almost all its principles upon the fact that existence implies not only eternity *post* but *ante*,—in the past as well as in the future. As to life, if we are to believe the theories of the savans, of whom Mr. Herbert Spencer is the exponent, it is only a metamorphosis of physico-chemical forces, whilst all forces, in their turn, are nothing else than life metamorphosed. If so, what our author calls existence, which he seems disposed to liken to a mushroom suddenly springing into being, is only a thing antecedent, and appearing to him for the first time under mere transitory aspects. Perhaps Mr. About will say that these aspects differ in kind, which is not incompatible with degrees. At all events, it is difficult to conciliate the absoluteness which the idea of The Good suggests, with transitory conditions.

But let that pass. If existence is the substratum of the Supreme Good, it is logical to infer, that the more we have of it, the better. Hence, a pæan, inspired by a knowledge of statistics. The average of life in France, before the great Revolution of 1789, was only twenty-eight years and a fraction. Man, now, lives thirty-nine years. The conclusion is obvious. Without disputing the correctness of these data, and although we may be traveling out of the docket, we crave leave to remark, that it is high time that the intimate nature of statistics should be looked into, with the view of ascertaining the exact relation which is often too confidently alleged to exist between a column of figures and individual facts.

Be that as it may, the reader can now easily detect the philosophical basis of Mr. About's book. Existence is synonymous with progress; there is a larger sum of existence in the world than at any time previous—*ergo*, progress is being more and more developed; and, so far as man is concerned, were this the whole of the theory of progress, Methusalah would be the type, and Cornaro the apostle, of progress on earth.

These premises afford the author a magnificent opportunity to expatiate upon the outward appearance of, what is termed, progressive civilization. History is fairly interrogated, and made to yield facts bearing upon the progress accomplished, from the time when man was "only a promising petty officer in the grand army of monkeys," to the nineteenth century, when, conceited and forgetful, he denies the pedigree, and confides his blood-relations to the tender, but mercenary, cares of Italian organ-grinders.

Taking the vast and intricate system called Society, Mr. About takes extraordinary pains to enable us to appreciate fully all the parts, great and small, simple and complex, of this vast machinery, and the wonderful improvements introduced therein. Mr. About may even be said to treat all these important topics in a kind of philosophico-historical manner, with a fair sprinkling of the inevitable statistics, which soon impress upon the mind of many readers the firm conviction, that this, after all, is a pretty good world; and that, though viewed from the stand-point of personal experience, the progress of the world is scarcely perceptible; yet, when historically considered, we can trace the progressive development of all human functions.

The one cardinal objection to Mr. About's work is, that it is not sufficiently philosophical. Whilst we are disposed to admit the existence of progress, Mr. About gives us no satisfactory explanation of the principles underlying this fact. The advocates of the theory of progress must never forget that the work they have in hand is not simply to lay before their readers a series of facts, from which the inference would seem to follow that the world has progressed in intellect, in refinement, and in culture; but to show the immutable principles, by virtue of which the progression is an inevitable one. The opponents of this theory, of which there are, alas, but too many, can cite numberless facts to prove the contrary; but principles once clearly defined and thoroughly argued, even if they do not force universal acceptance, lead the debate from a mere vicious empiricism to discussions upon fundamental axioms, test their truth, and, by every attack, call forth other truths, upon the basis of which Social Science may be founded and elucidated.

But critics must not judge an author by what he may do. What he has accomplished is the basis upon which all criticism must rest. What he should have done is likewise a matter germain to the subject. Now, we cannot forget that Mr. About was at one time the most promising pupil of the famous Normal School of Paris. He graduated with the highest honors in his class, and as a reward was sent to Athens. His archæological work on the island of Ægina, displays great aptitude for patient researches, and his *Rome Contemporaine*, places him in the light of a keen observer of men and manners. In many of his letters and pamphlets, there are indications, which prove to a certain extent, that he is capable of philosophical investigations. If so, we have a right to exact from Mr. About, something more than a superficial view of any subject which he is disposed to treat. He may choose to court popularity, and laugh to scorn any undertaking of an erudite, a scientific, or transcendent character; but when he assumes to discuss a question of such importance as that which forms the subject of his *Progrès*, he is in duty bound to consider it under more than one aspect, and to dive into it as deeply as his intellectual powers allow him; for in that mass of readers, for whom he is supposed to write, there are many more than people would generally suppose, who are fully able and disposed to follow the author everywhere. The book before us was not intended to fill the place of a romance; the title of it shows clearly what must have been the intention of the author: it was in fact a pledge, which he failed to redeem.

It is not sufficient, when treating of the progressive march of mankind, to demonstrate that progress does exist. We assume that it is incumbent on the author to tell us what progress consists in, not by an asseveration that it is synonymous with existence; and as to the sum of it, with comparisons which tend to place the alleged superiority of the elephant over the vibrion, on the fact, that the former lives a century or more, whilst the latter, apparently goes through all the periods of its existence in less than a day. But what is more important, is to give us the laws which preside over progressive manifestations. We must know what are the inner workings of all those incidents, which casual observers deem wholly disconnected, whilst in fact, they are incomprehensible, unless it is assumed that they bear relations of a positive character to the main facts. What they are, it is for science to determine. Modern philosophy has abandoned with great reluctance, nay, with feelings of regret, investigations into primary and final causes, believing that they are beyond the reach of the human intellect; but if we can never behold the vertex of the angle, let us at least ascertain the quantity by which lines starting from a well-known point, diverge from each other. Man will never rest satisfied with mere statements or generalities; a kind of irresistible force urges him constantly to probe the surface, and discover the basis which underlies the whole. And in this respect, Mr. About's book is sadly deficient.

Our author will probably reply, that he writes for the masses, and not for metaphysicians; that he must please before attempting to teach, and consequently, a stately philosophical treatise could scarcely find a publisher, whilst a work which only skims the surface, is sure to go through several editions. The masses are as likely to understand the workings of a law as its immediate results. Peter, Paul, and Robinson, are not so obtuse as certain authors would have us believe. Everything depends upon the form and the language. Use a periphrase rather than a technical term, resort to a comparison when the definition fails, and the most abstruse notion may easily be placed within the reach of any illiterate individual. On the other hand, if the author sees clearly himself, what he wishes to express, there will be no lack of words to convey his ideas. The benefit to be derived from such a course is worthy of the effort. We fail to perceive why a man of wit should exert himself to pave the way only for useless thoughts and platitudes. The only serious objection is, that the difficulty is tenfold greater for a French author than any other; and the reason, we confess, is sufficiently plain. The language in which Mr. About writes, does not admit of imperfectly digested notions; half-spun ideas, which the reader is expected to bring to a happy termination through his own ingenuity or imagination, are unknown and impossible in the vernacular idiom of Pascal, Voltaire, and Buffon. As Heinrich Heine was wont to say: When you attempt to write French, you must first know what you mean to say. We do not pretend to insinuate that Mr. About's literary abilities are not adequate to the task, or that the investigation of such questions is beyond the reach of his intellect. Far from it. We only charge him with having neglected to impart to his book the philosophical characteristics which the subject demanded.

It is certainly praiseworthy to show the immediate effects of progress in certain individual relations, but we deem it no less important to demonstrate how such individual progress affects the masses; and if it finds its counterpart or reflection in the well-being of humanity, viewed as a whole, we must likewise know whether this progress is due to a law pertaining to the human species. The definition of this law, if it exists, is of greater moment than the clearest exposition of its results. We may then enable entire communities, states and empires, to shape their course in accordance with that law, and thus obtain certain results, which can be duplicated, perhaps indefinitely. Nor is that all: the knowledge of one law may lead to the discovery of many more, and these combined, will perhaps give us leading principles, which, we scarcely need add, philosophers have not yet been able to determine.

Viewing simply the history of our own times, do we not seem to be living in the midst of a world teeming with contradictions? We see, for instance, a race alleged to be the only one on earth worthy of self-government, which it possesses as a boon for superlative wisdom and virtue. Its institutions represent the type of political progress, the highest point ever reached by any community or communities; and full of confidence in the future, proud of the past, and fully competent to appreciate the present, it advances steadily in the path of progress and perfection. It discards the errors and prejudices of other races as manifested in their political history. Being particularly blessed with the outpourings of a bountiful nature, it sets itself as an example to other nations. The rest of mankind naturally feel humbled and envious, but cannot refuse to admit the justness of the comparison, and admire the wondrous results achieved by this chosen people. Philosophers perceive at once, in such an extraordinary prosperity, proofs of the working of well-known and immutable laws. The most advanced scholars in other parts of the world, establish professorships to elucidate and perhaps apply these laws everywhere; and although they do not succeed, the belief gains ground that the failure is owing not so much to the principles or example, but to fundamental differences, which can disappear only under the influence of a greater admixture of goodness and virtue in their internal organization. Suddenly the scene changes; and in the twinkling of an eye the lofty fabric totters to its very foundation. The passions resume their full sway, and there is scarcely a single error or iniquity committed by less favored nations, in the present and in the past, which is not urged at once and carried into effect with an intensity altogether unknown, and a frequency which astounds and yet delights the gaping multitude. The question naturally recurs, are we moving in a circle? Do all these railroads, magnetic telegraphs, steam-engines, machines for peeling apples, etc., lead only to transitory benefits, affecting the individual, enhancing perhaps the physical welfare of the masses, but leaving the inner man untouched, and almost as wicked, as unjust, as blind, as when he roamed in the woods under the uninviting shape of the gorilla or chimpanzee?

On the other hand, the large class of philosophers to whom we stand indebted for a more cheerful view of the case, reply that the evolution of mankind is not altogether in the nature of that useful figure of geometry; whilst if we insist on quoting Euclid, it is not the *circle* but the *spiral*, which we should invoke, the assertion assumes an appearance of probability which deserves the attention of every desponding philosopher. In fact, what is called the progressive march of mankind resembles, like the spiral, a curve continually receding from a well-known centre. Now, that such a recession is really a progress, must be the conviction of all those who believe that the golden age is not behind us, but before us. In the meantime, we wish Mr. About had deemed it worth his while to study the law which regulates the recession, and demonstrated with tangible facts wherein the difference exists, why it is for the better, and whether it is of an immutable and inevitable character.

But we should not ask too much of Mr. About. He has already accomplished his task in the great work of progress. He may not be a theorist bold and profound, but if we may judge from the last chapter in *Le Progrès*, it is evident that he has done as much as any other man to promote the welfare and perfection of his own country and countrymen. In the first place, they stand indebted to him for the momentous reform introduced in the Paris *Bourse* or Exchange. Only a few years ago, the entrance to that Pandemonium was not simply a door, but a *tourniquet*, a kind of revolving frame, very similar to the turnstiles used in this country by perspicacious farmers, to keep the cows off the cabbage-patch. "*Où sont-ils?*" proudly asks Mr. About, who, after a controversy which will long be remembered, succeeded in having the tourniquets removed. Next in importance we find that he was the first to advocate the appointment of ministers without departments, secretaries simply ornamental, patient and loquacious puppets, set in motion by a wire and bandied in the Legislative Halls. It seems that the French people did not give him credit for this great innovation, and he asks in a sorrowful tone: "*Pourquoi ni la presse ni le public n'ot porté à mon avoir le succès,*" *&c.*, *&c.;* which certainly betrays the blackest ingratitude on the part of that chivalrous race.

In the field of political foresight and projects, destined to change the face of Europe, we find this retrospective but eloquent quotation:

"*Ressuscitons d'un commun accord cette belle nation polonaise, ce peuple chevaleresque entre tous, que la diplomatie et la guerre ont sacrifié tant de fois, sans jamais abattre son courage! Que la Pologne renaisse de ses cendres! Qu'elle soit grande! Qu'elle soit forte! Qu'elle touche par le nord à la Baltique, par le sud à la mer Noire!*"

"*On me trouva ridicule,*" says he, with the view of exhibiting in a stronger light the change of public opinion. But now, the case is very different. "*Ridicule!*" Who would dare make use of such an expression? Does not every student of history know that Mr. About's project and prediction have been carried to the letter? So with a congress of all the sovereigns in Europe, proposed to "*débrouiller tous les noeuds, tirer au clair tous les principes, constater tous les droits, redresser toutes les frontières, et fonder l'ordre Européen sur des bases inébranlables;*" in fine, to renew the epopee which has rendered the name of Don Quixote immortal. It has not been carried out, although Mr. About speaks as if he was not aware of this trifling circumstance; but the intention remains; we have not yet reached the end of time, and can afford to wait.

Withal, it is due to Mr. About to state, that several passages in his book betray a clear conception of the subject, considered from a practical and Economical point of view. Whether he only spins out a few suggestions, which, although hackneyed, are nevertheless true, or advocates them as if they were his own, he deserves credit for repeating what should never be forgotten. Let us share with him the merit of iterating notions which present themselves to the mind of every observer of men and manners. These truths, which almost pertain to the nature of axioms, if acted upon can only promote the welfare of all. No transcendent intellectual powers are necessary to perceive every gleam of hope which they contain; and there is no memory so refractory as not to retain what can be summed up in four words: PROGRESS, LABOR, ASSOCIATION, and LIBERTY!

THE LIMITS OF POLITICAL ECONOMY.

In the transactions of the *Société d'Economie Politique* published in the *Journal des Economistes*, we find a debate on the question: "Is there a reason for classifying Political Economists into Spiritualists and Materialists?" Is it clear language to use in Political Economy the words spiritualism and materialism, which in their philosophical meaning are so indefinite? Mr. Mannequin, in opening the debate, stated the circumstances which caused the question to be placed before the Society, and condensed his opinion upon the subject within a few words. No science, he remarked, could be said to be spiritualistic or materialistic. He contended that the words spiritualism and materialism have not a sufficiently scientific meaning attached to them; that the object of science is the search for, and demonstration of, truth; that truth is neither spiritualistic nor materialistic, but simply truth.

Four members of the Institute, in answer to these statements, declared that the words in question are well defined, that it will be necessary to employ them whenever it is intended to examine the principle and the reasons of things, when it is tried to condense and generalize a series of economical truths, to inquire into the destiny of man, or into the functions of spirit and matter and their essential distinguishing conditions. It was said, that from the moment that man is considered as the *principium et fons* of production, the question is decided: for then it is evident that Political Economy is a science intimately connected with mental philosophy and morals. Further, we find it stated that the idea of the immortality of the soul reigns over the social organism and influences the solution of the great economical questions; and, lastly, it was proclaimed that Political Economy, as a science, must embrace in its investigations all the conditions of human life, and that man must be considered from a double aspect of mind and matter. Finally, one of the orators asked, how it would be possible to justify heritage without the hypothesis of a future life?'

Our readers will perceive that even members of the Institute deal sometimes in assertions which have to be demonstrated--and not in arguments. One of them, M. Jules Simon, even went so far as to declare that in order to make a rational distinction between materialism and spiritualism it is necessary seriously to investigate and specially study the domain of philosophy and metaphysics. Thus the spiritualists, in this debate, do not directly meet the question at issue, but refer it, on the contrary, to a domain of knowledge other than Political Economy.

M. Mannequin considers the question a simple one. Science, he said, is derived from observation, and observation is based on the observable. Whether the observable be matter or spirit, it is always necessary to proceed in the same manner for the purpose of observing. It may be said of observers that they observe well or ill, that they derive from their observation truth or error. Spiritualism, he further states, is based on preconceived ideas, of which no true science can assume the responsibility. Whenever observers enter into scientific investigations with a desire to find confirmation of what they believed without previous examination, science is tortured and mutilated; and such is frequently the method of "spiritualists." For this reason, observers who wish to proceed with independence, and inquire into natural laws, without a pretension to dictate to nature the answer that they expect from it, are called Materialists, by Spiritualists. Thus Copernicus, Galileo, and Newton have been called materialists. As to the real meaning of the words materialism and spiritualism, M. Mannequin declared them to be void of scientific import; particularly, materialism cannot be considered a school, or a doctrine, or a sect. The spiritualists who gave the name of materialists to their antagonists, resemble the Mahometans—the *true believers*—who gave the epithet of *dog* to all Christians. A proof of this is the fact that many spiritualists are called materialists by those who are more spiritualistic than they.

In answer to some objections made by Mr. Rénouard, one of the four members of the Institute, already referred to, Mr. Mannequin concentrated his remarks in the following statements:—Science is composed of the observation of facts, and the laws and principles deducible therefrom. These laws and principles are not directly observable, but they are deduced from observation, and would not be understood without observation. For this reason, it is just to say, that there is neither materialism nor spiritualism in science, because the facts observed, and the laws and principles deduced from observation, are instituted by Nature. In order to classify observers into spiritualists and materialists, ideas would have to be divided into scientific ideas, founded on observation, and religious ideas founded on belief. Thus considered, spiritualists would be the men of faith—the believers.

Mr. R. de Fontenay declared it as his opinion, that Political Economy should pay no regard to the ideas of the immortality of the soul and of future life. He said, that whatever may be the unknown destiny which God reserves for man after this life, we positively know, that, on earth, man has to fill a destiny, a duty, a mission. These are clearly defined; they consist of the amelioration of the individual, and of the amelioration of the human species. The science which illustrates the laws of this triple mission, we call Social Science.

Morals can and must be considered as resulting from entirely positive considerations, and it would not be difficult for historians and essayists to show, that, regardless of myths, revelations, and religious poetry, morals have constituted themselves in history, and become modified and perfected, by following step by step the progress of human knowledge and activity. Mr. de Fontenay called morals the hygiene of humanity. Political Economy plays, in regard to this hygiene, the role of physiology and its accessory branches. In regard to a remark by one of the four members of the Institute, Mr. de F. observed, that heritage need not be justified by the hypothesis of a future life. It suffices, that, to qualify heritage, the family is, as in reality, the material and moral extension of the individual. The distinction of mind and matter as two different categories is void of sense. In its mystic or religious acceptation, spiritualism is a faith, a hypothesis—that is to say, an anti-scientific principle.

Mr. Lamê Fleury thinks that the words spiritualism and materialism, whatever their meaning may be in philosophy, correspond in Political Economy with two very different ideas, which are easily definable. When certain Economists call others spiritualists, they want to express a criticism as well, as when the others call the former materialists. Spiritualists and Materialists reproach each other with injuring the popularity of Social Science. But, on which side, the speaker asks, is the truth? According to him, the blame rests with the spiritualists, who have confused Political Economy—the science of interests and of morals—and the science of duties—Theology.

Mr. Fleury, in reference to the remarks on heritage, already reported, very justly proclaimed that the scientific problem here at issue is, the question, whether it is useful, from a social point of view, that the proprietor should have a right to do with his property, after his death, whatever seems best to him. The laws answer this question in many different ways; but laws cannot be considered as the test of morals. Mr. F. referred to A. Franck's work, on the "Philosophy of Penal Law," where the author, endeavoring to show the difference between the penal and the law of duty, observes, that the servant of a rich man, who takes a piece of money from his proprietor, commits a crime; while adultery, which infringes upon the rights of society so profoundly, is a slightly punishable offence. There exists between morals and Political Economy the same distinction as that between legislation and morals. Political Economy teaches the master of a sick servant to discharge him; morality forbids the leaving of the sick without aid.

One of the members of the Institute, at this juncture, protested against the materialistic doctrines proclaimed by Mr. Fleury. According to him, production is not a work of matter, but is only valuable on account of the spirit that directs it. The two foundations of wealth—property and capital—are, according to him, eloquent attestations of the moral force which governs Economical problems.

We, finally, reproduce here the remarks of Mr. Joseph Garnier, who coincided with the materialist participators in the debate. Mr. G. declared, that, according to his opinion, it is absurd to accuse Political Economy of Materialism, simply because it occupies itself with material interests, private and public wealth, production, consumption, and consumers; that there is no ground for the pretension on the part of some Economists, who believe themselves to be in possession of a more spiritual theory than those of the founders of that science; that there is no reason to classify Economists into spiritualists and materialists; and that it is not clear language in Political Economy to use the words spiritualism and materialism, which, philosophically considered, is always absurd.

This debate, it will be perceived, has led to no conciliation between the disputants; nor could it. The time has not yet come when scientists may leave the well-marked limits of the Knowable, to compass the shadowy outlines of the Unknowable. The field of Social Science is so vast, and even the raw material of it so little sifted, that time can be ill afforded to go out of its main course into these contentions. Inquiry should never be shirked from, whithersoever it might lead; for a refusal to seek the truth in nature, would be equivalent to irreligion. It is as though we were content to admire the Universe, without caring to examine it—a species of mock tribute which a reader of it would scarcely pay even to the author of a spelling-book. But the time for this kind of discussion has not yet come. Let us first know more. Meanwhile, let no one lose his equilibrium, if more be discovered than is expected.

"When Pythagoras wrought out his celebrated triangle problem," says Börne, "he sacrificed a hecatomb to the gods. Since then, the oxen tremble whenever a new truth is brought to light."

TO OUR SUBSCRIBERS.

An apology is due to our subscribers for the non-appearance of the Review on the day originally specified. Delays, almost unavoidable at the outset of a new enterprise, have prevented an earlier compliance with our promise in that respect. We trust that future promptness may atone for past shortcomings on the part of

THE EDITORS.

ERRATUM.

Page 48, first line—word "desirable" should read "derivable."

ERRATA.

Page 99, line 18, insert "to" in place of "and."
" 103, " 30, insert "career" in place of "history."
" 109, " 21, after "Islander," introduce "is a physical monstrosity."
" 144, " 8, after "times" introduce "persons within."
" 144, " 12, strike out "physiological."
" 161 " 29, insert word "hard," in place of "loud."

THE

NEW YORK

SOCIAL SCIENCE REVIEW:

A JOURNAL OF

POLITICAL ECONOMY AND STATISTICS.

APRIL, 1865.

THE PROGRESS OF SOCIAL SCIENCE.

I. *Histoire de L'Economie Politique.* Par Blanqui. Paris: Guillaumin et Cie., 1860.

II. *Ansichten der Volkswirthschaft aus dem geschichtlichen Standpunkte.* Von Wilhelm Roscher. Leipzig: C. F. Winterische Verlagshandlung, 1861.

Social Science, meaning thereby that branch of knowledge which is occupied with the elucidation of the natural laws that govern man in a social state, is of all sciences the most modern. Political Economy, a department of Social Science, though itself as a distinct branch of study but a century old, had first to make gigantic strides and advances, before the conviction forced itself upon the minds of thinking men, that man, as well as all else in creation, is governed by natural laws which impel him irresistibly forward in his march of progress; and that the progressive civilization of mankind is not a mere accidental phenomenon, but the necessary result of the forces which are at work in nature. To trace the history of ideas for the past fifty years in Social Science it is necessary to cast a birdseye view upon the historical progress of political economy, and its gradual development into something higher and better, than the mere study of the laws that govern the production, distribution, and consumption of wealth.

In stating that political economy is but a hundred years old, we do not claim that men had not devoted their attention prior to the latter half of the XVIIIth century, to the study of social subjects. There were prior thereto thousands of observers of manners and customs, hundreds of men in all ages, who observed isolated social manifestations with remarkable keenness, and delineated the ideas engendered by these observations with clearness and precision, and frequently with elegance. Seneca, Aristotle, Cicero, and Plato were men whose books teem with politico-economical reflections. During the middle ages, the republics of Italy exhibited such wonderful commercial activity and industrial enterprise as compared with the rest of Europe that it would appear marvellous, if, in the midst of all this activity, some men had not discovered some general principles which govern the production and distribution of wealth.

M. Daru, in his *Histoire de Vénise*, 2d volume, pages 293–314, quoted by Blanqui in his *Histoire de l'Economie Politique*, has translated from the archives of Venice a speech delivered to the grand council of Venice in 1421, by the Doge Thomas Moncenigo, in which he speaks of the threatening aspect of political affairs, and more especially of an anticipated war with Milan. In that address the aged doge uses language which would do honor to a legislator of the present day.

After exhibiting the budget of expenses and income of the republic, and giving a careful *resumé* of the financial resources of Venice, he says: "You are the only people to whom the sea is as open as the land. You are the canal of all wealth, and supply the entire world. The nations of the earth are interested in your good fortune. Happy shall you be if you preserve your own domestic tranquillity and peace, while the whole of Europe is in a blaze. As for myself, so long as a breath of life remains in me my voice shall be for peace. If you persist in the policy I recommend, you will continue to be the richest nation upon the earth. Avoid, as you would fire, aggressions upon the property of others or the levying of an unjust war. God will most assuredly punish you if you do otherwise. In that event he who had ten thousand ducats will have but one thousand, and he who was possessed of ten houses will have but one. You were masters and shall become subjects; and subjects to whom? To a class you detest—warriors, and a ribald soldiery. Other nations have frequently paid homage to your wisdom, by selecting you as their arbiters. Persist therefore, both in your own interest, and in the interest of your children, in the system which has bestowed upon you so much benefit and prosperity." And then upon the Milanese question he says: "And suppose you have ruined the inhabitants of Milan, what can they in the future give in exchange for your products? By ruining them you have most effectually ruined yourselves."

Thus the necessity of peace and commerce had attracted the attention of the enlightened men of Europe as early as the first half of the XVth century, but these mile-stones of the science stood as yet far apart, and their inscriptions were indistinct. It was only during the latter half of the XVIIIth century that men began to examine the rights of man upon principle, and that thinkers had the courage to make up an account current between the people of Europe and their governors.

The first great impulse to these studies was given by the much decried, but little understood, mocker, scorner, and laugher, Voltaire; a man who was all intellect, or rather what the French call, *esprit*, a word for which there is no English equivalent. Voltaire was in many respects a product of the age in which he lived, and a complete embodiment of the fashionable vices and intelligence of the period. The wars of Louis XIV., the complete centralization of power during his reign, and the withering and blighting effects of his so-called protection to literature, which robbed the literati of that independence of thought and freedom of spirit which alone can make their efforts valuable as guides to truth, caused a reaction under the reign of

Louis XV., in thought, similar to that which took place in England, in manners, after the Restoration. Independent thinkers began to examine the title-deeds of royal authority. The question of the rights of man was for the first time mooted in the *salons* of the great, and the forerunner of this reaction was Voltaire. Think of the position of France, then the foremost country of the world, when that great mocker and destroyer appeared upon the stage. France was then governed alternately by priests and harlots; the most shameful abuses and excesses did not even wear the cloak of hypocrisy to hide their ugliness from the public eye. Virtue was not only sneered at, but laughed at. The peasantry were oppressed in every conceivable form. Government, as then carried out, was a system (to use Voltaire's definition in his *Dictionnaire Philosophique*) by means of which as much money as possible was extorted from one class, to be squandered by another, in demoralizing the very class from which it was taken. Nothing was sacred. Religion, as we understand the word, was almost unknown. The blindest bigotry joined hands with the rankest infidelity. Society was almost in a state of disintegration. The ruins of all that was holy were strewn about, and served as the mere footballs and toys of the pampered children of luxury. Never have the blighting effects of centralization of power been better illustrated. Voltaire was the petted child of fortune. He was taken by the hand by the great, and became the lion of the *salons*. His biting, withering sarcasm, his skill at repartee, his constant and steady flow of wit, made him the welcome visitor in the palaces of kings and prelates, and gave him his opportunity to tear the masks from the faces, and the tinsel from the backs, of his hosts—and thus show the enormities which they but served to hide. Voltaire was heartless and venal, but he was the impersonification of intelligence. No fraud could impose upon him, and truth and falsehood were sharply and clearly defined in his own mind. His writings opened to the outside world an interior view of the condition of the nobility of Europe. He spared none, he exposed everything.

Voltaire's influence cannot be over-estimated. Montesquieu, D'Alembert, Baron d'Holbach, Condillac, Diderot, and Helvetius wrote for thinkers, but Voltaire's derisive laugh was understood by the great body of the people. To the last, however, he never lost his hold upon the affections of the great mass of the nobility. Though he attacked their power, though he undermined their tenures, they considered all he did in that direction but the sport of an erratic genius, and pardoned all his labors for the rights of man, in consideration of his shameless poem *La Pucelle d'Orleans* and his novel *Candide.* Then followed the period of the Physiocrates and French Encyclopedists. The Encyclopedists were a set of fearless thinkers, who stopped at nothing between premises and conclusions. It is charged against them that in pulling down the old structure of society, they at the same time destroyed many things that are holy and true. But those who make such a charge forget, that the holy and the true can never by the action of man be destroyed. The forms in which for the time being they may be embodied may be demolished, but the essence they contained will survive so long as man with his ever-present, constant aspirations for the sublime, the beautiful, and the true, holds a place upon earth.

When Adam Smith began his work, The Wealth of Nations, which forms the framework of what is called political economy at the present day, several important elements of political economy had already been ably investigated and elucidated. The questions relating to international commerce had been almost exhausted by Quesnay and Mercier de la Rivière. The former more especially deserves to hold a high rank as an economist. He it was who laid the foundation for the disproving of the Mercantile Theory upon which at that time the world was governed, by proving that money did not constitute the wealth of a nation. Quesnay and the writers who followed him claimed that all wealth was derived from the earth, that agricultural labor was the only productive employment, and that all persons who were devoted to other occupations simply consumed wealth and did not produce any. Though this theory has since been essentially modified, it nevertheless marked a great progress in the development of politico-economical ideas, and directed attention to the true sources of wealth. Up to the time when Quesnay wrote, it had never entered the minds of any class of thinkers that there were natural laws which governed and controlled the action of man in a social state. To him and his followers we owe the phrases of *laissez faire* and *laissez passer.* These phrases do not mean, as some persons vainly suppose, a counsel to wait upon Providence, and that we should simply fold our arms, and let things come to pass as they will; but they are a protest against the constant tendency on the part of philosophers and governments to devise systems for the government of the moral and industrial world, and artificially enforce them upon the people, in the vain idea of thus adding to their wealth and happiness. This philosophy, on the contrary, says to all these schemers, "You have believed until now that the industrial world was a body without mind, into which you must inspire the breath of life; that it was a sort of clay awaiting some Prometheus to quicken it into vitality. You have believed that the world would be one of chance or chaos if the regulating hand of some government would not order all things to be done or forbidden. Undeceive yourselves; under this seeming incongruity and disorder there are admirable natural laws which preserve the harmony of all things. Instead of devising your artificial combinations and quack panaceas, study these laws carefully, and as much as possible conform to them; do not interfere when you are ignorant of these principles, but *laissez faire* and *laissez passer* the manifestations of the laws of the Creator."

Adam Smith, though continuing the distinction between productive and unproductive labor, considerably extended the domain of political economy by classifying all laborers who are engaged in the production of a useful commodity as productive, and all others as unproductive. To him we are indebted not only for the fundamental axiom that labor is the source and origin of wealth, but he also completely demonstrated the fallacies of protection, and illustrated the advantages of free trade. His maxims in regard to taxation have become classical. His dissertations upon colonial government and the relations which should exist between mother country and colonies, though never fully recognized until a very recent period, and then only recognized through the force and logical acumen of Goldwin Smith, showed him to be one of those pioneer thinkers who are far in advance of their age. A long period elapsed between the publication of the Wealth of Nations and the appearance of any profound original work upon the subject of political economy. Ricardo followed the footsteps of Adam Smith in almost everything except in the theories of Value and Rent; in which particulars he remodelled the doctrines of Smith. He explained that the rent of land consisted in the difference between the least productive land in a community, and that which is most productive—a theory since disproved by Carey and Bastiat, as to the greater part of the world, yet one which holds strictly true as to England.

The Rev. T. B. Malthus made the next step in the progressive advance of Political Economy. His work on Population is a dissertation dismal enough in some of its aspects, yet a valuable guide to many important truths of political economy; more especially those truths which are related to the social questions of the moral, intellectual, and physical status of the lower classes. His theory of population is that mankind has a tendency to increase in a greater ratio than its means of subsistence. He admits that this tendency is constantly counteracted, yet he foreshadows a time in the distant future, when the whole habitable part of the globe may be so densely populated, that every additional individual shall consume proportionately more than he can produce. At the time when Malthus wrote, the mechanical arts were yet in their infancy. When the present century began its history, the steam engine, the railroad, and the magnetic telegraph had not yet begun their immeasurably beneficial missions of usefulness. The power of production has become hundred-fold since then. The impetus given to all branches of human industry, by the increased facilities of intercommunication, have made famines impossible, and great dearths improbable. The supply of the wants of any community no longer depends upon its own power of producing any special article of consumption. The cry of distress is heard at a distant quarter of the globe, and speculation at once supplies the want; even in the time of Malthus great progress had already been made. The difference between the present industrial status of the world and that of some centuries ago, can only be properly estimated when we take into consideration that during 600 years of the mediæval history of France, there were 300 years of distress and famine. That while certain districts in that country enjoyed a superabundance of the necessaries of life, in certain other districts the people were starving for the want of them. Not only this progress, but also the great increase of wealth since Malthus published his dismal view of the future of mankind, and the ameliorated condition of the lower classes, have created a doubt as to the correctness of the Malthusian law; yet the great merits of Malthus will incontestably ever be, that he is the first economist who drew attention to the fact, that the moral and intellectual status of the working classes mainly depends upon their physical well-being.

Jean Baptist Say is the next in order and importance of the thinkers on politico-economical subjects. His *Traité d'Economie Politique* is an admirable *resumé* of the subject up to the period when he wrote, and he extended the domain of political economy by clearer definitions, by more analytical examinations, and more happy illustrations of the truths of the science, than had theretofore been rendered. Contemporaneous with Say, is Charles Comte, a thinker whom the world has persistently ignored, but who stands on the threshold of that new system of philosophy of man now called Social Science.

Charles Comte has written two works, *Traité de Législation*, and *Traité de la Proprieté*, both of them works of imperishable worth and lasting value. It is a matter of no small surprise that these works have never been translated into English. His work, *Traité de Législation*, brought upon him the animadversion of the government, and his *Traité de la Proprieté* almost caused his expatriation. He lived in England when he concluded his last volume of the last-mentioned work, and while there cultivated the acquaintanceship of the master minds of that nation ; more particularly that of the great jurist, Jeremy Bentham, whose works exercised a powerful influence on his mind. On his return to Paris, after the fall of Charles X., he became a candidate for the position of professor of political economy at the college of France ; but P. Rossi succeeded in obtaining the post. The *Traité de Législation* and its continuation under the title of *Traité de la Proprieté*, form a commentary upon the legislation and systems of government of the world, and illustrate the basis of true liberty in its strongest possible light. Part of the third and the whole of the fourth volume is devoted almost exclusively to the subject of slavery. He examines that institution in all its details, and exhausts the subject completely, by the fulness of his illustrations and the irresistible force of his logic. It was the most powerful anti-slavery philippic ever written by man, and no one, nay, not even the most ardent defender of slavery can fail to be convinced, by the arguments of Comte, of the demoralizing effect upon both the oppressed and the dominant class, more particularly the latter, wherever slavery exists. An interval of seven years elapsed between the publication of the first and second part of his work. These years were employed by Comte in devotion to public affairs, as a member of the French chamber of deputies, but he withdrew from this position as a task uncongenial to his tastes. On retiring, he left the following opinion upon record in reference to the filling of public posts :

"After the revolution of 1830, having been called to fill various public posts, and having imagined that it would not be impossible for me to serve my countrymen in my new vocation, I suspended, for the time being, the execution of the project I had formed of completing the work of which four volumes had already been published, as early as 1826 and 1827. But experience soon dissipated these illusions, and served to convince me that there were epochs when men of independent thought, and who desire to preserve their liberties of conscience, should resign all participation in the active administration of government. I therefore returned with renewed pleasure to the execution of my original project, and the following volumes are the results of this determination." *

The principal object of the works in question was to show the natural bases of property, and the true spirit of legislation. In doing so, Comte combated both the *Contrat Social* of Rousseau, and *L'Esprit des Lois* of Montesquieu. It is almost needless to observe that the groundwork of Rousseau's speculations upon human government, in his admirably written but in many respects pernicious essay on society and government, published under the title of the *Contrat Social*, was the theory that the authority of all human government was derived from an original contract made by man to subject his individuality to the will of society.

Comte proved that this original contract is a fiction—a mere creation of Rousseau's fancy—and that on the contrary the whole authority of government rests upon the consent of the governed. The leading error of Montesquieu, which Comte devoted himself to combat, was the theory that property exists by virtue of law alone—is a creation of the law—from which follows the necessary corollary that law has absolute control and undoubted authority over individual property. Comte, on the other hand, proved that property existed anterior to law; that law was evoked by virtue of the existence of property; that property, therefore, is superior to law; and that all laws which impair the rights of property are laws made in opposition to the very objects of legislation and law; hence invalid and wrong—being then merely acts of spoliation under the guise and semblance of law.

---

* M. Charles Comte and Charles Dunoyer published together the *Censeur Européan*, a periodical devoted to social, politico-economical, and political subjects. The work brought upon its editors numberless difficulties. The independence of its tone became obnoxious to the government, and the editors having published an interdicted article, they were sentenced to pay a fine of 2,000 francs each, and to undergo imprisonment for the period of two months. Comte fled to Switzerland, where he received the appointment of Professor of International Law at the University of Lausanne. A demand having been made upon Switzerland by the French Government, to exile Comte, which demand was refused, and matters wearing a threatening aspect, Comte, urged by the desire not to involve the gallant nation which offered him an asylum, in any difficulties by reason of his presence, voluntarily departed from Switzerland for England, where he remained until a change in the government rendered it safe for him to return to France.

Comte was followed by P. Rossi, who was his successful competitor for the professorship of political economy at the French University. Though Rossi did not extend the domain of political economy, he is, nevertheless, entitled to great credit for the manner in which he elucidated the principles of the science as then understood. The clearness and freshness exhibited in his *Cours d'Economie Politique* is truly marvellous, when we take into consideration that French was not Rossi's native tongue; but further than this he did not go. To say that he was for the most absolute free trade is simply to declare that he was an economist who understood the principles of his science. He accepted the Malthusian doctrine of Population, and the Ricardo theory of Rent.

Charles Dunoyer, who was associated with Comte in the publication of the *Censeur*, in his *Liberté du Travail* held language to the people as bold as Comte did to their governors. He showed to them that the majority of their miseries arose not from the vicious organization of things, but from their own improvidence and ignorance. But his labors did not end here; he examined in detail the various industries of man, and arrived at one general conclusion, that liberty is the only means to further progress and general well-being. Political economy, however, entered upon a new sphere through the genius of Frederic Bastiat. Frederic Bastiat drew attention to his genius by a series of most delightful and witty pamphlets upon politico-economical subjects—more especially discussions and illustrations of the principles of Free Trade. The hitherto dry questions of political economy were handled by him with a skill and an address such as had never before been evinced upon kindred subjects. These pamphlets were published some time in the years 1848 and 1849, and attracted attention throughout Europe. He had a lengthy discussion with Proudhon upon the legitimacy of interest, and for once, that redoubtable socialist was vanquished with his own weapons. But the work upon which will rest the imperishable fame of Bastiat is his *Harmonies Economiques*, which he unfortunately never lived to complete. There remains, however, enough to have given a new phase to all politico-economical studies.

The basis of this work is the theory, then novel and original with Bastiat, but now accepted by all economists of merit the world over, that all the really legitimate interests of man are harmonious. That natural laws control as well the action of man as the rest of the domain of nature, and that legislation is, as a general rule, a mere hindrance and impediment to the full, free, and harmonious operation of these natural laws. Bastiat's work has served to tear down the arbitrary limits of the science, and extend its domain into that of Social Science.

In Germany, until quite recently, but little progress had been made in political economy. The German mind seems to have been so completely immersed in transcendental speculations and metaphysical studies, that the thinkers of that most thoroughly intellectual people of the globe seemed to have no time to devote to the mundane affairs of life. List's work on National Political Economy is a plea for protection ; therefore cannot be properly regarded a politico-economical work. Contemporaneously, Professors Rau and Roscher have advanced the study of political economy in Germany. Their works on the subject are excellent text books, and contain much statistical material for purposes of reference. The practical labors of Schulze Delitzsch should not be forgotten. Delitzsch has revolutionized the labor market of Germany by the organization of his trades, and popular loan and credit associations.

In England, of late years, nothing of importance upon the subject of Political Economy has been produced, except the publication of John Stuart Mill's work and Herbert Spencer's Social Statics.

Mr. Mill's work is a general *resumé* of the present status of political economy. A profound thinker, a close logician and conscientious critic, familiar with the languages and literature of modern Europe, he has given to English and American students of the science the best standard work on political economy. But he has not advanced its domain.

Herbert Spencer's works and merits as an economist and philosopher upon social questions, we have treated of in our last number. He has made political economy the groundwork for a thoroughly scientific and logical treatise upon

Sociology. His Social Statics is a philosophy of human progress, and illustrates the conditions essential to human happiness. Liberty is the alpha and omega of this philosophy. If there are any wrongs in the social system which require redress; if we see injustices and great inequalities in social conditions, the universal panacea is enlarged liberty. Spencer is a scientist of almost universal attainments, and as such, he could not help but enlarge the domain of thought in any particular department of science of which he may treat. The broader our knowledge of facts in every department of science, the wider will be our generalizations in any particular department. The man who is a mere lawyer, who has trained his mind to the conception of but one class of legal facts, whose faculties are trained to run in but a certain limit of empirically decided causes, becomes a mere machine, useful to society, and in all probability successful in a pecuniary point of view. Yet as a man he is a failure. Such a one is an intellectual monstrosity, precisely as one who has developed by gymnastic exercises solely the muscles of his arms, so that with the biceps muscular development of a Winship he has the trunk muscles of a Fejee Islander. It is the same in the case of any other profession or avocation. The division of employment, while, in an economical point of view, of the utmost advantage to the world, has drawbacks to the individual of a very serious nature.

A few years ago, Minghetti, the Italian minister of finance, president of the council, and one of the leading, if not the leading, economist of Italy, published a valuable treatise upon the relations of moral duty, law, and political economy. This work has since been translated into French by M. Saint Germain Leduc, with an introduction written by Hipp. Passy. The intention of the work is to show the interconnection between moral duty and the principles of political economy, and the harmony that should exist between them. Mr. Minghetti shows great familiarity with the principles of political economy, and has devoted himself to the task of combining moral science, law, and political economy into one harmonious whole.

The whole Italian school of political economists has been free from the artificial restrictions which have been imposed upon the study of this science elsewhere. In Italy, from the first, political economy was pursued more as a branch of moral science than as a distinct study. And there are a number of valuable works upon the subject written in this spirit in the Italian language. One of the leading thinkers of his day was Professor Antonio Genovesi, whose *Lezioni di Economia Civile*, published a few years anterior to the publication of Adam Smith's "Wealth of Nations," entitles Italy to an almost equal claim to that of Great Britain for giving birth to the science of political economy. Genovesi was a champion of free trade in cereals. He opposed the usury laws, and was one of the first to condemn the vicious systems by which the colonies at that time were governed. He foretold, as early as 1764, the separation of the American Colonies from English dominion.

The liberality of the Italian schools of political economists is illustrated by the remarks of Gaetano Filangieri, in his work entitled *Delle leggi Politichle et Economichle.* "Inasmuch as there are evils of mankind which are not yet cured, inasmuch as there are any number of errors and prejudices which perpetuate evils which still find partisans, inasmuch as the truth is known only to a privileged few and rests hidden to the great masses of mankind, and whereas she is still far from being heard at the foot of the thrones, it is the duty of the political economist to preach, discuss, agitate, and illustrate the truths of his science. If the light which he sheds is not useful to his age or to his nation, it may be useful to another age or another country. The political economist is a citizen of every country, and the contemporary of all ages. The universe is his nation, the earth is his pulpit, and his contemporaries and descendants are his disciples."

In Belgium the leading political economist is the able professor of political economy at the *Musée de l'Industrie*, M. G. De Molinari. Molinari's journal, *L'Economiste Belge*, is one of the ablest progressive journals of Europe, and has exercised considerable influence upon the formation of political opinions in Belgium. His *Cours d'Economie Politique* received the highest encomiums from the members of the *Societé des Economistes* in Paris, and possesses the merit of being more anti-governmental in tone than any other work on political economy that we know of.

Social Science for its future development and extension does not solely depend upon political economists. Within the past ten years a class of historians have entered upon the field of literature, who bid fair to do more than political economists proper, for the further development of its principles. Foremost among these are Buckle, Gervinus, Draper, Meyer, Martin, and Momsen. History is now no longer a simple chronicle of events, and which, as hitherto, simply served to give a detailed account of the fortunes of a few reigning families, and was almost wholly occupied with the pageants of war, and the idle chat and gossip of courts ; but it has become the history of peoples, tracing and showing their gradual development and the laws of progress which underlie this development. It is of less moment to the world to know at what precise period of time the battle of Austerlitz was fought, than to know the social conditions of mankind which made a Napoleon a necessary product of the age in which he lived. This system of study may lead to fatalism in philosophy, but we care not through the medium of what bugbears we arrive at truth. That the historian should do more to develop the principles of Social Science than political economists, may appear a strange paradox, but a like circumstance has occurred in the development of Esthetics as a science. While the teachers of Esthetics quarrelled about definitions and idle words, the science was advanced and its principles established by such men as Winkelman, Lessing, Goethe, Schiller, and Humboldt. This holds equally true in Social Science. What with the progressive advance of History, Statistics, and Medical Police, the progress of social science is no longer dependent upon any one class of specialists.

It is an old but ever true observation that, in progress of time, the sciences tend more and more to react upon each other in their respective developments. They interchange and compare notes with each other, so that it becomes daily more and more necessary for those who desire to achieve success in any particular department of science, carefully to heed the developments contemporaneously in progress in every other department.

S. S.

THE NATIONAL BANKING SYSTEM.

I. *The Political Manual;* being a Complete View of the Theory and Practice of the General and State Governments of the United States. By Edward D. Mansfield. New York: 1862.

II. *The Congressional Globe; XXXVIIIth Congress.* Washington: 1864.

III. *Essays.* By Herbert Spencer. New York: 1865.

IV. *Acts of Congress relating to Loans and the Currency from* 1842 to 1864 *inclusive.* Edited by J. Smith Homans, Jr. New York: 1864.

ADVOCATES of the National Banking System base their arguments mainly upon two grounds: its more perfect congruity with the social status of the times, and consequent influence in binding the people together; and its superiority as a currency measure. They argue, that as government, in common with all other human institutions, is a consequence of human imperfection; it follows that when men are perfectly organized—that is to say, all wise and all good—government will cease. But, that meanwhile, as mankind advances toward its ultimate condition, each stage of its general social progress should be marked by congruous institutions, and among them corresponding forms of government. Yet, as men, though they progress slowly, yet progress constantly, and as governments, being established by law, are of a nature more or less permanent and fixed, it follows that general social progress and government do not keep the same paces, but that sometimes one is in the advance, sometimes the other. Social progress as a whole advances by slow and unremittent steps; government by sudden leaps. The result is that we often possess forms of government fitted only for past generations, and as often remedy the evil by providing ourselves with forms of government fitted only for future ones. Thus the Constitution of 1787 having emanated from men who were strongly imbued with the radical tendencies of the French Encylopedists, is claimed to have been of a character in advance of its time, and the people for whom it was enacted are believed to have been and still to be unable to appreciate the almost unrestricted liberty which it conferred. Numerous instances are adduced to support this view. Amongst them is that of the universal suffrage granted by the Constitution. It is contended that this was a mistake. The theory was, that all who were privileged to vote, would hold the privilege too high ever to neglect its exercise, and that as consequently all men would vote, the men who would fairly represent the average intelligence and common interests of the whole people, would naturally be elected to office. But as this theory has been completely reversed in practice, it is believed that to do away with universal suffrage, and substitute in its place qualified suffrage, would be a step more in consonance with the social status of the times. The theory upon which the executive office was created forms another instance for the advocates of a strong government. The Executive was intended to be a mere cypher in the administration of the government. He was merely to carry into execution the wishes of the people as expressed by Congress. But, that as on the contrary, we find him called upon to prompt Congress as to what it shall enact, and that as he has been invested with powers much more ample than it was originally intended he should be, and strengthened by the disposition of a patronage that virtually makes him a monarch; it follows that the Executive Cypher was a mistake, and that the Executive Monarch is called for by the social evolution which has meanwhile taken place.

The application of these premises to the question of National Banks will soon be perceived. If universal suffrage is a mistake; if the limited powers of the Executive, and other provisions of the Constitution were mistakes; and the Constitution itself thus shown to be at variance with the spirit of the age; then whenever it prohibits something which is shown to be essentially congruous or ordains something which is shown to be essentially incongruous with the times, it is proper to go behind the Constitution, and modify it to suit the prevailing social status.

That the National Banking system is essentially congruous with the times, and that the State Banking systems were essentially incongruous with the times, is next sought to be demonstrated, and thus the desirability of adopting the one and destroying the other, and the legal power to do both, is logically deduced. But let us follow the argument.

First, a *national* existence is claimed for the people living in the United States. Though it is admitted that phases in the life of humanity all melt into one another; that new ones begin before old ones are extinguished; that no dividing line is discernible, no classification correct—yet classification is insisted upon notwithstanding. The people living upon this continent are termed a Nation; and this point once conceded, it becomes an easy matter to argue from it almost any desired conclusion.

Social progress, it is claimed, is divided into five classifications: I. The Individual: II. The Tribal: III. The National: IV. The International: V. The end of all Government. Having passed through the first two of these phases, and not having yet reached the last two, it follows as a matter of course, that we are still within the phase of progress distinguished by the term National. Forming part of a Nation, therefore, we are told that our highest duty is to preserve and prolong the Nation, that the Nation is all in all to us, that there is nothing so beautiful in this world as the flag of the Nation, and nothing so glorious as to die in defending it. That our happiness is nothing, our prosperity nothing, our lives nothing —after they have been put in the balance with that gigantic blessing called the Nation. Security of life, happiness, wealth, are only to be valued when they are derived as immunities conferred by the popular will of the Nation. In short, that the first of all mundane blessings is the defence, support, and prolongation of that artificial classification of social progress comprehended under the head of National.

Every institution, therefore, which operates to this end, is deemed to be of the required congruity; and every one that does not, is looked upon as a radical and dangerous experiment. The National Post-Office is pointed at with pride as an evidence of the success which attends the growth of institutions planted in congenial soil. "It almost pays for itself," they exclaim. The National Coast Survey is another. "It supplies our mercantile marine with reliable maps, for nothing." The National Mint is another. "And what a convenience to the miner! By all means let us have another at San Francisco." The National Pacific Railroad is another. "Besides binding the Californians all the closer to us, and enabling us to move an army quickly to the Gold Coast, observe what an advantage it will be to the Mormons!"

The evidences of success which appear to distinguish such of these institutions as have already been founded, and the unmistakable leaning of popular sentiment toward such of them as are yet only projected, are dwelt upon, and the National Banking system is shown to be eminently in harmony with them all—therefore to be a measure which fits the times with mathematical precision.

Next as to the incongruity of the State systems. It is claimed that the still prevailing lack of commercial integrity, rendered banking systems, which were exposed to the chicaneries of petty legislatures, and the designs of artful managers, too deficient of proper safeguards for the public upon whom they were to be imposed, to be trusted in. Something more was wanted, even after successive modifications had so improved the State systems that scarcely any of their original features remained. The want of this something more, is contended to be conclusive proof of their incongruity.

Without admitting this conclusion, a glance at the history of State Banking in the United States, would seem to furnish the advocates of National Banking considerable justification for desiring a radical change of system.

In 1784 the first State bank was established in Boston. Since that day bank panics and bank failures have not ceased periodically to afflict the people. In 1814 a suspension of specie payments lasted for three years, and was terminated only by great personal sacrifices. In 1820, and in 1825, bank panics occurred again. In 1837 the entire country was convulsed from end to end by the tremendous financial revulsion occasioned by the rotten systems of the State Banks. Such was the extent of the distress brought upon the country by this memorable crisis, that its calamitous consequences continue to be felt even at this distant day. The sod has not yet grown over all the commercial graves which the universal and desolating bankruptcy of 1837 opened in this country. Following this there were four years of partial suspension. In 1857 the State Banks again stopped payment, and numerous commercial failures ensued. Finally, in 1862, they once more proved themselves to be untrustworthy, by quietly suspending specie payments without even a color of necessity for so doing.* We have had State Banks founded on every conceivable security, good and bad, and they all resulted the same way. In their palmiest days their notes never had more than a strictly local circulation. An Indiana bank-note was worth but ninety-five cents on the dollar in New York, and a Kentucky bank-note but eighty-five cents in Pittsburgh—while the notes of banks located in more remote States would not pass current at the business centres for any price at all. Sometimes they fell to forty or fifty cents on the dollar, and occasionally they rose to par. They were largely counterfeited —it is said that there were five millions of counterfeit State bank-notes in active circulation previous to 1862†—and such was the multiplicity and variety of the designs upon their notes, that counterfeits were frequently impossible to be distinguished from genuine notes, even by experts. Counterfeit bank-note literature had become quite voluminous. We had six or eight semi-weekly periodicals in various parts of the country, exclusively devoted to the detection of counterfeit

* The Chemical Bank of New York was an honorable exception.

† The notes of over twelve hundred banks have been counterfeited or altered. There are in existence over three thousand kinds of altered notes; seventeen hundred varieties of spurious notes; four hundred and sixty varieties of imitations; and over seven hundred of other kinds; this arising from the great variety of bank notes; there being at a moderate estimate over seven thousand various kinds of genuine bills—some executed by good artists, and many in an indifferent manner.

The following statistics are from reliable data as to the years 1856 and 1862:

	1856.	1862.
Number of banks	1,409	1,500
Number whose notes are not counterfeited	463	253
Number of kinds of "imitations" .	1,462	1,861
Number of kinds of alterations . .	1,119	3,039
Number of kinds of spurious . .	224	1,685

—*Senator Sherman, Speech in Congress, Feb.* 10, 1863, *Cong. Globe*, i. 844.

notes and fraudulent bank issues ; besides standard works and books of reference without number.

No less than fifteen hundred banks existed in the Northern States. Each of these banks printed on the average five denominations of notes. Each of these notes were printed from different plates. The nature of the securities upon which these notes were issued in the various States was widely different. In order to become familiar with all these circumstances, a great deal of time had to be wasted in studying banking systems, learning to detect counterfeits, and keeping the run of insolvent institutions. But the truth is, that most people took this sort of information upon trust ; and thus the whole credit system of the country was thrown into the hands of a clique of publishers, who issued bank-note reporters, and who thus exercised all the authority of Insolvent Court judges.

Without reference to the numerous bank-note frauds, which, under the color of authority, have been time and again committed upon the public, and which are included under the convenient category of "wildcat," it is asserted that from no source whatever, have the people of this country suffered so keenly and so heavily, both socially and pecuniarily, as from the pregnant evil of State Banks : socially, in the reward to rascality which these systems are contended to have virtually offered ; and pecuniarily in the heavy losses which their failures are said to have entailed. Shrewd adventurers with a few thousand dollars in their pockets, have contrived to establish and manage banks with capitals of hundreds of thousands of dollars. It was a common thing to establish a bank in some remote locality ; then to issue notes based on the required security of State stocks, frequently purchased below par, and with the proceeds of these notes to purchase more stocks, and issue more notes, and soon, *ad libitum*, until the bubble would burst—the managers drawing interest all the time on the State stocks, and exposing the bill-holders to loss, whenever commercial depression happened to affect the value of the stocks. This system was perfected by keeping the notes in active circulation through brokers and agents in distant business centres, who paid them out in trade and to workmen and others, at par. Nor had this practice entirely disappeared after the establishment of the Suffolk and Metropolitan Bank systems of redemptions and clearings. Mention is made of individuals—owners of banks in this State and elsewhere—who ceased not to continue these dishonest practices, until the National Bank notes drove their uncurrent money out of circulation. Not only did they profit by drawing interest on a large capital, obtained as we have seen by a species of fraud, but they derived additional profits from the "shaves" to which, in league with brokers and bankers as unscrupulous as themselves, they compelled those who demanded redemption of their uncurrent notes at business centres, to submit.

What further proof, it is then triumphantly asked, is deemed necessary to establish the endemical nature of the National system, and the exotic character of the State systems? What says popular opinion, the embodiment of popular progress? Congress has voted for the National Banking system over and over again; the courts have upheld it; the press is in favor of it; and the people clamor for National Bank notes in preference to any other.

By these and kindred arguments not only are all Constitutional objections to the National Banking system swept away, but by gauging it and its rival system by their relative congruity with the present stage of social progress in this country, it is seen to harmonize more perfectly than the other with the various governmental institutions that surround the people.

The friends of progress are told not to take alarm at this necessary defiance of organic law.* Everything is going aright. Everything will be respected which proves to

* But there are not wanting those who find Constitutional authority to tax the State banks out of existence. By the provisions of that instrument, which interdicted the emission of bills of credit by individual States, it is contended to be a fair inference that the States were to permit no banking institutions to issue circulating money: or otherwise they might seriously impair the National resources, at times when they were most needed. That having done so, they did so not indeed in violation of the letter of the Constitution, but of its spirit, and therefore that their existence was only due to the forbearance of the general government. This being the case, the government possesses the right to destroy them by *any means* it chooses, not only by taxing them immoderately, but by peremptorily shutting them up if it deemed proper.—(*Mansfield*, § 246–249.)

be sufficiently congruous. There has been no union of Church and State, no religious persecutions, no religious disabilities, no law of primogeniture, and, in the midst of an era of paper money, no restraint placed upon the exportation of gold. All this shows that the Constitution, where it has not been too radical, has been duly respected. Where it has not been radical enough for the age, it has even been exceeded. Within a year or two an entire race of men has been raised from a condition of slavery to one of freedom. What more do we want? Is it general legislation? We have it. General incorporating acts have been enacted in many of the States. Mining and manufacturing associations, steamship lines, and insurance companies, are, to a considerable degree, freed from the control of legislation. The world has not stood still. Mankind has not retrograded. But in innovating "it is well to beware that it be the reformation which draweth on the change, and not the desire of change that pretendeth the reformation."

Not content with quoting Bacon, they drag in Herbert Spencer, and progress is actually sought to be felled by a weapon taken from the hands of its greatest living champion.*

As a currency measure the National Banking system finds additional support. First of all it is contended that as credit mobilizes and utilizes wealth, that while labor is the soil, credit is the sunshine which enables every grain of wealth to blossom into fruits of untold value, it follows that the more we have of it, the better.

If, therefore, credit is removed from the limited sphere it occupies in the State Banking systems and transplanted into that more extended and commanding one which it would occupy in the National system, endorsed as it is by the government, and fully confided in by the people, the same amount of currency which would effect a given number of transactions under one system, would effect a greater number under the other.

* "The most carefully framed Constitutions are worthless, unless they be embodiments of the popular character, and governmental arrangements in advance of the time, will inevitably lapse into congruity with the time."—(*Herbert Spencer:* Essay on Railway Morals and Railway Policy.)

This would stimulate commerce, and prove of the greatest benefit to the community. If it be objected that the National Bank currency, though it may possess a superior ratio of circulation to the State Bank currency, is not so well secured; its advocates at once reply that a superior ratio of circulation is the best proof of superior security. But, without insisting upon this principle, they are ready to show that United States bonds, upon which the National Bank notes are issued, not only form a large portion of the security upon which the State Bank notes are issued, and that therefore the security is to that extent the same in both cases; but that United States bonds are really a better security than State bonds. This is determined by their respective market prices. Thus while the six per cent. bonds of the various States are quoted at from 60 to par, only two of them, New York and Massachusetts, being above par—the one at 110, and the other at 120—the six per cent. bonds of the United States are quoted at 102.

If it be objected that, though the State six per cents. are temporarily depressed, in the end they will prove better than government six per cents.; they answer that the individual States, as well as the General government, are heavily in debt. They have equipped troops, paid bounties, furnished arms and ammunition, and performed many other important services for the General government. All this has been done on credit, and pay-day must shortly arrive. Their only means of payment is through taxation; but the General government being superior in authority, will forestall them in the appropriation of this source of revenue. The government will pump the well of taxation dry before the States will have a chance to raise a derrick over it. In what, then, does the superior security of the State Banking systems rest? It has been shown that State stocks do not furnish it. Is it to be found in the last of the three classes of securities upon which State bank notes are issued? Will real-estate bonds furnish it—bonds based upon a species of property daily depreciating, and destined to become still more depreciated, in value?

But if the fact of superior ratio of circulation is called in question, they instance the notorious truth that National Bank notes are invariably preferred to State Bank notes, and that tradesmen will often refuse the latter while they will always accept the former. Here we perceive in one case a limited confidence: in the other an unlimited confidence. And that this does not proceed from ignorance is evidenced by the fact that the same men who prefer National Bank notes to State Bank notes, prefer specie to anything else. What reason then have we to doubt that the same intelligence which causes a man to prefer specie to paper money, leads him to distinguish with judgment what sort of paper money is better? But it matters not whether intelligence and discrimination has had anything to do with it at all. The mere fact, which no one doubts, that the National Bank notes are universally preferred to the State Bank notes is conclusive evidence of their superior ratio of circulation. Depend upon it, say its advocates—depend upon it, that when the National Banks go down, as has been predicted, they will go down only under such a pressure of circumstances as would much sooner have caused the failure of the State Banks.

If you ask them of what service can this system possibly be to the government, apart from that ready power over the currency of the country, which it confers, and the social influence of which mention has already been made; they reply, that it furnishes a large market for United States bonds at a time when their absorption by the people is a matter of pressing necessity.

But the friends of the National system claim for it still another advantage—an advantage, which, in the estimation of many, is superior to all the rest. Every holder of a National Bank note is, as it were, a stockholder in the welfare of the system. The failure of a State Bank was hardly ever a matter of general concern and the public made no efforts to avert it; but as everybody, more or less, will become holders of National Bank notes, everybody therefore will be interested in maintaining the credit of the system, and of the securities upon which the system is based.

Finally, it is claimed that to the extent to which National Bank notes will supplant Treasury notes, this system will remove from the control of government officials, a great source of corruption, and disperse it among several hundred local banking institutions, who have pledged valuable securities for the privilege of using it, and will, therefore, neither throw it away, nor bestow it upon political partizans. Nor are these all the arguments in favor of this system : yet we believe that we have mentioned all, which have, or appear to have, any strength at all in them.

In fine, were we to believe the arguments of its defenders, there would seem to be no end to its virtues. It is a colossal Poor Man's Plaster ; warranted to cure all evils, and to remedy all disorders : and even those who do not need to use it, will find themselves a great deal better off after giving it a fair trial.

As the opinions of the majority are often erroneous, it would be manifestly injurious to the happiness and well being of the minority should the daily aberrations of the popular mind be suffered to take the form of law. It would also be injurious to the interests of the majority ; but we are willing that they should incur the penalty of their own errors.

It would therefore seem fit, and it has always been enacted in all systems of government, that changes in organic law should first pass through the ordeal of certain stipulated forms, before they are accepted. This is the only protection which the minority possess from the absolute tyranny of the majority. And this protection is eminently needful ; for otherwise the majority might possess the power to change the entire form of government by a mere vote. Now it is evident that this would be unjust ; for upon the same principle, a majority of the stockholders of an insurance company would possess the power to change the institution, by a mere vote, into a petroleum company, or a monte bank.

Organic law being therefore of paramount authority, it follows that any act in contravention of it, is *ipso facto* null and void, and no argument of expediency can avail to extenuate it. Should the National Banking law be unconstitutional, it were hardly worth while to discuss the question either of its social congruity or its financial expediency. But let us examine the point. Clause 2, Section VIII. Art I. of the Constitution confers upon Congress the power "to borrow money on the credit of the United States." Clause 18, Section VIII. Art I. of the Constitution provides that Congress shall have the power "to make all laws which shall be necessary and proper for carrying into execution the foregoing powers vested by the Constitution in the government of the United States, or in any department or office thereof," among which is the clause quoted above, and the one to declare war, &c. These clauses are held to authorize by implication either the emission of legal-tender notes, the charter of a National Bank, or the formation of a National Banking system ; or all of them.

Implied powers are prohibited to be exercised under our organic law ; for Art X. of the Amendments distinctly asserts that "the powers not delegated to the United States by the Constitution, nor prohibited by it to the States, are reserved to the States respectively, or to the people." But judicial decision, precedent, and authority are all in favor of the legality of the Act itself. The system, however, could never have found a footing unless it had been bolstered up by an invidious system of taxation which levied three to six per cent. per annum, and, after July 1, 1866, is to levy ten per cent. per annum on the circulation of the State Banks ; while the tax upon the National Banks is merely nominal. This is expressly prohibited by Sections VIII. and IX. of Art I. and Section II. clause 3 of Art I. The first-named section says that "all duties, imposts and excises shall be uniform throughout the United States." Then to make an invidious distinction, as the National Banking system does between State and National Banks, is clearly unlawful.* Upon this plea any particular interest may be taxed out of existence by a majority of Congress—the insurance interest, the railway interest, the shipping interest, the mining interest, the manufacturing, or the agricultural interest. The other sections say "no direct tax shall be laid unless in proportion to the census," and "direct taxes shall be apportioned

* The decision of the U. S. Supreme Court in Kentucky settled this point, if indeed any authority were needed upon a subject so plain to all understandings.

among the several States according to their respective numbers." But the tax lately put upon the State Banks *is* a direct tax, and is *not* in proportion to the census, or the number of people, in the several States. Another step in the same direction would enable a majority of Congress to tax the people according to their respective statures, or respective religions. Thus a man six feet high would be taxed a fifth more than one of five, or half as much again as a dwarf of four, or a fourth less than a giant of eight feet in height, and so on in proportion. Or a Catholic might be taxed more than a Protestant, or less than a Jew.

It would, therefore, appear that whatever pretext of law exists upon which the system itself is based, there is to be found no authority for that governmental patronage and preference without which it could never have maintained, and could not now maintain itself against the banking systems in vogue in the various States.

Passing over this point for the moment, let us examine the social aspect of this question. The argument upon which the advocates of the National Banking system rest, namely, that humanity has entered upon the so-called National phase of progress—no more, no less—is not correct. From the lowest form of barbarism, from the solitary and prowling Digger Indian, to the philosopher whose comprehensive eye has scanned the defects of all governments, and who has raised himself to that social position where government is virtually ended, so far as its effects upon himself is concerned, we may still find living instances of every possible form of human development, and all within the borders of this country. Tribes of aborigines, and troups of foreign emigrants wander about the western wilds, almost within call of the telegraph wires which civilization has stretched out to bring the remotest ends of society together. Territorial and State governments are every day formed from these tribal communities, and international communities already exist in the relations between the States. Thus the march of progress exhibits at once, even within the jurisdiction of a single government, every possible phase of social development, and the assertion that our present social status is the National, is erroneous ; and consequently all arguments based upon it are erroneous. With what sort of plausibility can it be contended that these varied forms of human progress shall be made to conform to one species of government, one set of laws, one religion ?

Human institutions can never be made to keep even pace nor be in perfect harmony with the natural laws of progress, and must ever be to an extent incongruous. But as the only complete remedy for this would be the entire abrogation of permanent government, while it is conceded that large portions of society still, and for a long time yet, require permanent government ; it follows that the more limited the duration, the territorial extent, and the jurisdiction of certain institutions are made, the better it must prove to be. For society being thus enabled to divide its endless phases into the smallest possible aggregations, each with its set of laws, its customs and its forms of religion most suitable to itself, it follows that a larger proportion of satisfaction will be produced than under any other arrangement. We see this in the disposition which human institutions make of themselves, when left perfectly free from governmental influence. While Catholicism is bound by its central authority to the observance of certain dogmas, and the unity of the church is by this means maintained inviolate, Protestantism, restricted by no ecclesiastical ruler, divides itself into a thousand sects, each including a batch of men who choose to seek their spiritual happiness by roads of their own making.

Even in the customs and in the dresses of men, we see that when left to themselves they exhibit the utmost possible diversity. One man eats his beef raw, another likes it cooked. The Cossack stuffs himself with mutton tallow ; the Frenchman gorges himself with confectionery. The Tartar lives on horseback ; the African burrows in the earth. The Zealander lives in the water ; the Laplander sits on a stove. The Algerine dresses in blue ; the Tyrolean in green ; the Morisco in yellow ; and the American in black. And in this, they but follow that example of infinite diversity which nature repeats in all her works. If the freedom to adopt what dresses, customs, laws, religions, etc., men may chose for themselves, is productive of the greatest happiness, as undoubtedly it is, then, next to absolute freedom in these matters, is the privilege to join whatever little knot of men exists who believe as we do, and among whom we can preach and practise those things which we believe : and the Constitution of the United States evidently regards this natural tendency to localization as a right belonging to the people. This at once disarms every argument in favor of enlarged empire, extensive jurisdiction of laws, National systems, etc.

What may be good for Delaware may not suit California. What may enrich Maine may not benefit Texas. What may exactly meet the requirements of Oregon may prove to be very ill adapted to Florida.

The State Banking systems, whatever their faults may have been, possessed this great advantage : they harmonized with the local institutions by which they were surrounded, and they probably to a great extent reflected in each particular locality the state of general social progress at which it had arrived.

Instead of laying across the land as the National Banking system does, like a huge plank, over which insolvency seems shortly destined to walk—resting on the shoulders of some, not touching others, unbending, unyielding, unaccommodating to local peculiarities—the State systems extended across the land, like a vast chain—a chain which bound the interests of the various parts in closer unity, a chain which in the suppleness and free play of its constituent links fitted itself to all but the minutest inequalities of every locality. To be perfect, even a chain is too unbending, for what was wanting was that entire freedom which in its action can only be likened to the elasticity of fluids. But next to a free banking system the State Banks were probably the best which could have been made to adapt themselves to the wants and the conditions of the people of the various States. And they possessed this striking advantage over any other system whatever : that they stood ready at any time to be further improved when occasion called for such improvement. The Suffolk Bank system in New England was the nearest approach to an absolutely free system which any part of this country ever possessed, and fairly reflected the superior education of the people among whom it flourished. The Clearing House system of this State was almost as perfect as the New England system, and fairly accorded with the public intelligence prevailing in New York. In Louisiana the State system was a very good one. So it was in Pennsylvania; and they, too, undoubtedly reflected the social progress which had been attained in the two great commercial cities within their borders; while the lax systems in vogue in the North-Western States were but the natural product of that backwardness which resulted from the influx of ignorant immigrants from abroad. The national system rubs all this out. It does not raise Iowa to the level of New York, but it lowers New York to the level of Iowa. It is a bed of Procrustes to which all statures are trimmed—the tall by having their legs cut off, the short by being racked to a proper degree of tenuity.*

---

* Union in the sense of harmony is perfectly possible, and is drawing nigh. Union in the sense of identity of belief, and faith, and government, and usage, is not only not near, but is, I am happy to say, further off than ever. You do not want it. The very thing that men have prayed for, and that the church has striven after, is just the thing that would curse the world.

The efforts for union have proceeded mainly upon a notion which is radically wrong and impossible; for the union sought after would have been a mischief, and not a benefit. It has been supposed that union required identity of belief; that it created a necessity for all men to believe the same things, and to believe them alike. They do not need to believe the same things, nor to believe them alike.

It has been supposed that union required that there should be oneness and universality of government; that it necessitated the having of one church, under one name, with one mode of worship, and one line of ordinances, and one system of administration. It would be a positive nuisance to have any such thing. I would not have the sects swallowed up and dissolved into one gigantic whale-sect if I could.

It has been supposed that there must be identity of service and religious offering, in order to make that which Christ desiderated, and which his disciples have been foolishly laboring for by mistake. This is a part of that illusion that has filled the world on almost every other subject. The whole race, it has been supposed, should be like a brigade of soldiers in line, uniformed, with one band of music at their head, all stepping together to one tune, and in exactly the same time. This is the picture that has been given to our religious fancy. Men have painted how blessed this world would be when there was not a sect left, and there was one great brotherhood called by one name, believing just the same things, following just the same way, and having just the same ordinances and usages, so that when the Sabbath morning came, all the successive latitudes should echo just the same worship, till the whole globe should be one vast unison. This may be pictorially and poetically beautiful, but practically it is one of the most consummate mistakes that ever could be brought to pass. We do not want men to think just alike; we do not want men to have just the same church governments; we do not want men to follow just the same rules and regulations. We would not thank any man who

We have now to consider the National Banking system as a currency measure. That credit is a blessing *per se* we deny. That it is beneficial when it arises naturally from

---

should attempt to do by heaven what men think that they are serving God and man by attempting to do by the church on earth. For, as it will appear, God made men according to different thoughts and patterns, and in attempting to rub out the divine creative idea you introduce confusion. Who would thank you, if you had the power to confine the fields to just one single product? Who would thank you to make every day just like every other day, so that there should be no checkered weather? Who would thank you to bring all the trees of the forest to one tree, and all their leaves to one leaf? Who would thank you to convert all flowers into one flower, no matter how gorgeous it might be? It is diversity that we want, and that God has provided for. It is so in the physical world, it is so in the commercial world, it is so in the political world, it is so in the social world, and, thank God, it is so in the moral world; and this great creative law has resisted every false and mistaken endeavor which has been made to bring about identity and call it union; to efface particularity, specialty, individuality, diversity, and difference, and put in their stead *one great stupid unison*.

The very efforts that have been put forth for union, then, have hindered it, because they have been in a wrong direction. They have sought a thing that not only was not union, but that was subversive of the only union that can ever take place according to the laws of our being.

Therefore we do not want, and cannot have, a union which sacrifices diversity and difference.

* * * * * * * * *

A pretty unity you would have if the legislature told you every day just when you should wash, how many pieces, and the manner in which you should do it; just when you should bake, how many loaves, and of what material they should be; just when you should go out, and when you should come in; just when you should spread your table, in the morning, at noonday, and in the evening, and what you should put on it; just when you should pray, and when you should not; just when you should undress your children and put them to bed, and when you should take them up; when you should flagellate them, and how much! If the whole procedure of our families was regulated by law, how discordant they would be! what scenes of conflict would be enacted in them! how like Babel let loose would they seem! And yet, how is it that the church has tried to secure unity? By giving up reason, and individuality, and peculiarity, and liberty. But churches can be harmonious just as families can. How? By letting every church think as it has a mind to, and by accepting every church into a neighborhood fellowship, provided the average of its doing is one that makes for virtue, and religion, and peace. Of this more in the sequel.

This attempt to unitize the human mind is a part of that universal blundering which has been undertaken upon theory in every department of society. In earlier periods, governments have tried to harmonize nations and empires by as far as possible reducing men to the kind of union which I have described. Earlier centuries have sought for identity in civil affairs by cutting off criticism, by discouraging debate, by denying large liberty, and by bringing men within the compass of laws and statutes. And the result of the experiment, it seems to me, has been such as to lead the church to imitate the example.

The same thing has been tried in the realm of commerce. There have been periods, in the wisest nations, when it was supposed that the public good required that commerce and manufacturing and husbandry should be held under legal restrictions and compressed to uniformity. But the progress of the development of civilization has taught men that the best way to promote the general welfare was to let industry alone. There are certain great bounds beyond which it is essential that commerce should not be allowed to go; but always commerce untrammelled by law is healthier than commerce meddled with and compressed and unitized by any fanciful or theoretic decree.

a certain state of things, we affirm. But the credit mobilized by means of the National Banks is an exotic credit, not a natural credit. It is brought into existence, not by the cheerful influences of honesty and trust, but by the artificial fertilizer, which in the shape of United States stocks is planted at its roots. The limited circulation of the State Banks was one of their best recommendations; for circulation if left to itself will never exceed the due wants of society; while circulation when artificially encouraged will not only exceed those wants, but, to the extent of such excess, will produce disorder and loss. The immense aggregate amount of services performed by the comparatively small circulation of the State banks, say from $60,000,000 in 1843 to $200,000,000 in 1860, was so great, that the people who employed this circulation during those seventeen years of active commerce, could afterward have afforded to lose every penny of it; yet during all this period the losses through bank insolvencies did not probably exceed one fiftieth part of that sum. After actively working a pack-horse for seventeen years, we can certainly afford to lose something in his price when we sell him; and so with the State Bank notes.

In attacking this feature of forced circulation created by the *quasi* legal-tender character of the National Bank notes, we know we are making a point out of a feature which it is agreed on all hands should be at once abolished; yet we think this feature of so much importance to the permanence of the National system, that we doubt if it ever will be repealed until

---

God has inspired the universe with diversity. He meant that difference should be a part of the sovereign beauty of the world and of human life. Foolish men have sought to eradicate this principle; but nature, still immortal and omnipotent, rises over each assault, and will to the end.

It has been just this that has been sought in morals and in religion. Not only has there been a real spirit of despotism in using the sanctions of religion, and the supposed authority which it confers; but the whole despotic power has sought to do an unnatural and impossible thing—a thing as impossible and unnatural in morals and religion as it has been proved to be in politics and in commerce. The worst thing that could have happened to the world would have been the fulfilment of that bright and beautiful dream of fools—the establishment of identity of belief, identity of church government, and identity of worship; but instead of these there have been variations in belief, variations in church government, and variations in worship. "There are diversities of gifts, but the same Spirit; and there are differences of administration, but the same Lord." Even so it is; but when will men learn it?—(*Henry Ward Beecher.*)

the system itself comes to an end. When these notes are deprived of the agency of government in putting them into circulation, we predict an immediate downfall of the whole system.

The main argument which establishes a superiority for the State Banks over the National Banks is this: that the former in emitting their notes, do so only when they receive for them *an equivalent in good commercial paper*. The security for the redemption of the notes is therefore doubled. Such an emission of paper is only the exchange of a well-known credit for one of restricted currency. When banking operations are conducted upon any other basis, they fall under the designation "kiting," and being known as such, either come to an early termination, as they did many years ago in this part of the country, and but a few years ago in the West—or, if they continue, as was until lately the case in the two instances mentioned in the first part of this article, the extent of the injury resulting from them is so limited as not to work any practical harm. But the National Banks are essentially *banks of circulation*, and nothing else. They do scarcely anything in the way of discounts, being furnished with a greater source of profit through the forced circulation performed for them by government. The relative soundness of the two systems is therefore so wide apart that the inferiority of the National Banking system is seen to be fatal to their permanency and solvency.

Let us take an example. We will suppose a National Bank with a paper capital of $500,000. This money is invested in government bonds at par. These bonds are hypothecated with the Comptroller of the Currency, and in obedience to the law, that officer issues to the Bank $450,000, or ninety per cent., in circulating notes—notes enjoying the quality of being legal tenders both to and from the government. The government is therefore compelled to take them at par in payment for more bonds, and in turn can compel its creditors to take them at par in payment for services or supplies. With such an amount of capital, let us see the extent of kiting operations which a National Bank can do.

Purchase of U. S. bonds at par.	Issues of quasi legal-tender paper.	Reserve required by law of 25 per ct. in "lawful money."
$500,000	$450,000	$112,500
337,500	303,750	75,937
227,813	205,032	51,258
153,774	138,397	34,599
103,798	93,419	23,355
70,064	63,058	15,764
47,294	42,565	10,641
31,924	28,732	7,183
21,549	19,395	4,849
14,546	13,092	3,273
9,819	8,838	2,209
$1,518,081	$1,366,278	$341,568

The limit created by law is $10,000. Having reached this figure, it must stop. Now what has been done? On a paper capital of $500,000 the enormous sum of $1,366,278 has been put in most active circulation; while the reserve of $341,568 has probably been mostly lent out on call loans, and thus made to contribute still further to the inflation. The profits of the Bank are, aside from what it may derive from temporarily lending out its reserve, six per cent. *in gold* on $1,518,081 worth of United States bonds; or, $91,084 per annum, payable semi-annually *in gold.* This is nearly twenty per cent. per annum in gold on its paper capital, and this is just what all these institutions with a few exceptions are now doing. They are put to no trouble, either. As government does all the drudgery of keeping their paper in circulation, the banking business of such institutions may legitimately be conducted in the garret rooms of a tenement house. Neither marble buildings, nor fireproof safes, nor plate-glass windows, nor gilded counters are required.

Should any popular disaster, or commercial panic, by creating a want of confidence, or even a return to peace, by creating a demand for that capital which now for lack of commercial enterprise is locked up in government bonds, largely occasion their sale, and precipitate a fall in their market value—should either of these events cause United States sixes to fall to 70, what becomes of the whole system of National Banks? Who can say therefore that this system is not fraught with dangers of a most momentous character? All the bank panics with which this country or any other country has ever been afflicted will bear no comparison to the ruin which will follow the stoppage of banks issuing in the aggregate three hundred millions of active currency. The only immediate remedy we still possess to avert this tremendous catastrophe is in depriving the notes of their character of quasi legal-tender. Neglect that precaution, and nothing can arrest the course of impending financial calamity.

It is no good argument to contend that because National Bank notes are preferred by the people, they are better than State Bank notes. While admitting the advantage they possess in being printed with a less number of designs than the State Bank notes had; it is manifestly absurd to suppose that their superior ratio of currency is due to this fact. For that matter, a little concert of management among the State Bank officers might have secured a similar advantage for the State Bank notes. The superior currency of the National Bank notes is unquestionably due to their quasi legal-tender character. So long as they are a legal tender to and from the government, and are receivable for taxes, &c., and payable for supplies, &c., they must, of course, while the National Banks remain solvent, continue to be preferred to State Bank notes. Their circulation is a forced one; and it is to this fact, and not to any intrinsic merit they possess, that they owe their superior ratio of circulation.

That the National system provides a large market for United States bonds when their sale is a matter of pressing moment, is true; but with less circumlocution and less injustice, a larger and readier market might have been created. The credit of the United States, when not bolstered up by such false expedients, would stand much higher than it does to-day. The bonds of the government need only to have been offered to the people *at what they were worth*—that is to say, at the price they would bring in open market—and they would have been absorbed in sufficient quantities for all practical purposes. But what has been the effect of this boasted system of absorbing United States bonds? For every bond absorbed there has been a National Bank note issued, and for every National Bank note issued, there has been a Treasury note retired. The effect of the whole operation has therefore been to convert what was a loan to the government without interest, into a loan with interest, and to transfer this valuable privilege, to the extent of three hundred millions of dollars, to the National Banks. Eighteen millions a year in gold as subsidy to a pernicious system!

And now as to the alleged tendency of this system to maintain the credit of the government by making every holder of its notes an interested party in upholding the government. If it could produce this result, which we deny, nothing would be more unjust.

Anything that tends to support and prolong social development in any phase, whether that phase be Individual, Tribal, National, or International, is an evil; for the artificial prolongation of any phase of progress is contrary to the laws of nature.

Unless the credit of the government is supported by means of equal interest and solicitude to all, it bears unequally upon those who profit little by it, and confers a disproportionate benefit upon those who profit largely by it. The man who holds a five-dollar National note is very little concerned by reason of this fact in maintaining the National credit, while he who holds thousands of dollars of such notes is by reason of this fact induced to submit to any abuse of power, no matter how onerously it may bear upon himself and others, rather than that his personal pecuniary interest should suffer. And experience supports this view, for it was seen in the case of the United States Bank, that while certain classes were largely interested in maintaining the abuse, the people at large rejoiced when it came to an end—notwithstanding that its bankruptcy entailed more or less loss upon all.

In its legal aspect, therefore, the National Banking system, taken in connection with the invidious taxation of the State Banks, is clearly unconstitutional; as a social and political institution it is remarkable only for its incongruousness and injustice; and as a financial measure it is deeply sown with the seeds of early and frightful decay.

All the disadvantages of the State systems which are included under the head of bank panics, were but those natural aberrations in systems which were gradually reconciling the benefits of credit with the still prevailing unscrupulousness of the age. They would have gradually led to a better state of things, as they did in New England and New York, and ultimately become more perfect.

In the matter of counterfeiting, it is by no means proved that the National Bank notes form a better safeguard against this crime than the State Bank notes did. The contrary would appear to be the fact; for counterfeits on State Bank notes could never hope to pass easily, both on account of the very circumspection to which the genuine notes were subjected, and the limited circulation to which they were confined; while the National Bank notes would appear to furnish an irresistible temptation to counterfeiting. The winding up of this system will doubtless reveal the existence of counterfeits to a very large extent. Some ten or twelve have been already noticed in the daily journals.

It will have been observed that we have said nothing upon the subject of domestic exchange, which the National system is foolishly expected to annihilate. We classed this among those arguments in favor of the system which did not merit a reply. It remains to be proved that any law can reconcile discordant interests, or furnish a bridge by which either time or distance can be spanned.

Since we have gone to the length of condemning this banking system, our adversaries may now fairly ask us to suggest a better one. To this we reply: The State systems are better. Let us go back to *them.* But if it be asked, is there no better method of banking than that provided by either of these systems? we reply, yes: that better method is found in having no system at all. "What! no system at all?" echo the true believers in governmental omniscience and prevision; "no discrimination as to who shall issue promises to pay, or not ?" No : it is time that tinkering with commercial affairs on the part of the government was ended. What right has the government to establish a standard or measure of any kind, whether it be of quality or quantity, and then to confer the privilege of supplying it to the public, upon a particular class ?

It has not been found necessary to restrict the emission of promises to pay on time. Why should there be any restriction upon the emission of promises to pay on demand ? Does the merchant or banker who is now free to emit his promissory notes at 30, 60, or 90 days, abuse the privilege ? No. And why ? Because he would gain nothing by it. As soon as it became known that he was issuing more paper than his wealth and social standing warranted him in doing, his notes would be refused ; and if he possessed neither wealth nor social standing, they would never be taken at all.* "But would the paper of any banking firm possess so high a credit that it would pass among all classes of people the moment it was offered ?" Unquestionably : we could name fifty firms in this city, and thirty more in Boston, and twenty more in Philadelphia, whose notes would be taken at once, provided they were designed so as to be mechanically safe from forgery and counterfeiting. "But what security would there exist for the redemption of these notes ?" The security of the original wealth of the firms who issued them ; the security of the specie or stock or other property for which they paid them out ; the security afforded by that horror with which every such firm regards a

* The current notion that bankers can, and will, if allowed, issue notes to any extent, is one of the absurdest notions—an illusion, however, which would never have arisen but for the vicious over-issues induced by law. The truth is, that in the first place, a banker *cannot* increase his issue of notes at will. It has been proved by the unanimous testimony of all bankers who have been examined before successive parliamentary committees, that "the amount of their issues is exclusively regulated by the extent of local dealings and expenditure in their respective districts;" and that any notes issued in excess of the demand are "immediately returned to them." And the truth is, in the second place, that a banker *will not*, on the average of cases, issue more notes than in his judgment it is safe to issue ; seeing that if his promises to pay in circulation, are greatly in excess of his available means of paying them, he runs an imminent risk of having to stop payment —a result of which he has no less a horror than other men.—(*Spencer's Essays*, p. 338.) And with banking left entirely free, there would exist the additional and still more potent restriction to over-issues mentioned in the text, viz., the natural limitation to the banker's credit.

failure to meet its engagements. "But how would it fare with the uneducated masses, who would be incapable of discriminating for themselves between the notes of good firms and the notes of bad ones?" They would refuse to have any of them at all, and use gold and silver money exclusively. And this is the kind of money the masses want. Hard Money has ever been their cry, but without Free Banking they will never obtain it. Those who required to use so much money that specie would prove inconvenient to handle, would hardly fail to acquaint themselves sufficiently with the security of the paper money in circulation before accepting it. Finally, should there be any one so foolhardy as to accept of paper money with the value of which he was not only ignorant, but which he was not obliged to accept at all, the loss of an occasional dollar or two would soon be the means either of teaching him a better discrimination, or of making him more prudent in the future, which dollar or two he could in all justice charge to the account of education, and consider it well spent. But this is not likely. No man makes the most inconsiderable purchase, or the most trivial contract, unless he is well able to drive his own bargain, or can rely, as in the case of attorneys and other agents, upon the judgment and probity of others. "But is it certain that houses of undoubted credit would find it worth their while to issue these circulating notes? Besides, would it not deprive government of a legitimate prerogative? Lastly, of what advantage would such an absence of system be to the people?"

There is no more doubt that firms of the highest standing would find it profitable to conduct a banking business then, than that such firms find it profitable to do so now, hampered as all their operations are by the mischievous interference of government. And as to depriving the latter (whether Federal, State, or Municipal it matters not) of a legitimate prerogative, we say, it does not. The days of government prerogatives have gone by, and none are any longer legitimate. The government has exercised this prerogative under the pretence of defending the ignorant from the designing; but when has it succeeded in doing so? Never. On the contrary, its mock guarantees have invariably lulled the unwary into a sense of false security, and so led them on to loss and sometimes to ruin. With a pretence equally as good, it might claim the prerogative of superintending every sale of goods or two-penny contract of hire, in order that the buyer might not be taken in, or the laborer cheated. But Herbert Spencer has fully treated this point in his admirable essay on "State Tamperings with Money and Banks," and to this authority we refer the reader for the evidences of the immeasurable advantages not only to the people, but to the government itself, of letting the business of banking alone.

This is what we would have; this is what we want—Free Banking. The aspirations of the human mind for freedom are insatiable. We are grateful for the abrogation of the right of primogeniture, of State religions, of special legislation concerning certain acts of incorporation, etc., but we want more. The history of mankind is the history of a struggle between subjection and freedom, and the relative proportion of each which enters into the condition of a given community marks with more or less precision the average phase of social progress to which it has attained: just as the relative proportion of specie and paper in circulation under Free Banking laws would mark with more or less precision the average state of credit which prevailed. If our adversaries quote Bacon, we reply that their quotation happens to be unfortunate, for the innovations effected by the Constitution of the United States were as nothing compared to the innovations effected by this National Banking system; and if they would derive from Spencer's words the true inference which he desired should be drawn from them, we answer by saying: that as it is impossible to frame constitutions which shall embody the popular character—and as all governmental arrangements must either be in advance of the time or behind it—it follows that fixed political forms are invariably mischievous in their effects, and that, consequently, the only rightful province of government is that important and comprehensive one which consists in the proper administration of justice. This is Spencer's meaning.*

* Thus all which the State does when it exceeds its true duty (the administration of justice) is to hinder, to disturb, to corrupt .... Take away the vicious

But without going to this extent, we may safely prognosticate, in view of the notorious and admitted inefficiency of government, whenever it interferes with trade, that the National Banking system will prove to be no exceptional case. And we may properly claim that this shall be the last governmental experiment upon a subject that, beyond the mere fixing of a standard measure of value, is as appropriately a matter of private enterprise, as is the manufacture and sale of yardsticks and peck measures.

In penning this article we know that we have run counter to the prejudices of a large class of readers, and that to every one who shall approve our course, there are hundreds whose convictions we shall offend. But, in the conduct of this Journal we have resolved at all risks to state the truth, and to stand by it, even though the truth be for the time unpopular, believing that there are no targets which so well invite the critic's shafts as those that are erected by the ignorance or the delusion of a whole people. A. D.

THE RIGHTS OF CHILDREN.

WHAT is the source of filial love? Helplessness. Why does the child nestle close to the bosom of the mother? Why is it happy in basking in her kind smiles? Because in that bosom it finds food, warmth, cosiness, protection; and in that smile it finds pleasure. The first four are essential to its existence, the last to its happiness. For this it returns all its possesses: filial love. It is popularly believed that filial love is a duty which the child owes to the mother for bringing

---

arrangements which now mostly prevent men from seeing the reactions that follow legislative actions. . . . . This faith in governments is in a certain sense organic, and can only diminish by being outgrown. It is a subtle form of fetichism. . . It is not simply that social vitality may be trusted by-and-by to fulfil each much-exaggerated requirement in some quiet spontaneous way—it is not simply that, when thus naturally fulfilled it will be fulfilled efficiently, instead of being botched, as when attempted artificially; but it is that until thus naturally fulfilled, it ought not to be fulfilled at all.—*Spencer's Essays.*

it into existence ; and as the father is equally instrumental in being the cause of its birth, it follows that this obligation is equally due to him. The effect of this is that the infant commences his career in this world with two creditors, to both of whom he owes all he possesses or expects to possess until he is twenty-one years of age, not only of the material things of this world, but of the passions and affections.

These two self-made creditors are equally importunate, and in most cases manage to keep up an incessant dunning ; until the statute of limitations sets the debtor free at the age of twenty-one. During this whole time his young life is frequently imbittered by the exactions of his parents. They monopolize his time and attention, and affect and exercise the right to direct his tastes and inclinations. The law which enables the child to escape this thraldom only when it is twenty-one, is a consequence of the popular fallacy we have mentioned—the fallacy that filial love is a duty. That this is a fallacy is easily demonstrable.

Clap the new-born child to the breast of a stranger, let it never know its natural mother, and where shall we look, except in the pages of romance, for any difference in the child's affection, between that which it entertains for its foster parent, and that which it would have felt for its natural one ? When the child grows older and its taste and inclinations become developed, there will undoubtedly be found more or less similarity in them to those of his parents ; and to that extent will an affinity of disposition exist between them, and this of course will promote filial affection. But it is not always that such affinities exist ; and it perhaps more frequently exhibits itself to any considerable degree between strangers, than between parents and children ; still, popular convictions run the other way, and it is generally believed that, even though separated at birth, there always exists between the mother and child some mysterious and potent affinity which is sure to exhibit itself whenever they might happen to come together in after life ? We know that many a fond and erring mother hugs this absurd delusion to her heart—we know that it has over and over again formed the theme of song and drama—but that it is a fiction is self-evident, and it is the part of science to assert its fictitious character.*

It would thus seem to be fairly established that the child owes nothing to its mother in return for her agency in calling it into existence. As for the father, we place him entirely outside of the question. A young infant cares nothing at all about its father ; often cries when first put into his arms ; frequently will not endure his presence for months after birth, and makes his acquaintance just as he does any stranger's—only after a hard-won familiarity.

Indeed, so far from being born in debt to its parents, it is often the reverse. In some cases it is more consonant with strict justice to regard the parents as being indebted to the child. For though existence has its compensations when obtained without conditions, it has not when saddled with any sort of parental incubus—such as that of a bad name, a despised class, etc. For this extra load which the child is obliged to carry through life, its parents are responsible. The child is therefore to be regarded as being born not only free from obligation to its parents, but as being sometimes even more or less their creditor by reason of their debts to society which custom has compelled it to involuntarily assume, and which it will have to pay some day or other. This great principle being once established, see how many important consequences flow from it. Not only is the enslavement of human offspring at once deprived of justification, if indeed it ever had any, but the Rights of Women and the Rights of Children at once advance to the front rank of principles to be maintained and reforms to be effected.

The young mother, who has just left school, to encounter, unprepared, all the trials of early maternity ; the poor, ignorant, doting little puss, whose passionate endearments to her first-born, returned by certain seraphic crows and sounds of an inarticulate nature, she would fain believe to be an inter-

---

* A curious physiological proof that moral and physical traits, so far as they *are* inherited, are due less to the peculiarities of parents than to the peculiarities of Wet-nurses, is adduced in the December number of the *London Social Science Review*, in an article upon that subject.

change of filial and maternal affinity, whose source was buried in the mysterious and the sacred, is not prepared for such a doctrine. She declares it to be savage, brutal, cold blooded, materialistic. It looks as though, to put faith in it, she were compelled to bid adieu to the tenderest of emotions, the sweetest of sufferings, the dearest of consolations, the very holy of holies of her fond beliefs. But this is not the case. Let us reassure her.

"Madam, a time will come, and before many months, too, when this helpless infant, whom you have borne, and nursed, and lavished so much care upon, will have other wants, will stand in need of other cares. Then, one of two things will happen. Either, as is most likely the case, you have never given any reflection to the subject, and will fail to perceive this change in your child, or you have, and you will perceive the change. In the former case, you will cry when you observe that he seldom looks to you, except for that protection which maternal sympathy is ever sure to afford him. When his food, his comfort, and his pleasure is derived from other sources, and his love and gratitude find their object in some laughing nursery-maid, you will rock yourself in despair, and ask heaven why it had been so unjust to you, why your child's love was turned away from you, why you do not die, etc., etc. Thus you will make yourself unnecessarily miserable, and lose an excellent opportunity to renew the affection that should exist between you. Perhaps you fall into another error. You take your baby to your heart again. You make him a nursling long after he has ceased to be a nursling, and continue his dependence upon you, in order that you may still reap his smiles and his love. All this is the clearest possible acknowledgment of the principle we are contending for; but what does it lead to? The child's growth, both mental and physical, is stunted; progress and development are at once retarded. Is this your design? Surely not. Either you do these things because you have never given any reflection to the subject, having been transferred from performing the duties of a school girl to those of a mother, without any intermediate preparation, or you have reflected upon it, and believing as you do, that the child is indebted to you for its existence, and bound to you by some mysterious tie of nature, attribute his conduct to the wiles of servantgalism.

"In the latter case, you will discharge some faithful domestic, whose only crime has been that she has deserved the gratitude of your infant, and employ a stranger in her place, who will try the other method, and ruin your child's temper by her moroseness and neglect. Perhaps you ascribe the child's conduct to his own perversity. In this case you will spoil him yourself, by making him a martyr to your fanciful code of filial ethics.

"Are these the alternatives you wish to encounter? On the one hand, make yourself miserable, or retard the child's development; on the other, do injustice to faithful domestics, and encourage bad ones who will ruin your child's temper? Or would you ruin it yourself? Will you hug this idea to your breast, which you will discern some day to be a delusion; or will you throw aside false sentimentality and imaginary emotions, to welcome truth in a knowledge of those laws of our existence which it is the task of philosophy to unfold?

"Start with the correct principle, and nothing will happen amiss. You will perceive the new wants of your child; you will supply them yourself, and you will earn that love which you so much covet, and which never can be obtained unless it is earned. Remember that, in becoming a mother, you have gone into an enterprise—an enterprise by which you cannot earn your living, to be sure—that duty pertains to your husband—but an enterprise by which you may earn an immense store of happiness for both of you—happiness, however, which is only to be reaped by diligently sowing that crop of tender and loving equivalents with which your sex is so beautifully and bountifully provided."

The child has therefore a Right to liberty—a Right to be born free. And this includes the Right to come into the world without taint, without blemish, without an heritage which must be to it either a source of mental or physical disquietude. It is not contended, should the child be born either tainted in character or blemished in health, that the parents thereby forfeit all right to his tutelage and maintenance; because in order that the child may be born free from hereditary disability a certain amount of self-abnegation is demanded of the parents, and this should have some reward. Furthermore, the taint or blemish inherited by the child will be sure some day or other to prove a source of unhappiness to the parents. But though the punishment of depriving the parents of their child whose right to be born free they have disregarded, is not demanded; yet the punishment brought upon them by the mental or physical deformity of the child should never be sought to be lifted from their shoulders in such cases. Let us now show how such mental and physical deformity is brought about by neglect or misconduct in parents.

Dr. Johnson, in his charming *Rasselas*, somewhere utters a caution against contracting marriage with persons in ill-health. No matter how much we feel drawn toward such persons; no matter how interesting and affecting their condition may appear to us by very reason of their delicate health or other physical misfortune, it is a duty we owe to our expected offspring that they shall be born without the liability of thus inheriting disease.

Ill-health in the parents is not the only physical defect which is almost certain to be inherited by the children. Intemperance, proneness to religious excitement, and ill-temper, &c., are also heritable. These misfortunes, when they once become common to the parents, manifest themselves in certain physical traits of the children. We shall presently see from the statistics of insanity what bearing these disabilities have upon the welfare of offspring.

Consanguineous marriages are a fruitful source of misfortune to offspring. Strange that we should be willing to devote so much attention to the crossing of breeds in cattle, and so little to the same subject, with human beings! Any stableman or drover can preach you an entire volume on blood-horses, Devon cows, Southdown sheep, and mettled hounds; yet the highest in the land pay no sort of attention to the immensely more important subject of consanguineous marriages. The Greeks had something of a correct idea when they sought with particular solicitude to perpetuate the race of their hardiest warriors, and a long line of distinguished posterity was the consequence—a race of heroes, of men who produced a civilization centuries in advance of their time. But their system was incomplete—the women were entirely left out of their calculations. It was a system of concubinage, doomed sooner or later to degeneracy and self-destruction.

In all countries and at all times certain degrees of consanguinity were forbidden to intermarry. But very little regularity has prevailed upon this all-important topic. Until modern days it has been considered totally within ecclesiastical jurisdiction; and as religions have differed, so have the physiological laws which they have seen fit to enforce. "The disposition to degeneracy, in some form, in the offspring of marriages of cousins or others near of kin," says the Introduction to the Census,* "has long been known, but comparatively recent investigations in both Europe and the United States, and particcularly those of MM. Boudin and Devay, in France, and Dr. Bemiss, of Kentucky, have more fully illustrated the subject and more satisfactorily demonstrated the fact." "Dr. Dahl states," we quote from the same volume, "that in Norway the most abundant sources of insanity are hereditary predisposition, the intermarriages of near relatives, and the use of spirituous drinks." Here we are introduced to a new source of misery to offspring—hereditary predisposition. We are disposed to pass this over—believing that no person would marry another where even a remote fear existed that the other might become liable to insanity. We are willing to ascribe the origin of the insanity thus stated to be so prominently imparted to offspring, to a period long after marriage. Yet not a few marriages of persons who prove to be insane, do occur; and we advert to the fact merely in order to induce greater caution in contracting alliances. But it has been shown by Darwin in his "Selection of Species by Affinity," that every marked peculiarity of an individual becomes intensified by marriage, and that unless these

* *Population of the United States in* 1860: compiled from the original returns of the Eighth Census, under the direction of the Secretary of the Interior. By Joseph C. G. Kennedy. Washington: 1864.

eccentricities are curbed by strong self-control, repeated intensification will be sure to end by producing insanity in the offspring of such marriages.

Dr. John S. Butler, of the Retreat, at Hartford, Connecticut, in his Report of 1862, compiled a resulting table of the causes of insanity at four different hospitals—the Worcester, the Philadelphia, the Bloomingdale, and the Retreat. This table shows that of 7,591 cases of insanity, 2,253 were occasioned by ill-health, 812 by intemperance, 740 by religious excitement, and 728 by domestic unhappiness. To appreciate the importance of these statistics it is necessary to know what proportion the insane bear to the whole population. According to the census of 1860, the number of insane persons in the United States was 23,999, or something less than one in every one thousand of population. But we think it would approximate nearer to the truth to place the proportion at one per centum of the whole population.*

Here, then, we have one per cent. of the population afflicted with well-recognized insanity. And of this number, the causes of more than one half of the cases are ill-health, intemperance, religious excitement, and domestic unhappiness—causes that are either heritable or in danger of being communicated by example to the young.

To be sure, the number of insane, even if allowed to be one per cent. of the population, is comparatively small, and for that reason the argument may be deemed frivolous; not that the principle is doubted, but that the extent of the injury it works is exceedingly limited. But we must ot forget that insanity is only the last refuge of the frame from burdens which it is unable to bear. It is only when we contemplate the many degrees of wretchedness, of suffering, and terror, through which the mind passes, the storms and breakers of human misery through which it battles and buffets before it is stranded on the shores of insanity, never to battle with life or share its sweets again, that we can realize what fruitful sources

* The reason for this is obvious. But a very small portion of the insane are given to the Marshals for enumeration. See page lxxix. of the Introduction to the Census.

of unhappiness these causes, and the previous one of consanguineous marriages, may become, to the offspring of inconsiderate, unsolicitous, or criminal parents.

What right has a parent to saddle its child with a bad reputation? None. Or with shame and dishonor? None. Or with constitutional ill-health, or with insanity, or with the misery, and sometimes worse consequences which are seen to flow from consanguineous marriages, and from the heritage or the example of the various exciting causes we have mentioned? None, none, none. Because Sykes is a thief and lives in the Five Points, must his unhappy child be a Sykes, and a thief, and live in the Five Points, too? Does he owe Sykes this fearful obligation until he is twenty-one, and entirely ruined; or has he Rights by virtue merely of his existence—and Rights which society is bound to recognize and defend?

Are consanguineous marriages to be any longer upheld, and the relations of such parents to their children to be maintained, that the child shall continue to suckle from its mother's breast that poison which it may have escaped at birth? Are marriages of unhealthy persons to be connived at? Are intemperate and quarrelsome persons, and those fond of religious and other excitements,* to have unquestioned sway over their offspring, to whom they are sure, more or less, sooner or later, to communicate these evils?

These are serious questions—questions involving the whole well-being of society—questions which go down to the very foundations of society. They are the road-bed, the tresselwork, the embankments, tunnels, bridges, culverts, and switches, over which society is travelling every day at railway speed, the derangement of any of which is sure to be followed by the most deplorable consequences. But let us carry this principle of the Rights of Children a little farther. The allegiance to their parents until twenty-one, or more, which the laws of most countries impose upon children, is productive of evil in other ways. A cook's son is certain to become a cook, a boot-black's son is almost sure to be a boot-black, an ostler's

---

* See page xc. *et seq.* of the Introduction to the Census.

son to be an ostler, a scavenger's son to be a scavenger. There is nothing essentially disreputable in these occupations. Cooks, boot-blacks, ostlers, and scavengers fill just as useful spheres in society as statesmen and financiers. Soyer was a cook, Rarey was an ostler, and the scavenger's occupation has recently attained dignity through the attention which has been directed to the valuable fertilizing qualities of street waste. But it is not to be denied that these occupations, as they are ordinarily conducted, are considered disreputable, and this is enough for our purpose. Why then should a child born of such parents be subjected for twenty-one years to all the influences and surroundings of a life which the world considers, whether right or wrong, to be disreputable? Carry this principle still farther. Not only occupations, but names and creeds, and many other circumstances of life, however agreeable to the parent, may become insufferable to the child. At twenty-one, the law allows him to seek an occupation agreeable to himself,* to change a vulgar or distasteful name by act of legislature, or to choose a creed upon his own responsibility. But after twenty-one years of vassalage, what chance is there that the newly made freedman will be prepared to exercise his rights? The cook is still a cook, the boot-black remains a boot-black, the ostler is fit for nothing but cleansing stables, the scavenger has no higher ambition than to sweep streets or clean out sinks. Yellowplush has become reconciled to his name, and the religious bigotry of his parents has, by dint of repeated lessons, been effectually transmitted to him and his posterity for generations to come. But the authority which clearly does not belong to the parent, still more clearly, belongs to no one else, unless, as may be the case, to parents by adoption. The child is free; not free to be dragged away from its parents, or its adopted parents, by somebody else, as Mortara's child was, or, as in a recent case in this city, where the natural parents of the child, who had never done anything for it, were allowed to force it from the embraces of its adopted parents, who had done everything for it; but free to follow his own bent.

* He may choose his own apprenticeship at sixteen.

Were it not certain to extend this subject beyond my present limit, a curious *ensemble* of that ignorance and superstition which is daily transmitted to children might be exhibited as one of the many evils that flow from the unreasonable continuance and extent of this sort of patriarchal government. Withholding a child from seeing a mirror, curing a ringworm by the use of a talisman, weaning a child by the signs of the Zodiac, and endless other absurdities, are daily transmitted from the old to the young, and so perpetuated *ad infinitum*—all owing to the unnatural authority reposed in parents, and with which nobody, as society is now constituted, dares to interfere.

I have purposely refrained from saying anything upon the subject of marriages between persons of opposite religions, because, as from a politico-economical point of view, the child's particular religion is a matter of no moment whatever, all the injurious consequences which flow from unions of this sort fall upon the parents themselves. I have also said nothing concerning the evils which flow from the power to restrict children from marrying whom they please, because in most countries a sufficiently liberal view of the Rights of Children has obtained, to accord them this liberty as soon as they become of suitable age.

Enough has been seen to show that the whole question of the Rights of Children, as defined by law, needs revision. The relations of parent and child, ward and guardian, foster parent and children, the case of runaway, orphan, or lost children—all these need the revision demanded by the modern researches of Social Science. When parents understand that their children have Rights, they will treat them better, and in return receive that filial love and gratitude which is so commonly complained of as being wanting.

But it is the important benefits which would accrue to society by that recognition of the Rights of Children which I have here only partially succeeded in setting forth the grounds of, that mainly challenge our interest. These benefits are most easily understood by an example.

A despotic government, even the best, is sure to have the effect of keeping its people ignorant and helpless; because such a government undertakes to regulate all their concerns. It watches all their movements, places such a man here and such a man there, bids this man do this, and this man that, compels them to wear just such clothes, to live in just such houses, keep just such equipages, make just such journeys, enter into just such contracts, with just such forms, and to eat, drink, and live in just such a manner as in its omnipotence it thinks most proper. This theory of constant watch over the individual is derived from the same source as is the notion that the Creator permits not even a sparrow to fall to the ground without especially ordaining the same. That the sparrow does not fall to the ground without the *knowledge* of the Creator is evident; that it does not fall without His *intention* is absurd; for this reduces the Creator to the necessity of intending every wrong and abomination which is daily committed on earth. But the doctrine of predestination is universally regarded to have been long since exploded. Be this as it may, despotic governments, in thus affecting to regulate every movement of their subjects, only succeed in making them abject and dependent. Deprived of the exercise of their most active faculties, they soon forget how to use them, and relapse into helplessness. Then that necessity for superintending their private affairs which was at first assumed by the government has become a real necessity, and they cannot do without it.

So it is with children. Govern them too much and they will soon be unable to live without government. Instead of lads of mettle and enterprise, your sons will sink into that automatic state so common to the offspring of over-watchful parents; and instead of women of independent character, your daughters will lapse into listlessness and apathy. Nor will the evil stop here. The greed of power displayed by the parents will be sure to be inherited by the children and perpetuated by them in turn—perhaps with interest.

EMILE WALTER.

MILL'S ESSAYS.

Dissertations and Discussions, Political, Philosophical, and Historical. By John Stuart Mill. 3 vols. Boston: William V. Spencer, 1865.

SOME six months ago one of the leading London weeklies stated that the degree of liberalism of which the general English mind seems to be capable is an assent to and obedience of the dictas of John Stuart Mill. We are inclined to doubt the truth of this compliment (though not intended so to be) to the liberal minds of England. Mill is but little understood by the great mass of the English. His works upon Logic and Political Economy are not used as text-books in the English universities, and his speculations upon and investigations of the forms of thought, and social manifestations, have not yet supplanted Locke, Aristotle, Paley, and Whateley. This, though, is hardly to be expected. The English universities are essentially theological institutions. Not only is there no professor, whose opinions do not conform to those of the Church of England, appointed to any chair whatever, but students themselves are still expected to pin their faith to the Thirty-nine Articles. To all the progressive intellectual movements of the century those institutions are dead. Even the galvanic influence of vigorous attacks from all sincere Englishmen who are ashamed of the figure that Oxford and Cambridge cut in the estimate of enlightened Germans and Frenchmen, have wofully failed of all effect. When, driven by the force of necessity, these falsely called institutions of learning are compelled to pay some heed to the progress contemporaneously made in the world of science, they do it with a view to make scientific discoveries conform to some preconceived idea of morality or religion ; precisely as the Church of Rome, after a useless struggle during the middle ages against art, determined to make it subservient to its own uses. Of any honest, dispassionate examination; of search for truth, for the sake of truth, and not for any prescribed ends; of a careful examination of their curriculum, and an earnest effort to place it in harmony with the age in which we live, there is not the slightest indication. It is just as impossible for such men as Spencer, Comte, Mill, or Moleschott, to get a fair hearing, before the bar of the universities of England, as it would have been for a William Lloyd Garrison to have been fairly tried by a jury of slaveholders. It is for that reason that men of independent thought, and who have cut loose either from all the prevailing theology or a part thereof, do not exercise that influence in England which independent thinkers exercise on the Continent. In England, the learned institutions not only refuse to accord to such men professorships, but deny admission into the university of any of their works. In Germany, the collegiate system of education is altogether different. A degree of intellectual tyranny such as is constantly exercised at the English universities, if attempted but for a single day at a German university would excite an insurrection of the students. Though Strauss was dismissed from his professorship at Heidelberg, after the publication of his "Life of Jesus," and Moleschott lost his position in the same university, in consequence of writing the "Kreislauf des Lebens," there was nevertheless no attempt made to prohibit or forbid the study of their works, and the day following the dismissal of either of these professors any "Privat Docent" at the university might with impunity have delivered panegyric lectures upon Strauss or Moleschott to all the students. The great merit of the German universities, and which gives to them their high intellectual position, is the principle of competition which is admitted in the delivery of lectures. The government simply appoints the regular professors, but anybody has the right to deliver lectures upon any particular subject, whether appointed or not, provided he can prove himself possessed of scientific attainments; and the university faculty are bound to furnish him with a hall wherein to deliver his lectures. Thus it may frequently happen that the lecture room of the regular professor upon any particular department of knowledge is completely deserted, while that of some "*professor extraordinarius*" in the same branch of science is crowded. This intellectual competition keeps the regular professors to their work, and up with their age. No new truth in any department of science can be regarded by them with indifference nor ignored; as their competitors will teach it to the detriment of the reputation, for learning or impartiality, of the regular professors.

The beneficial fruits of this system are easily discernible. In logic John Stuart Mill's work has long since supplanted Hegel and Aristotle. And in law George Spence's "Equitable Jurisdiction of the Court of Chancery" has taken the place of the "Commentaries of Blackstone" as a text-book on the English common law.

In this country, there are two obstacles to the rapid progress of truth—indifference and public opinion. The first is evidenced by the contemptible manner in which works of the highest scientific value are reviewed by the daily and periodical journals, if noticed at all; and the second, by the universal deference paid by all American writers on scientific, ethical, or metaphysical subjects, to the Moloch of Public Opinion. In England, the effects of public opinion, to stifle thought, are almost as severe as here. Mill, however, to his lasting credit, never bowed to this idol, and all he has said or written was said or written in total disregard of what Mrs. Grundy might say.

The Essays before us have all been published and printed in the English quarterlies and magazines, and are now, for the first time, collected together by the author Thus, the admirers of Mill are enabled to enjoy these Essays in a more durable form than the one in which they have heretofore existed. The further advantage of republishing articles originally contributed to the periodical literature of England is, that we thus discover to whom we are indebted for Essays, from which we have derived great pleasure, in the pages of the "Edinburgh" or "Westminster;" and we frequently have cause to regret that the English contributors to their magazine and review literature do not do voluntarily, what the French do from compulsion, sign each essay with the name of the author.

These Essays were written between 1833 and 1863. They therefore display the gradual progress made in thirty years, both in thought and style, by John Stuart Mill. Mill was born in 1808, therefore only twenty-five years of age when he contributed to the *Jurist* the first of these essays in order of time; and even in that essay, we can distinguish those characteristics of mind, and that independence of tone, which have since rendered the name of Mill familiar to all lovers of liberty.

The man who writes but one style is no master of style, but style masters him, says Quintilian. This truth is exemplified in Mill. We were not aware, until the reading of these essays, that Mill could wield a pen so steeped in gall, and deal controversial blows with such telling effect as he therein proves himself able to do. The article on "The French Revolution of 1848, and its Assailants," says some as severe things, in a most gentlemanly manner, as it has been our good fortune to meet with. According to that essay, Lord Brougham succeeded in misjudging the French Revolution of 1848 as effectually as he now misjudges our own war. We, in charity, attributed Lord Brougham's sympathy for the Southern rebellion and antagonism to the North to—as Moleschott would say—a gradual diminution, caused by his advancing old age, of the phosphoric element of his brain. But, in 1848, his lordship was 17 years younger, and he then already had cut loose from democratic and liberal principles, and had espoused the cause of the old and effete governments of Europe.

Mill defends the Revolution of 1848 against the aspersion and abuse of Brougham; and more particularly defends the motives of the men who stood at the head of the movement. Lord Brougham, in a pamphlet written against the Revolution, not only condemned the movement, but, also with very bad taste, impugned the motives of such men as Lamartine, Hugo, Blanc, and Marrast. In defence of the principles of the Revolution and its leading actors, Mill took up the rapier, and in an article in the "Westminster Review" of April, 1849, Lord Brougham, his aiders, coadjutors, and abettors are most effectually disposed of.

Mill was not confident of the ultimate success of the French Revolution in establishing, upon a permanent basis, a republican form of government for France; but he thought that the Revolution was necessary to remove the rotten system which preceded it; and we believe he was right.

The government of Louis Napoleon, bad as it is, in so far as it prevents the development of individuality—a characteristic in which the French character is most deficient—is not a sham and a cheat such as that of Louis Philippe had been. It is a government which, for administrative ability, is far superior to any other in the world. It does not pretend to a liberalism which it has not; whereas, the reign of Louis Philippe was a constant and steady system of demoralization of the hearts of the French people. No one who has carefully studied the history of France for twenty years anterior to the Revolution of 1848, can fail to recognize the truth of the picture drawn by Mill, when he says:

First, it was a government wholly without the spirit of improvement. Not only did it make an obstinate resistance to all and every organic reform, even the most moderate; to all merely legislative or merely administrative improvements, it was in practice equally inimical: it originated none itself, and successfully resisted all which was proposed by others. There are few instances of a government, in a country calling itself free, so completely sold to the support of all abuses; it rested on a coalition of all the sinister interests in France. Among those who influenced the suffrages of the bodies of two or three hundred electors who returned the ministerial majority, there were always some to whose interests improvement, be it what it might, would have been adverse. It made things worse, not better, that the most conspicuous instruments of the system were men of knowledge and cultivation, who had gained the greater part of their reputation as the advocates of improvement. In some of these men, it might be personal interest; in others, hatred of democracy: but neither scrupled, for the sake of keeping their party together, to make themselves subservient to the purposes of their worst supporters. In order to bind these together in an united band to oppose democracy, they were allowed to have their own way, in resisting all other change. This was of itself fatal to the durability of a government, in the present condition of the world. No government can now expect to be permanent unless it guarantees progress as well as order, nor can it continue really to secure order, unless it promotes progress. It can go on, as yet, with only a little of the spirit of improvement. While reformers have even a remote hope of effecting their objects through the existing system, they are generally willing to bear with it. But when there is no hope at all; when the institutions themselves seem to oppose an unyielding barrier to the progress of improvement, the advancing tide heaps itself up behind them till it bears them down.

This was one great characteristic of the government of Louis Philippe. The other, equally discreditable, was the more fatal to that government, because identified still more than the first, in public opinion, with the personal character and agency of the King himself. It wrought most exclusively through the meaner and more selfish impulses of mankind. Its sole instrument of government consisted in a direct appeal to man's immediate personal interests or interested fears. It never appealed to, or endeavored to put on its side, any noble, elevated, or generous principle of action. It repressed and discouraged all such, as being dangerous to it. In the same manner in which Napoleon cultivated the love of military distinction as his one means of action upon the multitude, so did Louis Philippe strive to immerse all France in the *culte des intérêts matériels*, in the worship of the cash-box and of the ledger. It is not, or it has not hitherto been, in the character of Frenchmen to be content with being thus governed. Some idea of grandeur, at least some feeling of national self-importance, must be associated with that which they will voluntarily follow and obey. The one inducement by which Louis Philippe's government recommended itself to the middle classes was that revolutions and riots are bad for trade. They are so; but that is a very small part of the considerations which ought to determine our estimation of them. While classes were thus appealed to through their class-interests, every individual, who either from station, reputation, or talent, appeared worth gaining, was addressed through whatever personal interest, either of money or vanity, he was thought most likely to be accessible to. Many were attempted unsuccessfully, many successfully. Corruption was carried to the utmost pitch that the resources at the disposal of the government admitted of.

Accordingly, the best spirits in France had long felt, and felt each year more and more, that the government of Louis Philippe was a demoralized government; that, under its baneful influence, all public principle, or public spirit, or regard for political opinions, was giving way more and more to selfish indifference in the propertied classes generally, and, in many of the more conspicuous individuals, to the shameless pursuit of personal gain.

One of the "Essays" is a dissertation upon the "Enfranchisement of Woman," written by Mrs. Mill. It is a very closely reasoned and admirably written composition, but it certainly does not prove that, as Mill says, the "general level of her faculties" "was so elevated that the highest poetry, philosophy, oratory, or art seemed trivial by the side of her, and equal only to expressing some small part of her mind." The hyperbolical manner in which the preface to this Essay is written is almost unpardonable in a man like Mill.

Every mother believes her "cherub" to be the wonder of wonders among babies, and it is to be hoped that the majority of men admire their own wives better, and believe them superior, to the wives of other people, but the expression of these preferences is a weakness from which great minds are expected to be exempt. We may even be willing to admit that Mr. Mill's admiration for his wife is well founded, yet this could not excuse language like the following:

"As, during life, she continually detected, before any one else had seemed to perceive them, those changes of times and circumstances which ten or twelve years later became subjects of general remark; so I venture to prophesy, that if mankind continue to improve, their spiritual history for ages to come will be the progressive working out of her thoughts, and realizations of her conceptions."

Several of the Essays in these volumes, such as "An Examination of Coleridge and his Tendencies," an admirable essay on Bentham, one on Dr. Whewell's Moral Philosophy, and an examination of Professor Sedgwick's Discourse, defend the Doctrines and Principles of Utilitarianism against the school which believes in innate ideas of right and wrong. But the Essays in which Mr. Mill's adherence to the doctrines of Bentham are best evidenced, and where in the "greatest happiness" principles are most ably set forth and most tersely argued, are those which are to be found at the end of the last volume, entitled "Utilitarianism." It is not expedient for us to enter, much as we would desire to, into the merits of this controversy; but we recommend to all who are truly anxious to search for truth in the great controversy between authority and reason, between morality as an inchoate belief and as a science, to read carefully these Essays of Mill as the last, and to our mind the most conclusive, words yet written upon the subject of which they treat.

The dissertation upon Armand Carrel we found unsatisfactory. Unsatisfactory, because it is the only one of Mill's Essays that is open to the charge of being verbose without being instructive. In this Essay Mill introduces to us one who, if he had not been prematurely cut off by an unfortunate duel, would, in course of time, have been one of the leaders of politics in Europe. Mill quotes largely from the biographies of MM. Nisard and Littré to prove that in the estimate of these contemporaries, Carrel was not only a man of indomitable courage, high purpose, and noble aspirations, but that his editorials made the *National*—from 1831 to 1834 considered merely as a monument of political literature—the most original production of the nineteenth century.

He is compared with Junius only to prove that he is far superior to that great master of style. The vocabulary of panegyric is exhausted for the benefit of Mr. Mill's object of admiration, and yet throughout this dissertation we have not a single translation of any article written by Carrel, nay, we are not even vouchsafed a single phrase as a specimen of Carrel's style or ability. This would be pardonable in a criticism upon any acknowledged leader in the world of letters, because every educated man is expected to be more or less familiar with his style and thoughts ; but when a critic introduces us to one whose merits the world has not yet acknowledged, one " whom the world must not be suffered to let die," it then becomes the duty of the critic to show to us by evidence stronger than the most boundless adulation, why the memory of his idol should be cherished, and wherefore some prominent niche in the temple of fame should be reserved for him. This Mill does not do, and he leaves us unsatisfied, because we are not willing to take the opinion even of Mill as conclusive as to the merits of any one. There is one sentence in the Essay which is unpardonable. Unpardonable because it is either, as Mill himself says of a similar sentence in Lord Brougham's pamphlet, " an unbounded reliance on the ignorance of the public," or he has written it without familiarity with the works of at least two of the authors to whom he does gross injustice by the following opinion:

"Just as Byron and the cast-off boyish extravagances of Goethe and Schiller which Byron did but follow, have been the origin of all the sentimental ruffians, the Lacenaires in imagination and in action, with which the continent swarms ; but have produced little fruit of that description, comparatively speaking, in these islands ; so, to compare good influences with bad, did Scott's romances, and especially Ivanhoe, which in England were only the amusement of an idle hour, give birth (or at least nourishment) to one of the principal products of our time, the modern French School of History." We cannot conceive what these boyish extravagances of Goethe and Schiller are, to which allusion is here made. It is true that Schiller's "Reuber" and Goethe's "Werthers Leiden" might not have been written at a more mature period of the lives of these poets, but they are by no means "cast-off boyish extravagances." Goethe certainly is not open to the charge here made. Even Germany complains that its greatest poet and writer is too conservative in tone, and that if he had espoused the cause of liberty he might, by the force of his genius, have advanced the political fortunes of Germany by half a century. Goethe, unfortunately, from the nature of his social and literary position was a *reactionnaire*. In counteracting in Germany the literary influence of Voltaire and the whole French School, he became conservative in tone and eventually in feeling.

There are several Essays in these volumes relating to our present struggle. One, written February, 1862, upon the Trent affair, and entitled "The Contest in America," in which he delivers a lecture to England upon the bitterness of its tone and feeling against the North, and its sympathy for, and moral support of, the slaveholders' rebellion. The other is a review—which originally appeared in the Westminster Review for October, 1862—of Professor Cairnes' book on "The Slave Power, its Character, Career, and Probable Designs." Mr. Cairnes' views were so well and thoroughly canvassed in the United States shortly after the appearance of this book that it is not necessary to enter at large upon its merits. Mr. Cairnes, at the time when he published his work—shortly after McClellan's defeats before Richmond—believed, in common with a great number of loyal and patriotic citizens of the United States, that the South would succeed in gaining its independence. Mr. Cairnes did not, however, believe that that would at all benefit slavery, but that in any event the system was doomed. On the whole, it was then the opinion of that ardent friend of the United States and of human liberty, which Mr. Cairnes has always proved himself to be, that the independence of the South was a probable and not very unfortunate event, and he questioned the expediency of coercing the South into an alliance with the North. Mr. Mill, in the review of Cairnes' work, to which he accords all the credit which its high merit deserves, with the prescience of a true statesman and philosopher says :

To prevent the extension of slavery, is, in the general opinion of slaveholders, to insure its extinction. It is, at any rate, the only means by which that object can be effected through the interests of the slaveholders themselves. If peaceful and gradual is preferred to sudden and violent emancipation (which we grant may in the present case be doubtful), this is the mode in which alone it can be effected. Further colonization by slaves and slavemasters being rendered impossible, the process of exhausting the lands fitted for slave cultivation would either continue, or would be arrested. If it continue, the prosperity of the country will progressively decline, until the value of slave property is reduced so low, and the need of more efficient labor so keenly felt, that there will be no motive remaining to hold the negroes in bondage. If, on the other hand, the exhaustive process should be arrested, it must be by means implying an entire renovation, economical and social, of Southern society. There would be needed new modes of cultivation, processes more refined and intellectual, and, as an indispensable condition, laborers more intelligent, who must be had either by the introduction of free labor, or by the mental improvement of the slaves. The masters must resign themselves to become efficient men of business, personal and vigilant overseers of their own laborers, and would find, that, in their new circumstances, successful industry was impossible without calling in other motives than the fear of the lash. The immediate mitigation of slavery, and the education of the slaves, would thus be certain consequences, and its gradual destruction, by the consent of all concerned, a probable one, of the mere restriction of its area ; whether brought about by the subjugation of the Southern States, and their return to the Union under the Constitution according to its Northern interpretation, or by what Mr. Cairnes regards as both more practical and desirable—the recognition of their independence, with the Mississippi for its western boundary.

Either of these results would be a splendid, and probably a decisive and final victory over slavery. But the only point on which we hesitate to agree with Mr. Cairnes is in preferring the latter to the former and more complete issue of the contest. Mr. Cairnes is alarmed at what he thinks the impossibility of governing the group of States after reunion, unless in a manner incompatible with free institutions—as conquered countries, and by military law. We are unable to see the impossibility. If reduced by force, the slave States must submit at discretion. They could no longer claim to be dealt with according to the Constitution which they had rebelled against. The door which has been left open till now for their voluntary return would be closed, it is to be presumed, after they had been brought back by force. In that case, the whole slave population might, and probably would, be at once emancipated, with compensation to those masters only who had remained loyal to the Federal Government, or who may have voluntarily returned to their allegiance before a time fixed. This having been done, there would be no real danger in restoring the Southern States to their old position in the Union. It would be a diminished position, because the masters would no longer be allowed representatives in Congress in right of three fifths of their slaves. The slaves once freed, and enabled to hold property, and the country thrown open to free colonization, in a few years there would be a free population in sympathy with the rest of the Union. The most actively disloyal part of the population, already diminished by the war, would probably in great part emigrate, if the North were successful. Even if the negroes were not admitted to the suffrage, or if their former masters were able to control their votes, there is no probability, humbled and prostrated as the Slave Power would be, that in the next few years it would rally sufficiently to render any use which it could make of constitutional freedom again dangerous to the Union. When it is remembered that the thinly peopled Missouri, Arkansas, Texas, and some parts even of the South-Eastern States, have even now so few slaves that they may be made entirely free at a very trifling expense in the way of redemption, and when the probable great influx of Northern settlers into those provinces is considered, the chance of any dangerous power in the councils of the United States to be exercised by the six or seven Cotton States, if allowed to retain their constitutional freedom, must appear so small, that there would be little temptation to deny them that common right.

It may, however, prove impossible to reduce the seceded States to unconditional submission, without a greater lapse of time, and greater sacrifices than the North may be willing to endure. If so, the terms of compromise suggested by Mr. Cairnes, which would secure all west of the Mississippi for free labor, would be a great immediate gain to the cause of freedom, and would, probably, in no long period, secure its complete triumph. We agree with Mr. Cairnes, that this is the only *kind* of compromise which should be entertained for a moment. That peace should be made by giving up the cause of quarrel, the exclusion of slavery from the Territories, would be one of the greatest calamities which could happen to civilization and to mankind. Close the Territories, prevent the spread of the disease to territory not now afflicted with it, and much will already have been done to hasten its doom. But that doom would still be distant if the vast uncolonized region of Arkansas and Texas, which alone is thought sufficient to form five States, were left to be filled up by a population of slaves and their masters; and no treaty of separation can be regarded with any satisfaction, but one which should convert the whole country west of the Mississippi into free soil.

The influence which Mr. Mill has exercised upon public opinion in England in reference to the American war is a very great one. He was one of the few enlightened men in Europe whose faith in our institutions never faltered despite their many blemishes and faults, and who believed that a great people could not and would not be balked in the pursuit of their high mission.

Let us now examine a little more closely the place that Mill should hold among the contemporary thinkers of the world. While we do not share the opinion expressed by Buckle, that if a jury of twelve of the most enlightened men of Europe were impanelled to decide by their verdict who had done most for the advancement of knowledge in Europe they should unhesitatingly pronounce the name of John Stuart Mill, we nevertheless believe that he has done more than any other thinker of England for the cause of liberal opinions, and the destruction of fetichisms in theology and politics. While Spencer is the bolder reasoner, and perhaps the greater genius Mill's high social position and practical turn of thought enabled him to exercise a greater influence. And herein lies the great difference between the thinker and the statesman. It may be wrong, judged from a lexicographical point of view, to call Mill a statesman, as he has never held any very exalted position in the council chamber of England, yet there is no other word which so fully expresses our meaning of Mr. Mill's qualities of mind. Familiar with the utmost limits of philosophical inquiry, conscious of the great truths on the side of those who hold that all governmental interference in any department of human activity is mischievous, he has nevertheless devoted his faculties and energies to the inculcation only of that part of these truths and the advocacy of such reforms as he believed immediately practicable. This, many would consider a defect. It is held, and with a great deal of reason, by men whose lives are devoted to the furthering of great social reforms, that it is our duty to exact the utmost farthing that governments owe to society, and to accept no compromise which does not admit the full justice of the whole of the claim. Such men hold with Emerson that we should speak our minds in words as loud as cannon-balls, and express our whole mind upon any question in which the interest of the whole of mankind is involved. Yet, in doing so, men of the greatest intellect, though useful as guides to truth, whose words of wisdom will benefit future generations, exercise but little influence upon their contemporaries. An argument logically pursued to its ultimate conclusion, a conclusion like Spencer's deduction of the Rights of Children from his first principle, repels rather than attracts the majority even of thinking men.

For that reason, the study of history in a philosophical spirit is absolutely necessary to one who desires to be useful to his fellow men in the inauguration and practical execution of social reforms. Neither error nor the institutions which are based upon it can be extirpated, branch and root, by one effort. Every reform is a compromise between truth and error, but this compromise expresses the intellectual standpoint of the great body of the people, and shows to what extent the truth will be accepted and acted upon. In that sense every great reform which history records may be considered a compromise. The reason why so many a great mind has failed to induce his contemporaries to coin his thoughts into acts, was because he forgot that progress was made only by a slow and tedious system of education, and not by sudden leaps and jumps. Such men generally forget the historical value of what in the abstract we may believe to be injustice or error. One of the most striking evidences of this in History is the fate of Charlemagne's Empire. Charlemagne attempted to govern barbarians by a system of law and order, fitted only for a comparatively civilized community. By the force of will, and indomitable energy, he succeeded during the brief space of his reign in bringing order out of chaos. Yet, hardly had he passed from the stage, when every vestige of his existence, in so far as public and governmental institutions are concerned, was blotted out also, and for several hundred years European society was in a position and condition as if he had never lived. The mistake made by the French Encyclopedists, and subsequently by the leaders of the French Revolution, was of the same character. They failed to accord to the various forms of religion their historical value and importance ; they therefore enthroned the goddess of Reason at a period when the people's ideas of reason were as imperfect as their ideas of religion, and their work failed because the spirit of the age was not in harmony with the intelligence and knowledge of a few hundred philosophers and statesmen. A reaction is only the necessary consequence of a premature development. Reactions never occur when the progress is in accordance with the true spirit of the age. Mill's sagacity, judgment, and breadth of philosophic view prevent him from attempting to force progress. He is a great reformer, not by boldness of theory and vastness of conception, for many have surpassed him in this, but by reason of advocating only such reforms for which he believes the people ripe. When judged from this standpoint, Mill looms up in gigantic proportions, for then and then only can we properly estimate his principal force. To compare great things to small, the influence of his words upon the thinking men of Europe is much like the influence of an honest lawyer who has never been known to have been engaged in an unjust cause. In course of time his causes are almost prejudged in his favor. Then begins the dangerous part of the influence of such an advocate ; prejudiced in his favor, judges no longer sift with the same care the evidence upon which the advocate relies for success, that they would exercise were they less satisfied of the honesty of counsel. Mill's influence in England has arrived pretty much at that stage. With a certain class of thinkers upon any knotty social or controversial question his words are almost conclusive. So long as Mill preserves the force of his faculties and the strength of his judgment, his influence is immeasurably more beneficial than it can possibly prove baneful ; but when we consider how in their old age such lights as Newton, Burke, and Brougham have been dimmed ; how conservatives in politics or religion have constantly cited such examples to prove the instability of man's attachment to reason, and his proneness to return with advanced experience to faith in authority, we are almost tempted to wish that such men would die when they have reached the zenith of their power, so that we should not be afflicted with the pitiable sight of the gradual decay of faculties and powers which have at one time been the wonder and admiration of the world.

We therefore regard with some misgivings the influence Mill exercises upon the intelligent classes of England. It is too overshadowing, and also exhibits the dearth of bold and original thinkers in that country. We trust, however, that our fears may never be realized. There are numerous examples in the history of literature that it is possible to grow old without growing intellectually weak. Goethe and Humboldt possessed in the evening of their long and honored lives the same, if not superior, intellectual vigor that they enjoyed at that period when both intellectual and physical force are supposed to culminate in man.

At all events Mill is entitled to the lasting gratitude of progressive men the world over for what he has accomplished. Born in a position which naturally might have led him to espouse the cause of governments, he voluntarily devoted his brilliant faculties to the service of the whole of mankind. From early life in a quasi-governmental employ, he never became the apologist of his superiors, and refused, though beset by every temptation so to do, to become the tool of party. Outside and above all partisanship, he has viewed his contemporaneous history from so elevated a standpoint, that at no time was the charge ever ventured upon, that he ever expressed an opinion from any but the most disinterested and pure motives. What he has done will always entitle him to be classed among the great benefactors of mankind, and consecrate his memory as one who at all times espoused the cause of the suffering part of humanity, though widely separated from them by wealth, social position, and culture. S. S.

PROCEEDINGS OF LEARNED SOCIETIES.

[UNDER this head we shall in future give quarterly reports of the Proceedings of Learned Societies in the United States. Officers of these associations will please send in a short *resumé* of their proceedings, up to within twenty days of the date of publication of this journal. We give in this number only the proceedings of two Societies, in consequence of our inability to obtain the rest in time.—EDS.]

THE SOCIETY FOR THE ADVANCEMENT OF SOCIAL SCIENCE.

THIS organization, founded October 9, 1862, has since continued to hold regular weekly meetings, except during the summer season, under the designation of *The Society for the Advancement of Social Science.* The place for meeting is at

No. 12 Union Square, New York, and the regular day is every Monday at 8 P. M. Communications intended for the Society should be addressed to Mr. SIMON STERN, Secretary.

The following papers are outlines of a few of the most recent debates.

REPUBLICANISM.

The question for discussion was :

IS THE UNITED STATES GOVERNMENT A REPUBLIC ? Debate opened by Mr. SIMON STERN.

Mr. STERN proceeded to give a *resumé* of Sir Geo. Cornewall Lewis' book on Government, because he agreed with the author in his estimate of the United States Government. Only in name is the United States Government a republic, because of the tyranny which the majority may exercise to the detriment of the wishes and interests of the minority ; because no form of Government whose province exceeds the administration of justice furnishes complete protection against tyranny ; because it exercises delegated powers liable to gross abuse ; because by some or other of its officers nearly every possible form of power is exercised ; and because neither women, nor pubescent minors, nor foreigners, nor Indians, nor negroes can vote. In effect, the Government is a constitutional monarchy. All my property is at its disposal—so is my happiness—nay, even my life. The only difference between our Government and an avowed monarchy consists in the manner that it is privileged to distress me.

Mr. THOMAS SMULL. Our Government *is* a republic ; not a perfect one, of course, but still a republic. If justice were better administered in it, and the people sufficiently alive to their true interests to oppose its constant tendency to centralize itself, we should be possessed of as pure a republican government as I would care to live under.

Mr. LEOPOLD RIESS. Kant defines republicanism to be that polity (Staatsprinzip) which separates the executive from the legislative power. We understand a state to be a republic, whenever the ruling power is vested in the people, whether executed by them direct as in the case of the Athenians (and called an absolute republic), or by their representatives as in modern governments, such as the United States, Switzerland, &c. Equality of civil and political rights is enjoyed in the United States by all classes. It is true that male adults under the age of 21 are excluded from suffrage ; but if this is open to criticism, the same applies as to women, who are denied the right of suffrage altogether. Human laws cannot be made sufficiently comprehensive to protect minorities. It has so far been recognized as a principle of a republic, that the majority should rule the minority. The perfect liberty of the minority can only be secured by decentralization, and not by any of our forms of government. Governors will ever overstep their functions, and, at times, make ill use of their power. If, therefore, in extraordinary circumstances, such as those which this country is in at present, more extended powers are assumed by the rulers, this cannot be considered a sufficient reason to deny to the United States the claim to be a republic.

Mr. E. Fezandié. The United States is no more a republic than Russia. Nay, even less, in one important respect. There, in case the tyranny of the ruler becomes insufferable, the people take care to strangle him. Here, we have no such resource. Even in regard to the Constitution, or the body of organic law which passes by that name, the English is more liberal than the American. What can be more indicative of a dominative tendency than the term "held to labor" which occurs in the Constitution of the United States. If it is so desired, the laws of this country may be used to elaborate tyranny to an insupportable degree. We have hitherto been more free under this Government than most others, but this has been owing less to the form of the Government, than to the fact that we had peace, and were free from taxation. As there is nothing in the form of the Government to repress usurpation and tyranny, we have yet to find an occasion to boast of our republicanism, when war and taxation, the two readiest levers of domination, shall have been placed long enough in the hands of authority.

Mr. Alex. Delmar. Instead of being *Is the United States Government a Republic*, were the question *Is the United States a perfect Democracy*, I could cordially agree with the last speaker; but the debate must be confined to the terms of the subject as stated. A republic is a form of Government in which the supreme power is vested, not in a single person or family, or a limited number of persons or families, but in the people or a large portion of them.

This definition I conceive to be more correct than the one given by Mr. Riess. Under his, France is a republic, Germany is a republic, so is Italy, so is Austria, so is every constitutional monarchy; every despotism which sets up the farce of a subservient Diet, or Chamber of Deputies, or Royal Parliament. Under mine, they are not. And as mine is the commonly received definition, and the United States Government agrees with it, it follows that it is a republic, and the question for debate is answered. But it seems to me that two further qualifications are needful to make even this definition correct; by adding: *and where that power is liable to be transferred at any moment*, and striking out, *or a large portion of them*, we have the definition of a republic, as follows: *That form of Government in which the supreme power is vested, not in a single person or family, or a limited number of persons or families, but in the people; and where that power is liable to be exercised at any moment.* The definition may be made more simple yet; but the antithesis furnished by this one, makes it more easy of comprehension. Were we to take this definition, our form of Government would not be deemed republican. The presidential, and other terms of office, are only limitations of the monarchical principle. The minority has no rights. Custom-houses and patent offices are royal prerogatives. Power over the currency, power to tax, power to legislate in derogation of private interests, power to appoint swarms of officers, are all forms of monarchical monopolies and tyrannies. But though it is time many of these abuses were swept away, some of them will always linger, until civic intelligence is universal. Pure democracy is impossible, until the tendency of education to a maximum has ceased to be one of unequal degrees in different individuals. This being the case, I conclude that, though a very imperfect one, the United States Government is, as we understand the term, a republic.

Dr. Julius Homberger. I concur with the last speaker. Many of Sir Geo. Cornewall Lewis' arguments against the republicanism of this Government are shallow. I admit that twenty-one years is too long an infancy for the citizen, but when he urges this as an objection to our assumption of republicanism, he should go farther. Why should not the madman, who, as is often the case, is sane enough on some subjects, politics for instance—why should this man not be permitted to exercise the right of suffrage? No one questions his sanity upon this point. He is a man, we will say, of rare intelligence on most subjects, this included; but unhappily, mad upon some one topic, not at all connected with that of Government. Why disfranchise this man, and permit the ignorant peasant or the besotted pauper to exercise a right which they can only exercise for evil, not only to themselves, but to society at large? Because the line has been drawn with less wisdom than it might have been, in regard to the right of suffrage, is no good reason for denying that this Government is a republic. And even were the line drawn with perfect justice, does it necessarily follow that the average conclusion of a large number of people upon any public subject is correct? Strictly speaking, the United States Government is beyond all question a republic. And looking back, it has been a successful one—looking forward is another thing. The present war is a trial out of which there is little hope it will emerge unscathed.

Mr. CHARLES MORAN. Instead of discussing a principle, we are discussing a name. Unless we free our minds from human laws and consult natural laws, it is impossible to know what conduces to the well-being of mankind. No true republic can consist of any community larger than that composing a single city, because where its domain is further extended, it would be impossible for the people to meet together and vote on public questions. The Greek republics were all cities and towns. Outside of these, the form of Government was anything but republican. Only where the rights of the minority are protected can true liberty exist, and the most important of these rights is that they shall choose what form of Government suits them best.

Mr. WM. P. LEE. The difference between a monarchy and a republic is, that in the former the king makes laws, not for himself, but for his subjects. There is no law over him. In the latter, the laws cover both the citizen and the executive. And though the majority make the laws, they make them for themselves as well as the minority, there is, therefore, no possibility of great oppression. All are alike amenable to them.

Mr. WM. B. SCOTT. Let us judge of the Government not by its name but by its acts. Is the conscription law republican? Is the legal-tender law republican? Are the tax laws republican? What claims then has this Government to be called a republic?

Mr. STERN. It is clear that in discussing this question we have followed in that path which the nation at large has chosen to travel. It has fixed its eyes not upon the true meaning of a republic, but upon the lexicographical definition of the term. So have we. The result is that neither they nor we can perceive what indeed is the true state of the case: that we live under as pure a form of despotism as it is possible to conceive. The only difference is, that the pill is sugar-coated, and the dose varied to meet the changing disposition and the vitality of the patient.

A little reflection will show Mr. LEE the error in his observation, "that there is no oppression in a government of the majority, because the laws made by the majority are binding upon them as well as upon the minority." In a community composed principally of Catholics, a law passed by the majority that all who are not Catholics shall be exiled, is a law binding upon the majority of the nation, as well as the minority, yet the oppression will be felt only by the minority. Take the conscription law as another illustration. If the United States is engaged in a war, believed to be right and just by a vast majority, and yet, if I stand alone in believing it to be wrong and iniquitous, a draft which takes me from my family, and compels me to fight in what I deem an unjust war, is an outrageous act of oppression and hardship, though it would not be as against persons who have decreed the inauguration or continuance of the war. The government of the majority can therefore be, and generally is, as oppressive as the most tyrannical form of government.

FREE TRADE.

The question for discussion was :

Do not all Taxes and Duties prejudice Home Industry, and operate in favor of Foreign Manufacturers and Producers? Debate opened by Mr. Wm. B. Scott.

Mr. Scott. There are, we will say, one thousand millions of population in this world. The least civilized portion of this population supplies the most civilized portion with raw products, which the latter either works up into manufactures, a part of which are sent back in payment of the raw products, or for which they give other products either in a raw state, or as is commonly the case, in a more or less manufactured state. It is clear that those of the most civilized nations who can sell their manufactures cheapest will become the successful competitors for supplying that vast portion of the world which is least civilized, and for receiving raw products in exchange—in a word, successful in commerce. That commerce is the life of a nation, needs no proof here. We are all aware of its abundant blessings. It confers peace, wealth, ease, education, liberty, and it indirectly leads to a true knowledge of God. Let us now suppose that one of these commercial nations, these competitors for the trade of the world, were to put a tax of five per cent. upon its domestic staples or fabrics ; is it not clear that by so doing it would stultify its own ability to compete with other commercial nations, to the extent of at least five per cent. in the price of its productions ?

Mr. C. E. Anderson. Though I may yet see cause for changing

my opinion, I am compelled at the present stage of the argument to disagree with Mr. Scott. Duties appear to me to injure only the foreign manufacturer, who supplies our markets, for it keeps him out of them. See what fortunes the Rhode Island manufacturers have been reaping since the tariff was raised. Duties also injure the consumer, who has to pay them. But that they do not injure our own manufacturers appears to me sufficiently plain.

Mr. Scott. Let me show you an instance where you are wrong. The cost of producing grain is increased by taxing the product itself, or by taxing something else which raises the cost of living, and so raises the cost of producing grain. This is in one country—the United States, for example. In some other countries, no such tax exists, or it is very much smaller. Is it not plain that the competition of these other grain-growing countries would successfully exclude us from the grain markets of the world, provided they could fully supply those markets; of which, of course, there is no doubt?

Mr. Charles Moran. What is essential to the manufacturing interests of this country? Capital and labor. Taxes increase the charges upon capital and the drain upon labor, without benefiting either. Protection to home manufactures, instead of being beneficial, has this effect: it throws industry into unprofitable channels. If iron could be got cheaper from England than it could be made here, no one would make it here. Put a sufficient duty upon its importation, however, and the manufacturer who had previously been in some occupation that was intrinsically profitable, leaves it to engage in the iron trade, which is only profitable because it has been protected. Protection causes all other than protected industries to languish. The effect of protection is to furnish hot-beds for the growth of puny and inconsiderable interests. Protection keeps us out from the commerce of the world. Protection reduces the wages of labor, and the interest of capital. Philadelphia successfully competes with New York in many branches of the inter-State commerce of this country, by reason of the local taxes there, being lower than they are here. So will this country be beaten in the commerce of the world, as New York in the instance mentioned, has been beaten in the commerce between the States.

Mr. Wm. P. Lee. John Stuart Mill says that protection may be proper and advantageous to certain manufactures which thrive in certain localities, owing to felicitous circumstances of climate, &c. For instance, a dry climate is not adapted to cotton-spinning. England possesses a moist climate, and is one of the few countries where this manufacture can be profitably conducted. Protection to cotton manufactures may therefore be proper to enable other countries to counterbalance this advantage which England possesses. I am an advocate of Free Trade, but I think that under certain circumstances Protection is desirable. In times of war we must do as we can, not as we would. War, by requiring taxes to be levied, increases the expenses of the citizen. This again increases the cost of manufacturing. If we are to devote so much consideration to commercial interests, we would forget what is more important—to support the war.

Mr. ISAAC C. KENDALL. There exists the greatest diversity of opinion concerning Protection. My own opinion is that American mechanical genius, so renowned all the world over, and which has so materially contributed to lessen the price of manufactures, owes its existence to Protection ; consequently Protection has really lowered the price of production. Whatever has been protected has fallen in price. This is certainly a good argument for Protection. And this can be proved to be in the nature of things. England supplies us with cotton prints. We now lay a duty on them. This stimulates home industry. Machines are invented to level the obstacle presented by the duty. The machines not only overcome this obstacle, but do more. They make the price cheaper than it was before the protective duty was laid on. This fall in price reacts to England, and lowers the prices of cotton prints there—all in consequence of the original protective duty. The first experiments in all improvements prove failures, but eventually the improvements succeed, and the loss occasioned by the first experiments is not felt. The mechanical genius of this country can overcome all the obstacles which high tariffs can furnish. We don't want to be confined to one employment, simply because that pays the best. Diversity of employments gives a chance to all. Protection makes new employments, and creates consumers for our agricultural productions, so that we can get along among ourselves without going to the rest of the world for supplies. In former times our markets were constantly disturbed, because the temptation to consume foreign luxuries led us to import more than we exported.

Mr. MORAN denied that we ever imported more than we exported. This was impossible. The speaker went on to exhibit the rationale of commerce, taking his starting point from the settlement of a new country by a band of colonists. He traced their growth and occupations, and showed, that, in the nature of things, inequality of international commerce could not happen.

Mr. KENDALL (continuing). Another advantage of Protection is, that it teaches a nation what occupations are the most profitable. Without Protection, this could not be discovered. It developes the mind of the nation. It fosters invention, and enables man to overcome nature.

Dr. JULIUS HOMBERGER. Industries when left to themselves flourish better than when artificially encouraged. Protected industries do not pay so well as those which exist without Protection. The Southern States found it to their interest to confine themselves almost exclusively to the cultivation of cotton. Had they done anything else they would have been false to their own interests. Reverting to the question for debate, it appears to me that there ought to be some discrimination made between the use of the terms duties and taxes. Duties open the question of Free Trade in its widest application ; while taxes only affect our relations with Europe. In this respect I believe the injurious consequences of taxation, in respect to this country, have been exaggerated. The taxes imposed here, only counterbalance taxes which have been long imposed in European countries. Without taxes we were better off than they, both as regarded the price of living and our ability to compete with them for the commerce of the world. With taxes we are only reduced to their level, not lower.

Mr. SCOTT. But we have other than taxed countries to compete with. Look at Canada, equal to our own country in extent of territory, and possessing the great advantage of freedom from taxation. Can we hope to compete with this new country in the race for commercial greatness ?

Mr. ALEX. DELMAR. I shall devote my remarks less to the question for discussion, which I answer categorically in the affirmative, than to a refutation of the extraordinary errors which I conceive to have been contained in the speech of Mr. KENDALL. The point which the gentleman dwelt upon with most emphasis, was that Protection fostered mechanical inventions. Now, the reverse of this is the truth ; for what inducement can there be to invent labor-saving machines when the tariff by means of Protection secures the manufacturer from foreign competition ? And if any inducement at all exists, how much greater would that inducement not have been had no Protection been laid ? But the speaker in the example of cotton prints claims that the hypothetical inventions he mentions go farther than to level the obstacle presented by the duty. He says, they make prices cheaper than they were before ; and that this reacts to England, &c. ! Having shown that under Protection there exists less inducement to invent than under Free Trade, it were superfluous to show that if an invention *is* made, under Protection, it is not likely to aim beyond the savings of the custom-house duties involved. The speaker assumes that certain manufactures hitherto enjoying Protection have become lower in price than the imported articles without Protection. But is this true? Are cotton prints cheaper here than in England? Is hardware cheaper? Is crockery cheaper? Is iron cheaper? Are pins and needles cheaper? Are cloths, cassimeres, vestings, hats, shoes, or gloves cheaper? Is paper cheaper? Is machinery cheaper? Is anything but a few corn brooms, cedar pails, and wooden clothes-pins cheaper? Look at the article of wood screws, on which the nation pays a profit to the New England manufacturer of, it is said, eight hundred per cent.—wood screws, which are as commonly used as nails are. As for the diversity of employments resulting from measures which force an agricultural country to become semi-mechanical, there is no advantage in this. Even was there no disadvantage, there is no advantage. The South, an exclusively agricultural country, has, when necessity demanded it, been able to prosecute home manufactures with success. And as for getting along among ourselves, can it be seriously claimed to be an advantage to follow the example of China and Japan? But to go back to Mr. KENDALL'S main point, that Protection would foster mechanical genius, so would cutting a man's legs off induce him to invent wooden ones; so would damming up a river induce it to overleap its barriers, and wander profitlessly over a whole country, instead of following its natural and direct route to the sea. Both of these are instances of a waste of power, and this is precisely the case with those inventions which are born of Protection. Putting a load on a horse's back will stimulate his invention to throw it off, but is it contended that the load will increase his speed? The speaker then showed that patents of invention were but another form of Protection, and instead of fostering mechanical genius, actually retarded it. As an instance answering not only to this point, but to the main one made by Mr. Kendall, and also to the question for discussion, he reviewed the history of the wood-screw trade, the protective tariff upon it, the patented machine for making wood screws, and the many other odious forms of monopoly combined in this manufacture.

EXECUTIVE POWER.

The question for discussion was :

ARE THERE ANY CIRCUMSTANCES IN A POLITICAL BODY WHICH MAY JUSTIFY THE TEMPORARY EXTENSION OF POWER VESTED BY THE COMMUNITY IN THE EXECUTIVE ? Debate opened by Dr. JULIUS HOMBERGER.

Dr. HOMBERGER. The Executive being created, and his powers defined and limited, by law, is he justified, in those cases not contemplated by the law, to extend his powers ; or must he go back to the people for a new warrant ?

Mr. WM. B. SCOTT. No government should confer power upon any one, or upon any class, which may be used to deprive others of their right to liberty, unless they have forfeited it by misconduct.

Dr. HOMBERGER. I had reference to measures which might momentarily please the whole people.

Mr. CHAS. MORAN. Or, whether a wrong measure may be used for a good purpose.

Mr. ALEX. DELMAR. The infraction of the organic law of a free people by its Executive is sure to be succeeded by something more than the immediate convenience which formed the excuse for its infraction ; but if in the framing of organic law the framers are not far-seeing enough to provide for all emergencies which may arise to tempt its infraction, then they are responsible for whatever evil consequence may ensue. It should never be forgotten that free government is local—nay, even individual, and that the moment it is centralized, it is in constant danger of destruction. Therefore to intrust the administration of any part of it to a particular man or set of men, is to expose that much, at least, to abuse.

Mr. E. FEZANDIÉ. All laws are laws of exception. They have all been made for a certain state of things—not upon principle. Of course, some time or other they become no longer operative. The caprice or fancy of the majority makes the law for the moment. Some men, to-day, if not checked by law or public opinion, would declare it treason even to harbor *thoughts* inimical to the measures of the hour. No laws are unexceptional. Governments are like banks : when you do not want money, they offer you plenty ; when you want it, there is none to be had. When you do not want freedom, government is exceedingly liberal with it. When you stand most in need of it, you are refused.

Mr. THOMAS SMULL. All governments are more or less experimental. The majority rules. Until the majority can know its true interests, misrule must result. A government of the people is the only true government, but the people must learn to be governors before their government can be good. A dictatorship is better than the misrule of a mob, because in the former case there is a better chance to overthrow it.

Mr. Erastus W. Benedict. There are times when a dictator is needful. The speaker instanced the case of the steamer *Arctic*, which was lost for the want of a Commander at the critical moment. But after all, a popular government is the strongest of governments. No government has been stronger than ours. Its strongest acts are provided for by law. The Constitution declares the object of the government to be the happiness of the people, and makes the President swear to support it. He can therefore lawfully do anything that is necessary to support it, and lawfully prevent anything that stands in the way of the people's happiness. "He shall see that the republic receives no injury." Who is to judge what constitutes the happiness of the people? The majority. The majority, therefore, must rule. If a policeman arrests me on a charge of crime, I must go with him, even though my submission temporarily robs me of my liberty. Why? Because the majority rules it. Upon this principle rests the whole theory of government. If the Executive does any unusual act necessary to the preservation of the government, without referring it to the decision of the majority, he is still excused; because he has sworn to protect the Constitution. How? By his own discretion. By what means? The army and navy.

Dr. Homberger. If the powers lately exercised by the President are vested in him by the Constitution, why should he have required the Bill of Indemnity passed to excuse him?

Mr. Benedict. Because he has enemies. No member of Congress can be arrested for debt. Why? Because the public good so demands. The principle is the same in the President's case.

Mr. Moran. Mr. Benedict has shown that this government was formed not for the people, but for the nation. Every man who has written upon government has said that government was for the people. But the moment the government was formed, it proved to be a government for the nation. It follows from Mr. Benedict's argument that this government is based on the same grounds as all others, and is not the exception which we fondly believed it to be.

Dr. Homberger. Even in despotic countries, the press is free in times of quiet. Up to a certain point freedom is undisturbed. That point is where the existence of the government is endangered. It has been the same here. That point of danger may be not in the same place ; but the principle is identical. It would therefore seem to follow that in principle, this government does not differ from a despotism.

INSANITY.

The question for discussion was :

WHAT LEGISLATION SHOULD THERE BE UPON THE SUBJECT OF INSANITY ? Debate opened by Dr. JULIUS HOMBERGER.

Dr. HOMBERGER stated the recent and notorious case of Miss Underhill, of Brooklyn, who, although a woman of acknowledged refinement and cultivation, was, at the instigation of relatives, and from interested motives, consigned to the dread horrors of a mad-house. Upon her release she brought an action at law against the offending parties ; and the only satisfaction she received was six cents damages from the jury. The law here in regard to the apprehension of insane persons is, that any person may be confined for insanity upon the affidavit of two physicians. If wrongfully detained, it is difficult, nay, often impossible to procure his release ; and when he is released, as shown in this case, ordinary juries are incapable to render him proper justice. The speaker then mentioned an instance where the cause of imprisonment was not the cupidity of interested persons, but the neglect of indifferent ones. The case was that of a Polish physician, who had filled honorable positions in his native country, and in France and Switzerland ; but who, subsequently, upon embarking for the United States, fell ill during the passage, and became weak and delirious. On the arrival of the vessel in New York, he was handed over the side into a boat, the sailors informing the persons who received him here, that he was "crazy." Upon this dictum he was consigned to the Insane Asylum on Ward's Island.

Here he remained some time, the keepers facetiously keeping him in ignorance of his whereabouts. The surrounding country, they informed him, was Switzerland ; the city of New York, whose spires could be seen in the distance, was Munich ; &c. Not until his release (through the accident of a letter), and his arrival in the city, did he know where he was. He never was mad. He was immured in this insane asylum without due process of law ; and an insane asylum is a place where even the writ of *habeas corpus* has no force. This same person is now a surgeon in the army. Now as to the legislation which this state of affairs seemed to demand. A board of

Commissioners of Insanity, with the power of judges or coroners, appeared to be what was wanted. This board was to pass upon cases of insanity.

Mr. Chas. Moran. Although publicity in such matters is often exceedingly painful and mortifying, yet publicity is the best safeguard for the accused.

Dr. Homberger. Under our present system it is often to the interest of relatives to keep the accused immured, and always to the interest of keepers. But in the town of Gheel, in Belgium, some twenty-five miles from Antwerp, where, from time immemorial, it has been the custom to send the insane, no such inducements exist. There they are at liberty to roam the town, a place of some 10,000 inhabitants, and even to leave it if they choose, though this they rarely do, unless recovered. They lodge with the peasantry, and pass their time in rural occupations, and the society of children. Overseers are at hand to minister to their wants, but not to coerce or restrain them, except in cases of confirmed violence.

Dr. Ellsberg confirmed the remarks of the preceding speaker in regard to Gheel. The insane were not obliged to work, but they preferred to do so, and the product of their labor paid the expenses of their maintenance. Insane persons like to be alone, and like to be free. They prefer agricultural employments ; for this combines both comparative solitude and freedom. An institution on the Gheel plan has for some time past been sought to be carried out here by Dr. Parego, formerly superintendent of the Gheel establishment, and now in this city. This is what we want—this and the Commissioners of Insanity advocated by Dr. Homberger.

Messrs. Moran, Smull, and Stern made remarks of a similar tendency, and favored a reform of this nature.

Mr. Fezandié. This question of lunacy has been much abused. How is it possible to determine in many cases whether a person is insane or not? It is said that all mankind is cracked up on some point or other. If after reading the late encyclical letter of the Pope, a question concerning his sanity was raised, it might go hard with the Holy Father. In the city of Naples, a head, said to be that of Saint Januarius, born A.D. 272, is exhibited in the cathedral, enclosed in a glass case. Two vials, containing a hard substance, believed to be his blood, are also shown. On September 19th, every year, the fête day of the saint, and on some other stated occasions, this alleged blood is seen to liquefy, to bubble, rise in the bottle, and fall again. On such occasions popular enthusiasm is raised to its height. Upon the occupation of Naples by the

12

French, the priests, designing to raise a tumult, declared on one of these days that the blood would not flow ; thereby leaving it to be inferred, which it readily was, by the populace, that the saint was displeased with the new *régime*. . Gen. Chomponniere, divining the true source of the trouble, commanded the priests on pain of death to cause the blood to flow ; and flow it did. Should anybody now put faith in such alleged miracles, would he not be considered a lunatic ? Yet the men who believed in them then, were considered sane enough. Like all others, this social question is decided by the first principle of Social Science—Utmost Liberty. Why should we deprive an insane man of liberty unless he is violent and dangerous ? The same justification would apply to confining a man in a hospital against his will because he was sick, or had a broken limb. Government has no right to interfere. If we could determine with precision when a man was insane, we should find that many a one who has been punished as a criminal, has only been unfortunate. Is drunkenness insanity ? Is spiritualism insanity ? Is mesmerism insanity ? Is Millerism insanity ? The hesitation to answer these questions proves incontestably that it is impossible always to determine upon alleged cases of insanity, and when it is not possible to determine, we should let the matter alone ; except where actual violence demands coercion.

Mr. Wm. B. Scott. No good can result from the establishment of public hospitals for the insane. Were there none such, it would be found profitable by private parties to provide them for the public. The rich would pay for the accommodation—the poor could be set to work, and their labor would be a sufficient recompense for their support, as in Gheel. In exceptional cases something else might be done.

Mr. Simon Stern. This is a subject which properly calls for governmental jurisdiction. It belongs to the proper administration of justice. Private insane asylums are invariably a means of injustice. Nothing would exist to prevent designing parties from consigning their personal enemies or troublesome blood relations to these irresponsible insane asylums. In Philadelphia, where a large asylum of such a nature is kept by a certain Dr. Kilpatrick, everything depends upon the Doctor's honesty. He may bury an innocent person alive if he chooses.

Mr. Leopold Riess. I am in favor of the doctrine of Utmost Liberty for insane persons, as well as for others. If private asylums are forbidden to be closed to the public, no such abuses could exist.

Mr. ALEX. DELMAR. I can see no valid objection to the establishment of an American Gheel; but it should be free from government interference. There cannot be too much liberty allowed to the insane. A man may be insane one moment, and sane the next. If he is not at liberty while he is insane, what chance is there that he will obtain his liberty when he becomes sane? Then, the determination of cases of insanity is altogether too delicate a matter to be intrusted to any formula. Is a man insane who, like Peter Simple's father, might think himself a balloon? Is another who conceives that he has squared the circle, or devised a perfect system of government, insane? Why not let the insane alone? We have no right to confine them. In violent cases, I confess that our own safety compels us to interfere; but only so long as the violence is imminent and dangerous.

After all, is not this tyranny over the insane, but another form of the tyranny of the majority; for what assurance have we that we are sane, and that those whom we immure in madhouses are insane, unless we derive that assurance from our greater numbers? As to the establishment of Commissioners of Lunacy, I am opposed to it. The thing has been tried in England, and has signally failed. Wilkie Collins' admirable novel of the Woman in White contains a graphic account of the shortcomings of this system.

Dr. ELLSBERG. The Commission of Lunacy is not designed to be like that in England; but to be a Court of Experts, in order that the accused may have a fair trial. Such a Court should be composed of men who are thoroughly familiar with the subject.

Mr. DELMAR. That alters the case. There are now 47 public Lunatic Hospitals in the United States. These establishments contain something like 11,000 patients. Surely something can be done for these unfortunates. Look at the reported "supposed causes" of insanity. We have "perplexities in business," "war excitement," "use of tobacco," "spiritual manifestations," "fright," "erroneous education," "political excitement," "mesmerism," "religious excitement," "Millerism," "fear of poverty," "slander," "ridicule of shopmates," "insufficient nutrition" (Grahamism), "ill-health," &c., &c. I am now quoting from an official report of one of these hospitals. Does there not appear to be room for investigation and reform here? Then look at another point. According to the Census, there are 25,000 insane persons in the United States. This can only be a small portion of the true number. These 47 hospitals are limited in their accommodations to 11,000 patients, while the private asylums, being few in number, cannot possibly extend the limit to over 12,500 patients. Now where are the remainder? At large. And there are probably not twice, but five times as many at large as there are confined. Then why confine any of them, if those who are at large behave so well as not to attract attention? I am convinced that this whole subject needs a thorough overhauling, and I trust that it will be reverted to again, in order that more light may be thrown upon it, and some lasting reform effected.

MONEY BASES.

The question for discussion was:

CAN THE PRECIOUS METALS BE ADVANTAGEOUSLY REPLACED AS MONEY BASES? Debate opened by Mr. THOMAS SMULL.

Mr. SMULL. Notwithstanding the assertion of some writers on the subject of Money—Chas. Moran, Stephen Colwell, and Lysander Spooner, for instance—it continues to be my belief that nothing can successfully replace the precious metals as money bases. It is true that gold and silver form but a small portion of the circulating medium in civilized countries; yet I conceive that portion, however small it may be, to be indispensable. Not that the precious metals vary less in value than most other things; but because they possess intrinsic qualities of usefulness and beauty which will always continue to make them desirable among men. You may make wheat a basis of currency; but as everybody does not want wheat, it would soon be replaced by the precious metals.

Mr. WM. P. LEE. Yet the precious metals are almost useless except for the use to which we put them as money. Demonetize gold and silver, and it will be seen that the labor expended in producing them is a sheer waste.

Mr. SMULL. No. Even conceding that the precious metals were demonetized, the fact that they would still be sought for, as I presume beyond all doubt they would, would be a sufficient proof that their usefulness was not impaired; for whatever men find to their interest to produce, is useful. Were we restricted to the production of only such things as were of absolute necessity to us, the world would never advance at all. New desires produce new resources, and the latter not only keep pace with the former, but actually outstrip them. The remaining part of what is produced, in excess of what is consumed forms, that wealth with which the world makes its most rapid strides towards perfection. Take the cloth which covers the table before us. The designs which are wrought in it might have been dispensed with ; the cloth itself might be considered a luxurious superfluity. But let us resolve to do without anything but what we actually need in order to exist, and I ask what progress the world could be expected to make ? So with the precious metals. They are useful as ornaments ; they are also consumed in the useful arts ; and this double use is so universal among men that these metals are in demand all over the world. One of the useful arts is the employment of money with which to effect exchanges. Mankind use gold and silver for this purpose more than anything else. It is this universal demand for the precious metals which makes them valuable, and so long as they remain thus universally valuable, they will be continued to be used, and will be the best things which can be used, even by those nations which are far enough advanced in civilization to know that they are not valuable for purposes of consumption, but only valuable principally as counters or checks for exchanging commodities. I mean, that after men have ceased to possess an exclusively specie currency, specie will continue to form—and nothing better can be used to perform—the function of a money basis.

Mr. WM. B. SCOTT. I agree with the remarks of Mr. SMULL. It is not correct, as some assert, that there is too much gold and silver in the world—that they might be dispensed with—that they are useless. When too much gold and silver has been eliminated from the bowels of the earth we shall know it. The very fact that men still want more of them is the best proof in the world that there is not too much of them. Until the demand for the precious metals is satisfied there never can be enough of them.

Mr. CHAS. MORAN. I am afraid the gentlemen are confusing the argument—or rather, they maintain it in a vicious circle. They confuse the use of the precious metals as money, with money itself. They apply the principles of money, to gold and silver ; and the principles which affect gold and silver, to money. What they say of one thing is only true of the other, and what they say of the other is only true of the one. Now what is the use of money ? Do we consume it ? Do we ever want it for use ? Not at all. We want it to effect exchanges. If I wish to exchange a hat for a pair of shoes, I first exchange the hat for a piece of money. Thus far, only half of my object is attained. Next, I exchange the piece of money for a pair of shoes. My object is then fully effected. But does it matter what the piece of money is composed of, whether it is heavy or light, useful or useless, perishable or imperishable, so long as it serves the purpose of exchanging the hat for the shoes? When we wish to carry a thing from one place to another, does it matter whether we use a golden wheel-barrow for the purpose, or a wooden one, especially if the wooden one is lighter, and more convenient for the purpose? Not at all. We do not propose to eat the money, or to clothe ourselves with it. Therefore what does it matter what it is made of, so long as it serves the only use it has—that of effecting exchanges? Now I contend that paper will do this, and do it not only as well as the precious metals, but better. Better, because paper costs nothing, and the precious metals cost a great deal of labor which might be otherwise expended; and better also because the precious metals are constantly varying in value, and paper would not vary at all. I know that it is claimed for gold and silver that their value rarely changes, and when it does, only a very little. But this is not true. The quantity of the precious metals continually changes its proportion to the quantity of commodities, the exchange of which is effected by these metals. Paper is the only thing which will answer the purpose of an unalterable medium, and it may be used without any basis of gold and silver. Let us suppose that all the precious metals suddenly disappeared from the world to-day. Then we should have no specie. Now I have a coat which I would exchange for a barrel of flour of equal value, only I do not want the flour for some time; while the owner of the flour wants my coat at once. What is more simple than that I should sell him my coat for a piece of paper, worthless in itself, but still representing the coat I have sold, and with which I can purchase the barrel of flour when I require it. No "basis" is used here. No gold or silver is required. Nothing but paper. For the sake of convenience you establish a unit, and give it a name. You call it a *sol*, a *machute*, or what not; and so many *sols* or *machutes* are worth a coat, and consequently so many, a barrel of flour.

Mr. LEE. Gentlemen, if we would come to a correct conclusion upon this important topic, we must make up our minds to dig deeper. What we want for a money basis is an unalterable measure of value, and we shall never possess one unless we take labor—raw, unskilled labor, as that measure. Here we have an unalterable measure, and from this we can build upwards. Even gold and silver are valued not by their usefulness or attractiveness to mankind, but by the amount of labor which was required to produce a given quantity of them. The average day's labor of a full set of human muscles unassisted by machinery, is the standard of value upon which I would base a currency, and nothing else will prove so invariable a standard. In fact, such a standard is absolute.

Dr. Julius Homberger. Mr. Lee's position is totally untenable. He contends that unskilled labor is the best standard of value. But unskilled labor is the product of food, and must increase its capacity to produce, with increase of food; and lose that capacity with decrease of food. Therefore the standard of value would be food. It would be much more correct to make the *result* of labor the standard of value, instead of labor itself; as might be done by using some product of labor, such as gold and silver for instance, as a common measure. And this is precisely the case now. In short, the whole argument is unscientific. I am afraid that Mr. Lee has "dug" a little *too* "deep."

Mr. Simon Stern. Finding a measure of value has been to political economists what the search after the philosopher's stone was to the ancient alchemists. Both attempts have proved futile, because neither a philosopher's stone, nor a measure of value exists in nature, and that which does not exist can never be found. That neither of them exist is provable—by negative evidence of course; yet the evidence is good enough. But the search for these myths has not been altogether fruitless. Incidentally, both attempts have been of some service to mankind. The one, in bringing to light many interesting and valuable laws of chemistry—the other, in eliminating critical discussions upon the nature and functions of money. A measure of value cannot exist. There is nothing fixed in nature. Nothing is of an invariable size or weight. Change is the universal law which rules all things. A measure of value is therefore an impossibility. If a barrel of flour which once cost ten dollars now costs fifteen, it may be wrong to affirm that the flour has increased in value. On the contrary, the flour may have fallen. A fall in the value of the dollar may account for the change, and this might occur not only with a paper currency, but with a gold one. Gold fluctuates in value just as all other things do; only, as we have decreed it to be a measure—which it is not—we reckon its fluctuations in the *prices* of other things,—and price is an element of money. And now to come back to the subject of discussion. I am of the opinion that nothing can advantageously replace the precious metals as money bases. The world is too dishonest for the employment of anything as a medium of exchange which does not carry its own value with it. That portion of mankind who are not dishonest, who may be trusted, who have credit, may issue paper to represent this medium of exchange, and the extent of the use of this paper will depend upon the extent of the recognition of their credit. To this extent paper may be used, and is used; but it merely represents specie, and unless it represents specie, or, in other words, unless specie is regarded as the basis of all money, commercial transactions would soon come to an end. Looking for a substitute for specie as a money basis, is like the search of Columbus for the mythical land of Cathay. He did not find Cathay, but stumbled upon America.. We will not find a substitute for specie, but we shall become more familiar with the principles which underlie the subject of money and its functions.

Mr. ALEX. DELMAR. Mr. Chairman, when the lamb lies down with the lion, when education and virtue are to the highest degree the attributes of all men, and peace and happiness the normal conditions of all races, then, and then only, shall we be able to dispense with money which has for its basis a thing that carries its own security with it. It is hardly necessary to relate why gold is preferred to any other thing which carries its own security with it; because you are already familiar with the reasons. But briefly, gold is a beautiful metal, wears well, is easily worked, is difficult to counterfeit, is indestructible, is portable, is readily divisible and reuniteable, is of uniform quality, &c. These qualities render it desirable for ornament and for use, and so long as it retains these qualities will it be sought for by mankind. So long as it is sought for, will it be valuable, and so long as it is valuable, will it be used for money. When it ceases to be valuable, paper may supersede it, but when that happens, the golden age, instead of being in the future, will have become a thing of the past.

It is a favorite idea with some that paper may be used as a medium of exchange without the use of specie for a basis. Mr. MORAN has advanced this idea with great ability. But does not the gentleman perceive his error? After supposing that all the precious metals had disappeared from the world to-day, he instances a barter. He would exchange a coat for a barrel of flour, the respective values being considered equal; but as he does not propose to use the latter immediately, he takes for the coat a paper token, with which he believes he may purchase the flour. But is this correct? In the first place, why will he sell the coat for one token? Why does he not demand two; or three; or fifty? "Because I choose to consider a coat worth one token," answers the advocate of universal paper money, "and I consider it worth one token because a barrel of flour is valued at one token, and a barrel of flour is valued at one token because a coat is considered to be worth one token. There we start: after that, everything will be priced or rated according to its value as compared with a coat or a barrel of flour."

"But suppose you would purchase something else, the price of which in your paper tokens you have not yet fixed; how will you determine its price?"

"By comparing its value with the coat or the barrel of flour which my token represents."

"Ah, your token represents something, does it? Very well. Then your scheme does not differ from the practice of to-day. Bank paper money is representative also; only instead of representing coats and barrels of flour, it represents gold and silver."

Thus the whole argument falls to the ground. Measuring two values without reference to a third value is like measuring ultra-mundane distances without triangulation. By the word dollar we mean twenty-five grains of gold—a certain quantity of a certain thing. Your "token," to be available as a medium of exchange, would also have to mean a certain quantity of a certain thing; and unless it does, it never can be a medium of exchange. It is claimed that gold is unnecessary for the purposes of money. I claim that it is the best thing for the purpose, because it is the most convenient of all those things which carry their own value with them. If it even be admitted that gold pieces are only checks or counters, still, for the same reason, they are the best of checks or counters. The security afforded by the possession of specie is satisfactory to all the world. That is the only kind of money which deserves the name. Paper, and even credit, may perform the same functions in civilized communities, and are highly useful in dispensing to some degree with the precious metals; but to be acceptable they must rest upon the precious metals as a basis. It is alleged that the precious metals do not constitute a correct standard of value, because the quantity of them in use as money is constantly varying. This is undoubtedly true; but the same may be said of paper. When credit is unimpaired, the quantity of paper is increased, and prices advance; when credit is impaired, the quantity of paper is decreased, and prices fall. Therefore to have a paper currency which would not change, we must have universal and continued credit. This, of course, is impossible. As to Mr. LEE's idea of labor forming the standard of value, I will merely say that this notion has long since been exploded. Labor varies in value as much as anything else, because it depends upon our wants and our capacities. Besides, everything is not the product of labor. Time is an essential ingredient in the value of many things.

For the rest I agree with Mr. Stern.

Mr. Erastus W. Benedict. "Unskilled labor," as it is termed, can never form a measure of value. What is unskilled labor? Is there any kind of labor which is unskilled? The carrying of a hod requires a certain amount of skill: neither you nor I could do it. We would not know how. The native savage has as much muscle as you have; nay more. But he cannot do any useful labor with it. Why? Because he does not possess enough skill. It is not unskilled labor, therefore, which produces anything useful; but skilled labor: and its product must vary with the skill that guides it. Labor as a measure of value is out of the question. It is the product of labor which we must use; and what product is so convenient for the purpose as gold and silver? These metals are the most convenient for the purpose, both on account of their intrinsic fitness and because all mankind repose the utmost confidence in their value. A measure of value must be valuable itself, or it will not carry security with it; and security is all-important. Confidence in its value, is the reason why we accept gold and silver. The only substitute we can employ for it, is credit, or paper based upon credit. But we cannot employ either credit, or paper, unless they in turn are based upon something that carries security with it—and of all things which are secure, the precious metals are the most convenient for the purposes of money.

Mr. Delmar. Gold is the only thing which never is without a large number of people who have confidence in it, and will always take it.

THE AMERICAN FREE TRADE LEAGUE.

On the evening of February 25, 1865, the following gentlemen were invited to meet at the *Maison Dorée*, for the purpose of forming an American Free Trade League:—William Cullen Bryant, Parke Godwin, John A. Dix, George Bancroft, Francis Lieber, Gulian C. Verplanck, Francis Cottenet, James McKaye, William Wood, Cyrus W. Field, David Dudley Field, Alexander Delmar, Charles Moran, William B. Scott, Thomas Smull, Simon Stern, Benj. F. Lee, Alfred Pell, Isaac H. Bailey, Charles Astor Bristed, William Kemeys, Edward Cooper, James A. Roosevelt, Alfred Beach, Robert B. Minturn, Charles Nordhoff, Joshua Leavitt, Charles H. Marshall, Vincenzo Botta, Edwin L. Godkin, John D. Van Buren, James E. Pulsford, and Jackson S. Schultz.

About fifteen of the number attended. On motion, Mr. Isaac H. Bailey was appointed chairman. After appointing a committee, consisting of Messrs. D. D. Field, Stern, and Bristed, to draft a constitution, a committee consisting of Messrs. Pell, Moran, Marshall, Delmar, Scott, Bailey, and D. D. Field, was appointed to nominate a list of officers for the League. The League then adjourned. On Tuesday, March 7, two of the Committee on Appointments met at the office of the London and Liverpool Insurance Company, and made the nominations. Upon a second meeting of the committee, five of the members being present, the original nominations were revoked, but subsequently confirmed, with one or two alterations. The nominations finally agreed upon were as follows:

For President, Alfred Pell; for Vice-Presidents, John A. Dix, David Dudley Field, Lucius Robinson, Isaac H. Bailey, and Moses Taylor; for Treasurer, William B. Scott; for Corresponding Secretary, Charles Astor Bristed; and for Recording Secretary, Robert Pell.

On Friday, March 17, a meeting of the League took place, at Clinton Hall, when the above nominations were agreed to, with the exception of changing the President, on motion of Mr. Pell, from Mr. Pell to William Cullen Bryant, and nominating Mr. Pell, on motion of Mr. Delmar, for Vice-President, in place of Moses Taylor, declined. The constitution was then presented by the committee, and formally adopted, and the nominees elected, when the League adjourned. The Executive Committee, consisting of Messrs. Rufus Prime, Moran, Wood, McKaye, Pulsford, John Cummerford, Schultz, Wm. H. Appleton, Delmar, Stern, Marshall, Leavitt, Godkin, Smull, and Godwin, then went into session, Mr. Delmar in the chair. After adding Messrs. Charles H. Bramhall, George Opdyke, A. Pell, R. Pell, Kemeys, and Bailey to their number, and electing Mr. Moran as permanent chairman, and Mr. Stern as permanent secretary, they adjourned.

The name of this organization is sufficiently expressive of its design. We await with much interest the first results of its operations. The ordinary membership is one dollar per year. Life members, fifty dollars. Subscriptions may be sent to the treasurer, William B. Scott, banker, 44 Pine Street, New York.

CARLISLE TABLE. (Joshua Milne.)

Age.	Living.	Dying.	Expectation.	Age.	Living.	Dying.	Expectation.
0	10000	1539	38.721	53	4211	68	18.927
1	8461	682	44.674	54	4143	70	18.275
2	7779	505	47.546	55	4073	73	17.580
3	7274	276	49.812	56	4000	76	16.892
4	6998	201	50.757	57	3924	82	16.209
5	6797	121	51.244	58	3842	93	15.545
6	6676	82	51.168	59	3749	106	14.918
7	6594	58	50.793	60	3643	122	14.337
8	6536	43	50.240	61	3521	126	13.817
9	6493	33	49.569	62	3395	127	13.311
10	6460	29	48.820	63	3268	125	12.809
11	6431	31	48.038	64	3143	125	12.299
12	6400	32	47.268	65	3018	124	11.787
13	6368	33	46.503	66	2894	123	11.271
14	6335	35	45.742	67	2771	123	10.749
15	6300	39	44.994	68	2648	123	10.225
16	6261	42	44.271	69	2525	124	9.699
17	6219	43	43.567	70	2401	124	9.174
18	6176	43	42.866	71	2277	134	8.646
19	6133	43	42.163	72	2143	146	8.156
20	6090	43	41.458	73	1977	156	7.715
21	6047	42	40.749	74	1841	166	7.327
22	6005	42	40.030	75	1675	160	7.003
23	5963	42	39.309	76	1515	156	6.690
24	5921	42	38.584	77	1359	146	6.401
25	5879	43	37.856	78	1213	132	6.111
26	5836	43	37.131	79	1081	128	5.796
27	5793	45	36.403	80	953	116	5.507
28	5748	50	35.684	81	837	112	5.201
29	5698	56	34.993	82	725	102	4.928
30	5642	57	34.336	83	623	94	4.652
31	5585	57	33.681	84	529	84	4.390
32	5528	56	33.023	85	445	78	4.125
33	5472	55	32.356	86	367	71	3.895
34	5417	55	31.679	87	296	64	3.709
35	5362	55	30.999	88	232	51	3.595
36	5307	56	30.315	89	181	39	3.467
37	5251	57	29.633	90	142	37	3.282
38	5194	58	28.953	91	105	30	3.262
39	5136	61	28.274	92	75	21	3.367
40	5075	66	27.608	93	54	14	3.481
41	5009	69	26.965	94	40	10	3.525
42	4940	71	26.335	95	30	7	3.533
43	4869	71	25.712	96	23	5	3.457
44	4798	71	25.085	97	18	4	3.278
45	4727	70	24.454	98	14	3	3.071
46	4657	69	23.814	99	11	2	2.773
47	4588	67	23.165	100	9	2	2.278
48	4521	63	22.500	101	7	2	1.786
49	4458	61	21.811	102	5	2	1.300
50	4397	59	21.107	103	3	2	0.833
51	4338	62	20.387	104	1	1	0.500
52	4276	65	19.676				

INSURANCE STATISTICS.*

MILNE'S CARLISLE LIFE TABLE. (SEE OPPOSITE.)

THIS Table was formed by the eminent actuary Joshua Milne, from the observations of Dr. Heysham on the mortality of Carlisle (England) for the years 1777–87. Though somewhat defective in graduation, it is far more satisfactory than the Northampton Table in its approach to accuracy; for which reason, it is extensively used in England, and very generally in this country. Although first published in 1816, it appears better adapted to the mortality of American life, than some later tables of more refined construction; and as an extensive system of convenient tables for the use of actuaries has been constructed on its basis by David Jones of London, and also by David Chisholm (the latter particularly remarkable both for convenience and elegance), it will probably long remain a favorite Mortality Table for this country.

RECENT PUBLICATIONS.

SOCIAL SCIENCE, POLITICAL ECONOMY, AND STATISTICS.

Law in Nature, &c. Four papers read before the Adelaide Philosophical Society. By R. D. Hanson, Chief Justice of South Australia. Printed at the request of the Society. Adelaide, 1864.

Etudes sur la Systême Penitentiaire Irlandais. Par M. Van der Brugghen. Berlin: Luederitz. London: D. Nutt, 1865.

The Financial Statements of. 1853, 1860–3. To which is added a Speech on Tax Bills and on Charities, 1863. By the Right Hon. W. E. Gladstone. Second Edition, including the Financial Statement of 1864. London: J. Murray, 1864.

La Réforme Sociale en France. Par M. F. Le Play. Paris: H. Plon, 1864.

The Confederate Secession. By the Marquis of Lothian. Edinburgh and London: W. Blackwood & Sons, 1864.

---

* From the Annual Report of the Superintendent of the Insurance Department of the State of New York. Albany: 1864.

The False Nation and its Bases: or, Why the South Can't Stand. By J. Arthur Partridge. London: E. Stanford, 1864.

England, the United States, and the Southern Confederacy. By F. W. Sargent, M. D. London: Hamilton, Adams & Co., 1864.

Our Resources. By a Citizen of Providence, U. S. London: Trübner & Co., 1864.

Italics. By F. P. Cobbe. London: Trübner and Co., 1864.

Brigandage in South Italy. By David Hilton. 2 vols. London: Sampson, Low, Son & Co., 1864.

Chemins de Fer de L'Europe. Recettes Comparatives des années 1862 et 1861. Publication du bureau de statistiques de la direction générale des ponts et chaussées et des chemins de fer au ministre de l'agriculture, du commerce et des travaux publics. En 4. Imprimerie impériale, 1864.

Deux Publications Nouvelles de M. Boccardo: *Locomagno o Gotardo?* Gênes, imprimerie de Pellas frères. *Le Colonie e l'Italia.* Turin, Franco et Pigli, 1864.

The Science of Exchanges. By N. A. Nicholson. London: Effingham Wilson, 1864.

Questione Delle Banche in Italia (*La Question des banques en Italie*) par le comte Ferdinand Trivalzi, de Milan. Brochure en 8. Turin, 1864.

Tout rentier peut-être banquier, par M. Victor Saussine. Brochure en 8. Paris, 1864.

Dictionnaire des Communes de la France. Par M. Adolphe Joanne, avec la collaboration d'une Société d'archivistes, de géographes et de savants. 1 vol. petit en 4. Paris, chez L. Hachette et Cie.

Causeries populaires D'Economie publique et de Morale. En 16 de 82 pages. La Rochelle, Chartier, 1864.

Les Banques d'émission et d'escompte. Par M. Maurice Aubry. Brochure en 8. Paris, Guillaumin et Cie., 1864.

Der Landwirthschaftliche Credit in Oesterreich. (*Le Crédit agricole en Autriche.*) Par M. Fr. Neumann. Br. en 8. Vienne, Gerold, fils, 1864.

Oesterreichs Handelspolitik (*La politique commerciale de l'Autriche*). Par M. Fr. Neumann. Br. en 8. Vienne, Gerold, fils, 1864.

Agricultural Value (the) of the Sewage of London, examined in reference to the principal schemes submitted to the Metropolitan Board of Works. 8vo. pp. 78. London: Stanford, 1865.

The Economy of Capital; or Gold and Trade. By R. H. Patterson. Edinburgh and London: William Blackwood & Sons, 1865.

Bradshaw's Railway Manual. Shareholder's Guide, and Official Directory for 1865; containing the History and Financial Position of every Company, British, Foreign, and Colonial; Statistics, &c. Vol. 17. 12mo. London: Adams, 1865.

Testimonies Concerning Slavery. By M. D. Conway. Second Edition. Post 8vo. London: Smith & Elder, 1865.

Considerations on Representative Government. By John Stuart Mill. 3d Edition. 8vo. London: Longman, 1865.

A Handy Book on the Law of Friendly, Industrial, and Provident Societies; with

Copious Notes. By Nathaniel White, Esq., of H. M. Civil Service. London: Virtue & Co., 1865.

Practical Hints for Investing Money. With an Explanation of the Mode of Transacting Business on the Stock Exchange. Third Edition. By Fr. Playford. London: Virtue Brothers, 1865.

Statistique Morale de l'Angleterre Comparée avec la Statistique Morale de la France. Par M. A. Guerry. Tours: Ladevéze, 1865.

A History of American Manufactures from 1608 *to* 1860. Exhibiting the Origin and Growth of the principal Mechanic Arts and Manufactures. Comprising Annals of the Industry of the United States, Statistics of Manufacturing Centres, &c. By J. Leander Bishop, A. M., M. D. 2 vols. 8vo. Phila.: Edward Young & Co., 1865.

Manual of Social Science. Being a Condensation of the Principles of Social Science of H. C. Carey, LL. D. By Kate McKean. 12mo. Phila.: H. C. Baird, 1865.

Statesman's Year-Book. A Statistical, Genealogical, and Historical Account of the States and Sovereigns of the Civilized World, for the year 1865. By Frederick Martin. 8vo. London: Macmillan, 1865.

Moralist and Politician. Or Many Things in a Few Words. By Sir George Ramsay, Bart. London: Walton, 1865.

Capital Punishment. Based on Professor Mittermaier's Todesstrafe. Edited by John Macrae Moir, M. A. 8vo. London: Smith & Elder, 1865.

Manual of Political Economy. By Henry Fawcett, M. A. Second Edition. 8vo. London: Macmillan.

Capital Punishment: Is it Defensible? By Philander. 8vo. London: Nisbet, 1865.

I. *The National Bank Act of June*, 1864. Containing—1. The Bank Act, approved June 3d, 1864. 2. Analysis of each section of the Act. 3. Alphabetical Index to all the subjects in the Act. 4. List of National Banks established under the Acts of February, 1863, and June, 1864. 8vo.

II. *Acts of Congress relating to Loans and the Currency from* 1842 *to* 1864. 8vo.

III. *The Railroad Almanac for* 1865. 8vo. By J. Smith Homans. New York: Published at the office of the Banker's Magazine.

Du Commerce et des Progrès de la Puissance Commerciale de l'Angleterre et de la France, au point de vue de l'histoire de la législation et de la statistique, d'après les sources et les données officielles, avec une Introduction comprenant un aperçu de l'histoire générale du commerce jusqu'à nos jours. Par M. Charles Vogel. Tome Ier. 1 vol. en 8. Chez Berger-Levrault, Paris et Strasburg, 1864.

Jurisprudence Electorale Parlementaire. Recueil de décisions du corps législatif (de 1852 à 1864) en matière de verifications de pouvoirs. Par M. Alphonse Grun, avocat, ancien rédacteur en chef du Moniteur universal, chef de la section législative et judiciare aux archives de l'empire, etc. 1 vol. en 32. Paris: Durand.

Grundriss du Volkswirthschaftlehre (Éléments d'économie politique). Par M. H. de Mangoldt. Stuttgart: J. Engelborn. 1 vol. en 8, 1863.

Essai Critique de la Philosophie Positive. Lettre à M. Littré (de l'Institut). Par Charles Pellarin. 1 vol. en 8 Paris: Dentu, 1864.

Annuaire des Sociétés Savantes de la France et de l'Etranger. Par le comte Achmet D'Héricourt. · 2 vols. en 8. Paris: A. Franck, 1864.

Journal de la Société de Statistique de Paris. Paris: A. Franck, 1864.

Legge sulla Richezza Mobile commentata col Regolamento e provvodimenti relativi. Cav. E. Bellono. Torino: 1864.

Grundlehren der Gesetze des Staates. F. Esshaver. 1 vol. Tübingen: 1865.

Corso teorico pratico d' economica politica. A. Gola Ferrero. Reggio: 1864.

Die Hexenprocesse. Ein cultur-historischer Versuch nebst Documenten. Tübingen: 1864.

Jahrbuch, Statisches, der österreichischen Monarchie für das Jahr 1863. Herausgegeben von der K. k., statistichen Central Commission. Wien: 1864.

Das Recht des Besitzes. Eine civilistische Abhandlung. F. C. v. Savigny. Ed. von A. F. Rudorff. n : 1865.

Lettres sur la Philosophie de l'histoire. Par M. Odysse Barot. En 8. Paris: Germer Baillère.

Les Débats sur la Banque de France. Résumé, conclusion. Par J. A. Rey, Paris: Guillaumin.

Almanach de Paris. Annuaire général de Diplomatie, de Politique, d'Histoire, et de Statistique, pour tout les Etats du globe. En 32. Paris: Amyot, 1865.

ANY OF THE ABOVE WORKS CAN BE HAD ON APPLICATION TO THE EDITORS OF THE NEW YORK SOCIAL SCIENCE REVIEW.

THE

NEW YORK

SOCIAL SCIENCE REVIEW:

A JOURNAL OF

POLITICAL ECONOMY AND STATISTICS.

JULY, 1865.

THE GROWTH OF NATIONAL WEALTH.

I. Debt and Resources of the United States. By Dr. William Elder. Pamphlet. Philadelphia: 1863.

II. The National Resources, and their Relation to Foreign Commerce and the price of Gold. Article VI. North American Review, for January, 1865.

There are many persons who derive both pleasure and profit from rummaging among the wild figures of the United States Census, and deducing therefrom what, with the most extraordinary complacency, are assumed to be exact logical corollaries concerning national resources, and their rate of accumulation.

Every now and then some wonderful statement appears in the newspapers which shows, with an air of accuracy that always accompanies a parade of figures, how wealthy this happiest of countries is sure to be by the middle of the next century, and how easy it will then be for the people to pay the interest on the National Debt.

This pictured affluence is found not in increased liberty, in wise legislation, in redoubled security to life and property; but is predicated upon the rate of the growth of national wealth which occurred previous to 1860, and then invariably heightened by other considerations which vary with the poetic taste of the statistician. Sometimes it is the gold mines of California; sometimes the petroleum wells of Pennsylvania. Sometimes it is the manufactures of New England; and sometimes the peppermint crop of Ohio.

There are many good-natured patriots who stand ready to gulp down these specimens of statistical imagery without mastication; satisfied if in the end they argue that the people of the United States are the most favored on earth. Did the statistical romances whose titles appear at the head of this article find no other class of readers, we should feel disposed to treat their productions in the same manner that the wits of Pitt's time disposed of one Perry's scheme to extinguish the national debt by means of a sinking fund based on a single penny, which, it was proved, would suffice for the purpose if put out at interest for a few thousand years or so.

But when either through the humbug of incomplete tables, or by dint of proofless statements, the people not only of these States, but of the whole of Europe are made to believe that the accretion of wealth in this country is quite beyond the reach of any other country, and is due to this industry or that "resource," to Yankee enterprise or to "inevitable destiny," it is time that the true sources of national wealth and the laws which determine its rate of growth, and control its accretion, should be sought by the exact light of science and not through magnifying glasses and magic lanterns. Questions like these are too serious to trifle with; their solution too intimately affects the business and happiness of mankind. The course of emigration is sometimes directed by these El-Doradic guides, and before actual experience can turn it back to less chimerical channels much mischief naturally ensues.*

It does not follow that because a man owns a gold mine he is therefore rich; any more than it follows that because another reckons all his worldly possessions in a garden patch he is therefore poor.

---

* The reader needs but to be reminded of Patterson's Darien scheme and Law's colonization of Mississippi to recognize the evil mentioned in the text.

So neither does it follow that because one country produces twice as much per head as another; that the former is wealthy, and the latter impoverished. Wealth results from overplus. Therefore to determine the laws which govern the accumulation of wealth it is necessary to look not only at production, but also at consumption. The gold mine may produce a million per day; but if to work it and support himself its owner expends over a million per day, instead of being rich he is on the road to complete destitution. The garden patch may yield but five dollars per day; but if to work it and support himself its owner expends only two, he is not only rich but is every day becoming richer.

In certain climates man and beast both require additional support, and consumption may follow so closely upon the heels of production that the excess of the latter over the production of less exacting climates may go for nothing. Contrariwise, the lesser producer may be the greater saver, and thus while one country remains stationary, another, producing but half as much, may daily become more opulent.

To obtain an insight into the laws which govern the accumulation of wealth it is necessary to study well the nature of savings, or, as they are called in countries where a system of barter and commerce prevails—profits.

Profit is resolvable into three parts: Interest, Insurance, and Wages. (The following diagram illustrates the analysis.)

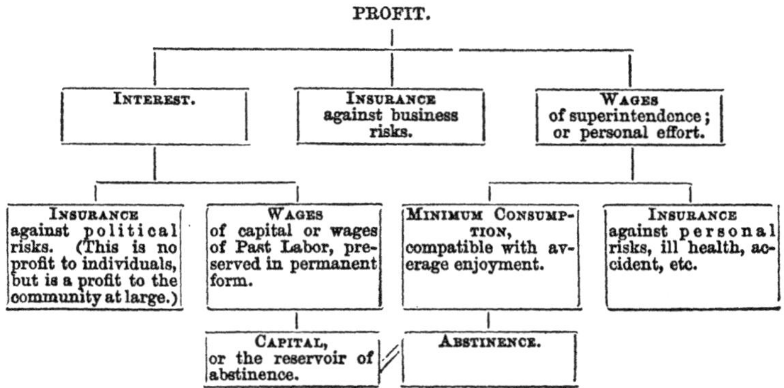

Make the earning of profit *absolutely secure*, and let it require no personal care or superintendence whatever; *and profit then becomes identical with interest; and the rate of possible profit is the possible rate of interest.*

But let us follow the analysis.

Interest is the wages of Capital: wages which are earned without human labor and without any further risk than that which may arise from the insecurity peculiar to the government and state of society prevailing in particular localities. Interest is therefore composed of Political Insurance and Past Labor. The rate of interest is determined by the demand and supply of loans, and these again depend " on the amount of accumulation going on in the hands of persons who cannot themselves attend to the employment of their savings, and partly on the comparative taste existing in the community for the active pursuits of industry, or for the leisure, ease, and independence of an annuitant." * As both the accumulation of capital and a taste for industrial pursuits depend upon security to life and property, and freedom of commercial action, it follows that the rate of interest in any locality is determined by the comparative security and freedom which prevails there. Accordingly we find that in countries where the greatest respect is paid to security of property and life, and where commercial restraint is gradually giving way to freedom, as in Holland, England, France, and the United States, the rate of interest is low; and that in countries where insecurity, despotism, or anarchy prevail and jeopardize life and property, the rate of interest is high. Thus in Turkey, a despotic country, the rate of interest ranges from 5 to 100 per cent. In California, where formerly the state of society was favorable to acts of injustice and spoliation, the rate was from 25 to 200 per cent. It is now but 10 per cent. at its business centre, San Francisco, and varies from 20 to 50 per cent. in the interior.†

---

* J. S. Mill.

† Sometimes the rate of interest in a country is higher or lower than what it should justly be from the state of security which property enjoys there, as compared with other countries. This is caused, 1st, by a sudden drain or a sudden heaping up of capital, in other words by an undue lack or an over supply of capital; or, 2d, by the prevalance of mistaken impressions concerning the state of security which exists for capital there; or by total ignorance on the subject.

In the various states of South America, where constant revolutions imperil the security of life and property, the rate of interest is ordinarily very high. In the free cities of Germany, on the contrary, freedom and tranquillity have made it very low.

In speaking of the rate of interest we of course make no reference whatever to the legal rate established in various countries by law; a rate of interest ordained by law being about as operative as a rate of temperature would be if ordained by law. It would be as ridiculous to be guided by it in a disquisition of this character, as it would be to consult the other in a treatise on the laws of heat.

Legal rates of interest are barbarisms—they deserve no more respect from publicists than they obtain observance from those who borrow and lend money. Yet they are not without effect; though in seeking the laws which determine the rate of interest no notice whatever need be taken of them. Like pieces of base metal ignorantly left near some magnetic compass, though they may cause the faithful needle to deviate from its course and to point erroneously, yet over other needles and other compasses their effect cannot extend. The aberrations which are traceable to usury laws apply only to particular cases, and once beyond their immediate influence the great principle of the identity of profits and interest must continue to indicate with unerring precision the true rate of national growth and accumulation.

Let us now sum up the results we have already attained.

Profit is resolvable into Interest, Insurance, and Superintending or Personal Wages. Divested of the last two factors: the remaining one is seen to be simply interest. Interest is the wages of capital, and its rate is determined by the demand and supply of loans, which again depend upon the prevailing freedom and security.

Now if the net profits upon capital employed by a single individual be identical with the prevailing rate of interest, so must be the net profits upon capital employed by any number of individuals; because the identity of net profits and interest does not proceed from the power or peculiarity of the person or persons through whose agency they may come into existence, for it is a function of capital itself.

We thus reach the important deduction which it is the especial object of this essay to unfold: namely, *that the net profits of a community, no matter how large or small it may be, no matter how civilized or barbarous it may be, amount yearly to precisely that percentage on the capital it employs which is indicated by the prevailing rate of interest in that community.*

Expressed more briefly, the law arrived at is this:

NATIONAL ACCUMULATION OF CAPITAL GOES ON AT THE RATE INDICATED BY THE PREVAILING RATE OF INTEREST; OR, NATIONAL ACCUMULATION AND INTEREST ARE IDENTICAL. Not to weary the reader with reiterations, the whole argument may be compressed into the following propositions:

Capital increases by means of profits. Profits consist of the difference between production and consumption. To ascertain the rate of profit it is necessary to analyze profit. Profit consists of Wages of Superintendence, Business Insurance, and Interest. Wages are composed of *work* Insurance and Minimum Consumption. Neither of these factors can be reduced any further. Business Insurance is also elementary. Interest is composed of Political Insurance and the wages of Capital. The former is uncompounded, and the latter is the earnings of Past Labor, which, entering into competition with, are always the same as the earnings of Present Labor. Capital is therefore Past Labor preserved in a permanent form. The preservation of past labor results from abstinence—we mean abstinence from that degree of enjoyment which is within the reach of all.

There is therefore no limit to profit, because abstinence may become general, instead of being, as it is now, only occasional. But the analysis proves that whatever that profit may be it must ever be identical with the rate of interest, less insurance against political risks. And as political risks are insured as it were by the country itself, and indeed go to make the differences which exist between what is called the rate of interest in various countries, it follows that if we take no account of the losses to the country which occur from these risks, that the Political Insurance is so much clear gain to it; consequently that national Profit or the rate of national accumulation is identical with the rate of Interest.

We look upon the deduction thus made as one of such practical and immediate value, bringing home as it must to the apprehension of all, the noble truth that wealth, and security to life and property, are inseparable, that the reader will pardon us, we hope, for endeavoring to fortify it by yet additional arguments.

Let us take an illustration. Jones, a draper, sells during the course of a year a quantity of cloth for $5,000 which cost him $3,000. He has therefore made $2,000 profit. But the time and labor which he personally devoted to the sale of the cloth might have been applied to some other employment at which he might have earned without any risk, and without the use of any capital, say $1,800. Deducting therefore this amount, which represents his "wages of superintendence," there would remain a profit of $200 which his capital of $3,000 had earned for him. But in earning this profit of $200 he has run several risks. First, he might have bought the cloth and been deceived in regard to its quality. It might have perished in his hands. It might have been burned or stolen. He might not have been successful in selling it; the market price might have fallen after he bought it and before he sold it, and he might thus have lost upon it instead of making a profit. In a word, a variety of risks attends every enterprise and frequently causes it to fail and all the capital invested in it to be lost. Let us say, in a hundred similar enterprises to the one instanced, that but two of them fail. The risk of failure is therefore two per cent. and this should be deducted from the $200 profit made. This would leave the net profit $140. The prevailing rate of interest, we will say, was four and two thirds per cent. Now had Jones remembered that he might have earned $140 simply by putting out his capital at interest, he would scarcely have bothered himself about entering into this cloth enterprise when he would have been as well off by keeping out of it.

But the fact is, business enterprises are never insured by outside parties. Besides preferring to serve himself, than to be in somebody else's employ, in order to earn the $1,800 a year which we have assumed his labor to be worth, Jones *takes the risk of insurance on his capital himself.*

He trusts to luck, and hopes thus to pocket the two per

cent. insurance. It is this confidence in being able to propitiate fortune where others have failed, which is the real incentive to all business enterprises; and again are we forced to perceive that it is only where FREEDOM opens the widest door to personal effort that this hope can lead men into industrial pursuits. Jones knows as well as we do that in the long run, among a great many men like himself, the net profit, that is, the profit divested of insurance and the wages of superintendence, cannot amount to more than four and two thirds per cent. upon the capital invested productively. The rate of interest proves this to him: *for were more to be earned, capitalists would at once engage their funds in whatever pursuit afforded a greater net profit than the rate of interest at which they were then loaning them out.* But Jones hopes and believes that *he*, at least, will net more profit than would equal the prevailing rate of interest on his capital, and it is that hope which induces him to go into the business. He concerns himself not with what may befall his competitors; but looks only to himself. This particular Jones may be successful or may fail, but it is evident that among a hundred or a thousand similar Jones's engaged in similar enterprises in the same locality, that but a percentage equal to the prevailing rate of interest in that locality can be amassed by them from their enterprises, in the shape of net profit. If more could be netted, the rate of interest, as we have already seen, would rise; if less it would fall.

Having by this illustration again shown the identity of net profit and interest, we are now ready to proceed with more direct arguments.

1. Suppose the people of the United States borrow from the people of England a million of dollars with interest at six per cent., which we will say is the average prevailing rate of interest throughout the whole of the former country. The rate in England being, we will say, but three per cent., it is evident that so long as that relative state of security to capital which existed in the two countries at the time of the transaction, continues, that not only will the same proportional difference in their respective rates of interest continue, but loans like the one instanced will practically never be recalled. The people of England will be quite content to receive from the

people of the United States the yearly interest upon their capital without caring at all for the return of the principal, because to have it returned would terminate transactions which to them are sources of constant profit. It may be argued, if the net profit derived from this capital by the people of the United States be identical with the rate of interest, and consequently only six per cent., then, after paying to the lenders the six per cent. stipulated, no gain will be left to the borrowers. Profit is composed of interest, insurance, and wages. Deduct the interest, and what remains? Insurance and wages. Insurance pays only for itself. Therefore deduct Insurance also, and what remains then? Wages. Would wages be all the advantage that the borrowers would ultimately derive from the loan? *No; Wages, and Political Insurance.*

Why do English lenders prefer to send their capital to the United States for investment, when, deducting the risk of insurance, they could invest it in England at the same rate? From precisely the same motive that induces Jones to become his own insurer—the hope which forms the mainspring to each individual enterprise—the hope of success and of exemption from misfortune.

2. Capital is said to flow towards a low rate of interest. Why should this be, when whatever risks which may attend its employment appear to be provided for in the analysis given in the argument? *Answer.* Capital flows towards a low rate of interest, it is true: it flows there for security. But it also flows towards a high rate of interest—for investment. Thus there are two currents of capital which are constantly flowing—the one towards security, the other towards investment. But in barbarous countries, or even in civilized countries when convulsed by political disturbances or war, the risk of employing capital equals, or perhaps even exceeds, the entire profits which the industry and skill of man, aided by the creative powers of nature, can produce. Therefore, after deducting Minimum Consumption, and after deducting the various insurances—Business, Personal, and Political—nothing is left; or perhaps even a loss is shown. Capital turns away from such countries and flows back towards more favored ones, countries which are less barbarous, less disturbed by war, or more favored by nature and

human skill; in a word, towards security. Fear, ignorance, sumptuary laws, all these may divert or prevent the free flow of capital; and they do. Capital does not find its best place of investment so readily as it finds its best place of security. This is seen from the undue heaping up of capital which occurs in all secure countries. The current towards security is therefore in the end greater than that towards investment; so that capital is truly said to flow towards "a low rate of interest."

3. We have said that, in countries where the risk of destruction to capital approximates the reproductive powers of nature, &c., capital never remains. An instance of this is Turkey; though of late years, under the influence of the wise measures of its enlightened Sultan, much has been done there towards political and commercial reform. Investments of foreign capital are no more often made in Turkey than equal amounts escape from its borders to seek security in more favored countries. There was a time when the amounts that escaped from her were even greater than the amounts which were entrusted to her. During that time, therefore, she must have retrograded in wealth. But let us look beyond Turkey. Look at China, from which every year escape immense sums which seek investment at low rates of interest in England, where political freedom prevails, in France, where wise laws are administered with promptness and impartiality, in Holland where commercial restrictions no longer exist. Look at the interior countries of Asia; look at the entire coast of Africa, indeed at almost all barbaric or semi-barbaric countries which the adventurous standard of civilization has ever invaded. From all these countries a steady stream of wealth keeps flowing towards Europe, never again to return until an era of security and freedom shall be inaugurated, at whose sign obedient capital is ever ready to move.

4. Unless it is contended that the laws which govern national accumulation are different from those which govern individual accumulation, our theorem cannot be gainsaid. That they *are* the same, is easily perceived by reflecting that if wealth grew faster in one country than another, deducting risks, capital would naturally flow from countries where the earnings were small to those where the earnings were large.

But the rate, whatever it was, in the more favored countries, would soon be reduced to a common level with the others, through the influence of the competition of capital. Now is this not the exact casė as regards the rate of individual accumulation, or the Rate of Interest?

5. Suppose a country so fruitful, and its populace so skilful and yet withal so abstinent that they saved up every year an amount equal to one fourth of their previous capital. This would be a national accumulation of twenty-five per cent. per annum. Suppose another country, older and richer, where the rate of accumulation was but ten per cent. Now let free intercourse for the exchange of capital, &c., exist between the two countries, and what will follow? The lowering of the rate of profit in the first country, and the raising of the rate of profit in the other. The rate common to both would become twelve and a half per cent. if the risk of the employment of capital was the same in both—and if different, the rate would differ correspondingly.

6. Suppose that the people of a certain nation possessed all they needed in this world. There would then be no employment for capital, *no accumulation of wealth*, no business, no profits. Labor would cease, and human action be at an end. There would likewise be *no rate of interest.* Suppose a contrary state of affairs—poverty, distress, wanting everything, possessing nothing. In this condition, whatever the nation produced would be an *infinite degree of profit*, since it would be something which resulted from nothing. Now in the condition described, what rate of interest would this nation be willing to pay in order to at once possess the means of satisfying its hunger, providing itself with shelter, clothing, &c? *An infinite rate of interest.*

Here again the rate of interest and the rate of national profit is plainly seen to be identical.

Guided by this now indubitable theory that the rate of the growth of national wealth is determined by the average rate of interest prevailing in a nation, if we now examine the rate of this growth in various countries, as established by actual enumeration, whatever discrepancy occurs is due, 1, to errors in the enumeration, or, 2, to the flow of capital from or to other countries. There is no other possible explanation. If the growth of wealth within a country is undeniably going on at the rate indicated by the rate of interest prevailing, then should the increase or decrease of wealth in that country, as ascertained by actual count, be more or less, it follows that if the count be correct, the increase or decrease is owing to the flow of capital to or from that country.

"The first attempt to obtain the capital wealth of the United States by actual investigation, was made by the United States Marshals in 1840. Since that time we have official valuations more and more complete at the end of each Census decade. *That these three inventories of the property of the Union are all defective in the matters intended to be embraced, and understated also in valuation, is well known.*"

* * * * * * * * * * *

"An unquestionable deficiency in the reported products occurs in the following particulars, for which the census-takers are not responsible :—

"They take no account of the current consumption of our agriculturists and of their families and employees. In 1840 this class amounted to three-fourths of the total population, and approached the same proportion in 1850 ; *nor are any manufacturing or mechanical products of the year returned whose annual value falls below* $500. *Besides all this, which probably amount to one-fourth of the total annual product, no account is taken of * * * * * * the products of the fine arts, nor of a large portion of the products of the useful arts ; all of which may be very safely stated as equal to half the value of the agricultural and manufacturing products noticed by the census-takers.* Some of these appear in the valuation of the property of the country in the decennial census appraisements, and help to swell the obvious disparity." *

In addition to the above, no account was taken, nor could any account ever be taken of the wealth which consisted of the food, clothing, and personal ornaments belonging to the thirty millions of inhabitants which formed the population of this

* From an article by Dr. Wm. Elder, in the National Almanac for 1864.

country and which were on hand at the time of the taking of the Census. This alone would amount to a colossal sum in the aggregate. Indeed, it needs no long argument to show that the count was wrong. It must be very evident that if the count was right, the late war could never have continued as long as it did. It would have stopped from mere exhaustion of means to carry it on. If the Census of 1860 is right, there was in the whole country at that period property valued at $16,159,616,068. From this should be deducted $2,000,000,000 for the value of the slaves, which was included in the aggregate, "holding them," as the *National Almanac* very properly observes, "for all the purposes of our inquiry as producers and consumers of wealth, and not as property, otherwise than the laborers of any other country are a part of their national wealth and resources." This leaves $14,159,616,068. Of this sum $9,350,000,000 represented the value of the real estate, and $4,809,616,068 that of the personal estate. If no allowance is made for foreign accessions or diminutions of capital, the whole waste occasioned by the war must have come out of this sum of $4,809,616,068, and its increase from 1860 to 1861, the year when the war broke out; because the real estate could neither directly nor indirectly contribute towards maintaining armies and fleets. This proposition, if we take into account the waste both North and South, and on the high seas, is manifestly absurd. The debt of the United States is at the present moment, say $3,000,000,000; of this sum, say that but $2,000,000,000 represents property absolutely destroyed, or capital put into unproductive shape, as into cannon, uniforms, harness, caissons, pontoons, fortifications, men-of-war, &c. Add an equal amount for towns burned, farms and railroads destroyed, vessels captured or sunk at sea, and other devastation committed on the property of the Northern States (and which is not included in the sum of the national debt of the United States), and we have $4,000,000,000. The Confederate debt at the close of the war stood somewhere about $3,000,000,000. Adding the large amounts due to soldiers and others, it was considerably more. Of this sum probably not over $1,000,000,000 represented actual value, and of this we shall not allow over $750,000,000 for military consumption and waste; though it is hard to believe that the rebels kept up a four years' war for one third what the same cost the United States. This adds $750,000,000 to the $4,000,000,000 already enumerated. Now whatever the destruction amounted to which occurred in the Northern States, in Maryland, Pennsylvania, Western Virginia, Kentucky, Tennessee, Missouri, &c., it is very plain that the destruction in the Southern States must have been much greater. From the James River to the passes of the Mississippi the Union armies swept like a whirlwind over the land, and in their track towns were left burning, and farms and railroads torn up. The retreating rebels, too, often laid waste their own homes, and desolation thus marked the path of both combatants. Hundreds, nay almost thousands of towns were utterly ruined, while vast stores of cotton and other property, such as bridges, steamboats, &c., were committed to the flames without mercy. To sum up all this destruction at $2,000,000,000 is very moderate indeed, and yet, for that matter, our argument is sufficiently strong if we leave it out of account altogether. Adding this, however, to the rest, and the grand total of actual destruction is seen to be, even when estimated very moderately, no less than $6,750,000,000.*

The correctness of the census figures would therefore seem to involve the problem of destroying property to the amount of $6,750,000,000, out of a capital of $4,809,616,068, and still retaining as much wealth as before!

The census is, therefore, clearly wrong; but though wrong as to the entire sum of wealth in the United States, it may still be of some value in determining approximately what the rate of growth was from 1850 to 1860. This follows from the fact that these two censuses were taken in a different and more complete manner than the previous ones, and contained both of them the same class of items, and made the same class of omissions.

---

* See an estimate of like character in Hunt's Merchants' Magazine for June, 1865, which brings it by a different course to about the same amount.

The following table is from the United States Census of 1860, page 195:

The true value of Real Estate and Personal Property according to the Seventh Census (1850) *and the Eighth Census,* (1860,) *respectively; also the increase, and increase per cent.*

STATES AND TERRITORIES.	REAL ESTATE AND PERSONAL PROPERTY.		Increase.	Increase per cent.
	1850.	1860.		
Alabama	$228,204,332	$495,237,078	$267,032,746	117.01
Arkansas	39,841,025	219,256,473	179,415,448	450.32
California	22,161,872	207,874,613	185,712,741	837.98
Connecticut	155,707,980	444,274,114	288,566,134	185.32
Delaware	21,062,556	46,242,181	25,179,625	119.54
Florida	22,862,270	73,101,500	50,239,230	219.74
Georgia	335,425,714	645,895,237	310,469,523	92.56
Illinois	156,265,006	871,860,282	715,595,276	457.93
Indiana	202,650,264	528,835,371	326,185,107	160.95
Iowa	23,714,638	247,338,265	223,623,627	942.97
Kansas	....	31,327,895	....	......
Kentucky	301,628,456	666,043,112	364,414,656	120.81
Louisiana	233,998,764	602,118,568	368,119,804	157.31
Maine	122,777,571	190,211,600	67,434,029	54.92
Maryland	219,217,364	376,919,944	157,702,580	71.93
Massachusetts	573,342,286	815,237,433	241,895,147	42.19
Michigan	59,787,255	257,163,983	197,376,728	330.13
Minnesota	Not returned.	52,294,413	....	......
Mississippi	228,951,130	607,324,911	378,373,781	165.26
Missouri	137,247,707	501,214,398	363,966,691	265.18
New Hampshire	103,652,835	156,310,860	52,658,025	50.80
New Jersey*	200,000,000	467,918,324	267,918,324	133.95
New York	1,080,309,216	1,843,338,517	763,029,301	70.63
North Carolina	226,800,472	358,739,399	131,938,927	58.17
Ohio	504,726,120	1,193,898,422	689,172,302	136.54
Oregon	5,063,474	28,930,637	23,867,163	471.35
Pennsylvania	722,486,120	1,416,501,818	694,015,698	96.05
Rhode Island	80,508,794	135,337,588	54,828,794	68.10
South Carolina	288,257,694	548,138,754	259,881,060	90.15
Tennessee	201,246,686	493,903,892	292,657,206	145.42
Texas	52,740,473	365,200,614	312,460,141	592.44
Vermont	92,205,049	122,477,170	30,272,121	32.83
Virginia	430,701,082	793,249,681	362,548,599	84.17
Wisconsin	42,056,595	273,671,668	231,615,073	550.72
District of Columbia	14,018,874	41,084,945	27,066,071	193.06
Nebraska Territory	....	9,131,056	....	......
New Mexico Territory	5,174,471	20,813,768	15,639,298	302.24
Utah Territory	986,083	5,596,118	4,610,035	467.50
Washington Territory	....	5,601,466	....	......
	7,135,780,228	16,159,616,068	8,925,481,011	126.45

* Partly estimated.

If this table were correct, the rate of interest, provided no movements of capital in and out of the various States occurred, was eleven per cent. in Connecticut, while it was but three and a half in the adjoining State of Massachusetts; and eighteen in Illinois, while it was but ten in the adjoining State of Indiana.

The following table exhibits the various States in groups, and the respective rates of yearly accumulation from 1850 to 1860, according to the census:

Three to Six per cent.		Seven to Ten per cent.		Eleven to Fifteen per cent.		Over Sixteen per cent.	
Maine	4½	Alabama	8	Connecticut ..	11	Arkansas	18
Maryland......	6	Delaware.....	8	Florida	12	California	25
Massachusetts .	3½	Georgia	7	Missouri	14	Iowa	27
New Hampsh. .	4	Indiana......	10	Dist. Columbia	12	Minnesota ...	16
New York. ...	5½	Kentucky	8½	New Mexico. .	15	Oregon	18
North Carolina.	5	Louisiana	10			Texas	22
Rhode Island. .	6	Mississippi....	10			Wisconsin....	21
Vermont	3	New Jersey...	8½			Utah Territory	18
Virginia	6	Ohio	9			Illinois.......	18
		Pennsylvania .	7				
		South Carolina	7				
		Tennessee ...	9½				

These discrepancies all prove one thing: that during these ten years of peace, movements of capital were constantly gravitating toward the least settled and least secure States, from the most settled and the most secure. This capital was sent for investment in order to reap the benefit of the high rates of interest prevailing at its various points of destination West and South. That capital constantly flowed in that direction in times of peace is evidenced from the fact that, while Western and Southern merchants were in debt to Northern and Eastern merchants, the latter were never known to be in debt to the former. So much for the flow of capital in times of peace.

Now for the reflux in times of war and insecurity. Without going into a minute argument to prove a fact well known to everybody, it will be sufficient to say that the abnormal increase of deposits in the savings banks and banks of issue in the Northern and Eastern States after the war began, the heaping up of specie hoards, the course of the exchanges with Western and Southern cities, the shipments of gold to Europe, indeed, all those familiar indications of a backward tide of wealth, avoiding investment and running panic-stricken toward peace and security, which appeared at that period, incontestably prove the existence of the reflux we wish to establish.

The flow of capital toward investment and its reflux toward peace and security are thus clearly seen to have occurred in this country to a marked degree, the first during the decade ending 1860, and the latter during the semi-decade ending 1865. This wealth, wherever it goes, being reckoned, as a matter of course, a part of the wealth of the country in which it is found,* helps to augment the natural rate of accretion demonstrated by the prevailing rate of interest; and a country thus grows richer or poorer accordingly as she is blessed with peace and good government, or war and insecurity. The census of the State of New York for 1865, now in course of being taken, will, if made in the same manner as the last one, undoubtedly demonstrate that the State has greatly increased in wealth during the war. The bogus statisticians whom we have already noticed will, of course, ascribe the increase *to* the war, and piling error upon error, will argue that, as New York increased in wealth by the war, so did the whole country! And all from using figures instead of brains. For, if the latter were but called into service, the movements of capital to and from security and investment could scarcely remain undiscerned.

We have one more hill to climb, before indulging in a glance at the new views which on every side surround the theory we have surmounted.

Emigration and capital flow in the same direction, and to a great extent they flow together.

The same causes which invite the investment of capital invite also the emigration of labor; and were all things equal, the movements of the two would be identical. But in the first place the movements of men do not obey new impulses so readily as the movements of capital; and in the next place artificial restrictions of law and custom are placed much more numerously around the former than around the latter.

* "It must be borne in mind that the value of all taxable property was returned *including that of foreigners as well as natives*, while all was omitted belonging to the State or the United States."—*Census of* 1860, *p.* 80.

14

The following table shows the population of the various States in 1850 *and* 1860 *respectively; also the increase and the increase per cent.:*

STATES.	1850.	1860.	Rate of decennial Increase.
Alabama	771,623	964,201	24.96
Arkansas	209,897	{ 435,450 / *14,555 }	107.46
California	92,597	365,439	310.37
Connecticut	370,792	460,147	42.10
Delaware	91,532	112,216	22.60
Florida	87,445	140,425	60.59
Georgia	906,185	1,057,286	16.67
Illinois	851,470	1,711,951	101.06
Indiana	988,416	1,350,428	36.63
Iowa	192,214	674,913	251.14
Kansas	....	107,206	....
Kentucky	982,405	1,155,684	17.64
Louisiana	517,762	708,002	36.74
Maine	583,169	628,279	7.74
Maryland	583,034	687,049	17.84
Massachusetts	994,514	1,231,006	23.79
Michigan	397,654	749,113	88.38
Minnesota	6,077	172,123	2,760.87
Mississippi	606,526	791,305	30.47
Missouri	682,044	1,182,012	73.30
New Hampshire	317,976	326,073	2.55
New Jersey	489,555	672,035	37.27
New York	3,097,394	3,880,735	25.29
North Carolina	869,039	992,622	14.20
Ohio	1,980,329	2,339,511	18.14
Oregon	13,294	52,465	294.65
Pennsylvania	2,311,786	2,906,115	25.71
Rhode Island	147,545	174,620	18.35
South Carolina	668,507	703,708	5.27
Tennessee	1,002,717	1,109,801	10.68
Texas	212,592	604,215	184.22
Vermont	314,120	315,098	0.31
Virginia	1,421,661	1,596,318	12.29
Wisconsin	305,391	775,881	154.06
Total	23,067,262	31,148,047	35 04
TERRITORIES.			
Colorado	....	{ 34,277 / * 2,261 }	....
Dakota	....	2,576	....
Nebraska	....	28,841	....
Nevada	....	{ 6,857 / *10,507 }	....
New Mexico	61,547	83,009	51.94
Utah	11,380	{ 40,273 / * 426 }	253.89
Washington	....	11,168	....
District of Columbia	51,687	75,080	45.26
Total	23,191,876	31,443,322	35.59

* Indians.

The analogy between the movements of population here given and that of capital before given, is very remarkable.

Were the official tables of imports and exports in years past of any practical value, the course of trade between this country and Europe would undoubtedly exhibit in times of peace an immense flow, and in time of war a great ebb of foreign capital. But these tables are unfortunately of scarcely any value at all:

First. Because "from the absence of penalty for deficient or untrue outward invoices, or of special necessity from any cause requiring the record of the export manifests to be complete and full, there has been more or less of failure, either to clear outward shipments of domestic produce, or to secure the record of such clearances when the ship obtains its general clearance and leaves the port." * Copies of outward manifests are required to be left at the Custom-house before clearance papers are given. In order to avoid the delay of keeping a vessel awaiting the plodding steps of official routine, these manifests are sent in a few days previously. Meanwhile the vessel continues to take freight, and not unfrequently the great bulk of it is taken after the manifest has been sent in. The latter is left to be made out by a junior clerk who frames it entirely in accordance with his fancy. "Sundries" always forms the chief item, and the whole ends with a row of figures which bear as much relation to the truth as the Julian calendar does to the price of whiskey cock-tails, but which, nevertheless, enter into the grave totals of the official column of exports.

Second. Because the imports, "undoubtedly, are always short not only of the true valuation when entered, but still more deficient in the valuation they should have as one side of the commercial exchanges. The increase over the invoice price at which they are entered, resulting from transportation across the Atlantic and the advance properly charged on them on arrival (when they are sold) by the importer, add twenty per cent. to the recorded aggregate values at the point and time of actual exchange." †

---

* North American Review, January, 1865, p. 131.

† Ibid.

Third. Because of the immense values which are constantly smuggled into the country not only by false swearing in valuations and by the concealment of valuable goods within packages of grosser material, and about the person, but by whole cargoes landed along the coast in boats, or run across the Canadian border in wagons.

Fourth. Because no account is taken of cargoes which, after leaving the country, are wrecked and are wholly lost.

Fifth. Because, owing to the popular confusion which surrounds the subject of money, the precious metals have not been recognized as merchandise, and shipments of gold and silver have been and are still made to and from the country, which are never entered upon the official tables. These shipments amount to sums of very great magnitude. In the case of some San Francisco transactions alone they amounted in 1862–'3–'4 to $54,000,000.*

Sixth. Because, concerning goods which enter free of duty, the valuation is either not reported at all, or, if reported, it is done without the slightest regard to accuracy.

Seventh. Because no account is taken either of the wealth brought into the country by foreign emigrants, or of that which is taken away by persons going abroad. These items are of great importance. The wealth brought into the United States since its settlement, by emigrants, amounted up to the year 1860, in cash alone, to the enormous sum of $1,400,000,000. Of that which has been taken away in times of insecurity or alarm, we have no means of knowing the amount.

The official tables of imports and exports being thus abundantly shown to be worthless as a basis of computation of the international flow and ebb of wealth, we must dispense with the assistance which they might have afforded to us in our investigation and endeavor to find some better data.

Let us take for this purpose the very item last mentioned as an important omission from the import and export tables—the accession and loss of capital accompanying immigrants and emigrants. "From 1790 to 1819 there arrived in

---

* North American Review, January, p. 133.

this country about 50,000 immigrants.* In the next ten years the foreign arrivals were about 70,000; and in the ten years following ending with 1820, 114,000." From 1820 to 1860 they were 5,459,421. This makes a grand total of 5,693,421.†

"It appears of the emigration from Prussia to America and other countries in the fifteen years ending with 1859, it was ascertained that 183,232 of the emigrants carried out their property to the amount of 45,269,011 Thalers, being an average of 242 Thalers, or $180 to each individual." ‡

Allowing for the usual want of accuracy in official statistics, and particularly in a case where ignorance and fear would naturally influence the emigrant to conceal all but a small portion of his hoard; allowing also for the sums of money brought by cabin passengers, into whose affairs official inquiries are never made; and finally allowing for the bag and baggage, tools, and clothing, that every emigrant brings with him, the sum of $250 would appear to be a low estimate of the amount of capital brought into the country by each of them. This, for 5,693,421 immigrants, amounts in the aggregate to $1,423,-355,250.

The largest accession of capital from this source during any one period of five years, was from 1850 to 1854, which corresponds to a period of remarkable prosperity in the affairs of this country. The immigration and accession of wealth during the period mentioned were as follows:

Year.	Immigrants.	Immigrants' Capital.
1850	310,004	$77,501,000
1851	439,442	109,860,000
1852	371,603	92,901,000
1853	368,645	92,161,000
1854	427,833	106,958,000
Total	1,917,527	$479,381,000

* Dr. Adam Seybert computes the number who arrived during this period at 120,000, or an average of 6,000 per year (see Appleton's Cyclopædia, article *Emigration*); but we have preferred in the text to follow the census.

† But this only includes passengers who arrived by sea. The large immigration by way of Canada, as well as the numerous trifling accessions to our population by immigration from Mexico, besides the many who have entered the country after working their passage hither as seamen, are taken no account of whatever.

‡ United States Census, 1860. Introduction, pp. xviii and xxiii.

Enough has been shown through the synchronical movements of emigration and capital to prove that peace and security invite their accession. We shall now briefly endeavor to show how the opposite conditions drive both away.

From 1850 to 1854, the period of the most remarkable accessions to our population and wealth from abroad, Europe was either engaged in war or convulsed with political disturbances. In 1850 the Hungarian war was just subsiding. It had convulsed the whole of Hungary, Russia, Austria, and Italy. Kossuth had been appointed governor and afterward overthrown. Rome was declared a republic and was captured by the French. Venice surrendered. The Schleswig-Holsteiners and the Danes were at war. In 1851 Louis Napoleon dissolved the National Assembly of France and overthrew the Constitution. In 1852 he made himself emperor, by the celebrated *coup d'état*. In 1853 Italy was very much disturbed. The Porte declared war against Russia. In 1854 Great Britain, France, Sardinia, and Turkey were engaged in war with Russia, while Austria and the other monarchies of Europe were constantly agitated by the proximity of the allied operations and those of their antagonist.

During all this time entire peace reigned in this country, and the result was an immense ebb of population and capital from Europe and its flow towards this country. Upon the declaration of peace in 1856 the current slackened. The immigration into the United States from 427,833 in 1854 fell to 200,877 in 1855 and 200,436 in 1856. In the early part of 1857 it began to increase, but the financial troubles in this country of that year checked it again, and though by the end of the year it had reached 251,306 it fell to 123,126 in 1858 and to 121,282 in 1859. In 1860 it again revived and amounted during the year to 153,640; but then the American war broke out, and immigration entirely stopped and began to flow the other way. In 1861 the arrivals were 91,919, in 1862 91,987, in 1863 156,000, and in 1864 182,000; making in all, during the four years of the war, but 521,906; which number is perhaps fully counterbalanced by the numerous departures of persons from the United States who fled thence to avoid the consequences of civil war.

Thus, with emigration, streams of capital of the saved-up wealth of the abstinent and the thrifty of all the world, are seen to be constantly moving to and fro, flowing in times of peace towards investment and in times of war towards security. No country can be so rich but that its riches may be all tempted to desert it for better investment or better security; and no country so poor but that, if it affords superior employment or security for capital, it may be filled to the brim with the choicest wealth of the earth. This mobility of capital makes it the common property of mankind, and not, as shallow politicans would have us believe, the gift of particular nations. While an immediate loss of wealth must necessarily ensue from wars or other public calamities, yet this does not hold good in the long run; for with the means of once more inviting the investment of capital through peace and security, which all wise governments possess, the wealth so lost comes not out of the fund of the nation who directly lost it, but from the common fund of civilization. It is the world which suffers—not a country. It is mankind in common—not some particular aggregation of men who adopt a piece of colored bunting as their political symbol and call themselves a nation. While, therefore, wars and other public calamities undoubtedly cause loss of wealth, it is one which, though it temporarily affects the prosperity and wealth of a country, yet, in the end, only affects the general prosperity of the civilized world. Cessation of war will not always bring it back. Capital, like a creditor whose debtor has once defaulted, requires guarantees. A mere peace will fail to invite its stimulating flow. A peace which is not followed by increased security—which means improved protection to person and property—and an improved administration of justice—which means the undivided attention of government to its only proper function, and the relinquishment of its assumed right to meddle and interfere in matters with which it has no concern—a peace not followed by new concessions of governmental prerogatives, might as well for these purposes be no peace at all: for it will surely fail to attract either wealth or population.

It is now time to return to our theorem. The rate of the growth of national wealth being seen to be identical with the prevailing rate of interest, we possess at all times a key to that growth; and when we find it by actual count to exceed or fall short of the rate which we know must be the true one, we are furnished with a better set of import and export tables than the ingenuity even of a customs-officer can devise. With peace, with security, with liberty, we need have no fears neither of the harvest nor the "balance of trade;" the nation will grow rich in spite of them; but with Lynch-law in one part of the country and pettifoggery elsewhere, with the tyranny of the majority hanging like a pall over the heads of the timorous few, with the rule of the party in power over the opposition, of the white over the black, of man over woman, of the strong over the weak—not all the wealth which the imagination can conjure up would, if converted into palpable realities, suffice to redeem the country from that comparative poverty which will surely await her.

Let treasures be poured into her lap never so fast, and they will flow to other countries, as water will through a sieve.*

But we have faith in the progress of mankind toward the right. Education must eventually open the eyes of the populace to the important truths which, as yet, are only discussed in the domain of social science; and when it does, all the conditions favorable to a high rate of interest must disappear. In this country, more than in any other, exist the elements of popular instruction and the means of popular education. Travel and intercourse are common and cheap, and public schools are numerous. It cannot be long, therefore, before the people will

---

* "Let us say that the condition of affairs to-day *is* not changd: that men with a minimum allowance of brains are continued to be appointed to public office; that passion and injustice shall rule the country; that five-and-thirty years hence our form of government, no matter what it may be in name, shall be as strong and as despotic as that of Turkey; that the very name of free trade shall be abhorred; and that commercial intercourse between this and Albany shall be as toroughly tied up and *protected* as that between this and Europe now is. What then will be our condition?

"Though California should yield mountains of pure gold, tough petroleum should spout up from the earth in volumes that would shame Niagra itself, though coined money rained from the clouds as manna rained upon the Hebrews, though wealth of every kind sprang up upon every side to feast the greey eye and water the longing lip, the nation will grow poorer and poorer, and finlly lapse into a state which, if compared to the progress made by other nations in the mean time, will closely resemble that which we now call barbarism."—*Hunt's Merchants' Magazine for June*, 1865, *p.* 424.

place themselves upon the right road; and then will follow that career of prosperity which is indicated, not by the high rate of interest so glowingly foreshadowed by our friends the "statisticians," but by a contemptibly low one—the lower the better.*

Another thing this principle should teach us—that we are not so little interested in the affairs of other countries nor other countries in our affairs, that we need to maintain an affected and stupid attitude of unconcern while improved legislation abroad is diverting capital away from us for investment, nor when our own passion for territorial acquisition or civil tumult is jeopardizing the capital which foreigners have invested on this continent. With the rate of interest in England at three

---

* Two curious tables are published in the number of Hunt's Magazine quoted above; one showing that on her present capital the country may, during the present century; increase her capital to the enormous sum of $175,466,000,000; or lose it, until at the end of the same period it is reduced to $11,000,000,000, or $3,000,000,000 less than it is assumed to be now. The following is the first table:

RESOURCES OF THE UNITED STATES, No. 1.

[All the following sums are stated in millions, except the percentages.]

Period.	Capital.	Average yearly accession of foreign capital.	Average yearly rate of net accumulation.	Increase of capital and profit at end of period.	Remarks.
1865–68....	14,000	2 per cent.	6 per cent.	3,630	Over Legislation.
1868–78....	17,630	3 "	5 "	22,130	Reform.
1878–88....	39,760	3 "	4 "	39,240	Continued reform.
1888–98....	79,000	2 "	3 "	52,600	Stationary state of freedom and security, same being a little more perfect than elsewhere.
1898–1900..	131,600	1 "	2 "	43,866	
1900	175,466				

The enormous aggregate assumed for the year 1900, it will be seen, is reached by *a rate of accumulation constantly decreasing*. The other table is as follows:

RESOURCES OF THE UNITED STATES, No. 2.

[All the following sums are stated in millions, except the percentages.]

Period.	Capital.	Average yearly accession of foreign capital.	Average yearly rate of net accumulation.	Increase of capital and profit at end of period.	Remarks.
1865–68....	14,000	2 per cent.	6 per cent.	3,630	Over Legislation.
1868–78....	17,630	None.	7 "	17,000	Continued do.
		Capital yearly sent abroad.			
1878–88....	35,000	5 per cent.	8 "	12,000	Worse and worse.
				Decrease.	
1888–98....	47,000	10 "	9 "	12,000	Insecurity.
1898–1900..	35,000	15 "	10 "	24,000	War, &c.
1900	11,000				

Here it will be seen that the falling off of wealth occurs in spite of *a constantly* INCREASING *rate of accumulation*. These calculations are very remarkable, and had the writer perceived the identity of the rate of interest with what he calls the "rate of accumulation" or "profit" his theory had been perfect.

per cent., it were expedient to examine into our code of laws, and their administration, with a view of discovering wherein British freedom and security exceed our own; and with French and British capital invested both in this country and in all the countries of America to the extent of thousands of millions, it is high time we renounced that superlatively arrogant assumption which is contained in the so-called "doctrine" of President Monroe.

But, above all, let it impress upon us the axiom which we have already repeated over and over, but which, had we the power, we would drum for everlasting into the ears of men, that: wealth is security; security is peace; peace is Liberty!

A. D.

THE ETHICS OF VENGEANCE.

It is not strange that, in an hour of intense excitement, passion should get the mastery over reason; but it is strange that when the hour of reason returns, passion should still be accepted as its master. It is not strange that the murder of the President should rouse in the masses of the people a thirst for blood; but it is strange that, when the horror occasioned by the crime has subsided, the thirst for blood should be accepted as, in any sense, or in any degree, a substitute or an equivalent for justice. It is not strange that, coming out from the fierce struggle of a civil war, the people should be animated by a spirit of vengeance toward the men who brought the civil war on the country; but it is strange that, on the restoration of peace, when the recuperative forces are all at work again, and the danger is past, the spirit of vengeance should be solemnly accepted as a principle on which loyal and patriotic men ought to act in their dealing with the criminals.

When the assassin of the President met his miserable end, a general feeling of disappointment was expressed that justice had been cheated of its victim; justice being, in common speech, another name for the gallows. The implication was that, horrible as the man's death was, it had not that "awful" horror that is associated with the gibbet: and, merited as it was, it lacked that judicial character which a deliberate public execution would have given to it. Behind this, again, lay the implication that no such thing existed as a natural or social law of justice which unswervingly executed itself, and did its work most thoroughly when it was free to avail itself of all the avenging, retributive, corrective, and restraining powers which nature and society have at their command. The operation of these powers is not reckoned into the process of retribution. All that they effect is counted as something incidental, secondary, and aside from justice; sometimes as a palliation of justice; often as a reprieve from justice. It "cheats justice of its victim."

As diligent students of the natural and social laws, as profound admirers of their exact and beautiful working, as vehement haters of crime and earnest friends of the powers that restrain, convict, doom, and eradicate it, we feel bound to protest against the notion just described. We believe that the very opposite doctrine is the truer; that human justice is rather in the way of the justice that is executed by the decrees of the individual and social organization; that our punishments are under some aspects best described as rewards; that in cases of real crime—against which nature enacts penalties as well as we—the penalties which we enact are in a certain sense remissions, reprieves, pardons, absolutions, devices by which criminals escape from doom. The pain we inflict is a dispensation from pain. Society, by means of its natural constitution, will inflict more agony on a peccadillo than we can inflict on a crime, and will punish a foible more terribly than we can punish a guilt. In the presence of the compensating laws we are babies with bunches of flowers, instead of instruments of torture, and bundles of feathers instead of whips of cords.

To illustrate: If the President's murderer had been taken alive, he would have been shut up in a cell, dark, lonely, cramped, it is true, but securing to him certain immunities. He would have been maintained at the public cost, and spared the trouble and humiliation of supporting himself in a community that regarded him as an outlaw. He would have been sheltered from the violent hands, the angry looks, and the bitter words of men. No rage could reach him. To a great many in the community, he would have been an object of sympathy, and he would know that he was. A morbid interest would have been excited in him and his fate. The elements of romance would have clustered about him, and would have clung to him. He would have been the subject of conversation in all circles, a figure of importance in the public mind; in a word—a hero. As his career drew to a close, the demonstrations of interest in him would have been intense. His occupations would have been detailed in the papers. What he said and did from day to day would have been reported for his own edification and entertainment, as well as the public's. Very little opportunity or disposition would he have had for reflection on the nature and consequences of his deed. He would have been too much preoccupied with the current speculations about himself to suffer severely in his mind either on his own account, or on the account of others who might be suffering innocently through his crime. So far from being humiliated or convinced, he would be put upon his pluck as a careless, reckless, dare-devil. The days of his trial, would be days of tremendous nervous excitement of thought and temper. The days preceding his execution would have been spent, probably, in real or mock bravado, or in stupid indifference to everything that concerned society, his friends, or himself. The last hour would, at all events, have been but an hour. The last moment, however hideous, would have been but a moment; then all, so far as his relations to his fellow men were concerned, would have been over forever. Suffering, atonement, amendment and achievement would have been from that moment impossible.

Yet this would be called a just punishment. Just, however, it hardly would be; for it does not satisfy the conditions which society exacts from those who commit offences against its order. For the moral shock it had sustained, for the loss of property and life it was subjected to, for the discomfiture into which it was thrown, the criminal makes no reparation in this process of terminating his career. He merely adds to them all another shock—a new loss of property and life; a new excitement that deranges the mental calm which is so necessary to social well-being. Punishment, he has scarcely met with. His actual end was far more terrible than any end to which the law could have brought him. His physical tortures alone were agonizing, and were continued for days. His mental tortures are fearful to imagine. He was a fugitive—an outlaw—with a price set on his head; every moment of his life was steeped in fear; his pursuers lay in wait for him at every turn. The air he breathed was full of maledictions. Who his friends might be he did not know; he knew that all men might be his enemies. Burning with rage and hate, he flies from one hiding place to another. He is brought to bay at last like a wild beast; like a beast he is shot; and the physicians say that, from the nature of his wound, his sufferings, before death released him, must have been inconceivable.

But if the wretch had escaped, his sufferings, we imagine, would have been vastly greater than they were. What if he had lived to be poor, ragged, outcast, the companion of desperadoes; lived to see his fatal mistake—to see how his boyish fury had defeated itself, how he had made a martyr, when he meant to murder a man, how he had strengthened the Government he designed to overturn; what if he had lived to hear the last sigh of his broken-hearted mother, to know that he had blighted a noble brother's career, to be stunned by the roar of execration bursting upon him from both hemispheres and rolling up against him like a storm whichever way he turned; what if he had lived to be shunned and pointed at as the perpetrator of a deed without a name, the head of a new line of monsters, living for the purpose of saving his life from violent and shocking death. This would have been infinitely worse as punishment than anything that men could have inflicted on him, than anything he actually did endure. It would have met the requisitions of justice better; for if he was made of no use to his fellow men as a worker, he would have done good service as a scarecrow, and would have illustrated fairly in his fate the action of that tremendous law which guards the order and welfare of society with a jealousy that cannot be eluded, and shows nature's estimate of the worth of human life by the unflinching severity with which it pursues and overwhelms its violators. The evil would have worked itself out naturally, and all men would have seen the full process of its working out.

Speaking of punishment, therefore, there is some reason for thinking that it would have been more severe if the criminal had been permitted to escape, and to meet in the world the natural consequences of his atrocious deed in the neglect and hatred of his fellow men. But it is a question whether we have any right to speak of punishment at all; whether, in fact, we are competent to speak of it under any aspect, to say what it ought to be, how much, how little, of what kind, to adjust it to persons or even to offences; or to apply it in such a manner as to insure beneficial results to the individual criminal, to the general class of criminals, or to the community at large. To punish wisely—and certainly no one would advocate unwise or unreasonable punishment—supposes a knowledge of circumstances, of motives, intentions, dispositions, elements of character, the bearing of experiences on character, that men do not possess, and perhaps never will possess. Herbert Spencer's plain and sensible remarks on the moral education of children opened a new field of thought to the minds of most people in our communities, and are calculated to effect a revolution in domestic discipline. If we have not yet learned how to punish teasing children, we must be very far indeed from having learned how to punish guilty men.

Besides, the idea of punishment includes the idea of retaliation, it implies that suffering is inflicted for the suffering's sake, a compensation for harm done, trespass committed, or rule broken. There is just a touch of revenge in it always, or of anger which borders on revenge. The element of passion enters into the composition of all punishment. The passion may not be active in the form of feeling; it may be perfectly cool, calm, and collected. It may have a judicial look; but if it appears so, it is merely because the passion, by long use, has become inveterate, and has settled down into a steady regularity of action, which has also the air of a principle. It is passion with the emotion worn off, and the impulsiveness stiffened; in other words, stale passion.

It is true, no doubt, that sentiments of indignation and horror, varying in intensity all the way from a feeling of moral disapprobation to a feeling of moral detestation, spring up immediately on the commission of crime, and prompt some measure of retribution on its perpetrator. To most people this fact seems to settle the whole question, by affording a justification as by human nature herself for the retribution which is everywhere visited on guilty men. But the human nature that gives voice to such sentiments, we must bear in mind, is not human nature in its normal condition, as it will appear one day, when the social relations are adjusted to laws of natural equity, and sympathy takes the place of antipathy in the feelings which men bear toward one another. It is human nature in its wild state, unregulated by reason, ungoverned by principle, untaught by experience, and unsoftened by kindness. It is human nature as formed under the influences of barbarism that announces itself in doctrines of retaliation. Such shall not be the human nature of an enlightened age, such as is now dawning on us. The ideas of punishment that still obtain in modern society may have been suitable enough to the times out of which they sprung; but that they are not suited to these times is indicated clearly in the protests that are made against them in intelligent circles, in the vehement repudiation of them by social reformers, in the uncomfortable sensation which they create in the better part of the community, and in their palpable failure to accomplish any purposes of personal amendment or even of social security. That a thing exists, is no reason why it should exist longer. That a thing has existed a thousand years, is no reason why it should continue to exist another day. It may be a sufficient reason why it should cease, on the spot, to perpetuate its ignorance and foolishness. The more like an unalterable fact it looks, the less an unalterable fact it should be. There is a great deal of thoughtless talking about "human nature." In simple truth, it remains to be seen what human nature is to be under the influences of a noble civilization. Certain it is that it will be something very different from what it is now. And certain it is that one of the elements it will drop with the least hesitation, is this element of passion, in the administration of discipline to its refractory sons. It is not a question whether the usages demanded by this element of passion, and sustained by it, should be at once abandoned. They cannot be till the passion is outgrown by the intelligence of the community. The "institutions of justice" are not the only institutions existing among us that belong to another age, and which yet cannot be remanded to the limbo where the things characteristic of that age should be. Customs change more slowly than character, and then go on perpetrating inconsistencies and absurdities long after they suspect them to be what they are, having no other customs better suited to their moral development to take their place. There should be constant effort to promote accord between sentiments and practices; and it is in the course of such effort that things hallowed by usage and by antiquity are pushed aside. The question is, can this work be accelerated too fast? Is it not timely now to say that "punishment" for crime does not come within the province of government, or of society, however constituted and represented? Is it not timely now to say that, as barbarism is not civilization, so the usages of barbarism cannot stand as the usages of civilization; and as vengeance is no longer regarded as a safe or wholesome quality in man, so the customs which it originated and perpetuates can no longer be the customs approved by men who understand what manly duties are. Inconsistencies are demoralizing. The persistency in them involves indefinite harm. There is a species of sanctity in logic, which enforces itself by severe penalties if it is disregarded.

In dealing with criminals, there are three ends which society may, as it seems to us, legitimately have in view, and may aim at attaining:

1. The first is the reformation of the criminal, the counteracting of his evil propensities, the fostering of his good tendencies, the restoration of him to the position of a useful and worthy member of society. Justice and pity, too; a regard for the individual's work as a man, and for society, which may turn him to some good account in its service—all conspire in urging this end upon us. But plainly it is an end which cannot as yet in any considerable number of cases be reached. The science of human nature is as yet in its infancy, and the

adaptation of circumstances to dispositions in such a way as to develop the better qualities and suppress the worse, is a matter that has been hardly approached. A few instances of successful moral education are detailed in English reports; but they bear no proportion to the cases in which moral education has been tried and failed, and you can hardly see them in the multitude of instances where the moral education has never been so much as dreamed of. They are merely occasional and incidental studies in the moral treatment of crime, establishing no rule that can safely be followed on a large scale, and laying the basis of no philosophy of the question.

There is nothing to encourage the belief that the cases we have in hand now, and shall have in hand by the quantity for some time to come, will yield to any moral treatment that this age can apply. The attempt to make good men, of characters like the assassins of the President and the Secretary of State, would probably end very near its commencement. What regenerating arts have we that will enable us to convert the chiefs of the Southern slave-holding aristocracy into peaceful, law-abiding citizens of a republic? Criminals whose deed is born of a sudden impulse, or of some single passion which circumstances have stimulated to excess, and whose motives are only skin-deep, may have their personal equilibrium restored by judiciary management, so that the social order will seem friendly to them as they will be friendly to it. But where deeds are born of inveterate dispositions, and motives are powers that sway every part of the moral man with a constant rule, and tendencies have become fixed by the exercise of years; when, in a word, the criminal is the product of an old and recognized order of things, which is about passing away, amendment is out of the question. To think of it is waste of time.

2. The second end that may be legitimately kept in view in the treatment of criminals, is the mechanical use of them as artisans and laborers, at different occupations, that will keep them still in the ranks of contributors to the general productive industry of the community, and will help them to make some amends for the loss that society has sustained at their hands. This mode of treatment is now generally recognized, though

it has not been scientifically applied on any large scale. It would be quite impossible to apply it on a scale commensurate with the demands of the country in an exigency like the present. The Government cannot undertake to "turn to use" a hundred thousand men. No work-house smaller than nature's own would be big enough to employ them in their various capacities. No stimulus weaker than nature's own would be sufficient to drive them to their labor. Whatever benefit is to be derived from them must be drawn out by social necessity, on penalty of starvation in case they decline the conditions of industry. The presumption is, or well may be, that this penalty will be fully as effective from its terror as any pain that can be invented and artificially brought to bear. Nature has a way of making men work which art has found it impossible to improve upon, and will surely never supersede. Her rule is: If a man will not work, neither shall he eat; and she holds rigidly to it. She is never caught throwing so much as a dry crust of bread stealthily to any idle loon whom she has taken a fancy to. On the whole, she may be trusted to turn all material to account that is committed to her.

3. The plan of converting assassins and traitors and slaveholders being unpractical, and the scheme of putting them to some good use not being evidently feasible under the circumstances, but one other resource is left. Society, in dealing with them, must consult, not their moral well-being, not their social value as persons or powers, but simply its own safety. It must confine its efforts to the task of protecting itself against further harm from them. It is not in its power to punish them. Nothing less terrible than the social laws can do that. It is not in its power to reform them; nothing less merciful and persuasive than the social laws can do that. Its province is to draw their fangs, and make it impossible for them to do harm again.

This is by no means as easy a task as it might seem; and in entering on it, by the old methods, simply adopting the old barbarism with a new intention, we may be easily duped by appearances. The methods which vengeance devised in the interest of the retributive theory, will be out of place in the interest of the security theory, and will effect but partial and unsatisfactory results. Shall we be saved from the men who have plotted treason and murder, by taking away their political and civil rights, and allowing them to live in the country as men disfranchised? But though disfranchised, they are alive, and in the midst of us, in full possession of their faculties of personal persuasion. Will banishment make their harmlessness sure? But in these days there are no foreign lands. The continents are interlinked; the shores touch; the oceans are conductors; populations intermingle. One may live in America though his residence be in Russia, France or Spain. He may interfere with our affairs from Vienna almost as directly as from New York; and may do as much harm from London or Constantinople as from Boston or Cincinnati.

Will the State prison make our State secure? But prisons can be broken; and in this country are sure, sooner or later, to be opened. Or, leaving such possibilities out of the question, the inmates of them are objects of thought and speculation. They excite commiseration as long as they exist; and exciting commiseration, they exert more or less influence.

Will the gallows procure for us the sense of safety which is so important for the people to have? Will the criminals be harmless if put under the ground? Dead men tell no tales, says the proverb. True; but do dead men exert no influence? In these days, when the moral sentiment is humane, to execute malefactors is to transfer the popular sympathy from the law to the offender. In our case the execution of traitors would, beyond a doubt, transfer the sympathy of Europe from the Government to the traitors. Their prestige would rise; ours in the same proportion would fall. We should be charged with needless cruelty and vindictiveness; they would be credited with undeserved manliness, valor, and honor, and so their reputation heightened by pity; and the prevalent abhorrence of deliberate blood shedding would do us more harm, possibly, than living they themselves could personally effect. Here is a new danger to be guarded against—a danger to our national character, which is as well worth considering as danger to our political State. The assaults of hostile criticism, misconception, and censure, are as much to be dreaded as an attack with swords; and if, by taking the lives of our conspirators, we are going to weaken our own moral position in Christendom, it is not safe to do it.

These considerations may be deemed exceedingly fine-spun. We are not answerable, people will say, for such remote and ideal contingencies as have been here presented. If men are disfranchised and cut off from direct political power, we have no concern with their personal magnetisms. If they are out of this country, it is none of our business to imagine what they may be doing in other countries. If they are in prison, and well bolted in their cells, we will let their power over the popular imagination take care of itself. And if they are in their graves, we will not disturb our minds about the predictions of spiritualists, or the comments of the foreign press. This is all very well, and is undeniably sound in its place. But even if these remote and ideal dangers can be escaped, and our political security can be maintained as fairly and completely as if they were incurred, is it not worth while to consider their weight? We live in an age where fine-spun considerations do have influence, and are worth taking into account. It is an age of refined speculation, and somewhat rarefied sentiment. The blind, blunt policy does not answer now in civilization. The more a government consults courtesy and kindness, the safer it will be. Even the ostrich has discovered that its broad inhumanities cannot be concealed simply by hiding its head in the sand.

We make these general remarks mainly in the way of criticism. Our points have been negative. We have contented ourselves with indicating the courses which, in our judgment, should not be pursued toward its old enemies. In regard to the course that should be pursued, we make no suggestions, beyond this: that the minimum of pain inflicted is the maximum of wisdom practised. The more is left to the social laws and the less is undertaken by artificial tribunals the better, in our conviction. Extract the lion's teeth and claws with no more ado than is necessary, and let him go. They will be tolerably well extracted when the evil actually done is weighed, measured, and exhibited; when the individual's complicity in it and responsibility for it is fully shown, and when a large placard, advertising his history and character, to all whom it may concern, in capital letters, is authoritatively printed and, as it were, strongly sewn to his back.

O. B. FROTHINGHAM.

LAW AND LAWYERS IN THE UNITED STATES.*

"Es erben sich Gesetz und Rechte wie eine ew'ge Krankheit fort."

THE author of the above work, the Hon. George Sharswood, presiding Justice of the District Court of the city of Philadelphia, and Dean of the faculty of the Law Department of the University of Pennsylvania, has in a small compass attempted to give us his views on the practical importance of the profession of the law, and an exposition both of the line of conduct and of study which, according to his opinion, should be pursued by a lawyer for the purpose of achieving success, or, to do what is better than success itself—deserve success.

To say that Judge Sharswood is a fair specimen of the American lawyer is to do him much less than justice. He is far superior to a great majority of our lawyers, and may be deemed a representative man of the best that the American Bar has produced. The words of such a man are always to be listened to with respect, and even if we derive no positive information from him, we can at all events in a negative way discover in what respect the class which the Judge represents is deficient, and in what particular its education has been inadequate and insufficient. We purpose to examine this work from its negative side only. Its deficiencies are such as it has in common with every law book, or quasi literary work written by a lawyer, that has issued for the past quarter of a century

---

* An Essay on Professional Ethics, by George Sharswood, second edition, Philadelphia, T. & J. W. Johnson.

from the American press—want of originality and absence of philosophical spirit or breadth.

In the first place, it strikes us strangely that it should be deemed necessary for a particular class of professional men to possess a code of ethics specially framed for and adapted to their use. The whole of professional ethics may be comprised in a short sentence. "Be a gentleman in all your relations with the bench, bar, and fellow-citizens," and your professional ethics are all laid down. It is supposed that the adoption of a code of ethics aids in promoting an *ésprit de corps.* This position we believe to be a mistake. All the codes of ethics combined will neither transform blackguards into gentlemen, nor convert opinionated fools into scientists. And for a true gentleman and scholar a code is useless, as his accomplishments, knowledge, and acquirements will of themselves tend to develop that self-respect and true dignity of character which codes of ethics in vain attempt to maintain and encourage.

It is the universal complaint that the profession of the law is degenerating. If that be true, it is because learning is deemed less essential and less important than heretofore; that the members of the profession no longer regard the development of the law their true object and aim, but deem the making of money and acquirement of a large practice of first importance. In New York city, at all events, law is not pursued as a profession, but followed as a trade.

A sense of this degeneracy was brought home to us a short time ago, as we accompanied a distinguished member of the German bar through our Halls of Justice, for the purpose of showing to him our law and lawyers in operation. The general term of the Supreme Court was just then in session, and by a happy accident, the majority of our leaders of the bar were assembled ready with their printed cases and points, at the proper time, "to distinguish and divide a hair betwixt south and southwest side." Upon having the various legal celebrities of our city pointed out to him, our friend completely confounded us with the question, "What have these gentlemen done for the development of the law to justify that hold on the public esteem, and that standing at the bar that you claim for them?" "Done? done? why they have argued cases with a great deal of skill, and have won controversies involving large sums of money," was our awkward reply. "And is that all! Do you in America call men great because they have shown great ability in earning large fees; because they have settled a dispute between John Doe and Richard Roe, involving half a million, and in which their *jus honorarium* amounted, probably, to a fifth of the sum involved? Have these great lights you have shown me expended their rays solely upon old parchments, or to illuminate some question of practice or of evidence? Have they not devoted their faculties and energies in making law more certain and more scientific?" Alas, no! Nothing of the kind. Practitioners, simply practitioners, almost all of them. Not a score of scientists among a bar of three thousand members. With this confession in our heart, if not upon our lips, we bowed our head with shame, and left the court room.

Were we wrong to feel this sense of humiliation? Has the bar of the United States produced anything worth mentioning in the way of juridical *science* within the past thirty years? Has law become more of a science in America than it was thirty years ago? Has the combined activity of thousands of lawyers resulted in anything higher than the pursuit of a lucrative business? Have they, as a class, felt themselves called upon to remedy the incongruities of our juridical system, to raise the moral and scientific standard of the profession, to increase the knowledge of principles, or to cultivate and develop a knowledge of the natural laws that govern man in a social state, and to harmonize human law with the natural coördination of things? Alas, no! Go into court at any time when our Titans of the bar are engaged in debate; hear an argument upon a railroad case which has become celebrated by reason of the amount involved, and the ability of the lawyers engaged in it; admire the skill with which arguments are advanced, met and refuted; and when you have heard thas, you have heard all and seen all that the leading minds of the American bar have done since Chancellor Kent published his commentaries. Now, we ask in all seriousness, is this not disgraceful? Is it not a repetition of the labors of Sisyphus, with the sole distinction that the members of the bar are paid for their routine toil? Does such a scene take place in any department of human activity whatever, other than in the law? In medicine, every year witnesses new discoveries and new remedial agents, and methods for the curing of disease. Our roll of honor among practising physicians in our midst, who have advanced the science of medicine, is a long and well-filled one, and though their discoveries may not in the majority of cases have been as important as those of their brethren in Europe, they have worked with equal zeal and equal disinterestedness. Our engineers are constantly making new discoveries of natural properties, and new applications of natural forces. Every science progresses: works that ten years ago were regarded as text books are now thrown aside as lumber. Similarly the mechanical arts constantly improve and advance. We now make better tables, better pianos, better steam engines than we did ten years ago. Everywhere activity, enterprise, novelty, and movement—everywhere progress, except in the law, which has stagnated into immobility, a stagnation which is demoralizing little by little the bench and the bar, a stagnation which has already converted our lawyers into practitioners, and our judges into—well, at all events, into something less than Marshalls.

When we diligently search for the cause of all this degeneracy, we find it in the insufficiency of the preparatory training for the duty and function of the advocate. We find its cause, like the cause of almost every social evil, in ignorance. An ignorance with which the practitioner of forty years' standing, and with an income of fifty thousand per year, is equally chargeable with the veriest tyro who, with his Columbia College Law-school diploma in hand, stands ready for admission—an ignorance which is the common property of the "learned judge" upon the bench, and "my learned brother" at the bar.

Education for the profession of the law, in any true sense of the word, that is to say, the cultivation of the faculties, so as to enable the aspirant to forensic honors to understand the principle underlying any given case; the logical training of the mind, so as to enable the student to grasp an idea and follow it to its ultimate conclusion; the cultivation of his moral faculties, so as to enable him to draw closely the line between right and wrong; and a knowledge of the organization of society, are neither aimed at nor thought to be necessary. In saying that a legal education, in any true sense of the words, is non-existent, we assure our reader that we do not even forget that there are colleges in our midst, where students matriculate with the titles of LL.B. But we have little respect for parchment titles, and we shall justify our disrespect by incontrovertible evidence of the contemptible character of our system of legal culture.

We have two law schools in our own city—the law school of the University of the City of New York, and the law school of Columbia College.

The faculty of the former is composed, nominally, of four professors; of whom three do nothing, or almost nothing—the whole of the labor devolving upon Professor Pomeroy, the "Dean of the Faculty." And this gentleman, within two academic years, is expected, in the pretentious language of the prospectus of the institution, "to give a *thorough and complete* training in legal science to gentlemen intending to enter the bar of any State." The other institution, which is also designed, as its prospectus unblushingly declares, "to afford a complete course 'of legal education' for gentlemen intended for the bar in any of the United States," has a faculty of five professors, whose respective duties we shall briefly state. Charles King, LL.D., the president of the college, performs his task toward affording "a complete course of legal education," &c., by being the president of the college. Theodore M. Dwight, LL.D., professor of municipal law, like Professor Pomeroy at the University, is the working man of the "college." He delivers one lecture per day, Saturdays excepted, to each class, of which there are four or six, thus making an average of between seven to eight hours' labor per day, of which time each student, however, receives but one hour and a half. A large amount of labor for the professor, but a small amount of instruction for each student. Francis Lieber, LL.D., professor of political science, condescends to deliver about twenty lectures per year to all the classes. Charles Murray Nairne, M.A., professor of the ethics of jurisprudence, exhausts his branch of jurisprudence, or himself, by delivering from two to four lectures each year. John Ordronaux, LL.B., M.D., professor of medical jurisprudence, delivers about twenty lectures per year. In two academic years from the time of entering college, each academic year lasting about seven months, the student, after having his powers of endurance taxed by an average of two hours of instruction per day, is graduated as a bachelor of laws, upon the strength of which he is admitted, without examination, to practise as an attorney and counsellor in all the courts of the State of New York. Out upon such shams! "Colleges" such as these do not even give the shadow of a proper legal education.

Without at all deprecating the labors of the professors of these colleges—or rather the single professors, because, as before stated, the bulk of the labor at Columbia is performed by Professor Dwight, and at the University by Professor Pomeroy, both of whom we sincerely believe to be conscientious men, determined and willing to perform their duties as far as they understand them, and no one can do more—we claim that the education above detailed is no education at all. That its only result is to tax the memory with a few so-called principles of law. Principles, forsooth! We cannot recall to mind any of these "principles" which are paraded as such in the law books, that would not provoke a smile of contempt from any logically trained mind.

But in the majority of instances the practitioner has not even had the advantage that such a system affords. He enters a law office, begins his career with copying papers, eventually is raised to the dignity of drawing pleadings, reads Blackstone's Commentaries, Kent's Commentaries, studies some of the provisions of the Revised Statutes, and the Code, and if possessed of a good memory, this preparatory education is more than sufficient for the applicant to pass a triumphant examination before examiners who have passed through the same routine to fit themselves for the bar.

Medical education, bad and insufficient as it is in our medical colleges, is, at all events, based upon a knowledge of what is to be acquired in the way of information by one who is to devote himself to the curing of disease. They have chairs on anatomy, physiology, pathology, chemistry, therapeutics, materia medica, and surgery, without mentioning the specialties, such as instructors for the diseases of the eye, ear, respiratory organs, genital organs, etc. The truth is felt and practised on in the medical profession, that the education of the physician would be incomplete, vicious, and totally false, if it were confined to materia medica, therapeutics, and surgery. In other words, that success in a knowledge of materia medica is impossible without a knowledge of chemistry and physiology; that surgery is butchery without a knowledge of anatomy. And a medical education in any university or college aims not only at giving the student a proficiency in the arts by means of which he is to gain a livelihood, but also inculcates a knowledge of the sciences upon which these arts are based. But it may be urged that there are no such sciences upon which the law is based. That is not true. Sir James Mackintosh has said that constitutions grow, but are not made. That remark means, if it means anything at all, that law has that intimate interconnection with the growth and development of society that it must keep pace with the development of every other department of human activity. Therefore, he who wishes to know the reason of the law, which Lord Coke calls the life of the law, must understand the laws of nature by virtue of which society is that wonderfully complex but simple, heterogeneous yet harmonious whole that it is. What chemistry is to materia medica, history and comparative statistics are to legislation. What anatomy and physiology are to the art of surgery, political economy and social science are to jurisprudence. What pathology is to medicine, psychology and a knowledge of the causes of crimes are to criminal law. And, precisely as any well-educated physician would call any one a quack who would presume to make the diagnosis of and prescribe for a disease without having been grounded in the sciences before detailed, so, in our estimate, every one who is ignorant of the sciences which we claim to be necessary for the education of the lawyer, may justly be called a pettifogger.

Do we require proof of the inadequacy of education to fit the members of the bar for their duties, and the consequent vicious empiricism practised by them? We have it all around us. In the work cited at the head of our article, the author seriously recommends as a system of Education for the lawyer the course of legal study indicated below,* and which is copied from his book.

---

* Course of Legal Study.

"*Non multa sed multum,*" is the cardinal maxim by which the student of law should be governed in his readings; at the commencement of his studies—in the office of his legal preceptor, Repetition—Repetition. Blackstone and Kent should be read—and read again and again. These elementary works, with some others of an immediately practical cast—Todd's Practice, Stephen's Pleading, Greenleaf's Evidence, Leigh's Nisi Prius, Mittford's Equity Pleading, well conned, make up the best part of office reading. Of course, the acts of Assembly should be gone over again and again. I do not say that this is all. The plan of reading which I am about to recommend may be begun in the office. Much will depend upon what may be termed the mental temperament of the student himself, which no one but the immediate preceptor can observe; and he will be governed accordingly in the selection of works to be placed in his hands. No lawyer does his duty, who does not frequently examine his student, not merely as a necessary means of exciting him to attention and application, but in order to acquire such an acquaintance with the character of his pupil's mind—its quickness or slowness—its concentrativeness or discursiveness—as to be able to form a judgment whether he requires the curb or spur. It is an inestimable advantage to a young man to have a judicious and experienced friend, watching anxiously his progress, and able to direct him, when, if left to himself, he must wander in darkness and danger. "There be two things," says Lord Coke, "to be avoided by him as enemies to learning, *præpostera lectio* and *præpropera praxis.*" Co. Litt. 7 Ob.

I prefer presenting a certain order of subjects to be pursued; observing, however, that it may be somewhat irksome to pursue any one branch for too long a period, unvaried. When that is found to be the case, the last five heads may be adopted as collateral studies, and pursued simultaneously with the first three.

These heads or branches are—1. Real Estate and Equity. 2. Practice, pleading, and Evidence. 3. Crime and Forfeitures. 4. Natural and International law. 5. Constitutional law. 6. Civil law. 7. Persons and personal property. 8. The law of Executors and Administrators.

I. Real Estate and Equity.

The following works are recommended for perusal: Lord Hale's History of the Common Law. Reeve's History of the English Law. Dalrymple's Essay towards a general history of Feudal property in Great Britain. Sullivan's Lectures on Feudal law. Sir Martin Wright's introduction to the Law of Tenures. Craig de Feudis. Robertson's History of Charles the V. Hallam's History of the Middle Ages. Sir Henry Finche's Law, or Nomotechnia. Doctor and Student, by St. Germain. Prefaces to the several volumes of Lord Coke's Reports. Littleton's Tenures. The First Institute, or Lord Coke's Commentary on Littleton's Tenures. Preston's Elementary Treatise on Estates. Fearne's Essay on the Learning of Contingent Remainders. Sheppard's Touchstone of Common Assurances. Preston on Abstracts of Titles. Preston's Treatise on Conveyancing. Treatise on Equity, by Henry Ballow. Jeremy's Treatise on Equity, and Story's Commentaries on Equity Jurisprudence. Powell on Mortgages, with Coventry's notes. Bacon's Reading upon the Statute of Uses. Sanders on Uses and Trusts. Hill on Trustees. Lewis on Perpetuities. Sugden on Powers. Chance's Treatise on Powers. Sugden on Vendors and Purchasers. Bacon's Abridgment on Leases. Woodfall on Landlord and Tenant. Roscoe's Treatise on the Law of Actions relating to Real Property. Cruise on Fines and Recoveries. Powell's Essay on the learning of Devisees. Jarmin on Wills. Reports by Plowden, Hobart, and Vernon. Johnson's Chancery Reports. Smith's Leading Cases. Binney's Reports.

What else, we ask, than empiricism can a system be called which requires such cramming as this. Truly, any one who is tortured by obedience to the directions of Judge Sharswood, may be said to be in the position of Rabelais' Prince Gargantua, who, having been placed under the tuition of an old pedant, and being compelled to study the hobgoblin discussions of the early scholastiques from morning till night, soon gave

---

II. Practice, Pleading, and Evidence.

Sellon's Practice. Fourth Part of the Institutes of Lord Coke. Tidd's Practice. Stephen on Pleading. Saunder's Reports, with notes by Williams. Broom's Parties to Actions. Greenleaf on Evidence. Selwyn's Nisi Prius. Leigh's Nisi Prius. Mitford's Pleading in Equity. Story's Equity Pleading. Barton's Historical Treatise of a Suit in Equity. Newland's Chancery Practice. Gresley on Evidence in Equity.

III. Crimes and Forfeitures.

Hale's History of the Pleas of the Crown. Foster's Crown Law. Yorke's Consideration on the law of forfeiture for High Treason. The third part of the Institutes of Lord Coke. Russell on Crimes and Misdemeanors. Chitty on Criminal Law.

IV. Natural and International Law.

Burlamaqui's Natural and Political Laws. Grotius de Jure Belli et Pacis. Rutherford's Institutes. Vattel's Law of Nations. Bynkershoek's Questiones Publici Juris. Wicquefort's Ambassador. Bynkershoek de Foro Legatorum. McIntosh's Discourse on the Study of the law of Nature and Nations. Wheaton's History of International Law. Wheaton's International Law. Robinson's Admiralty Reports. Cases in the Supreme Court of the United States.

V. Constitutional Law.

The Second Part of Lord Coke's Institutes. Hallam's Constitutional History of England. Wynne's Eunomus. De Lolme on the English Constitution, with Stephen's introduction and notes. The Federalist. Rawle on the Constitution. All the cases decided in the Supreme Court of the United States, on Constitutional questions, to be read methodically, as far as possible.

VI. Civil Law.

Butler's Horæ Juridicæ. Gibbon's History of the Decline and Fall, chapter 44. Justinian's Institutes. Savigny's Traité de Droit Romain. Savigny's Histoire du Droit Romain au Moyen Age. Taylor's Elements of the Civil Law. MacKeldy's Compendium. Colquhoun's Summary of the Roman Civil Law. Domat's Civil Law.

VII. Persons and Personal Property.

Reeves on the Domestic Relations. Bingham's Law of Infancy and Coverture. Roper on Husband and Wife. Angel and Ames on Corporations. Les Œuvres de Pothier. Smith on Contracts. Story on Bailments. Jones on Bailments. Story on Partnership. Byles on Bills. Story on Promissory Notes. Abbot on Shipping. Duer on Insurance. Emerigon, Traité des Assurances. Boulay-Paty Com. de Droit Commercial. Story on the Conflict of Laws.

VIII. Executors and Administrators.

Roper on Legacies. Toller on Executors, and The Law's Disposal, by Lovelass.

unmistakable evidence that the harder he studied, and the more sedulously he worked, the more stupid he became.

> "Mir wird von alle dem so dumm,
> Als ging mir ein Mühlrad im Kopf herum."

"What," will indignantly exclaim some lawyers—if perchance they should read this review—"have we not advanced the law in our State, by means of codification?"

We assure our readers that we do not forget that we have in our State attempted, yes, and succeeded after a fashion, the codification of the laws. And that lawyers of reputation and standing were charged with this codification. But what have they done? Have they *renovated* the law? Have they laid down broad general principles to which almost every conceivable case may be referred, and the logical deductions from which must be accepted by every well-balanced mind as conclusive, and authoritative? Have these commissioners removed the incongruities of the law, or recommended the practical application of the well-known principles of political economy? Did they recommend free trade in money, and a repeal of the usury laws? Did they recommend an application of the principles of free trade in banking, and cause the abolition of our banking laws? No. Nothing of the kind. They have combined the separated particles of absurdities, scattered throughout our law and statute books, into one combined system; but in so far as any evidence of true juridical science is concerned, they have done nothing, absolutely nothing. Codification is useful, very useful, if by means of codification we make law less complex and more certain. It serves no other end than to give employment to some few lawyers, if it does not answer that purpose. That in our State, at least, codification has not resulted in greater certainty of the law, every lawyer who has practised under the system of the common law and subsequently under the revised statutes and code, can bear witness. Rulings are as conflicting as theretofore, technicalities abound, a decision upon the substantial merits of a cause is as difficult to arrive at as under the common law; and law, as a science, has not advanced at all. Nay, worse, our system of codification, when completed, will not only not exercise a beneficial influence upon the student of the law, but a positively pernicious one. Under the common law —the *lex non scripta*—the student was compelled to refer each decided case to some broader generalization, to which, we contend, the name of principle was given by an abuse of language; yet this generalization was a step nearer to a principle in its logical signification, than the rule laid down in any special case. Thus the student's mind experienced some enlargement, and habits of thought were formed which may have led an original thinker to wider and wider generalizations; but under a code which, as Kossuth expressed it, is "a cast-iron system," no such habits of mind are formed at all. To become learned in the law, the student is simply to tax his memory, and when this absorbing, in opposition to the reasoning, process has continued a sufficiently long time, when this walking pneumotechnic machine has been sufficiently well filled, it is a lawyer. Truly, under such a code it is easily possible to conceive of a sufficiently well constructed mechanical instrument to perform every function of the lawyer.

We trust that we are not misunderstood; we do not favor the old common law system with its manifold technicalities, such as fines, common recoveries, entails, mortmain, &c. What we ask is, that when a code is framed in the year 1865, for the government of the people of the State of New York, it should be framed at least in accordance with the enlightened spirit of the day. "Time there was, when the brains were out the"—measures—"would die"; but to such times our own decade can certainly not be reckoned. Over a half a century ago Jeremy Bentham, in his admirable "Defence of Usury," has beaten the brains out of the usury laws, nay, he cracked their skulls, and showed that they had no brains, but notwithstanding this complete demonstration of the fallacy of all restrictions upon free trade in money, and although there have been repeated revisions of the laws of New York of late years, the usury laws still disgrace our statute books. To demonstrate many other like instances of incongruity between the spirit of the age and our laws, would lead us too far from the object of our criticism. We therefore refrain; but at once apply the best test of the viciousness or benefit of any system of education; the fruits which it bears. Here our probe sinks into an abyss of corruption, and proves the existence of a disintegration so general and wide-spread that our heart sinks within us for fear that the patient is beyond remedial agency.

The past four years has been fruitful of illustrations of the low intellectual and moral status of the Bar of the United States.

Four years of civil war; four years within which have been crowded all the evil popular passions of a century of ordinary years, four years within which party feeling ran higher than ever before in the history of our country; four years of almost unbridled power and license on the part of the administration; four years within which the bar of the United States might have won for itself imperishable renown and glory, by forming the breastworks of the liberties of the people, but which alas! are years to which no lawyer can look back with feelings other than shame and humiliation.

From the outset of our civil war, the Legislative and Executive branches of our general government exercised many powers which in the opinion of a large class of the community were never delegated. Congress passed act after act, which raised doubts of their constitutionality, at the time of their passage. Had law been pursued, in our midst, as a science; had lawyers been scientists, they as a class should at all events have been almost unanimous upon the question of the constitutionality or unconstitutionality of any of these acts of Congress or exercise of executive powers. But alas! sad experience has taught us that upon almost every question of constitutional law, lawyers were as unsafe guides as laymen. That their, so called, principles of law led to as widely different conclusions, as Smith and Jones arrived at, in the discussion of the same question over a bottle of whiskey, in some bar room. The legal tender question may serve as an illustration of our charge against the American bar. The powers under which the legal tender act purported to have been enacted were clearly before us in the Constitution of the United States, and yet upon this very question, the bench and the bar were as divided as were their political opinions, and the conclusions arrived at by the courts upon the constitutionality of the act corresponded to the political complexion of its members.

If our lawyers had been educated in the principles of political economy, they never could have made the mistake that Judges Denio and Selden made, when they said that they regretted that they were compelled to decide against the constitutionality of the legal-tender law, *because they believed in its necessity and expediency.* Had they understood principles, in our sense of the word, they would have understood that a thing cannot be good in theory and bad in practice; they would have known that if a principle is correct its application must in the long run tend to produce beneficial effects, and that laws making governmental paper money a legal tender were vicious in principle. And those judges who prostituted the ermine by deciding the question from political motives or the supposed expediency of the measure would, if they had been properly educated lawyers, have known their duties sufficiently well to have been aware of the fact that as judges they were to decide a cause in accordance with the law, their province, and not upon the question of its expediency, the province of the legislator.

It may be urged in reply that partisanship ran so high; that in a time of public excitement and popular passion, our lawyers as well as the rest of the community were seized by the frenzy of the hour and their judgments were carried away with their prevailing passions. Here we answer that a legal education which is so superficial, which exercises the judgment so little, and gives it such unsafe moorings that its decision *upon a legal point* can be turned by any political breeze or gale, is no education at all, but a vicious empiricism no more reliable, upon any question higher than whether Hodge owes Snooks a thousand dollars or not, than the opinion of a pot-house politician or brawling demagogue.

Our own city suffers under a government of the worst description. We are most shamelessly plundered in spite of the law, through the forms of the law, and by means of the law. Our departments are heterogeneously organized, and irresponsible in their management. Powers of self-government which should be vested in the city, are exercised by the legislature.

The taxing power is used as a means to confiscate the property of A for the benefit of B, and not, as intended, as a payment to the State for positive benefits conferred. Yet while lawyers have felt these evils, know, or should know, their remedies, have they done anything to check them; have they as a body protested against their continuance, and have they tried to secure a reform by means of new constitutional provisions? They have not. The Constitution of the State of New York of 1846 expires, if the people so will it, in 1866; and by virtue of its own provisions a new constitutional convention, to frame another constitution for our State, can be convened in the latter year for that purpose and to that end. Such a convention might frame for us an instrument more stringent in its provisions and better tended to protect us from the encroachments of power than the one under which we now live. We all know the corrupting, blighting effects of special legislation. Why do not lawyers move in a body and insist that special legislation shall be put an end to by means of a constitutional provision to that effect? Lawyers know to what a pass the system of electing judges for a short term of years has brought us. Whether the admittedly low state of the bench is due to the elective system, or to the short term of years for which judges are elected, is not for us to determine here; at all events we do know that an evil exists, which should be remedied, and a constitutional convention is clearly the proper body to seek out the cause and to find the remedy of so crying an evil. In short, here again the bar of New York would have a magnificent opportunity for good, but, like other similar opportunities, it will be permitted to escape without a single effort being made to grasp it and use it for the benefit of our fellow citizens. The members of the legal profession are either so oblivious of their duty in the premises, or so immovable in all matters in which a large fee is not immediately in perspective, that unless some influential class outside of the profession moves and agitates the necessity for such a constitutional convention, no steps will be made to effect a reform.

If we would deem it necessary to offer still further proof to sustain our bill of indictment against the American bar, and the degeneracy of its members consequent upon the vicious system of legal education in our midst, we could cite other and equally forcible examples as those already adduced. Enough however, we believe, has been shown to awaken attention to this monstrous evil, an evil more dangerous to the welfare of our own country than a like state of affairs would be to the happiness of any other people. If in England lawyers were to degenerate, the bad consequences would be more confined to the comparatively narrow circle of the bench, bar and suitors; whereas with us the pestiferous influence of the degradation of the bar permeates every class of society, as our legislators, both State and national, are, in nine cases out of ten, lawyers.

The practical legislation of Great Britain would proceed pretty much in the same fashion as theretofore, because the lawyers are not the governors of that empire. The reins of government are in the hands of the landed aristocracy and gentry; and conservative and narrow-minded as those classes have frequently shown themselves to be, they are, nevertheless, composed of men of liberal educations, wide culture, and who by means of ample fortunes are placed above the temptation to practise the more contemptible vices of humanity. In France the governing class is semi-literary and semi-military, with a slight sprinkling of scions of old aristocratic families. The few lawyers whom we find in the French chamber, such as Berryer, Favre, Cremieux, are not merely lawyers, but have taken an active part in every public movement which has agitated France for thirty-odd years.

The governors of Germany are princes, assisted by diplomats and statesmen by profession—a thorough bureaucracy totally distinct from the bar. The bar, however, of Germany, is composed of a body of thoroughly learned men. To become aware of the intelletual activity of the German bar, one need but look at the catalogues of the Leipzig publishing houses of law books that they have newly published. We have but lately received from Germany two law-books of very considerable philosophic merit, logical accumen, and critical research. One entitled "Lehrbuch der Gerichtlichen Psychologie, von Dr. F. J. Julius Wilbrand (Text-book of Juridical Psychology, by Julius Wilbrand, LL.D.), the other written by the celebrated

Professor Mittermayer, of Heidelberg, one of the leading if not the leading jurist of Germany, entitled, "Über die Wirksamkeit der Schwurgerichte in Europa und Amerika, über ihre Vorzüge, Mängel, und Abhülfe. (The jury system in Europe and America, its advantages, evils, and their reform.) That works such as those cited should be written in Germany, and not written here, would in itself not prove any very great superiority of the German bar over that of our own country, as there are, at all events, some lawyers in our midst who can do equally well; but that law-books of so philosophical a character readily find publishers, and that a continuous stream of books of a like nature issues from the book-centres of Germany is a proof of a wide-spread and constant demand for them, and incontestably places the jurists of Germany above those of America.

Among civilized nations we, as a people, are certainly the readiest talkers and the most unphilosophical thinkers. And this principally arises from the fact that we have abnormally cultivated the "gift of the gab." Many of our readers will recollect the bitter but decidedly clever reply sent some time in the year 1855 by Horatio Hubbell, Esq., of the Philadelphia bar, to the Professors of Yale College, who desired a contribution of five dollars from him toward the building of a hall for the debating club of that institution. Mr. Hubbell says in his letter:

"Do you not know that, of all the besetting sins of this sinning nation, the most innate and original is this propensity for gab? that by it we have wasted more time, spent more money, and paralyzed more decision than can be rightly estimated? Instead of being encouraged, it should be repressed. Do you not know that, under the influence of this mania, tinkers, rowdies, and snobs throughout the land are rushing to the bar, the pulpit, the stage, and the halls of legislation? And that these windy sons of Eolus, under a supposed inspiration, are howling like midnight wolves from one end of the continent to the other, "*Clamor ibat ad cœlum!*" It is the fatal epidemic of republics. What distracted Greece? Gab! What fractionized Rome? Gab! What anarchized France? Gab! What will dismember this Union? Gab! This eternal propensity of gabbling, on all occasions, and at all times, is the curse of our country. Ask me to subscribe to support the dead languages—to raise a deaf and dumb institution—to build a Quaker meeting-house—to erect some monumental stone—in short, to do anything that implies or promotes silence, and my purse strings will in all probability be opened."

We are decidedly of opinion that the propensity for gabbling animadverted upon by Mr. H. is one of the incidental causes of the degeneracy of the bar. But properly educated men do not gabble, and the only way to get rid of this propensity to talk at all times and on all occasions is to teach people the value of ideas, and a proper respect for them. And that can only be done by a proper system of education.

The question, therefore, presents itself to us, at all events, with terrible earnestness, how to remedy an evil so wide-spread and general? An evil which, unlike the wrongs of the negro or of women, can find no class of philanthropists ready and willing to undertake its remedy, and inaugurate a reform.

After criticism such as we have indulged in, it is perhaps incumbent upon us to show something that might be a remedy, if the bar were ready to accept any medicine for its disease. It is an old and ever true adage that it is easier to criticise than to construct. Yes; but that is no reason why one who is fitted to criticise, but who may not be able to show the path to reform, should not indulge his vein, and exercise his faculties. We believe that we have benefited our fellow-citizens, and more especially the members of the bar, if we show to them that the road they are now pursuing leads to moral and intellectual degradation, as there is enough native power of intellect among our professional men to discover the true path when once convinced that they are in the wrong one. But we believe that a remedy can more readily be found than the nature of the evil would seem to warrant us in believing.

We do not even ask that the legislature be requested to interfere and pass a law that no man shall be admitted to the bar without an education sufficiently thorough, and a culture sufficiently wide, to insure his being both a gentleman and a scholar. We distrust legislative panaceas for social evils. Remedies such as those resemble in their action alteratives in medicine, and it frequently becomes difficult to determine whether the disease artificially called into existence to supplant the old one be not in reality more difficult to cure and more dangerous to the body politic than the one supplanted. A State educational programme would be well enough, provided legislators were up with their age, and mankind would remain *in statu quo;* but neither miracle has ever yet happened.

Except to remove such causes of the evils complained of as have been directly created by legislation, we deprecate all legislative interference. For we are firmly convinced that much of the demoralization of the profession is due to pernicious legislation. We believe, for instance, that the whole system of costs should be radically abolished; and we would thus, at one blow, get rid of all those hangers-on at the outskirts of the legal profession—the ragged fringes of a not very clean garment—who subsist solely by means of the costs—who, to use the parlance of lawyers, "practise for costs." A spontaneous and voluntary movement on the part of a few enlightened lawyers would be the only way to improve the profession. Let us organize a law college wherein the educational course shall be five academic years instead of two, and the faculty be composed of ten professors instead of one. The men who, for the first five years, would assume the position of professors, would have to work hard and without pay. Only a genuine devotion to the task and a thorough belief that they are performing a sacred duty to the profession and the public generally could sustain them in such a course. But is the goal to be reached not worth the effort? Is the elevation of the dignity, character, and learning of the bar, and the many collateral benefits which will flow therefrom not worth the gratuitous labors of ten men? Why ten? How find labor for all of them? The necessity for ten professors is readily discernible upon a division of the subjects which should be daily taught in such a college. The studies might embrace the following subjects, and be divided as follows: 1st Chair, Social Science and Political Economy; 2d Chair, Philosophy of History and Comparative Statistics; 3d Chair, Logic, Rhetoric and Elocution; 4th Chair, Juridical Psychology and Moral Philosophy; 5th Chair, Medical Jurisprudence; 6th Chair, Comparative Law, Conflict of Laws, and International Law; 7th Chair, Constitutional and Federal Law (and if thought advisable, an introduction into the *corpus juris civilis;*) 8th Chair, Common and Statute Law—Municipal Law; 9th Chair, Practice and Pleading; 10th Chair, Evidence.

As the system here recommended differs materially from any pursued in any university whatever, it is perhaps incumbent upon us to show why it is that social science, political economy, logic, etc., should be taught in a law-school. To those ignorant of a science, it is impossible to make clear its importance. Therefore such of our fellow-citizens who imagine political economy to be a series of abstruse speculations upon the best means of getting the largest amount of benefit for the smallest return in services, or, how to gain advantages over our neighbors, will not see the propriety of such studies in any college for the education of youth. But those who know what gigantic strides have been made of late years by political economy and social science, who know what these sciences teach, will comprehend how important it is for every one to understand the true relations of capital and labor, to understand the true distinction between monopoly and freedom, and such will perceive that the education of a lawyer is of necessity incomplete and vicious, if he rest ignorant of those fundamental principles of political economy which, were he cognizant of them, might enable him to trace the consequences of laws, and to perceive their beneficial or deleterious social influences. By reason of the teachings of these sciences and the lessons to be derived from the philosophy of history every student, graduated at such a college, would be more or less of a legal reformer. He would understand the law not only as it is, but as it should be; and would, at all events, comprehend the direction that reformatory measures should take, and the end to be had in view in constitutional, legislative and legal reforms so as to promote the object of all human effort—human happiness.

It would not only be an act of supererogation, but a direct insult to the understanding of our readers to undertake at this late day to show the advantages of a thorough training in logic, rhetoric and elocution. The disease of gabbling would not rage so fearfully in our midst if those studies were more thoroughly appreciated and pursued.

We are not so sanguine as to believe that the mere existence of a college offering thorough instruction in those branches of human knowledge which we deem essential to the proper education of a lawyer, will at once effect the desired reform. The reform will be gradual and hardly appreciable during the first five or ten years. The reform would make itself felt only after the superiority of the graduates of such a college over their brethren at the bar will become so manifest, that the latter, by means of that ever-active law of competition, would be soon thrown out of employment, and stricken from the roll of attorneys by want of something to do. The law of competition is an invisible but all-powerful legislator who places every man in his proper position, and removes him from an improper one. Society's notice to quit must be obeyed or suffering will follow. The impetus once given for the supply of a superior commodity or a superior service, and the inferior commodity and inferior service will in the long run find no market. It is this natural law of competition that we desire to set at work, and we may rest assured that in course of time it will accomplish the desired reform, far better than any human legislation could possibly do.

One of the immediately beneficial effects which would be produced by the inauguration of the reform herein urged, is the restoration to the profession of that *ésprit de corps* which it now so much lacks. It would give rise to that feeling of fellowship and mutual courtesy, which can only exist among scientists, never among tradesmen. Lawyers would feel that they have a mission to perform higher than the mere conducting of a controversy between Jones and Smith. They would feel that, by virtue of their education and position it is their duty and their right to be foremost in every reformatory social movement, as they are the exponents of a circle of sciences which in their practical application are of the utmost possible importance to humanity, and not, as now, the mere followers of a business, in which a more or less respectabe living can be earned.

As every cause produces more than one effect, and as the collateral advantage of every beneficial action are generally even more fruitful of blessings than the direct ones, it is difficult to foretell how great a progress in the social scale we should make by reforming the bench and bar of the city of New York alone, and thus by force of exmple effect a reform in the character of the bench and bar in the whole of the United States. S. S.

NEGRO SUFFRAGE.

It appears unfortunate that social progress should manifest itself unevenly—that the order of development should not be uniform—that ages, which have been distinguished for their philosophical acuteness, should also be distinguished for their general barbarism—that Socrates should have lived in the days of human sacrifices, and Galileo surrounded by the creatures of the Inquisition. While on the one hand we perceive the highest advancement—on the other we recognize the lowest order of fetichism. The most opposite forms of progress live cheek by jole. Thus, much that is good would appear to run the risk of perishing for want of appreciation, and much that is bad retains its hold on humanity for want of that general enlightenment which would lead to its detection and exposure. But this is only a superficial view of the case. Let us look closer, and we shall find that the good is never wholly lost, but springs up again in some neglected spot, like seeds which are dissipated by the wind, and carried to remote localities, there to germinate and blossom. And the bad, though it flourishes for a time, it is better that it should so flourish, because if it is eradicated before the time when ordinary intelligence will condemn it on sight, its resurrection and future permanent existence may surely be looked for.

It is deemed a sort of telescopic philanthropy which seeks to ameliorate the condition of the blacks, while so many wrongs remain unalleviated at home. Against this it will be said that whatever good is done, no matter in what direction, is never lost. The march of progress is in the direction of the least resistance, and though this direction may not appear at the time to be the most profitable, yet in the end it will undoubtedly prove to be so. It is nearer round than over an obstacle. When the blacks shall have been freed, then the wrongs of women and the needs of those nearer to home will have to be redressed for very shame. In freeing the blacks, therefore, we indirectly contribute to free woman, etc. There is great strength in this argument; and if the advance so made could be deemed certain, the inference could scarcely be doubted. But who doubts that the advance is irrevocable. Even if the negroes, who, having taken no part in their own enfranchisement, should recede into barbarism under some coolie system, it can scarcely be apprehended that slavery will ever again be established in this part of the world. Then, so far as the whites are concerned, the advance from slavery to freedom, is a fixed fact, and we may now turn our attention to home affairs.

Turn we then to home, and let us see what chance there is of success. Alas! none. The public mind is still engrossed with the negro. Having freed him, the next step is to give him the right to vote. This has been done already in Connecticut, Minnesota, and some other States, and is now proposed to be done as a national measure for all the States.

As a national measure we oppose it—oppose it at once and emphatically—first, because all human enactments having an extended jurisdiction, are injurious; sitting too lightly, as they are sure to do, on the shoulders of some, and too heavily on those of others; and next, because under the Constitution, the Federal Government has no right to settle the status of electors.*

In this determination we are gratified to find ourselves supporting the policy which the President has already publicly announced.

Only as a measure for the action of the individual States, therefore, do we mean to discuss this question; and as such a measure we heartily approve it. Our approval is based upon the following grounds:

1. It is the inalienable right of *every* human creature to be FREE.

2. Negroes are human creatures, and negroes are therefore entitled to be free.

3. The right to freedom involves the right to vote.

---

* Says the Constitution, art. I. sec. 2: "The House of Representatives shall be composed of members chosen every second year by the people of the several States; and the electors *in each State shall have the qualifications requisite for electors of the most numerous branch of the State Legislature.*"

4. Negroes are therefore entitled to vote.

So much for principle; now for expediency; for although THE SOCIAL SCIENCE REVIEW never bases its views upon reasons of expediency alone, yet when both expediency and principle are shown to point the same way, there would seem to be no good reason against using as an illustration of the correctness of a principle, all those arguments which flow from the expediency view.

In most of the Northern States, and some of the Southern, free negroes have now, and for years past have had, the right to vote, when seized of a certain amount of real property. Any objection to allowing negroes to vote which is based on distinction of color is therefore invalid: for it would be manifestly absurd to contend that: 1. A black man should not have the right to vote because he is black; 2. The possession of property does not alter the black man's color; 3. But the possession of property should give the black man a right to vote!

What is the objection then? Is it the fear that men so lately liberated from a state of bondage will be unable to appreciate the great boon which the franchise confers, and will so use it unwisely; or is it because they do not ask it themselves, but it is sought to be conferred upon them by a political party?

Let us examine these points. It will hardly be denied that far beneath the rudest forms of barbarism which we import in emigrant ships, stands the Southern negro. To every one of these negroes who possess an ordinary amount of intelligence there are hundreds and thousands of grovelling slaves, rude buffoons, mere laughing stocks of humanity, but a single remove in point of intellect from the aboriginal gorilla, from whence, according to the philosophers of the Development Theory, all mankind have, some time or other, descended. But so far as the exercise of the franchise is concerned, they are no further removed from that degree of intelligence, the possession of which causes it to be accorded by all the world as a right without question, than are many of the Russian serfs and Polish Jews and Italian lazzaroni and Zingaras and Paddywhacks, to whom the franchise is now open; because many among all these classes know nothing whatever about theories of government, nay, not even the rights of property itself, but like the downtrodden field-hands of the South, are brutal, vindictive, cunning, revengeful, and ungrateful—possessing all the bad attributes of the lower animals and but one of their good ones—that last least glimmering spark of good, that attribute of humanity, so low that even the brute creation shares it with them—the love of offspring.

But what measure is so powerful to eradicate ignorance and implant knowledge as the elective franchise! What lever so tremendous to lift up poor, ignorant, brutalized humanity, from the depth to which prejudice and caste and tyranny has reduced it! Let experience answer.

Over and over again have the champions of suffrage reform in England triumphantly demonstrated that no educational influence is so strong as that of the elective franchise. It is the only school which all men have time to attend to; because it is a school which they can carry with them into their fields and workshops; it sets them to thinking, and mental activity is the means whereby they are turned into useful and valuable members of society. Besides this, to deprive the uneducated of the right of suffrage simply because they are uneducated, not only divests the educated of any further interest in their welfare, but creates a radical antagonism between the two classes, which it is desirable to avoid: and to confer upon the uneducated this great privilege compels the educated, for their own safety and prosperity, to look after their poorer brethren, and to see to their advancement. It is true that suffrage without an educational qualification tends to pull the educated down to the level of the uneducated—in other words, impedes the further intellectual advancement of the latter class; but it is equally true that it tends to raise the masses to the level of the educated—in other words, to assist their intellectual advancement. And as it is the welfare of the greater number, which in this instance it is desirable to seek, because the welfare of the lesser number, the latter may, without injustice, be left to secure for themselves; it follows that, as a means of well-being and advantage to the vast majority of a nation, universal suffrage may be regarded the most potent of all, because it constantly educates and trains a people to the discharge of their duties as citizens and their functions as rulers.

Above all, what measure, in this instance, so just, when viewed in the light of moral compensation! When we reflect that these men and their forefathers have been condemned to slavery through our own ignorance and brutality, what form of indemnity for these wrongs would be so complete as to lift them up to the level of our own political privileges, even if in doing so we suffered the consequences of *their* ignorance and brutality?

But we are not of the opinion that any more evil effects will flow from the admission of negroes to the franchise than have resulted from the admission of immigrant whites to that privilege. A similar term of probation will undoubtedly secure the same degree, or nearly the same degree, of benefit; and if good has resulted, and no man will endeavor to deny that good *has* resulted from the extension of the suffrage in this country to all white men, regardless of origin or extraction, regardless of mental or physical qualifications, then good must result by extending the same privilege to the blacks. Out of four millions of irresponsible, lazy creatures will be made four millions of responsible, and therefore industrious creatures. Out of four millions of discontented, turbulent people, will be made four millions of contented and law-abiding citizens. Out of four millions of oppressed men and women, who will some day or other violently burst the bonds which restrain them, and which bonds may now, in this moment of kindness, be quietly removed, will be made four millions of grateful and willing citizens.

Only,—let this great act be consummated by the Southern people themselves. Let not the black man's gratitude be reserved for a party of men which, beyond a few individuals among it, has been working, not from principle, but from interest, not for the good of the country, but for party power. The negro loves his native home and its surroundings too well to carry his gratitute to any distant market. And when, amid the toil and trouble and vexations of life, he compares the difficult path of independence with the easy, irresponsible condition of slavery, to whom will he look with respect and gratitude so readily as to those who, in his days of bondage, nursed him when he was sick, fed his aged parents long after they were able to work, and brought up his piccanninies to manhood. He will learn what his masters should have learned long ago—that slavery does not pay—and that a slaveholder is actually a practical philanthropist, though a wofully mistaken one. This philanthropy he will repay.

As a question of expediency, therefore, we think that negro suffrage will prove of great and immediate benefit to such of the Southern States as may choose to adopt the measure.

One thing is certain: if the negroes are desirable inhabitants, the Southern States will not fail to bid high enough to persuade them to remain within their borders, and as they must bid against the radicals, who on this question now have the ascendancy at the North, their bids will doubtless be high enough for the purpose. If they are not desirable inhabitants, the Southern States will allow themselves to be outbid; and the negroes will, in course of time, all remove to the North.

This arrangement, however it may fall out, cannot fail to be a happy one: the negroes will settle where they are most appreciated, and those who most appreciate them will enjoy their companionship.

And this consideration is one of the best arguments in favor of having this question determined by local authority: not by national. Local acts, like silk garments, fit the figure with ease and precision—national acts, like suits of armor, fit nobody, and are always irksome to the wearer.

But we go still farther than the advocacy of conferring the right of suffrage upon the blacks.

We contend that the right of representation should go with the right to vote. We base this view upon three grounds.

1st. Principle. The right of representation follows as a logical sequence to the right to vote. Therefore, if the first is right, and we have already shown that it *is* right, the second is right; and if it is right, it should be practised.

2d. Justice. Were the suffrage made universal to all men, that great reform which has so cruelly been deferred until it would appear to have passed away from men's minds forever, that reform, for the accomplishment of which we would personally have willingly sacrificed all the darkies in Christendom, and considered the loss a cheap one; that reform, the studied retardation of which makes our manhood blush for itself—THE ENFRANCHISEMENT OF WOMAN—will immediately press itself upon the attention of the people of these States, and demand practical recognition.*

3d. Expediency. There would seem to be ground for believing that the momentum which progress has acquired in the direction of negro equality will not abate until all opposition to it has ceased. The Southerns evinced their wisdom by ceasing to oppose our armies when they saw that opposition was hopeless. Let them again show their wisdom by ceasing to oppose negro agitation. Let it run its course. Let them not give any political party this only remaining peg on which to hang its hopes of ascendancy. Let niggerism be "run into the ground," and let the next reform be one which, like that of Woman's Rights, they can themselves originate. By this means they will not only cheat Mr. Chase of the Presidency, but elect a President of their own. The race for supremacy should in the future ever be toward further reforms.

Let but this sort of rivalry exist, and men need no longer fear for the perpetuity of free institutions from sectional agitation.

But if even this view should prove unfounded—if the momentum which progress has acquired in the direction of negro equality, instead of being yet in full vigor, should even now be undergoing retardation—still, we think, as a measure of expediency, that the South can do no better than to keep

* I know that it will be said: Woman herself does not ask for the right of suffrage. She knows that her sphere of action does not include attendance at the polls, and she does not even ask for the privilege. Neither did the Southern negroes ask for liberty. Why? Because they did not know the value of it. So with woman.

If you give her the right to vote, she will, in all probability, never exercise it; but in possessing that right she will possess many others, which she *will* exercise, and will exercise for good. But I am not now discussing the question of Woman's Rights. I am satisfied to believe that woman is not indifferent to her own elevation and advancement, when I know, that two thousand years ago, she stole disguised in the dresses of men to listen surreptitiously to the divine words of Plato in his garden at Athens.

up the momentum, and carry the movement forward until it is fully accomplished.

First, let us examine the grounds for believing that the movement is undergoing retardation.

It cannot be doubted that such men as Wendell Phillips, Gerrit Smith, Charles Sumner, Horace Greeley, and other equally renowned philanthropists, desire that this movement should go forward to completion; but there are not wanting indications which would seem to show that politicians generally and the vast rank and file who follow where politicians lead, because they expect to be politicians one day themselves—that these men do not wish to see negro representation become a law. They want the negro votes for themselves. They would be slow to place themselves in competition with some popular Pompey or ambitious Cæsar from the Everglades, or to run on a split ticket with some war democrat of the African type who rejoiced in the appellation of Hannibal Lincoln or Napoleon Grant Gingerbones. No. Having gained two millions of votes, and filled up to the brim the bitter cup of mortification and insult which they intend that this measure shall prove, and which to some extent it would prove if carried out as they now demand it shall—namely, as a national measure—having done this, these abolitionists of expediency would stop short and deprecate any further agitation of the question. They would paint a negro representative in congress, elected from some band of Obi worshippers in South Carolina, who but yesterday was the vilest of slaves. They would put rings through his nose, and clothe him in his Ashantee dress of reeds, naked to the waist, with a log drum in one hand and a fetich in the other. Blood, feathers, parrot beaks, dogs' and alligators' teeth, broken bottles, grave mould, egg shells, cats' claws, snakes' skulls, and all the elements of plantation barbarism would be dragged in to give the background to this picture. "Shall this man," they will then triumphantly ask, "shall this man become a representative in the congress of the United States?" meaning this, of course, as a mere preliminary to the exordium: "Oh, take me in his place!"

But reason teaches us that there is no more chance of this man being elected to congress than there is of the election to that office of some scab-covered mendicant of the Levant, to whom the liberality of our laws has extended the right of citizenship. If any negro is ever elected to congress, an event which we very much doubt will ever happen, that negro will be a man whom no white man will be ashamed to engage in political debate.

We therefore approve the principle of conferring the suffrage upon negroes, and trust the subject will engage the attention of the legislatures of the various States as soon as they are in session, so that it may go into effect as a State measure, and not in the way certain political partizans would wish—as a national measure.

The object of these men is not the welfare of the negro, but their own elevation. Their purposes are sufficiently manifested in the following authoritative programme of their policy:

"Let the States be kept under military supervision until their loyalty can be safely trusted with civil government. Meanwhile, let the military authority in each State take a census of all loyal citizens—without distinction of color, and including both old residents and new settlers—and at a proper time let these loyal citizens, and none others, but all these, represent themselves in a State convention, enact a free and equal constitution, and so restore the State to its true dignity in the Republic." *

It is power, power, power—the old craving, that actuates them. Let the Southern States hasten to act in accordance with principle, let them practise that which justice demands, let them heed the voice of wise expediency, and they will forever block this new game for Federal centralization. To do all this, it is only necessary to erase the word "white" from their statute qualifications for electors and representatives.

EMILE WALTER.

---

* From the *New York Independent*, which journal presented the above as the programme of the Chase party. *The Nation*, a new party organ of the same stripe, also advocates the same policy.

SPECIALTIES IN MEDICINE AND THEIR RELATIONS TO QUACKERY.*

"Ever since society existed, Disappointment has been preaching, 'Put not your trust in Legislation,' and yet the trust in legislation seems scarcely diminished," and "in their efforts to remedy specific evils, legislators have continually caused collateral evils they never looked for."

The text of our remarks, shall be these two sentences, taken from Herbert Spencer's Essay on Over-Legislation.

Previous to the adoption of the Code of Ethics of the American Medical Association, the sense of professional duties and responsibility was, there can be no doubt, as keen among professional men as to-day. We do not think that there was a physician, who, being at the same time a gentleman, needed the recommendations contained in the first chapter of that code to be written out for him in the shape of paragraphs, seriously telling him, "that he ought to unite tenderness with firmness, and condescension with authority;" "that he shall treat his cases with attention, steadiness and humanity;" "that he shall observe secrecy and delicacy;" "not make too many visits;" "not make gloomy prognostications;" "not abandon hopeless cases;" and a host of other advices which are perhaps well meant but cannot be regarded but as absolutely unnecessary and useless.

Whoever is fit to be a physician must certainly know from the intuitive knowledge of propriety which a gentleman pos-

* This article formed in substance a report made by the author at the annual meeting of the American Medical Association, held June 7th, 1865, at the city of Boston. The report was not favorably received, but as it presents a correct application of the principles of free trade, to questions of professional ethics and legislation, we have prevailed upon the author to permit us to publish his very able paper. We have seen proper to preserve throughout the article, the second person, as the arguments are mainly addressed to the members of the American Medical Association, though we trust they may prove of interest to the public at large.

Eds. S. S. Review.

sesses, how to behave himself at the bedside; and only gentlemen can be physicians deserving the name; the idea to inculcate propriety by a code of ethics, voluntarily adopted, to others than gentlemen, is preposterous. Was it ever supposed necessary by the respectable women in the community, to fortify their respectability by publishing a code of ethics and demanding conformity thereto on the part of their virtuous sisters so as not to be confounded with prostitutes? It strikes us as equally absurd that it should be necessary to embody for the government of physicians the common rules of gentlemanly propriety in a code of ethics so that they should not be confounded with quacks!

It might be, perhaps, profitable and timely to expose the puerility of embodying also an article of ten paragraphs on the duties of patients towards their physician, a proceeding about as ludicrous as if there was an Essay there on the "duties of Sandwich Islanders to the Crown of England;" but we refrain, as we are not appointed to criticise the laws of Ethics of the American Medical Association: nevertheless, we desire to show by these examples, and those which we cite hereafter, that from a practical and scientific point of view, that document does not require to be handled with the piety and esteem which some old books, though obsolete, are sometimes entitled to, either for their intrinsic merit, or for the care bestowed by the authors upon their production.

We only therefore allude to the bad taste of articles in which it is laid down as a rule, "that physicians ought to attend gratuitously to physicians, their wives and children;" attempting to define whether and to what extent vicarious offices should be rendered by one physician to another; the barbarous proposition to refuse consultations with physicians who are not recognized as "regular" by the "Association;" the unnecessary hints given in the chapter on Consultations to behave decently at the bedside, etc., etc., etc.

While satisfied that the American Medical Association will agree with us that all these attempts at legislation are superfluous and practically inoperative, and that we will not be gainsaid, if we utter our belief, that it is not in consequence of the adoption of these rules as a code of laws, if the good feeling and understanding between practitioners have improved since their publication, we now beg leave to enter upon the essential subject matter of our Essay, to which the whole of the second chapter has the most intimate relation, but particularly the third paragraph, which reads as follows :

" It is derogatory to the dignity of the profession to resort to public advertisements, or private cards, or hand-bills, inviting the attention of individuals affected with particular diseases ; publicly offering advice and medicine to the poor, gratis, or promising radical cures ; or to publish cures and operations in the daily prints or suffer such publication to be made ; to invite laymen to be present at operations ; to boast of cures and remedies, to adduce certificates of skill and success, or to perform any similar acts. These are the ordinary practices of empirics and are highly reprehensible in a regular physician."

It would be an insult, we think, to the common sense of this body to defend before it the right of a physician to pursue special studies. We trust there is no one among you sufficiently prejudiced or ill-informed not to know that the strides which our science has made of late years have been the consequence of some of the best minds in the profession concentrating their thoughts on one particular branch of medical science. We feel that to defend, in the year 1865, the principle of division of labor, would be considered by an enlightened profession to be a ridiculous act of supererogation. It strikes us as equally superfluous to defend the right of a well-educated physician to make use of the results of his special observations and practice ; in other words, the right and liberty to reap the fruits of a special study in a special branch cannot with a shadow of justice be denied to specialists.

Take from the specialist the right to use every honorable means in his power to extend his practice, and you practically do the same thing as if you would forbid a general practitioner to make his numerous calls in a carriage. Say to a specialist, you have no right to put your name in a newspaper, and in reference to him your law works quite differently, and produces different results, than the same interference produces upon the general practitioner. The latter more or less expects his practice from his immediate neighborhood ; he moves there where the majority of his patients reside, and every family he visits professionally yields to him a proportion towards his yearly average of income ; the specialist, on the contrary, in order to render himself useful to society, in order to advance his reputation and income, must spread his name in wider circles ; his reputation must extend over a larger surface : for a circle or community which would yield a splendid return for the services of a general practitioner would suffice neither properly to support a specialist, nor to secure a practice sufficiently large to stimulate his scientific energy.

To this position may be urged the objection that, the specialist necessarily being at the same time a physician of general attainments and knowledge in medicine other than his mere specialty, he may and should in the commencement of his career attend to general practice and gradually devote more and more special attention to some special class of diseases. This idea is radically vicious. For in the first place the cultivation of those branches of medical science which are sufficiently advanced to be practised as specialties, demands unremitting zeal and undivided attention on the part of those devoted to them, and faculties which would produce by their exercise splendid results would be dissipated in the routine and drudgery of general practice. Need we cite any examples to prove so plain a proposition ? Universal experience has taught us that, with man as with machinery, the more perfect his adaptibility for the successful performance of any special function, the less will he be enabled to perform any other. Well does Herbert Spencer say : " An instrument intended to perform the double function of shaving and carving will not shave as well as a razor nor carve as well as a carving knife."

In the second place, it is but fair and proper that specialists should leave the field of general practice to those whose intelligent aid they covet and desire for the purpose of securing a special practice.

It must not be inferred from this that we hold it necessary or even desirable that general practitioners should lend their support and patronage to specialists on condition only that the latter do not interfere with their general practice. We would deprecate any such bargain as undignified and improper. We would not admit that specialists should offer any such petty inducements for patronage on the part of physicians in general practice; but we may safely assert that specialists will not find it to their interest to undertake general practice, and they certainly must always feel that their limited experience does not justify them in attempting to practise indiscriminately.

This brings us to a vital point of our argument. We would most emphatically lay down the proposition that no physician has a right to attend any case, unless he is satisfied that he is able to do it full justice. A village doctor may set a limb, he may perform tracheotomy, or operate on a case of vesico-vaginal fistula, precisely for the same reason that the captain of a ship in an emergency cuts off the leg of an injured sailor, no surgeon being present or readily procurable; or a physician may be justified in doing his best for such patients whose circumstances forbid them to resort to the most competent authority, but the moral right to attend to patients who apply for relief does not extend any further. If a blind man applies for a delicate operation on the eye to a practitioner in whom he has confidence, that confidence is only then justified and rewarded if the medical adviser indicates to the inquirer the safest mode of gaining his eyesight; and it is an abuse of this confidence, and breach of the trust reposed in him, if the physician undertakes the operation if not fully competent for the task. It cannot be denied, that then it is the duty of the practitioner to send the patient to a specialist in order to discharge his obligations to his patient.

It is hardly necessary to point out the various circumstances which may make the existence of competent specialists a source of comfort and a blessing to the general practitioner, for, fortunately, the special branches have already borne such brilliant fruits that we need not fear their being ignored by the scientific physician and surgeon. We must rather turn now to the most important of the points at issue, the question of advertising as a means of publicity.

The New York State Medical Society (we may hope not after anything like mature reflection, for a deliberate enactment of illiberal propositions is hardly to be expected from a body of intelligent scientists,) has discountenanced and prohibited the advertisement on the part of a specialist, of his residence in a medical paper, and has even gone to the length of objecting to the indication on business cards of the specialties which practitioners may choose to follow. The Boston Medical Journal, on the other hand, thinks those advertisements in medical journals, which, in Boston, are sanctioned by usage, not only justifiable, but even advantageous to professional and public interests. But no orthodox paper or orthodox practitioner has hitherto been found who dares to assert the right of the physician to advertise wherever he pleases, and as much as he pleases, in the mistaken belief that advertising in itself is derogatory to professional dignity. When we ask why, we are answered, because it is known that the advertisers of medical commodities are generally men without education, mountebanks and pickpockets in disguise. How absurd! For the same reason the respectable merchant might give up advertising because would-be merchants every day try to get money by pretentious announcements. The auctioneer who sells thousands of pieces of goods of all kinds should cease to announce his sales because Peter Funk, next door, sells brass watches for gold chronometers, and advertises his sales. A mining company conducted by a score of men of untarnished reputations, should abstain from advertising the sale of their stock, or refrain from giving any public notice of their existence, because a bubble company, with a lot of bogus names, or a set of adventurers at its head attempts to extract, by means of the public press, money from the pockets of the ignorant. Because Mr. Snow, the prophet and medium, or Mrs. Hatch, the celebrated spiritualist, invites the "believers" to attend a discourse on Sabbath evening, the Right Rev. Bishop Potter and the Rev. Mr. Beecher evidently tarnish the dignity of the body clerical by allowing the advertisements of their sermons to be published in the very same paper and in the very same column!

You see here to what incongruities the establishment of

illogical laws leads. Because impostors illegitimately and improperly use one of the most glorious and beneficial results of the art of printing, the inestimable advantages of public advertisements by means of the daily journals, you lay down as a law that on account of such perversion, the same instruments must not be used for good and legitimate ends. It is obvious that an advertisement containing a true representation of the commodities which a member of the community has for sale and exchange, cannot be considered in any way but legitimate, while it is equally clear that a misrepresentation must reflect discredit on its author.

When we examine the reason why prejudices which are so clearly demonstrable to be prejudices, should have taken such firm hold and be so deeply rooted in the minds of an intelligent class of the community, a class which, from the nature of their studies, should be the strongest exponents of liberal opinions, we find that they have their root in an hallucination with which physicians have flattered themselves, and that is, that the nature of the services of a medical man differs essentially from all other services rendered by members of the community to each other.

Why the medical profession should believe that the service which they offer to the public—advice—is distinguishable in its nature from other services, is difficult to understand. A physician gathers his knowledge of disease like an engineer gathers his knowledge of the laws of mechanics, or an artist his knowledge of esthetics. They sell to their clients, patients, or patrons those special inferences which their general knowledge enables them to draw. They are paid according to the value of their services. Such transactions the public justly consider to be strictly commercial. But the profession believe that the patient owes them, even after the fee is paid, an eternal debt of gratitude. There is no reason that such a belief, nourished as it is by illusions and conceit, should any longer be upheld.

There is no reason why the laws of free trade should not be applicable to medical services, as well as to all others. The plea that the public must, in its ignorance, be protected against quacks and empirics, is no more valid than the laws which in despotic countries protect the people from liberal newspapers and "dangerous" religious dogmas; laws which require the baker and butcher and carpenter to have passed an apprenticeship and journeymanship before he has the right to make bread, or shoes, or tables.

Whoever sells bad commodities, whoever sells them at too high a rate, must, as experience has shown, invariably be beaten and supplanted by the competition of those who sell good commodities at a reasonable rate. Now, therefore, if there is not sufficient superiority in the advice of an experienced and competent physician over that of a quack and empiric to guarantee a better success to the former, then there is no occasion to warn the public and protect the public from the practices of the latter, a proposition which certainly would not be endorsed. But if, as we may safely assume, the practical results of scientific medicine and surgery are sufficient to ensure a success to the scientist which the quack can never obtain, then there is no valid argument which can be advanced to prohibit the practitioner of medicine, as well as the specialist, from proceeding with the view of securing practice in the same way as the dealers in commodities or the vendors of other services. We have already alluded to the fact that the interests of the general practitioner and the specialist are different, and we would have a practical demonstration of this fact, if to-day it would be declared legitimate for a medical man to advertise. The general practitioner would not avail himself of his right, because he knows that it is necessary for him only to establish his reputation within a small circle; he knows that only a limited number of patients can make use of his services, because it is almost impossible for a patient to employ, as a regular physician, one who resides from him even the distance of a few miles. We will admit that it is already different, to some extent, in the case of the surgeon. He also draws his patients from long distances, and it might be urged that an oculist, aurist, or a specialist in the diseases of the chest or of the womb, can establish his reputation in the same manner as a surgeon. But this is not so easy under the present circumstances. Charlatans, who reset jaws and knee-joints, tie the carotid artery, and perform staphyloraphy, do not exist, as immediately fatal effects would too clearly expose their ignorance ; while those who attempt to cure cataracts by eyewaters or needle operations, or deafness by taking out fictitious polypi, consumption by blowing medicated steam into the mouth, and hypertrophy of the womb by cauterising its neck, are innumerable, and because their manipulations so closely imitate to the eye of the inexperienced the operations of the regular practitioner, that many of the public, who are accustomed to seek for celebrities in the daily prints, and unaware of the existence of higher authority than that of the "advertising quack," must needs believe, after having been deceived, that there is no help for them. But it is not necessary to dwell on all the disadvantages which the unphilosophical legislation of the "Code of Ethics" has fostered and created, and, unless abolished, will continue to engender and to perpetuate. If we ask you whether quackery has increased or diminished, it will unanimously have to be declared that humbug and imposition were never carried to a higher pitch than at the present moment ; that the consumption of patent medicines is on the increase ; and if we inquire whether the social influence which physicians enjoy or ought to enjoy, has increased, whether it is sufficient for one of the profession to say that he is a physician, in order to impress every one with the certainty that he is dealing with a gentleman, if we inquire for an answer to this, we are afraid candor will force the admission that the title of Doctor is too frequently prostituted to insure regard by the mere fact of being possessed.

Homœopathic and Eclectic Colleges and practice have spread in spite of innumerable—perhaps often unwarrantable—accusations from the members of the American Medical Association, and the legislatures of the different States have never been ready to recognize the influence and rights of the "regular" medical profession. We would therefore in vain seek in that direction for any beneficial results of the code of ethics.

Did you expect by means of the Code of Ethics to elevate the dignity of the profession ? Confess yourselves disappointed, and if the profession stands higher than it did twenty years ago, admit that your law on advertising did not produce that effect! Did you anticipate that it would annihilate quackery? Then look at the columns of our newspapers and candidly state that you have been mistaken; that, as Herbert Spencer says, you have in your attempt to remedy a specific evil, the low state of professional dignity, caused a collateral evil in the unrestricted and uncontrollable spread of imposition and quackery in all its forms! Nay, you have done worse; you have not only not prevented quackery, you have not only not protected the public from imposition and injury at the hands of the quacks; but your code of ethics has had for inevitable effect the protection of quackery by leaving it the free and uninterfered-with monopoly of the public press. You have said to the regular physician and specialist: If you avail yourself of the public press to announce to the community the achievements of your scientific attainments, and the success of your treatment or operations, we will read you out of the profession; and that same prohibition and threat was equivalent to saying to the charlatan: "Now is your time to ply your profitable but dishonorable calling; gull the public by advertisements inserted in the daily journals by the yard, and we will carefully watch and guard your interest by preventing any advertisement of a respectable physician or specialist to enter into competition with you."

Up to the present time specialists have not been very numerous, and the time that has elapsed since some of them have been bold enough—for it was boldness in the face of stubborn and unreasoning opposition—to be specialists, and to attend to their specialty exclusively, dates back but a few years. Within a few more years they will form a strong minority, nay, they may, in the larger cities at least, even be in majority. What will be the necessary consequence of an increase in their numbers if the profession continues by legislation to interfere with their interests? Depend upon it, that we do not make the demand unadvisedly or inconsiderately for the recognition of the right of the specialist to advertise. The specialists have more at stake, and are more interested to preserve the distinction between the scientific physician and the quack than general practitioners can be. If quack eye and ear doctors, clap doctors and abortionists are a disgrace to the profession at large, they are much more so to scientific specialists, the latter being in a greater danger to be confounded with them, than the members of the profession at large. Suppose we would for a moment admit that the medical profession in general might put down quackery by its influence in the legislative bodies of the country, or by act of Congress, would it then not be the duty of the profession immediately to rally and to carry through the measures necessary to effect that end; especially if they hold specialties and specialists in sufficient esteem to deem them worthy of the effort? If they do not do so, is it not an insult to every specialist, as such inactivity would show that the profession neglected the interest of and repudiated those upon whom at the same time it thinks proper to impose laws. But as we have already stated, it is likely that the influence of the whole profession would not suffice to carry such laws through our legislative halls, as instances innumerable have proved the insufficiency of professional influence in legislation, or at least have proved that the gold of non-professional purses weighs heavier in the balance of Minerva than the humanitarian arguments of medical reformers, and at all events it is certain that many years would have to elapse before adequate laws could be enforced throughout the whole of the United States.

What we would ask, is not a vigorous pursuit of lobbying in all its details, but simply that you abolish the rules which in your wisdom you have created twenty years ago, and abolish your prohibitions against advertising, and we are convinced that the natural laws of competition will work out the end desired by us all; the abolition of quackery. Medical men in this country have, though medical practice is virtually open to all, attained a fair average of knowledge and skill, and may with pride be compared to the physicians and surgeons in countries where examinations and certificates without end are requisite to procure a license for practising; druggists in this country, without State examinations, know how to put up prescriptions as well as in France, England or Germany, and find it, without the occasional visits of a body of supervisors of drugs, to their interest to keep good preparations. Bankers and business men are as honest as in Europe, though they cannot be imprisoned for debt, and may escape payment of money they owe by a number of dishonest practices ; clergymen are as learned as in Europe, without examination and obligatory education ; bakers bake bread equally well, and shoemakers make as good shoes, though there is no law requiring the proving of capacity before making an attempt to bake bread or to make shoes.

It is certain that there are many among the profession who will doubt the possibility to throw quacks out of employment by competition. Those will say that the public wants to be deceived ; that the greatest liar among advertisers will attract the greatest number of patients, that scientific physicians will never have the cunning possessed by charlatans, and which is requisite and essential to make advertising profitable ; that scientific and honest men, when they stoop to advertise, will soon be impregnated with the mercenary spirit characterizing the irresponsible advertiser, and lapse into the same meretricious practices. Of those we would ask, whether the achievements of modern surgery, ophthalmology, gynecology, &c., are not brilliant enough to impress every one, even if soberly and simply stated, with admiration and esteem ? Whether they actually believe that medicine is so fictitious a science, that success must be always a boast, and that lying is necessary to attract the public ? Whether in medical matters the old adage that honesty is the best policy must be reversed to be true ? Whether, as it is undeniable that advertising attracts patients, it is not more certain that a specialist who advertises and thus attracts many patients, can more easily afford to be candid and honest than those who get but scanty practice without advertisements, and thus may have in their effort to earn a living almost an excuse for hiding the truth ?

It would be vain to attempt to answer these questions otherwise than by the stale arguments which a conservative but unreasoning spirit has opposed to liberty of the press, liberty of speech, free trade, and innumerable other reforms which have been achieved, or partially achieved, within the last century, and which will one day be so completely and fully recognized that a more enlightened age will wonder at the comparatively slow pace of their progress and condemn their opponents as we do now the persecutors of religious dissenters, the institutors of the "holy;" inquisition, and the upholders of errors without number which were considered the indestructible framework of society during the feudal ages!

With great justice there may be adduced another forcible argument in favor of the right to advertise. There is no influence which paralyzes energy to such an extent as the impossibility to exercise faculties for want of material to exercise them on. Take from the artisan the wood, stone, or paper necessary for his work, limit the supply of cotton to the spinner, impoverish the painter so as to make him unable to buy colors and canvas, leave the sculptor without marble and the musician without his instrument, and his faculties and energy, however brilliant they may be, will suffer from the want of being exercised. What to these material, colors, marble, piano, or violin, is to the practitioner the patient. Prevent him from having patients, and he will lapse into inactivity, while nothing will stimulate his energy, his scientific zeal and thirst for knowledge, like a continuous demand upon them. The general practitioner who enters the profession may settle in a remote village, and secure a practice without difficulty, only perhaps not a very remunerative one, while the specialist, who must select a large city, is again aggrieved by the working of your Code of Ethics, which has been framed without regard and esteem for him—like the framers of the Constitution of the United States forgot the interests and rights of the negro.

The Code of Ethics was drawn up at a time when scientific specialization of medicine was so much in its infancy, that those who presumed to devote themselves to a special class of diseases on the pretence that they had discovered new processes of curing the "ills that flesh is heir to," were looked upon, perhaps properly, with disfavor and distrust by the profession. You have therefore, by means of your code, attempted to combat what you feared would eventually flower into charlatanism. But continuing your code formed under circumstances no longer existing, continuing prohibitions originally directed against charlatanism, against a class of men whom you must confess to be scientists, and who, by their achievements, have wrung from you tributes of praise and admiration, is a proceeding which must prove as inoperative and injurious, as would be the attempt to govern society of the present day by a system of laws applicable to a state of barbarism.

The only position which the profession could take against the specialist insisting upon the recognition of the rights claimed for him in this report, would be the following. General practitioners would say to specialists: "You have a right to exist, and to follow your pursuits, because as specialists you are enabled to heal certain classes of disease with better success than we are. We admit your right, we approve of its exercise. You want to guard your interest by abolishing our Code, but we believe that you would only injure yourselves, and consequently the whole profession. You complain that your interests are infringed upon by laws which were launched against quackery, and which you believe to have been abortive, and have only injured you. You insist upon our incapacity to destroy quackery by the means that we have adopted. You attack our opposition to what we deem the doubtful right of advertising on your part. Let us try to conciliate our interests and views, and compromise the matter. If you waive your right, or what you deem such, we will richly compensate you. We will exhibit our willingness to help you in your pursuits. We will use our influence to forward your interests. Every patient who applies to us with a disease of the eye we will send to an oculist, every case of syphilis to a syphilidologist, every case of disease of females to a gynecologist, and so on. We will thus by our united patronage enable you to put down quacks in the manner you propose, by competition. We are able to send you, by canvassing your merits, as many cases as the quack now attracts by his advertisements. We will solemnly pledge ourselves to leave the field of legitimate specialism to specialists, if specialists will pledge themselves on their part to abide by our code, to respect what we choose to call dignity, and to avoid what in our opinion is detrimental to the social standing of our profession."

Observe that we do not assume that you are prepared to speak to specialists in this manner, because we know that you could not be induced to relinquish the treatment of what you call simple diseases of the eye, the womb, or the nervous system; because we know that it is often impossible to define the limit between general disease and special disease. But should you even go so far as to abrogate your right of attending to a disease of the eye, ear, throat, womb, or chest; should you, in order to bind us to abide by the code of ethics, make a proposition so undeniably against your interests, we would emphatically deprecate any such arrangement, because in our opinion it is not in conformity with the dignity of specialists to accept it. Such a new law would within a short time work as detrimentally to your interests as the Code of Ethics now works against that of specialists. You cannot be deprived of your right to treat whatever case you think yourselves able to do justice to; and that you should send those patients, whom you cannot or dare not take under your care, to specialists whom you know to be competent, instead of leaving them to the searching of newspaper celebrities, is simply a matter of justice, but not a compensation which can be held out to induce us to compromise. And besides it is of paramount importance that specialists should not be mere *protégés* of the general practitioner nor dependent on him for patronage, but simply competitors pursuing a similar calling, circumscribed within narrower limits. An arrangement such as the one supposed would make specialists entirely dependent on the profession. Your patronage would be accorded to those of their number whom you would like best, and to those who would force themselves upon your notice. The personal dignity of specialists would suffer more in this manner than by advertising their cards in every newspaper. And finally, it would not by any means abolish quackery by competition. The public would misinterpret your intentions. Physicians would appear to have formed a Trades-Union against the great men of the eighth page of the newspaper. The quack would thrive and flourish in spite of the Protective Association, and not fail to take the air of a persecuted genius, who cannot succeed in inculcating the advantage of his new system upon an "obstinate old fogyish and illiberal body of men." This being already a dodge resorted to by the advertising fraternity, how much more would such a charge assume credibility in the eyes of the community, in the face of what would seem an organized opposition to "the great medical inventions and discoveries of our age"!

And now, gentlemen, concluding our plea for the abolition of that part of the Code of Ethics animadverted upon, we beg for our views your earnest and careful consideration. We do not expect that propositions so startling and radical should be accepted by your body without considerable opposition and debate. We know well the clogs and hindrances which conservatism has ever laid in the path of reform. History has furnished us with examples too numerous and too recent to be lightly passed over or forgotten, that truth however plain and undeniable, that rights however sacred and just, cannot force their immediate acceptance in the face of moss-grown prejudices and vested interests! But it is useless to attempt to organize resistance to reform, the correctness of the basis of which must be admitted by the very men who oppose its introduction! Laws and rights, the poet says, are transmitted like an hereditary disease from one generation to another, and what the poet paradoxically proclaimed years ago, the history of the last few decades has spendidly vindicated as an eternal truth.

The great thinkers and social reformers of our time have directed their attention to thousands of questions, and achieved reform in matters innumerable; but the basis of their efforts was always the restriction of law within its proper sphere—the administration of justice. The abolition of the corn laws, the gradual abolition of international restrictions of trade, the emancipation in Ireland, the abolition of slavery in Russia and the United States, the freedom of the trades and abolition of the guilds in Germany and Holland—all these glorious results of the collective experience and wisdom of two thousand years

18

are based on the recognition of the principle, *that every man has a right to be free, and that being free he is capable to work his way and to achieve his ends in the best manner, if laws* (created with a view, as has been cleverly said, to guard by present wisdom against future folly) *leave him unfettered and untrammeled.* Give to the specialist, gentlemen, the right to exercise his faculties and to find a market for them, and be assured he will not only be able to keep up his dignity without an ethical guide, but he will also, by his scientific knowledge, according to the law of competition, irresistibly throw out of existence that spurious article and sham of a service, the advice of the quack! Give to the specialist his freedom and he will seek out for himself the most expeditious road to fame and fortune, as general practitioners have always done, and in the exercise of this freedom he will no longer feel, as heretofore, that his association with the profession is a source of limitation and restriction of his legitimate rights, but he will exhibit that he feels it a duty to himself, and due to the generosity of a noble and honorable profession with which he is associated, and which frankly accorded to him his rights, that neither he nor the profession shall suffer by the slighest sacrifice of the true dignity of the scientist and gentleman!

JULIUS HOMBERGER.

WHAT IS FREE TRADE?

It is to answer this now frequent question that the following adaptation has been made. Yet, like the most charming of Bourcicault's plays, like the familiar air of "Home, sweet Home," it is only an adaptation. To the genius and wit of Frederick Bastiat do we owe the keen and cogent original. But to better answer the demands of the present day, it has been so much altered, so much Americanized, that the adaptor has considered it due to the memory of Bastiat that his share in the work should be acknowledged in this manner, rather than by doing him the injustice of placing his name as the author of what is, at best, but a mere shadow of his incomparable *Sophisms of the Protective Policy*.

In the preface to a translation of this work by Mrs. D. J. McCord, dated New York, 1848, appears a letter from Dr. Francis Lieber, now of New York, but then of South Carolina. Dr. Lieber, who appears to have been an ardent Free Trader, embraces in his letter several illustrations of the mistaken selfishness which pervades protection, and these illustrations are too good to be passed over. Says Dr. Lieber:

"Individual instinct has always led men to abridge labor, as we naturally seek the shortest road to our object. But when the aggregate labor of a community is considered, there are ever many persons who fix their exclusive attention upon the immediate inconvenience which must necessarily result from every change, and cannot or will not discern the greater ultimate good. Where railways are introduced, post-horses are thrown out of work, and their owners, as well as the farmers who supplied them with oats, will suffer for a time. When that great agent of civilization and conductor of human affections, the mail, was established, all the old messenger women, who once used to carry letters even from the students at Paris to remote parts of Germany, were deprived of their honest and hard-earned profits; and when the Croton aqueduct infused health, cleanliness, safety, comfort, and even delight, into every dwelling of New York, all the water-carriers were obliged to look out for other employment. The King of Oude was persuaded by the British residents to build water-mills; but soon after the prince had done so, he ordered them to be destroyed, from a sincere pity for the many decrepit people who had been employed in grinding grain at the hand-mills; thus depriving his whole people of cheap bread, who, by saving money upon this article, would have obtained means to employ additional labor, and that of the decrepit people among the rest. So, on the introduction of hops into England, the city of London petitioned against their use, lest they should injure the beer; and with equal wisdom the Kentish farmers, whose land was overrun with coppice, and who are now so largely benefited by their cultivation, objected to their growth 'because they occasioned a spoile of wood for poles.' Nay, when Parliament, under Walpole's administration, was passing an act to improve the roads, serious riots disturbed the peace of London, because provisions would be brought to the city from distant parts, and leave the metropolitan gardeners unprotected; and Shaftsbury was treated as a traitor to his country by the ruling party of the 'country gentlemen,' in parliament and out of it, because he had proposed to lower the duty on Irish beef! Many improvements, indeed, have been opposed upon grounds as rational as those stated by old Mause, in objection to her son Cuddie Headrigg's use of the barn-fanners for winnowing wheat, when lately introduced at Tillietudlem: 'Your leddyship and the steward hae been pleased to propose that my son Cuddie suld work in the barn wi' a new-fangled machine for dighting the corn frae the chaff, thus impiously thwarting the will of divine Providence, by raising wind for your leddyship's ain particular use by human airt, instead of soliciting it by prayer, or waiting patiently for whatever dispensation of wind Providence was pleased to send upon the sheeling-hill.'

"Now what else is Free Trade, but another name for road, canal, machinery, natural agent, railway, mail, wagon, plough, or whatever other abridgment of toil, removal of impediment, victory over elements, and increase of enjoyment and civilization can be named? All have but this one end, to get as much for as little labor as possible, so that the labor thus saved may be applied for the attainment of other objects, and that capital may not be wilfully wasted.

"It appears, then, that the publication of Mr. Bastiat's work, unmasking sophisms which are still diffused over many countries, will have a beneficial effect here, as it has had in a high degree in France. The perspicuity and raciness of the style, garnished at times with graceful irony, will make those parts of the work acceptable to the general reader, which otherwise might have remained uninviting to him. The petition of the French tallow-chandlers to the Chamber of Deputies, to exclude the sunlight, as being highly injurious to all the great tallow interests, I regard as a rare specimen of irony, quite equal to Dean Swift's cucumber man, cited by Mr. Webster in 1824, and worthy of all notice, not so much for the ingenuity as for the intrinsic truth of its satire.

"This petition brought back to my mind an occurrence of which I have been a witness. When the protective fever was in one of its paroxysms in our country, a meeting was held in a populous northern city for the purpose of digesting a petition to Congress. One resolution after the other, to protect yet an additional article, was adopted, when at last a person rose and claimed protection for coffee. The meeting was struck with astonishment. The proposer explained, and stated that he was the owner of green-houses containing some coffee plants, on several of which he had actually observed beans in the progress of formation. He thought that we ought to try at least to produce coffee; that it was a disgrace for a free and powerful nation to pay annually so much money out of the country to enrich foreigners; that with proper protection hot-houses would spring up all over the country; that labor confers all value; that it indicated a state of semi-barbarism to allow the sun to ripen the bean for us, when we could do it ourselves, and that, the sun of a foreign country, too! True civilization and national defence required the work to be done by man, and by man at home. The gardener, the carpenter and mason, the wood-cutter, the forest-owner and miner, the glazier, the potter, and the tinner, would all receive their profits. Coffee would rise in price, and thus enable the owner of hot-houses to pay high wages; this in turn would enable the receivers of wages to pay proportionably high for all necessaries of life; the shoemaker and tailor, the grocer and baker, would flourish; capital thus abundantly created would flow back and seek new investment in the hot-houses, competition would reduce the price of coffee, and the necessary ultimate effect of this patriotic protection and republican coffee production must be the reduction of this valued article to a degree of cheapness unknown at any previous period. All these blessings might be obtained by a single prohibitive word of Congress.

"This argument, though closely resembling the reasoning which had found favor with the meeting when applied to other products, and under other resolutions, was answered, not by arguments, as might have been expected, but with hisses."

Plenty and Scarcity.

Which is better for man and for society—abundance or scarcity?

What! Can such a question be asked? Has it ever been pretended, is it possible to maintain that scarcity is better than plenty?

Yes: not only has it been maintained, but it is still maintained. Congress say so; many of the newspapers (now happily diminishing in number) say so; a large portion of the public say so; indeed, the *scarcity theory* is by far the most popular one of the two.

Has not Congress passed laws which prohibit the importation of foreign productions by the urging of excessive duties? Does not the *Tribune* maintain that it is advantageous to limit the supply of iron manufactures and cotton fabrics, by restraining any one from bringing them to market, but the few manufacturers in New England and Pennsylvania? Do we not hear it complained every day: our importations are too large; that we are buying too much from abroad. Is there not an Association of Ladies, who, though they have not kept their promise, still, promised each other not to wear any clothing which was manufactured in other countries?

Now, tariffs can only raise prices by diminishing the quantity of goods offered for sale. Therefore, statesmen, editors, and the public generally, believe that scarcity is better than abundance.

But why is this; why should men be so blind as to maintain that scarcity is better than plenty?

Because they look at *price*, but forget *quantity*.

But let us see.

A man becomes rich in proportion to the remunerative nature of his labor; that is to say, *in proportion as he sells his produce at a high price.* The price of his produce is high in proportion to its scarcity. It is plain, then, that, as far as regards him at least, scarcity enriches him. Applying, in turn, this manner of reasoning to each class of laborers individually, the *scarcity theory* is deduced from it. To put this theory into practice, and in order to favor each class of labor, an artificial scarcity is forced in every kind of produce by prohibitory tariffs, by restrictive laws, by monopolies, and by other analogous measures.

In the same manner it is observed that when an article is abundant, it brings a small price. The gains of the producer are, of course, less. If this is the case with all produce, all producers are then poor. Abundance, then, ruins society; and as any strong conviction will always seek to force itself into practice, we have seen in many countries the laws struggling to prevent abundance.

Now, what is the defect in this argument? Something tells us that it must be wrong; but *where* is it wrong? Is it false? No. And yet it is wrong? Yes. But how? *It is incomplete.*

Man produces in order to consume. He is at once producer and consumer. The argument given above, considers him only under the first point of view. Let us look at him in the second character, and the conclusion will be different. We may say:

The consumer is rich in proportion as he *buys* at a low price. He buys at a low price in proportion to the abundance of the articles in demand; *abundance*, then, enriches him. This reasoning, extended to all consumers, must lead to the *theory of abundance.*

Which theory is right?

Can we hesitate to say? Suppose that by following out the *scarcity theory*, suppose that through prohibitions and restrictions we were compelled not only to make our own iron, but to grow our own coffee; in short, to obtain everything with difficulty and great outlay of labor. We then take an account of stock and see what our savings are.

Afterward, to test the other theory, suppose we remove the duties on iron, and the duties on coffee, and the duties on everything else, so that we shall obtain everything with as little difficulty and outlay of labor, as possible. If we then take an account of stock, is it not certain that we shall find more iron in the country, more coffee, more everything else?

Choose then, fellow country-men, between scarcity and abundance, between much and little, between Protection and Free Trade. You now know which theory is the right one, for you know the fruits they each bear.

But, it will be answered, if we are inundated with foreign goods and produce, our specie, our precious product of California, our dollars, will leave the country.

Well, what of that? Man is not fed with coin. He does not dress in gold, nor warm himself with silver. What does it matter, then, whether there be more or less specie in the country, provided there be more bread in the cupboard, more meat in the larder, more clothes in the wardrobe and more fuel in the cellar?

Again, it will be objected, if we accustom ourselves to depend upon England for iron, what shall we do in case of a war with that country?

To this I reply, we shall then be compelled to produce iron ourselves. But, again I am told, we will not be prepared; we will have no furnaces in blast, no forges ready. True; neither will there be any time when war shall occur that the country will not be already filled with all the iron we shall want until we can make it here. Did the Confederates in the late war lack for iron? Why, then, shall we manufacture our own staples and bolts because we may some day or other have a quarrel with our iron-monger!

To sum up:

A radical antagonism exists between the vender and the buyer.

The former wishes the article offered to be *scarce*, and the supply to be small, so that the price may be high.

The latter wishes it *abundant* and the supply to be large, so that the price may be low.

The laws, which should at least remain neutral, take part for the vender against the buyer; for the producer against the consumer; for high against low prices; for scarcity against abundance; for protection against free trade. They act, if not intentionally, at least logically, upon the principle that *a nation is rich in proportion as it is in want of everything.*

Obstacles to Wealth and Causes of Wealth.

Man is naturally in a state of entire destitution.

Between this state and the satisfying of his wants there exists a number of obstacles which it is the object of labor to surmount.

I wish to make a journey of some hundred miles. But between the point of my departure and my destination there are interposed mountains, rivers, swamps, forests, robbers; in a word—*obstacles.* To overcome these obstacles it is necessary that I should bestow much labor and great efforts in opposing them; or, what is the same thing, if others do it for me, I must pay them the value of their exertions. IT IS EVIDENT THAT I WOULD HAVE BEEN BETTER OFF HAD THESE OBSTACLES NEVER EXISTED. Remember this.

Through the journey of life, in the long series of days from the cradle to the tomb, man has many difficulties to oppose him. Hunger, thirst, sickness, heat, cold, are so many obstacles scattered along his road. In a state of isolation he would be obliged to combat them all by hunting, fishing, agriculture, spinning, weaving, architecture, etc., and it is very evident that it would be better for him that these difficulties should exist to a less degree, or even not at all. In a state of society he is not obliged personally to struggle with each of these obstacles, but others do it for him; and he, in turn, must remove some one of them for the benefit of his fellow-men. This doing one kind of labor for another, is called the division of labor.

Considering mankind as a whole, *let us remember once more that it would be better for society that these obstacles should be as weak and as few as possible.*

But mark how, in viewing this simple truth from a narrow point of view, we come to believe that, obstacles instead of being a disadvantage, are actually a source of wealth!

If we examine closely and in detail the phenomena of society and the private interests of men *as modified by the division of labor*, we perceive, without difficulty, how it has happened that wants have been confounded with riches and the obstacle with the cause.

The separation of occupations, which results from the division of labor, causes each man, instead of struggling against *all* surrounding obstacles to combat only *one;* the effort being made not for himself alone, but for the benefit of his fellows, who, in their turn render a similar service to him.

It hence results that this man looks upon the obstacle which he has made it his profession to combat for the benefit of others, as the immediate cause of his riches. The greater, the more serious, the more stringent, may be this obstacle the more he is remunerated for the conquering of it, by those who are relieved by his labors.

A physician, for instance, does not busy himself in baking his bread, or in manufacturing his clothing and his instruments; others do it for him, and he, in return, combats the maladies with which his patients are afflicted. The more dangerous and frequent these maladies are, the more others are willing, the more, even, are they forced, to work in his service. Disease, then, which is an obstacle to the happiness of mankind, becomes to him the source of his comforts. The reasoning of all producers is in what concerns themselves, the same. As the doctor draws his profits from *disease*, so does the ship-owner from the obstacle called *distance;* the agriculturalist from that named *hunger;* the cloth manufacturer from *cold;* the schoolmaster lives upon *ignorance*, the jeweler upon *vanity*, the lawyer upon *cupidity*, the notary upon possible *breach of faith*. Each profession has then an immediate interest in the continuation, even in the extension, of the particular obstacle to which its attention has been directed.

Theorists hence go on to found a system upon these individual interests, and say: Wants are riches: Labor is riches: The obstacle to well-being is well-being: To multiply obstacles is to give food to industry.

Then comes the statesman;—and as the developing and propagating of obstacles is the developing and propagating of riches, what more natural than that he should bend his efforts to that point? He says, for instance: If we prevent a large importation of iron, we create a difficulty in procuring it. This obstacle severely felt obliges individuals to pay, in order to relieve themselves from it. A certain number of our citizens, giving themselves up to the combating of this obstacle, will thereby make their fortunes. In proportion, too, as the obstacle is great, and the mineral scarce, inaccessible, and of difficult and distant transportation, in the same proportion will be the number of laborers maintained by the various branches of this industry.

The same reasoning will lead to the proscription of machinery.

Here are men who are at a loss how to dispose of their wine-harvest. This is an obstacle which other men set about removing for them by the manufacture of casks. It is fortunate, say our statesmen, that this obstacle exists, since it occupies a portion of the labor of the nation, and enriches a certain number of our citizens. But here is presented to us an ingenious machine, which cuts down the oak, squares it, makes it into staves, and, gathering these together, forms them into casks. The obstacle is thus diminished, and with it the fortunes of the coopers. We must prevent this. Let us proscribe the machine!

To sift thoroughly this sophism, it is sufficient to remember that human labor is not an *end*, but a *means*. *Labor is never without employment.* If one obstacle is removed, it seizes another, and mankind is delivered from two obstacles by the same effort which was at first necessary for one. If the labor of coopers could become useless, it must take another direction. To maintain that human labor can end by wanting employment, it would be necessary to prove that mankind will cease to encounter obstacles.

Effort—Result.

We have seen that between our wants and their gratification many obstacles are interposed. We conquer or weaken these by the employment of our faculties. It may be said, in general terms, that industry is an effort followed by a result.

But by what do we measure our well-being? By our riches? By the result of our effort, or by the effort itself? There exists always a proportion between the effort employed and the result obtained. Does progress consist in the relative increase of the second or of the first term of this proportion—between effort or result?

Both propositions have been sustained, and in political economy opinions are divided between them.

According to the first system, riches are the result of labor. They increase in the same ratio as *the result does to the effort.* Absolute perfection, of which *God* is the type, consists in the infinite distance between these two terms in this relation, viz., effort none, result infinite.

The second system maintains that it is the effort itself which forms the measure of, and constitutes, our riches. Progression is the increase of the *proportion of the effect to the result.* Its ideal extreme may be represented by the eternal and fruitless efforts of Sisyphus.*

The first system tends naturally to the encouragement of everything which diminishes difficulties, and augments production,—as powerful machinery, which adds to the strength of man; the exchange of produce, which allows us to profit by the various natural agents distributed in different degrees over the surface of our globe; the intellect which discovers, the experience which proves, and the emulation which excites.

* We will therefore beg the reader to allow us in future, for the sake of conciseness, to designate this system under the term of *Sisyphism*, from Sisyphus, who, in punishment of his crimes, was compelled to roll a stone up hill, which fell to the bottom as fast as he rolled it to the top, so that his labor was interminable as well as fruitless.

The second as logically inclines to everything which can augment the difficulty and diminish the product; as, privileges, monopolies, restrictions, prohibitions, suppression of machinery, sterility, &c.

It is well to remark here that the universal practice of men is always guided by the principle of the first system. Every *workman*, whether agriculturalist, manufacturer, merchant, soldier, writer or philosopher, devotes the strength of his intellect to do better, to do more quickly, more economically,—in a word, *to do more with less.*

The opposite doctrine is in use with theorists, congressmen, editors, statesmen, ministers, men whose business is to make experiments upon society. And even of these we may observe, that in what personally concerns themselves, they act, like everybody else, upon the principle of obtaining from their labor the greatest possible quantity of useful results.

It may be supposed that I exaggerate, and that there are no true *Sisyphists.*

I grant that in practice the principle is not pushed to its extremest consequences. And this must always be the case when one starts upon a wrong principle, because the absurd and injurious results to which it leads, cannot but check it in its progress. For this reason, practical industry never can admit of *Sisyphism.* The error is too quickly followed by its punishment to remain concealed. But in the speculative industry of theorists and statesmen, a false principle may be for a long time followed up, before the complication of its consequences, only half understood, can prove its falsity; and even when all is revealed, the opposite principle is acted upon, self is contradicted, and justification sought, in the incomparably absurd modern axiom, that in political economy there is no principle universally true.

Let us see, then, if the two opposite principles I have laid down do not predominate, each in its turn;—the one in practical industry, the other in industrial legislation. When a man prefers a good plough to a bad one, when he improves the quality of his manures; when, to loosen his soil, he substitutes as much as possible the action of the atmosphere for that of the hoe or the harrow; when he calls to his aid every improvement that science and experience have revealed, he has, and can have, but one object, viz., to *diminish the proportion of the effort to the result.* We have indeed no other means of judging of the success of an agriculturalist or of the merits of his system, but by observing how far he has succeeded in lessening the one, while he increases the other; and as all the farmers in the world act upon this principle, we may say that all mankind are seeking, no doubt, for their own advantage, to obtain at the lowest price, bread, or whatever other article of produce they may need, always diminishing the effort necessary for obtaining any given quantity thereof.

This incontestible tendency of human nature, once proved, would, one might suppose, be sufficient to point out the true principle to the legislator, and to show him how he ought to assist industry (if indeed it is any part of his business to assist it at all), for it would be absurd to say that the laws of men should operate in an inverse ratio from those of Providence.

Yet we have heard members of Congress exclaim, "I do not understand this theory of cheapness; I would rather see bread dear, and work more abundant." And consequently these gentlemen vote in favor of legislative measures whose effect is to shackle and impede commerce, precisely because by so doing we are prevented from procuring indirectly, and at low price, what direct production can only furnish more expensively.

Now it is very evident that the system of Mr. So-and-so, the Congressman, is directly opposed to that of Mr. So-and-so, the agriculturalist. Were he consistent with himself, he would as legislator vote against all restriction; or else as farmer, he would practise in his fields the same principle which he proclaims in the public councils. We would then see him sowing his grain in his most sterile fields, because he would thus succeed in *laboring much*, to *obtain little.* We would see him forbidding the use of the plough, because he could, by scratching up the soil with his nails, fully gratify his double wish of "*dear bread* and *abundant labor.*"

Restriction has for its avowed object, and acknowledged effect, the augmentation of labor. And again, equally avowed and acknowledged, its object and effect are, the increase of prices;—a synonymous term for scarcity of produce. Pushed then to its greatest extreme, it is pure *Sisyphism* as we have defined it; *labor infinite; result nothing.*

There have been men who accused railways of *injuring shipping;* and it is certainly true that the most perfect means of attaining an object must always limit the use of a less perfect means. But railways can only injure shipping by drawing from it articles of transportation; this they can only do by transporting more cheaply; and they can only transport more cheaply, by *diminishing the proportion of the effort employed to the result obtained;* for it is in this that cheapness consists. When, therefore, these men lament the suppression of labor in attaining a given result, they maintain the doctrine of *Sisyphism.* Logically, if they prefer the vessel to the railway, they should also prefer the wagon to the vessel, the pack-saddle to the wagon, and the wallet to the pack-saddle; for this is, of all known means of transportation, the one which requires the greatest amount of labor, in proportion to the result obtained.

"Labor constitutes the riches of the people," say some theorists. This was no elliptical expression, meaning that the "results of labor constitute the riches of the people." No,—these theorists intended to say, that it is the *intensity* of labor, which measures riches; and the proof of this is that from step to step, from restriction to restriction, they forced on the United States (and in so doing believed that they were doing well) to give to the procuring of, for instance, a certain quantity of iron, double the necessary labor. In England, iron was then at $20; in the United States it cost $40. Supposing the day's work to be worth $2.50, it is evident that the United States could, by barter, procure a cwt. of iron by eight days' labor taken from the labor of the nation. Thanks to the restrictive measures of these gentlemen, sixteen days' work were necessary to procure it, by direct production. Here then we have double labor for an identical result; therefore double riches; and riches, measured not by the result, but by the intensity of labor. Is not this pure and unadulterated *Sisyphism?*

That there may be nothing equivocal, these gentlemen carry

their idea still farther, and on the same principle that we have heard them call the intensity of labor *riches*, we will find them calling the abundant results of labor, and the plenty of every thing proper to the satisfying of our wants, *poverty*. "Every where," they remark, "machinery has pushed aside manual labor; every where production is superabundant; every where the equilibrium is destroyed between the power of production and that of consumption." Here then we see that, according to these gentlemen, if the United States was in a critical situation it was because her productions were too abundant; there was too much intelligence, too much efficiency in her national labor. We were too well fed, too well clothed, too well supplied with every thing; the rapid production was more than sufficient for our wants. It was necessary to put an end to this calamity, and therefore it became needful to force us, by restrictions, to work more, in order to produce less.

All that we could have further to hope for, would be, that human intellect might sink and become extinct; for, while intellect exists, it cannot but seek continually to increase the *proportion of the end to the means; of the product to the labor.* Indeed it is in this continuous effort, and in this alone, that intellect consists.

Sisyphism has then been the doctrine of all those who have been intrusted with the regulation of the industry of our country. It would not be just to reproach them with this; for this principle becomes that of our administration only because it prevails in Congress; it prevails in Congress only because it is sent there by the voters; and the voters are imbued with it, only because public opinion is filled with it to repletion.

Let me repeat here, that I do not accuse the Protectionists in Congress of being absolutely and always *Sisyphists*. Very certainly they are not such in their personal transactions; very certainly each of them will procure for himself *by barter*, what by *direct production* would be attainable only at a higher price. But I maintain that they are *Sisyphists* when they prevent the country from acting upon the same principle. A. D.

GOVERNMENT.

PART II.

OUR previous article on Government closed with a sketch of some of the leading systems of Governments which had existed in the Old World prior to the French Revolution.

We shall now attempt an analysis of the Government of the United States.

It was in the school of the French Philosophers, that the great American statesmen who established the independence of the United States, imbibed their ideas of liberty. No Government was ever based on so ample a recognition of human rights as that of the United States. Thomas Jefferson, the most eminent statesman our country has ever produced, in his original draft of the Declaration of Independence said: "He, (the king of Great Britain), has waged cruel war against human nature itself, violating its most sacred rights of life and liberty in the persons of a distant people who never offended him; captivating and carrying them into slavery in another hemisphere, or to incur miserable death in their transportation thither. This piratical warfare, the opprobrium of infidel powers, is the warfare of the Christian king of Great Britain. Determined to keep open a market where men should be bought and sold, he had prostituted his negative, for suppressing every legislative attempt to prohibit or to restrain the execrable commerce; and that this assemblage of horrors might want no fact of distinguished die, he is now exciting those very people to rise in arms among us, and to purchase that liberty of which he has deprived them, by murdering the people on whom he also obtruded them: thus paying off former crimes committed against the LIBERTIES of one people with crimes which he urges them to commit against the LIVES of another.

In regard to this paragraph, Jefferson says: "The clause

reprobating the enslaving the inhabitants of Africa, was struck out in complaisance to South Carolina and Georgia, who had never attempted to restrain the importation of slaves, and who, on the contrary, still wished to continue it. Our Northern brethren also, I believe, felt a little tender under those censures, for though their people had very few slaves themselves, yet they had been pretty considerable carriers of them to others."

As we have here a full recognition of the rights of the Africans by the writer of the Declaration of Independence, there is evidently no foundation for the claim so constantly made that that celebrated instrument was only intended to apply to the white inhabitants of the United States. It is true that the paragraph which most distinctly asserted the rights of the black race was stricken out; but there still remains a sufficient acknowledgment of these rights, not only by Jefferson, but also by most of the prominent statesmen of that day, who believed that all the slaves would, ere long, be freed either by the action of the State Legislatures or by their masters; so earnest was the conviction that the institution of slavery was injurious to the true interests of the community. In consequence of the introduction of the culture of cotton in the Southern States, these expectations of the eminent statesmen of the Revolution were not realized, and the people of the United States are now reaping the terrible fruits of the surrender by their forefathers of the rights of a portion of humanity, to please the supposed interests of South Carolina and Georgia. Should we not all, both North and South, be to-day a happier and more prosperous people, had the Constitution fully recognized and carried out the principles for which Jefferson and others so nobly contended? Jefferson, with the usual correct prevision of those who look to principles as the only safe guides on all occasions, said that the day was not distant when the slaves must be liberated, or worse would follow. Nothing, said he, is more certainly written in the book of fate, than that these people are to be free.

The Constitution of the United States is undoubtedly the most perfect system of human government ever organized by man, because it grants more liberty to the individual, and therefore attempts to govern less, than any government that has ever existed. The preamble to the Constitution is an admirable declaration of the true source and objects of Government. It says: "We, the people of the United States, in order to form a more perfect union, establish justice, ensure domestic tranquillity, provide for the common defence, promote the general welfare, and secure the blessings of liberty to ourselves and our posterity, do ordain and establish this Constitution for the United States of America."

A careful and thorough analysis of the Constitution of the United States establishes clearly, that all its undoubtedly beneficial provisions are those which prohibit the exercise of power, or recognize some inherent right of man—which is also a limitation or a prohibition of the exercise of power by Government; and that all the provisions which are of doubtful utility, or which have proved injurious in practice, are precisely those which confer power or authority, or deny some inherent right of man—which is also a delegation of power to Government. Is not this a striking confirmation of the correctness of the principles established by the investigations of social science?

The people of the United States have been greatly benefited by the following provisions of the Constitution:

ARTICLE I, SECTION 2. Representatives and direct taxes shall be apportioned among the several States which may be included within this Union, according to their respective numbers.

ARTICLE I, SECTION 8. All duties, imports, and excises, shall be uniform throughout the United States.

ARTICLE I, SECTION 9. The privilege of the writ of habeas corpus shall not be suspended, unless when in cases of rebellion or invasion the public safety may require it.*

No bill of attainder, or ex post facto law shall be passed.

No capitation, or other direct tax shall be laid, unless in proportion to the census.

No tax or duty shall be laid on articles exported from any State.

No preference shall be given by any regulation of commerce or revenue to the ports of one State over those of another; nor shall vessels bound to or from one State, be obliged to enter, clear, or pay duties, in another.

No title of nobility shall be granted by the United States.

* The latter portion of this clause, which grants authority to suspend the habeas corpus in exceptional cases, has given rise to serious abuse during the past four years.

ARTICLE I, SECTION 10. No State shall enter into any treaty, alliance, or confederation, grant letters of marque and reprisal, emit bills of credit, make anything but gold and silver coin a tender in payment of debt, pass any bill of attainder, ex post facto law, or law impairing the obligation of contracts, or grant any title of nobility.

No State shall, without the consent of Congress, lay any impost or duties on imports or exports, except what may be absolutely necessary for executing its inspection laws.†

No State shall, without the consent of Congress, lay any duty of tonnage, keep troops, or ships of war in time of peace, enter into any agreement or compact with another State, or with a foreign power, or engage in war, unless actually invaded, or in such imminent danger as will not admit of delay.

ARTICLE III, SECTION 2. The Judicial power of the United States shall extend to controversies between two or more States; between a State and citizens of another State; between citizens of different States; between citizens of the same State claiming lands under grants of different States; and between a State, or the citizens thereof, and foreign states, citizens, or subjects.

The trial of all crimes, except in cases of impeachment, shall be by jury, and such trial shall be held in the State where the said crimes shall have been committed.

ARTICLE IV, SECTION 2. The citizens of each State shall be entitled to all privileges and immunities of citizens in the several States.

ARTICLE I, of the Amendments. Congress shall make no law respecting an establishment of religion, or prohibiting the free exercise thereof; or abridging the freedom of speech, or of the press; or the right of the people peaceably to assemble, and to petition the Government for redress of grievances.

ARTICLE III. No soldier shall, in time of peace, be quartered in any house, without the consent of the owner, nor in time of war, but in a manner to be prescribed by law.

ARTICLE IV. The right of the people to be secure in their persons, houses, papers, and effects, against unreasonable searches and seizures, shall not be violated; and no warrants shall issue, but upon probable cause, supported by oath or affirmation, and particularly describing the place to be searched, and the persons or things to be seized.

ARTICLE V. No person shall be deprived of life, liberty, or property, without due process of law; nor shall private property be taken for public use, without just compensation.

ARTICLE VI. In all criminal prosecutions, the accused shall enjoy the right to a speedy and public trial, by an impartial jury of the State and district wherein the crime shall have been committed, which district shall have been previously ascertained by law, and to be informed of the nature and cause of the accusation; to be confronted with the witnesses against him; to have compulsory process for obtaining witnesses in his favor, and to have the assistance of counsel for his defence.

---

† This exception led to the enactment of State inspection laws, which proved so burdensome and oppressive that they have been entirely repealed in many States.

ARTICLE VIII. Excessive bail shall not be required, nor excessive fines imposed, nor cruel and unusual punishment.

ARTICLE IX. The enumeration in the Constitution of certain rights, shall not be construed to deny or disparage others retained by the people.

ARTICLE X. The powers not delegated to the United States by the Constitution, nor prohibited by it to the States, are reserved to the States respectively, or to the people.

But is it not more than doubtful whether they have been benefited by the following ones?

ARTICLE I, SECTION 2. Which stipulates that the numbers upon which the representatives and the direct taxes shall be apportioned, "shall be ascertained by adding to the whole number of free persons, including those bound to service for a term of years, and excluding Indians not taxed, three-fifths of all other persons."

ARTICLE I, SECTION 8. The Congress shall have power to levy and collect taxes, duties, imposts, and excises, to pay the debts, and provide for the common defence and general welfare of the United States.

To borrow money on the credit of the United States.

To regulate commerce with foreign nations, and among the several States, and with the Indian tribes.

To coin money, regulate the value thereof, and of foreign coin.

To establish post offices and post roads.

To promote the progress of science and useful arts, by securing for limited times, to authors and inventors, the exclusive right to their respective writings and discoveries.

To declare war, grant letters of marque and reprisal, and make rules concerning captures on land and water.

To raise and support armies.

To provide and maintain a navy.

To make rules for the government and regulation of the land and naval forces.

To provide for calling forth the militia to execute the laws of the Union, suppress insurrections, and repel invasions.

To provide for organizing, arming, and disciplining the militia, and for governing such part of them as may be employed in the service of the United States.

To make all laws which shall be necessary and proper for carrying into execution the foregoing powers, and all other powers vested by this Constitution in the Government of the United States, or in any department or officer thereof.

ARTICLE I, SECTION 9. The migration or importation of such persons as any of the States now existing shall think proper to admit, shall not be prohibited by the Congress prior to the year 1808, but a tax or duty may be imposed on such importation not exceeding ten dollars for each person.

ARTICLE IV, SECTION 2. No person held to service or labor in one State, under the laws thereof, escaping into another, shall in consequence of any law or regulation therein, be discharged from such service or labor, but shall be delivered up on claim of the party to whom such service or labor may be due.

The stipulations which declare that representation in Congress and direct taxation shall be apportioned among the several States according to population, recognize the important truth that the only proper basis, both of representation and of taxation, is population. The Constitution here, precisely like the laws of nature, admits no difference in the duties of men on account of either their wealth, their intelligence, their education, their occupation, or their location. Nature makes no difference, on these accounts, in the punishment she inflicts on those who disregard her laws ; nor in the reward she bestows on those who conform to them. Taxation in proportion to population is the only basis that strictly accords with the well-being of all. It is evident that no one should be excused from contributing his full quota to the general expenditures of Government merely because he chooses to remain ignorant, or to live in idleness, or to consume or waste all he earns or produces, or to occupy himself at a less productive, which invariably means, a less necessary, occupation than others. If a man from ignorance, indolence, or any other cause, continues at an occupation not necessary to the community, and therefore unprofitable, he should not be relieved of any of the evil consequences to himself of this disregard of the wants of others. He cannot, in justice, ask those who are more industrious, more intelligent, or more economical, —those who render greater services to the community—to bear the burthen of a portion of his share of the Government expenditures. All taxes imposed on capital inflict penalties on those who confer benefits ; they act on the thriftless like premiums for inflicting injuries on the thrifty. Human laws, like natural laws, should offer incentives to effort, to intelligence, to economy, to virtue ; and constantly impose penalties on idleness, ignorance, extravagance and vice ; but unfortunately nearly every human law does the very reverse of this ; and the laws enacted by Congress, in regard to taxation, are no exception. The just and beneficial stipulation of the Constitution in regard to direct taxation, has been rendered null and void from the beginning, by raising all taxes by indirect taxation, the most expensive, as well as the most oppressive and injurious system possible, because it requires an enormous number of government officials, and interferes with the legitimate and beneficial operations of industry and commerce, to the great injury of the entire community. The reasons generally offered for resorting to indirect taxation, are, that direct taxes will not be submitted to by the people, and that it would be unjust to levy the same amount upon a poor agricultural population, as upon a rich manufacturing and commercial community. Now the truth is, that agriculture is the most productive of all occupations, in proportion to the capital and intelligence it requires; and there is no portion of the United States where direct taxes for State and local purposes, have not long been levied and collected to an amount much greater than that necessary to meet the ordinary expenditures of the Federal Government.

The stipulations which prohibit the States from laying any impost or duties on tonnage, or on the commerce between the States, as well as the one which prohibits the Federal Government from imposing a tax on articles exported from any State, are a recognition of the inherent right of man to dispose of the results of his labor or of the labor of his ancestors, as well as all property legally acquired, wherever he may deem best, without obstruction or interference from Government. These stipulations have greatly benefited all sections of the Union, by leaving the commerce and intercourse between the inhabitants of the different States entirely unfettered, thus permiting their full development; and the principle, if extended to the commerce of the world, would be as beneficial to humanity at large as its application in the United States has proved beneficial to the people of the various States.

The stipulations which prohibit the Federal Government and the States from granting any title of nobility, are a recognition of the equality of all men in their relations to Government, and leave, as the only attainable distinctions, intelligence, virtue, industry, and wealth, the attainment of which by the individual, is as beneficial to the community as to the persons who acquire them.

But the most important stipulation of the Constitution, the one that forever crowns with glory the great men who were the authors of that noble instrument, as well as the generation which accepted it as the regulator of their future actions, is that which does away with every excuse for war between States by establishing a system of settling international disputes, as well as disputes between States and citizens of other States, and between citizens of different States, by means of tribunals which examine all differences which may arise between them, and decide them without recourse to violence.

If a boundary question between New Jersey and New York, or between Massachusetts and Rhode Island, can be properly and advantageously determined by tribunals, why cannot similar questions between Canada and the United States, or between any two European states, be settled in the same manner by tribunals to be created for that purpose, composed of eminent jurists of all nations? It will be said that there is a great difference between the two cases; that in one case the Government of the United States is supreme over the States, and can, therefore, enforce the decisions of the United States courts; whereas in the other case, there is no supreme authority that could enforce the decisions of any tribunal that might be appointed to decide between nations. But why cannot all the European states, just as well as the several States of the Union, agree to submit their disputes to a tribunal of eminent jurists of all nations, whose decisions could be enforced by their united power? This is precisely what the States of the Union have done by means of the Constitution, which binds States to the principle which has so long been applied to individuals: that they shall not be judges and redressors of their own wrongs. The general acceptance, by all nations, of this principle would confer greater benefits on humanity than any reform ever made or suggested in regard to government. The opposition to it will, as usual, come mainly from the governing classes. The armies and navies, as well as the numerous administrations necessary to supply their wants, provide too many easy sinecures for the governing classes, for them to consent to their abrogation if they can prevent it. Mr. Legoyt, chief of the statistical bureau of the French ministry of agriculture, commerce and public works, reports that, in 1862, Europe, although wholly at peace, and with no appearance of war, maintained the enormous number of 3,875,847 armed men!

which represents the entire adult males in a population of 20,000,000! the cost of which, even at the very low renumerations which are allowed in the forced military service imposed in most of the states, was over 700 millions of dollars!

The ordinary expenditures of Great Britian and France are divided as follows:—

PROPORTION OF YEARLY BUDGET.

Public debt, ...	50 per cent.	38 per cent.
War, ...	34 "	35 "
State, ...	16 "	27 "
	100	100

As the public debts of all countries have been created to meet war expenditures, it follows that even in times of peace, only 16 per cent. of the yearly expenditures of Great Britain, and 27 per cent. of those of France, are for the purposes of civil government, and this in monarchical countries. In 1856, during the Crimean war, 92 per cent. of the yearly expenditures of Great Britian were for past and present wars. Do not these figures prove that it is impossible to exaggerate the benefits that would be conferred by any system which would bid fair to close the dreadful temple of Janus?

The stipulations in the Constitution of the United States which prohibit States from engaging in war, from maintaining troops or ships of war in time of peace, from issuing letters of marque, and from entering into alliances with other states, are the natural and beneficial consequences of the adoption of the principle of settling international disputes by means of tribunals. This renders armies and navies unnecessary; prevents the enormous outlays they require; and returns to industry the immense number of men in the prime of life, who would otherwise be employed in preparations for the destruction of life and property.

The civilizing effects of peace and a termination of the brutal scenes and results which invariably accompany war, are beyond all price.

The stipulation that no State shall emit bills of credit (paper money), nor make anything but gold and silver coin a legal tender, is absolutely necessary to maintain the sacredness of contracts, which the States are expressly prohibited from impairing, as well as to ensure a sound currency, which is an indispensable instrument to the beneficial operations of commerce and industry. The recent deviation from these sound principles by Congress, in the enactment of the legal-tender act, has already produced consequences which fully prove the importance of maintaining inviolate these wise provisions of the Constitution.

The stipulation that the citizens of each State shall be entitled to all the privileges and immunities of citizens in the several States, wisely secures many important rights from being any longer dependent on the will of the Government.

The amendment which forbids Congress to enact any law prohibiting the free exercise of religion, or abridging the freedom of speech or of the press; or the right of the people peaceably to assemble; is an acknowledgment that there are things which man has the inherent right to do, and which government therefore has no right to interfere with. Why should not the right to labor at any occupation, and to make any proper use of the result of labor, be added to those enumerated in the Constitution as not subject to governmental control or interference? The interference of government with industry and commerce is no more necessary or excusable, than its interference with the religious opinions of the citizen.

The 8th and 9th Amendments of the Constitution clearly stipulate that the people and the States are sovereign in regard to all the rights and powers not expressly delegated to the United States, and completely dispose of the pretended right of Congress to enact laws or exercise powers not granted in the Constitution, merely because, in the opinion of Congress, they are necessary to the exercise of the powers granted, to the maintenance of the Government, or to the well-being of the people. The reservation of any power or right is a strict prohibition to its exercise by others, no matter what may be the consequences that are to follow. An amendment of the Constitution is the only legal mode of enlarging the powers of Congress or of the Executive, and if it be permitted to enlarge these powers by any but the proper and legal means, for a beneficial object, it establishes a precedent which will soon be exercised to do the same thing for objects injurious to the people.

The exceptions to the full recognition of the rights of man which are *implied* rather than expressed in the 2d Section of Article I, and in the 2d Section of Article IV, in regard to the Indians and slaves, have been dearly paid for by the people of the United States. The treatment of the Indians as outcasts, and the ignoring of their rights, have caused numerous expensive and murderous wars—wars which were disgraceful to our people, because generally consequent on the invasion or disregard of the inherent rights of that terribly wronged and unfortunate race. The continuance of slavery after the acknowledgment of its heinousness, not only prevented the full development of the wealth, and the general progress, of the States in which slavery continued to exist, but also led to the terrible civil war which has raged during the past four years, the full effects of which have not yet been felt. Do not the disastrous effects of deferred emancipation in the United States conclusively prove that natural laws are never infringed, that injustice can never be committed, without entailing evils and sufferings which might have been avoided by submission to these laws?

It must not be forgotten, that the words "slave" and "slavery" are not to be found in the Constitution. This certainly indicates that its framers shared the then prevalent opinion that slavery was to be only of short duration; that it would soon be annulled by the voluntary action of the States or of the slave owners. The studied absence of the words "slave" and "slavery" in a Constitution drawn up when slavery was generally prevalent, goes far to prove that its authors felt the impossibility of reconciling that unjust institution with a form of government based on liberty; and this must have led to the desire that the Federal Government should in no manner sanction slavery or be responsible for its existence. It is true the 2d Section of Article IV says, "No person held to service or labor in one State under the laws thereof, escaping into another, shall in consequence of any law or regulation therein, be discharged from such service or labor, but shall be delivered upon claim of the party to whom such service or labor may be due." But even Southerners themselves have admitted, in their State conventions or Legislatures, since their secession, that this provision was only mandatory on the State authorities, whose duty it was to return the fugitive slaves, but that it in no way required the action or interference of the Federal authorities, being strictly an affair of comity between the State Governments, and consequently that all the fugitive slave bills passed by Congress, which so greatly irritated the North and contributed to the estrangement of the two sections now at war, were unconstitutional.

In virtué of the power to collect duties, Custom Houses have been established which interfere with the inherent right of every individual to dispose of his property to whomsoever, and wheresoever he pleases. This interference with the exchange of commodities is excused on the plea that it develops home industry and makes us independent of foreign nations. But the interdependence of nations, like that of individuals, should be encouraged and not prevented, because it is one of the natural and surest preventives of war. Custom Houses, instead of developing home industry, retard and diminish its progress, by inducing capital and labor to quit the most profitable occupations, to engage in others less renumerative.

This retards the production of Capital, and upon the amount of existing capital depend both the occupation and the renumeration of labor. Every person willing and able to work can always find employment in a free community, except perhaps in moments of crises and panics. Man does not seek labor, but the results of labor. If greater results can be obtained through exchanges of commodities, than by direct production, the true interests of labor, as well as of the whole community, require that they should be procured by exchanges. By imposing discriminating duties on imports, Congress aims to benefit—uses the power delegated "to establish justice and promote the general welfare of the people of the United States," with a view to benefit—a small portion of the people, occupied in certain industries, at the expense of all the other classes. And even if this really benefited the persons occupied in the protected industries—which it certainly does not—would it "insure domestic tranquillity, establish justice, and promote the general welfare" which the preamble to the Constitution declares to be its object? Has it not, on the contrary, been a constant cause of discord and jealousy between the different sections of the country? Did it not almost produce an insurrection in South Carolina during the administration of Jackson, and did it not greatly aid political demagogues in estranging the North and the South, of which the final result has been our present conflict? The numerous government officials required to collect duties on imports, are withdrawn from useful productive occupations, whilst the cost of maintaining them becomes a burden on the industry of the country. Besides which, the increase of the government patronage that Custom Houses entail, is one of the principal causes of the corruption and demoralization of political parties, who seek to obtain possession of the government solely for the sake of the power and patronage it confers.

Under sanction of the power to regulate commerce and to coin money and regulate its value, the Government claims, and some courts have decided that it possesses, the right to interfere with contracts, even after one of the parties to them has fulfilled his part of the obligation. The Government also claims that it possesses the power to authorize the liquidation of an obligation in a different currency from that stipulated in it; and that it can replace money by mere government promises to pay money at a future indefinite period of time! This not only impairs the obligations of contracts, which the framers of the Constitution evidently never intended to sanction, since they expressly forbid the States from doing so, but it further deprives the community of a sound currency, an instrument indispensable to the exchanges of commodities and services, the want of which invariably diminishes production; for production is affected by everything that impedes exchanges.

The power to establish post-offices and post-roads, although one of the functions exercised by all governments, is certainly a very needless and improper one. Private enterprise, if permitted, will carry letters more promptly and more economically than any government. The Post-office greatly increases the patronage of Government, and therefore the means of corruption within reach of political demagogues.

The people of the United States have not been benefited by the power to grant patents to inventors. Patent laws are now condemned by the most intelligent thinkers of Europe, as well as of this country. Michel Chevalier has recently expressed himself as entirely opposed to patent laws. Science and art require no protection from governments. They, like industry and commerce, flourish best when uninterfered with, in any manner, by governments.

Nor have the people of the United States been benefited by the stipulation that the importations of slaves should not be prohibited by Congress prior to 1808, but that a duty of $10 per person might be imposed on their importation. Here again we find human law and government sanctioning and legalizing that which the individual condemns. The perpetration of a crime was here made the source of revenue to the Government!

The clause authorizing Congress "to make all laws which shall be necessary and proper for carrying into execution the powers vested by the Constitution in Congress and in the Federal Government," has been made the source of the astounding claim that Congress can enact any law, and the President of the United States exercise any power, which may be deemed conducive to the well-being of the people! If this assumption be warranted, what is the meaning and intent of the ninth and tenth articles of the amendments of the Constitution, which expressly stipulate that "the enumeration in the Constitution of certain rights, shall not be construed to deny or disparage others retained by the people," and that "the powers not delegated to the United States by the Constitution, nor prohibited by it to the States, are reserved to the States respectively or to the people"?

The Constitution has thus been considered to authorize a centralized national government, whereas its great merit is really as a compact between independent States—as a new and almost perfect code of international law, based on a fuller and broader recognition of the inherent rights of humanity, as established by natural laws, than is to be found in any code of international law. Were the principles of the Constitution recognized by all nations, and accepted as the rule of action of all states, most of the evils of human governments, as heretofore conducted, would disappear, and humanity would realize a happiness and well-being hardly dreamed of by the most sanguine.

It is as a compact between independent States that the Constitution has conferred most of the benefits which the people of the United Sates have enjoyed under it, whilst all its evils and difficulties have risen, without exception, from those parts which are applicable to the functions of an ordinary government, and which attempt to control the individual actions of the people. We know that the doctrine that the States are sovereign is unpopular at this moment, and will be said to be the Southern State rights doctrine; but when correctly understood it will be found that there is a radical difference between our theory and the Southern doctrine of State rights. The latter holds that a State, when dissatisfied, may withdraw from the Union, and resume the powers delegated to the Federal Government; whilst we hold that there is nothing whatever in the Constitution to warrant this. The only thing that can have given rise to this theory appears to be, that portion of the Declaration of Independence which says that "Governments derive their just powers from the consent of the governed; that whenever any form of government becomes destructive of these ends (the protection of life, liberty, and the pursuit of happiness) it is the right of the people to alter or abolish it, and to institute a new government, laying its foundations on such principles, and organizing its powers in such form, as to them shall seem most likely to effect their safety and happiness." But the Declaration of Independence preceded the Constitution by more than eleven years, and, very naturally, defended the right of revolution, to which the States had just resorted. The Constitution itself is really a new code of international law, to which all the States gave their deliberate assent; and one of the well-established principles of international law is, that it can neither be abrogated nor modified by the will of one or more states. Every alteration in international law requires the unanimous, or nearly unanimous, assent of all the states that are to be controlled by it. But even if the Constitution be considered as the organic law of an ordinary government, it must be remembered that no government can recognize in its fundamental structure the right of any one to destroy it by violence. The Constitution, therefore, neither recognizes nor authorizes the right of secession; in fact, it even allows no possible excuse for the resort to revolution, since it establishes legal modes of redressing every possible grievance that may arise, by means of amendments to the Constitution itself, and by resort to the United States courts, which possess the power to declare unconstitutional any law of Congress or any act of the Government officials. All the powers conferred by the Constitution on Congress and on the Federal Government were undoubtedly intended to be supreme; to be exercised by no other authority, and to be neither resisted nor annulled by the individual action of the States. Nothing whatever can be found in the Constitution to sustain the Southern doctrine of State rights. But the States, nevertheless, were sovereign states previous to the adoption of the Constitution; and after its adoption still remained sovereign in regard to their reserved rights, precisely as the individual remains sovereign in regard to his natural rights delegated neither to the State nor to the Federal Government. That this is so, is beyond all question, for articles IX and X of the amendments to the Constitution are clear and explicit on this subject. And the rights they expressly reserve to the States and to the people are infinitely more numerous and important than those delegated to the Federal Government, since they comprise nearly all those which affect the actions and the property of the citizens.

The Federal Government was undoubtedly organized mainly with a view to the foreign relations of the States, and for the common defence against foreign aggressions. The War of Independence gave importance to these relations, otherwise it is doubtful whether any confederation would ever have been formed between communities so thoroughly imbued with ideas of local and individual liberty and independence as were the old colonies.

The Constitution of the United States created a central government, to which were delegated certain powers, to be exercised for the common good of all the States. All powers not expressly delegated are reserved to the States or to the individuals composing each State. In both the State and Federal Governments, the individual is recognized as the true and proper source of all power.

The real effective powers delegated to the Federal Government are merely:

1st. The power to negotiate with foreign nations.

2d. The power to declare war and maintain an army and navy.

3d. The regulation of commerce.

4th. The right to coin money.

5th. The transportation of the mails.

The States are prohibited from maintaining armies and navies—from levying taxes or duties on commodities imported or exported—from making anything but gold and silver a legal tender—and all questions between the States are to be submitted for adjudication to tribunals, the United States courts, whose decisions are final.

Now it is evident that if the principles of the Constitution of the United States were incorporated into a code of international law—and if this new code were recognized and submitted to by all civilized nations, nearly all the powers delegated to the Federal Government would lapse from non-use; for,

1st. All states or nations consenting to submit their grievances against each other to the decision of tribunals, *no standing armies or navies would be required.* The local police and the local militia would be ample to maintain local order everywhere.

2d. All states or nations being prohibited from imposing any obstacle to the free exchange of commodities, all custom houses, and all necessity for regulating commerce, would disappear at once.

3d. The moment all international disputes are to be settled by tribunals, there would be no negotiations to be carried on between states, and consequently there would be neither ambassadors nor consuls to be maintained at the expense of the people.

4th. As to the right of coining money, the several States being prohibited from making anything but gold and silver a legal tender, this power might be transferred to the States without danger or inconvenience, as a universal currency of uniform weight and fineness would then soon be adopted.

5th. As to the transportation of the mails, they should be left to private enterprise, which will perform this service far better and more economically than it will ever be done by any government.

The only sessions of Congress necessary under such a system would be when a modification of the code of international law became desirable, which would not often be the case after wars cease and the inherent rights of man are fully recognized and protected, because these rights ever remain the same.

With the cessation of the necessity for the use of the powers delegated by the Constitution to the Federal Government, would cease also all necessity for the present expenditures of that Government, and for the numerous officials it now employs. The people would thus save these enormous expenditures, and be further benefited by the return of the Government officials to productive occupations.

With such a code of international law as the arbiter of nations, what injury would there be in permitting the subdivision of States, *ad infinitum*, as long as each subdivision recognized the supremacy of the law of nations? Without a limit to the right of subdivision of States, would there be the slightest danger that any community would withdraw from a State unless a gross attack on individual or local rights were made by the State authorities? And would not this right of withdrawal from a State be the best and most efficient check on the usurpation of power by State authorities? Would not all government then soon become reduced to local governments, kept in check by the tribunals maintained by the code of nations? Would not all the present difficulties arising from Federal and State patronage, from Federal and State corruption, from Federal and State intervention with the rights and freedom of the individual, disappear at once, never to return under such a code of international law?

Under such a state of things, let us suppose that Long Island should decide to secede from the State of New York;

what injury or evil could this produce to the inhabitants of any portion of the State of New York or of any other State? Each citizen of every other State would continue to have the same rights in the new State of Long Island that they had there when it formed a portion of the State of New York; commerce between Long Island and the rest of the world would continue on precisely the same footing as before its withdrawal from the State of New York. The only difference would be that the former State jurisdiction of New York would be divided into two distinct jurisdictions, each exercising control over one of the new divisions, but both subject to the controlling influence of international law and of international courts.

The conclusions established by a careful and dispassionate analysis of man, of government, and of the natural laws which control both, are:

1st. That man, like everything else that exists, is perfect for the object for which he was created, and that he is constantly and efficiently controlled by just and perfect natural laws, the effects of which he cannot escape.

2d. That every attempt of man to counteract or escape from the effects of natural laws invariably injures him; whilst his submission and conformity to them invariably benefits him.

3d. That the individual is, at all times, when of sound mind, more competent than any one else to decide which of his numerous wants are, for the time being, most imperative, and in what manner they can be best supplied; but that he cannot do this properly and beneficially in regard to the wants of others.

4th. That as man is endowed not only with wants, but also with faculties which enable him to supply them, each individual should look for the supply of his wants to his own faculties and efforts, and not to those of others or of Government.

5th. That the only legitimate basis of government is the natural law of the division of labor.

6th. That, therefore, nothing should be done through Government, unless it secures greater results with the same effort than can be obtained from individual action.

7th. That the only proper object of government is the well-being and happiness of the governed—not that of any class or classes, but of all the members of the community.

8th. That the happiness and well-being of all are best secured by limiting government to the mere protection of life and property and the dispensation of prompt and equal justice to all. Every other proper object can be better and more surely attained by the individual through his own efforts, than by relying on the action of Government.

9th. That all individuals of sound mind are entitled to perfect freedom in all their actions, so long as they do not infringe on the like freedom of others.

10th. That the necessary imperfection of all human laws, which can never be made to adapt themselves, like the perfect laws of nature, to every varying circumstance, requires that they should constantly be modified in accordance with the variations in the circumstances they are intended to regulate or control.

11th. That these necessary alterations in human laws can only be made as promptly as is necessary to the well-being of the governed, by leaving each locality, the more restricted the better, to legislate for itself in regard to all matters that only affect local interests.

12th. That the more general interests of humanity can only be properly regulated by general conventions of nations, which should establish and recognize the inherent rights of man, and incorporate them in the law of nations, to which all should be made to conform.

13th. That all and every centralization of power is injurious to humanity, because a distant authority can never become properly acquainted with the varying wants of each locality. The laws of a centralized government must encounter varying circumstances in each locality in which they are to be enforced, and thus a law which is beneficial in one locality, may prove injurious in other localities. Therefore, local laws alone can prove beneficial to man.

Thus far every system of human government ever organized has proved a failure, if we consider the well-being and happiness of humanity the proper object of government. Is there not something very significant in this constant failure in the attempts to insure the happiness of man through the action of governments? Why has not man deduced long since the true principle it reveals? Does it not prove that arguments and examples are the only power which man should exercise over his fellow men? When we perceive that the actions of humanity are constantly and efficiently controlled by the natural laws of the Omniscient and Beneficent Ruler of all things, how can we continue to believe that the well-being of man is dependent on the short-sighted laws enacted and enforced by fallible men? * * *

ABRAHAM LINCOLN.

THE character of Abraham Lincoln is not an easy subject to discuss at this day. The effects of much that he has said and done remain yet to be seen. Beneath the good-humored, kind-hearted manners of Mr. Lincoln lay much that was stern and unsolvable. He was no unsophisticated man, nor yet was he a man of profound analytic powers. In all his public addresses it will be noticed that he addressed himself to the masses—"the plain people," he called them—and that provided enough was said to gain their approbation very little more was said. In this way Mr. Lincoln said many shallow things—things which at this time may to many of his fervent admirers seem profound and oracular enough, but which time and history will condemn as wanting cogency and breadth. Such, for instance, was that much-quoted paragraph of his in favor of revolution delivered in the House of Representatives, January 12, 1848:

"Any people, anywhere, being inclined and HAVING THE POWER, have a *right* to rise up and shake off the existing government, and form a new one that suits them better. This is a most valuable, a most sacred right—a right which, we hope and believe, is to liberate the world. Nor is this right confined to cases in which the whole people of an existing government may choose to exercise it. Any portion of such people that *can*, may revolutionize, and make their own of so much of the territory as they inhabit. More than this, a *majority* of any portion of such people may revolutionize, putting down a *minority*, intermingled with, or near about them, who may oppose their movements. Such minority was precisely the case of the Tories of our own Revolution."

Reduced to plain language, this is equal to saying: Both the right to revolutionize and to counter-revolutionize is derived from the power to do so. Therefore the greater the power the greater the right: which is an absurdity.

In his first message to Congress Mr. Lincoln said, "Again: if one State may secede, so may another; and when all shall have seceded, none is left to pay the debts." Surely the Union required no such feeble argument to prop it up.

Mr. Lincoln was not incapable, when it served his purpose, of addressing himself successfully, not indeed to the convictions but, to the emotions and sentiment of the better classes. What can be more impressive, for instance, than the italicized lines in the following address of his, recommending the adoption of the Emancipation proclamation to Congress?

"*I do not forget the gravity which should characterize a paper addressed to the Congress of the nation by the Chief Magistrate of the nation. Nor do I forget that some of you are my seniors; nor that many of you have more experience than I, in the conduct of public affairs.* Yet, I trust that in view of the great responsibility resting upon me, you will perceive no want of respect to yourselves, in any undue earnestness I may seem to display."

"Is it doubted, then, that the plan I propose, if adopted, would shorten the war, and thus lessen its expenditure of money and blood? Is it doubted that it would restore the national authority and national prosperity, and perpetuate both indefinitely? Is it doubted that we here—Congress and Executive—can secure its adoption? Will not the good people respond to a united and earnest appeal from us? Can we, can they, by any other means, so certainly or so speedily assure these vital objects? We can succeed only by concert. It is not 'can *any* of us *imagine* better,' but 'can we *all* do better?'

"The dogmas of the quiet past are inadequate to the stormy present. The occasion is piled high with difficulty, and we must rise with the occasion. As our case is new, so we must think anew, and act anew. We must disenthrall ourselves, and then we shall save our country.

"*Fellow-citizens, we cannot escape history. We, of this Congress and this Administration, will be remembered in spite of ourselves.* No personal significance, or insignificance, can spare one or another of us. *The fiery trial through which we pass will light us down, in honor or dishonor, to the latest generation.* We *say* we are for the Union. The world will not forget that we say this. We know how to save the Union. The world knows we do know how to save it. We—even *we* here—hold the power and bear the responsibility. *In giving freedom to the slave we assure freedom to the free—honorable alike in that we give and what we preserve. We shall nobly save, or meanly lose, the last best hope of earth. Other means may succeed; this could not fail. The way is plain, peaceful, generous, just—a way which, if followed, the world will forever applaud, and God must forever bless.*

Nay, besides being impressive, it possesses many of the elements of a high order of poetry. But here his power to sway the thinking classes ended. He was incapable of employing abstract arguments—he never used generalizations, but supplied their place with familiar illustrations and homely morals. Called to execute the wishes of thirty millions of people, Abraham Lincoln was altogether too original a character to permit his individuality to be lost in his official life. It constantly displayed itself in the quaint stories with which he interlarded all his speeches—stories of pioneer life, of Western experience—stories of humble men and humble things.

Guided by his strong good sense, Mr. Lincoln groped his way through many difficult situations with safety, but he must have sadly felt the want of more thorough training in social science. Many of his political convictions were anti-scientific. He was a protectionist. He was a centralizationist. In the last message which he ever sent to Congress, he invites the attention of that body to the principle of exempting Government bonds from taxation and seizure for debt—a principle which, though already partially reduced to practice, would, if wholly carried out, not only furnish a premium to extensive rascality, but would set up an additional stake in the enclosure of legislation which now hedges in the Government and centralizes its functions beyond the intentions of its original founders.

The death of Mr. Lincoln could only have been planned by a madman, because, for many reasons, no person in his place could have been disposed so kindly toward the Southerners as himself. He had fought them for four years, and not always with success. With inferior means and fewer numbers the South had kept the field, and defied all his efforts to subdue them. Only after one hundred thousand negro troops had been added to the Federal army was any serious impression made upon the enemy. Mr. Lincoln not only admitted this himself,* but being in a position where the truth concerning both combatants was always within his reach, it would have been singular had he not learned to admire his antagonists both for their earnestness and bravery. Nobody about him was known to be so well inclined toward the South as Mr. Lincoln himself. And had the plan been carried out of killing all those who by law might have immediately succeeded him in office, the uncertainty of gaining by the operation is very manifest.

The political consequences flowing from the death of Mr. Lincoln are very few. The country is happy in possessing for his successor a gentleman who not only seems determined to carry out, for the present, Mr. Lincoln's policy to the letter, but is also gifted with the talent of avoiding to do it in a servile way. The plan of reconstruction pursued by Mr. Johnson is precisely that which had previously been marked out by his predecessor. The late amnesty proclamation was sketched by

* Message of December 8, 1863.

him a year and a half before his death. In his message of December, 1863, both of these subjects will be found to have received Mr. Lincoln's careful reflection, and to have been disposed of in the manner subsequently adopted by his successor in office. Mr. Johnson has followed directly in his path. So quietly and easily has he done this that the country scarcely feels that its late Chief Magistrate is dead but little over two months.

The social consequences which must follow the death of Mr. Lincoln are more important. Mr. Johnson is an anti-centralizationist and a free trader. These are salient points in his political character, and when the questions which came up for settlement during Mr. Lincoln's life are settled in accordance with Mr. Lincoln's opinions, and new questions are presented for executive consideration, Mr. Johnson will apply to them the principles of a school of statesmanship differing very materially from that of his predecessor.

From the many difficulties which lay in Mr. Lincoln's path, the late lamented President found an easy refuge in depending on Providence.* This is all very well, provided you are sure that Providence thinks it worth its while to have anything to do with the difficulty, and also provided Providence was consulted before the difficulty was raised. But Mr. Lincoln was very superstitious. His superstition went so far that, upon the testimony of one who professes to have been his intimate friend, he suffered a trifling optical illusion to worry his mind, and to assume the character of an evil foreboding, "making him wish he had never seen it." †

---

* His practice of being controlled by events is well known. He often said that it was wise to wait for the developments of Providence; and the Scriptural phrase that "the stars in their courses fought against Sisera" to him had a depth of meaning.

* * * * * *

The honesty of Mr. Lincoln appeared to spring from religious convictions; and it was his habit, when conversing of things which most intimately concerned himself, to say that, however he might be misapprehended by men who did not appear to know him, he was glad to know that no thought or intent of his escaped the observation of that Judge by whose final decree he expected to stand or fall in this world and the next. It seemed as though this was his surest refuge at times when he was most misunderstood or misrepresented. There was something touching in his childlike and simple reliance upon Divine aid, especially when in such extremities as he sometimes fell into; then, though prayer and reading of the Scriptures was his constant habit, he more earnestly than ever sought that strength which is promised when mortal help faileth. His address upon the occasion of his re-inauguration has been said to be as truly a religious document as a state-paper; and his acknowledgment of God and His providence and rule are interwoven through all of his later speeches, letters, and messages.—*Harper's Magazine for July*, 1865—*Personal Recollections of Abraham Lincoln.*

† Shortly after the presidential election, in 1864, he related an incident which I will try to put upon paper here, as nearly as possible in his own words:

So far as there are any means of knowing, Mr. Johnson's character is of an entirely different stamp. He is a man capable of framing a correct policy long in advance of the time when it is to be acted upon, and possessed of resolution and firmness enough to carry it through, even though in so doing he might excite the emnity of the leaders of his own political party. A man possessed of this independence of character must rely for his support upon the people, and to rely upon the people he must favor popular measures. Such measures are those which Mr. Johnson has already expressed his intention to espouse—Free Trade and Local Rights. Mr. Lincoln acted upon the sympathies of the people through the acts of the eminent men about him, whom he suffered to influence his official career—through the diplomacy of Seward, the firm administration of Dix, the great military ability of Grant, the extraordinary genius of Sherman, and the courage of Farragut. These were the means which he took to gain the support of the people. And with these he excited their discontent by employing the reckless and ambitious Chase and the iron-heeled Stanton. Mr. Lincoln was a man full of pathos and humor, a soft-hearted man—a good man—an honest man; but we fear history will scarcely give him credit for strength of intellect, or far-seeing statesmanship. Mr. Johnson, we venture to predict, will prove to be a man of very different calibre. He will not act through his cabinet ministers, not rely upon circumstances, but will form his policy at the start, and carry it out inflexibly to the end. Provided this policy discards expediency and stands fast to

---

"It was just after my election in 1860, when the news had been coming in thick and fast all day, and there had been a great 'Hurrah, boys!' so that I was well tired out, and went home to rest, throwing myself down on a lounge in my chamber. Opposite where I lay was a bureau, with a swinging-glass upon it"—(and here he got up and placed furniture to illustrate the position)—"and, looking in that glass, I saw myself reflected, nearly at full length; but my face, I noticed, had *two* separate and distinct images, the tip of the nose of one being about three inches from the tip of the other. I was a little bothered, perhaps startled, and got up and looked in the glass, but the illusion vanished. On lying down again I saw it a second time—plainer, if possible, than before; and then I noticed that one of the faces was a little paler, say five shades, than the other. I got up, and the thing melted away, and I went off and, in the excitement of the hour, forgot all about it—nearly, but not quite, for the thing would once in a while come up, and give me a little pang, as though something uncomfortable had happened. When I went home I told my wife about it, and a few days after I tried the experiment again, when [with a laugh], sure enough, the thing came again; but I never succeeded in bringing the ghost back after that, though I once tried very industriously to show it to my wife, who was worried about it somewhat. She thought it was 'a sign' that I was to be elected to a second term of office, and that the paleness of one of the faces was an omen that I should not see life through the last term."

The President, with his usual good sense, saw nothing in all this but an optical illusion; though the flavor of superstition which hangs about every man's composition made him wish that he had never seen it.—*Ibid.*

principle, the country will have cause to be as grateful to him for thus restoring it to prosperity after the war, as it has to be grateful to his predecessor for pulling it successfully through the war.

Had Mr. Lincoln survived the return of peace, there could scarcely be any doubt that his policy would have been eminently conservative. The gentlemen who surrounded him as official advisers, the party leaders to whom he was indebted for his unlooked-for elevation, the numerous friends and chums of his humble early life who had obtained office under him, all these people, either from conviction or from interested motives, would have urged upon him a strong government, a centralization of power, protection, exclusion, monopoly, Pacific railroads, branch mints, debased coppers, three cent stamps, forms, oaths, red tape, and circumlocution. Tariffs framed by Thaddeus Stevens, and tax systems by Mr. Boutwell, would have found favor with the kind and easy nature of Mr. Lincoln. He was indebted to all these people. They had helped him to power, and supported him afterward. Under their influence he had risen to eminence; and (let us say) *in spite* of their measures he had brought the country safely through a great war. Could he turn his back upon them now, and particularly when his own leanings towards protection offered no obstacle to the elementary principles upon which all their measures were based? Decidedly not.

With Mr. Johnson the case is different. He is at liberty to cut loose from all these entanglements; and he has cut loose from them. We are convinced that the existing retention of Mr. Lincoln's cabinet ministers in office is only due to motives of delicacy. Mr. Johnson said, in a late speech to a Southern delegation, seeking civil government for their State:

"He had no hesitation in saying that before and after he entered public life he was opposed to monopolies and perpetuities and entails. From Magna Charta we had derived our ideas of freedom of speech, liberty of the press and unreasonable searches, and that private property should not be taken for public uses without just compensation. He had these notions fixed in his mind, and was therefore opposed to class legislation. Being providentially brought to his present condition, he intended to exert the power and influence of the Government so as to place in power the popular heart of this nation."

These words are very remarkable. They show the drift of the Executive mind. And under the system of government into which the Constitution of the United States has been tortured, the drift of the Executive mind is a matter of no little consequence to the destinies of the entire people. These words indicate to the American people that a time is at hand when the ruinous and blighting restrictions now laid upon the industry of the country will be removed. They point toward popular rights and popular freedom. The "popular heart of this nation is to be embodied in the measures of Government," and a career of prosperity is indicated which will so far eclipse all former eras in our history, that even the great war we have passed through will be speedily forgotten. Prosperity will make us forgetful. Over the graves of the myriads who fell in the struggle, and over the ruin of private fortunes and the desolation of homes, the great harvest of future wealth which peace and free trade are now sowing will wave its golden head till the ashes which moulder beneath are completely hidden both from view and remembrance.

Another melancholy consolation may be drawn from the occurrence of Mr. Lincoln's death and the accession of Mr. Johnson to office. During the war, Mr. Lincoln had leaned too plainly towards the exercise of doubtful powers ever to hope for the support of the Democratic party at the North, even though the only questions which separated Democrats from Republicans were settled by the war. Pride alone would have made them his enemies. The case is different with Mr. Johnson. Not only is he a different person from Mr. Lincoln, and for that reason alone not objectionable to the Democratic party, but, being a Democrat himself, his official acts will obtain the votes of the entire South; and thus encouraged by the combined support of the late opposition and the late insurgents, as well as that of the Republican party, his administration can only prove inimical to the wishes of a few political discontents who are never pleased with anything.

For these reasons, and for many others, which yet only assume the shadowy outlines of argument, should the American people feel that the cruel death of Abraham Lincoln is not an unmitigated misfortune to them. E. P.

STATISTICS.

THE CUSTOM-HOUSE SYSTEM.

As the subject of the customs revenue would appear to be destined to become the point at which the opposing tides of the now mooted questions of Free Trade and Protection will meet, we think it desirable at once to dip into the official statistics of receipts and expenditures concerning custom houses, so that we may know exactly what they cost us and what they yield. Though confident that the official figures only reveal a small portion of the expenditures, made directly or indirectly on account of the revenue service, because many of the Treasury expenditures under the head of "Miscellaneous," have a strong suspicion about them of belonging to revenue matters, and for other reasons, yet we shall not go outside of the published figures for our data. Our intention is to only embrace the periods from 1860 to 1865; but in order to divest our exposition from any suspicion of being special or unfair, we commence by giving the total amounts received for duties during each year since 1855.

TOTAL REVENUE COLLECTED FROM CUSTOMS, DUTIES, IMPOSTS AND TONNAGE BY THE UNITED STATES GOVERNMENT FROM THE YEAR 1855. (*See Finance Report* 1864, *p.* 238.)

Fiscal year.	*Amount Collected.*
1855	$ 53,025,794
1856	64,022,863
1857	63,875,905
1858	41,789,620
1859	49,565,824
1860	53,187,511
1861	39,582,125
1862	49,056,397
1863	69,059,642
1864	102,316,152
1865	76,000,000
Total in ten years	$661,481,833
Average yearly collections	66,148,183

We now proceed to give the Custom-House budget of receipts and expenditures for each separate year:

CUSTOM-HOUSE BUDGET, 1859-'60.

Receipts	$53,187,511

EXPENDITURES, (*Finance Report* 1860, *pp.* 17 *to* 20.)

Expenses of collecting the Revenue from Customs	$3,324,430
Repayment to importers of excess of deposits for unascertained duties	814,827
Debentures or drawbacks, bounties or allowances	585,158
Refunding duties on foreign merchandise imported	3,275
Refunding duties under act to extend the warehousing system	464
Refunding duties on fish and other articles under reciprocity treaty with Great Britain	82
Refunding duties collected in Mexico from military contributions	3,902
Debentures and other charges per act of Oct. 16, 1837	8,187
Proceeds (loss on) the sales of goods per act April 2, 1844	843
Salaries of special examiners of drugs and medicines	5.917
Additional compensation to collectors, naval officers, &c.	5,467
Building Custom Houses	455,276
Annual repairs of Custom Houses	6,875
Total	$5,214,703

Items included in which it is believed are some expenses for the support of the Custom House system.

Surveyors and their clerks	$109,080
Supervising and local inspectors, &c.	82,626
Contingent expenses under the act for the safe keeping of the public revenue	10,334
Compensation to persons designated to receive and keep the public moneys	1,388
Building vaults as additional security to the public funds in sixty-six depositories	3,594
Continuation of the Treasury building	248,023
Lighting and ventilating same	3,568
Building post-offices, court houses, &c., (in some localities one building is used for a Custom House in connection with the above purposes)	110,307
Payment of mortgage and interest on property in Pine street, New York	10,362
Relief of sundry individuals	256,175
Sundry items	8,358
Total	$843,815

We now proceed to the next year's budget.

CUSTOM-HOUSE BUDGET, 1860-1.

Receipts	$39,182,525

EXPENDITURES, (*Finance Report* 1860, *pp.* 37 *to* 40.)

Expenses of collecting the revenue from customs	$2,834,764
Repayment to importers the excess of deposits for unascertained duties	764,575
Debentures or drawbacks, bounties or allowances	640,115
Refunding duties under act to extend the warehousing system	1,045
Debentures and other charges, per act of Oct. 16, 1837	8,526
Salaries of special examiners of drugs and medicines	4,990
Additional compensation to collectors, naval officers, &c.	9,669
Building Custom Houses, including repairs	364,631
Analyses of 88 specimens of iron, &c.	6,984
Total	$4,635,299

DOUBTFUL ITEMS.

Supervising and local inspection, &c.	$81,550
Contingent expenses under act for safe keeping of public revenue	32,952
Compensation to persons designated to receive and keep the public revenue	3,486
Building vaults as additional security to the public funds in sixty-six depositories	2,180
Alterations and repairs of buildings in Washington, &c.	72,782
Relief of sundry individuals	374,587
Sundry items	12,997
Total	$580,534

The following year is the first one of the late war.

CUSTOM-HOUSE BUDGET, 1861-2.

Receipts,	$49,056,397

EXPENDITURES, (*See Finance Report*, 1862, *pp.* 37 *to* 40.)

Expenses of collecting the revenue from customs,	$3,284,724
Repayments to importers the excess of deposits for unascertained duties,	1,642,940
Debentures or drawbacks, bounties or allowances,	637,224
Debentures and other charges per act Oct. 16, 1837,	6,918
Salaries of special examiners of drugs and medicines,	4,122
Additional compensation to Collectors, naval officers, &c.,	6,355
Refunding duties on fish, &c., under reciprocity treaty with Great Britain,	2,609
Refunding duties on arms imported by States,	65,173
Building custom houses, including repairs,	26,066
Total,	$5,676,131

DOUBTFUL ITEMS.

Supervising and local inspectors, &c.,	$57,756
Contingent expenses under act for safe keeping of public revenue,	48,120
Compensation to persons designated to receive and keep public revenue,	938
Building vaults as additional security to public funds in sixty-six depositories,	1,282
Continuation of Treasuary Building,	294,511
Public Buildings in Territories,	7,217
Alterations and repairs of public buildings in Washington,	31,125
Total,	$440,949

The following year is the second one of the war.

CUSTOM-HOUSE BUDGET, 1862-3.

Receipts,	$69,059,642

EXPENDITURES, (*See Finance Report*, 1863, *pp.* 35 *to* 37.)

Incidental expenses in changing location of New York Custom House, fire-proof file cases for collector at New York, &c.,	$166,562
Expenses of collecting the revenue from customs,	3,238,936
Repayments to importers the excess of deposits from ascertained duties,	2,262,770
Debentures or drawbacks, bounties or allowances,	1,026,135
Debentures and other charges under act of Oct. 16, 1837,	7,027
Refunding duties on arms imported by States,	11,703
Refunding duties under act extending the warehouse system,	4,837
Additional compensation to Collectors, naval officers, &c.,	4,118
Salaries of special examiner of drugs,	4,537
Building custom-houses, including repairs,	100,174
Total,	$6,826,799

DOUBTFUL ITEMS.

Supervising and local inspectors, &c.,	$63,310
Contingent expenses under act for safe keeping of public revenue,	44,550
Compensation to persons designated to receive and keep the public revenue,	1,049
Building vaults as additional security to public funds in sixty-six depositories,	2,686
Building post-offices, court houses, &c., (custom-houses, warehouses, revenue offices, boat-houses, &c., are often included under this head),	83,740
Alterations and repairs of buildings in Washington, &c.,	59,369
Sundry items,	15,221
Total,	269,925

We now approach the third year of the war, and the last year for which we have as yet definite figures.

CUSTOM-HOUSE BUDGET, 1863–4.

Receipts,	$102,316,152

EXPENDITURES, (*See Finance Report*, 1864, *pp.* 35 *to* 40).

Incidental expenses in changing location of New York Custom House, constructing fire-proof file cases for collector, &c.,	$73,492
Expenses of collecting revenue from customs,	4,146,584
Repayment to importers of excess of deposits from ascertained duties,	2,597,891
Debentures or drawbacks, bounties or allowances,	1,051,331
Refunding duties under act to extend warehousing system,	491
Debentures and other charges,	9,184
Salaries of special examiner of drugs,	4,249
Additional compensation to collectors, naval officers, &c.,	1,120
Building custom-houses, including repairs, &c.,	83,068
Building marine hospitals and custom houses,	1,014
For unclaimed merchandise (loss),	2,490
Proceeds of sales of goods, wares, &c., (loss)	405
Repairing Government warehouse at Staten Island,	39,550
Purchase of steam or sailing revenue cutters,	377,666
	$8,388,535

DOUBTFUL ITEMS, 1864.

For supervising and local inspectors, &c	$63,362
Contingent expenses under the act for safe keeping the public revenue	70,061
Compensation to persons designated to receive and keep the public money	1,611
Building vaults as additional security to the public funds in sixty-six depositories	12,786
Continuation of Treasury building	655,491
Building Post-offices, Court Houses, *et cetera*, including purchase of sites	39,842
Alterations and repairs of buildings in Washington	478.257
Relief of sundry individuals	48,550
Total	$1,369,960

We come now to the budget of the fiscal year which has just expired, and as no official report has yet been made of the transactions of the Treasury Department, we must rely for our figures partly on accounts which have reached us from Washington and partly on estimate.

CUSTOM-HOUSE BUDGET, 1864–5.

Receipts $76,000,000

EXPENDITURES (ESTIMATED.)

Items directly charged to Custom-House expenditure on the books of the treasurer.. $9,785,000

DOUBTFUL ITEMS.

Amount included in various charges made according to official formula, but applicable in part to Custom-House expenditures $1,149,000

We now present a summary of the past five years' transactions, charging to the account of custom houses one-third of the amount embraced under doubtful items.

SUMMARY.

Fiscal Year.	Total Receipts from Customs.	Expenses of Collecting same as per Treasury Reports.	One third of "Doubtful Items."	Total Expenditure.
1860........	$ 53,187,511	$ 5,214,703	$ 281,272	$ 5,495,975
1861........	39,582,125	4,635,799	193,511	4,828,810
1862........	49,056,397	5,676,131	146,983	5,823,114
1863........	69,059,642	6,826,799	89,975	6,916,774
1864........	102,316,152	8,388,535	456,653	8,845,188
1865........	76,000,000	9,785,000	383,000	10,168,000
Total......	$389,201,827	$40,526,467	$1,551,394	$42,077,861

From the above summary it will be seen that the expenditures on account of our external revenue system bear on the average the proportion of about eleven per cent. to the receipts—falling to ten per cent. under a moderate tariff, like that of 1860, rising to thirteen per cent. under a high tariff, like the present one, and varying considerably under such changeable tariffs as prevailed during the intermediate years between those last mentioned.

But eleven per cent. of the sum raised from duties on exports is not all that the custom-house system costs the Government. It costs it the interest and the insurance risks on those permanent investments of capital which, in order to support the system, are necessary to be made in public buildings, ships, etc.; it costs it that portion of the expenses of the Naval Department which are incurred in fitting out, repairing, manning, and officering revenue cutters and blockaders; and it costs many other Governmental expenditures, which would here be tedious to relate. But let us see what those amount to which we have already enumerated.

The total cost of the various public buildings which the Government has erected since the year 1807, such as custom houses, warehouses, boarding stations, buildings used partly for these purposes and partly for other purposes, etc., amounts to about $30,000,000. The capital invested in these buildings being unproductive, the Government loses the interest which the capital is worth to it, and which, gauged by the rate which it is now paying for loans at par, is seven and three tenths per cent. The Government also takes upon itself the risk of insuring these buildings against fire and other casualties. That these risks run by the Government are very imminent is perceived from the fact that many of the buildings used for these purposes in the Southern States have lately been destroyed by act of war. In addition to these charges there should be one to balance that amount of revenue which the Government would derive from this property if it were in private hands, and subject to taxes under the internal revenue laws. In a word, the cost of holding this real estate should be reckoned at the same rate that city property now generally costs to hold when in the hands of private parties. This rate we put at ten per cent. per annum. Ten per cent. per annum on $30,000,000 amounts to $3,000,000 per annum.

The annual cost of maintaining the vessels usually employed in the revenue service, including steam and sailing cutters, boarding skiffs, etc., counting interest and risk on investment, wages of men and officers, repairs, outfits, etc., is about $2,000,000.

We can now make a pretty correct summary of what the custom-house system costs the Government; and having done this, we shall next proceed to examine what it costs the people.

SUMMARY OF COST OF CUSTOM-HOUSE SYSTEM TO THE GOVERNMENT.

Average yearly income for past six years	$64,866,988
Average yearly expenditures as stated in reports of the Treasury Department	7,012,977
Expenditures connected with maintaining public buildings for collection of duties on imports ten per cent. per annum, or..	701,297
Expenditures connected with maintaining public vessels for collection of duties on imports	2,000,000
Total average yearly cost of the system to the Government, being over 14 per cent. on the income derived from same	9,714,274

What this system costs the people shall be told in a future article.

THE

NEW YORK

SOCIAL SCIENCE REVIEW:

A JOURNAL OF

POLITICAL ECONOMY AND STATISTICS.*

OCTOBER, 1865.

OUR FIRST VOLUME.

THE present number completes the first volume of THE NEW YORK SOCIAL SCIENCE REVIEW; and the Publishers embrace this opportunity to address themselves directly to its readers.

On publishing this periodical they held forth the following language in its prospectus:

> To trace and examine by the light of science the social evolutions which are constantly transpiring; to critically examine every law having for its object the raising of revenue and the distribution of the burthens of taxation; to discover in what manner our National and State legislation can be improved so as to further the best interests of humanity; to exhibit the ignorance and venality of politicians, and show the futility and mischievous tendency of their measures; will be the special aims and objects of this Review.
>
> THE NEW YORK SOCIAL SCIENCE REVIEW will never degenerate into an advocacy of partisan policy. Its province will be extended not only to our own affairs, but to those of all nations; and it will represent the best views on Political Economy, come from what quarter they may. From time to time carefully prepared Statistics will appear in its pages, and every effort will be made to render the work valuable alike to the student of Political Economy and to the practical Legislator.

It is believed that these pledges have been fully lived up to. Furthermore, without promising to do either thing, the work has been enlarged, and the price lowered. But the reading public can form no idea of the difficulties with which the Publishers have had to cope. Notwithstanding the vital importance to our people of organized knowledge on the subject of Social Science, but few works pertaining to it are published in this country. Those that come from other countries are very useful to us (and herein they are invaluable,) in the discussion of general principles. Whenever they apply these principles to practical affairs, it is to the affairs of other countries ; not to those of our own. Our Editors have, therefore, been obliged mainly to confine themselves to the reviewal of current official documents, relating to the political and social condition of the country. If, in discussing the character and tone of these papers, the prejudices of political partizans have sometimes been shocked, the fault should be ascribed to the nature of the documents themselves, and to their well-known lack of philosophical breadth; and not to any partizanship on the part of the Editors.

Not only books for review, but reviewers also, have been difficult to obtain. Among the political economists of the United States, but few are not committed to principles which we cannot fully endorse, and to these few, accordingly, have we been mainly indebted for the matter which has appeared in our pages. They comprise the names of Charles Moran, Esq., Rev. O. B. Frothingham, Dr. Julius Homberger, Henry Harrisse, Esq., Emile Walter, Esq., and those of the two Editors, Messrs. Delmar, and Stern. Principles which lead to the centralization of the powers of government and to increased restraint, we cannot support—for these lead to social degeneration, to social poverty, to social annihilation. The plan which we adopted—that of attaching the names of the writers to their articles—we thought would invite contributions from the best talent in the country. We have received contributions enough, it is true, but not of such value in a scientific or literary point of view as would warrant their publication.

Another source of difficulty to the Publishers has been in the absence of appreciative and discriminating criticisms from the press. Such notices as have been given to our work, and so far as numbers are concerned we have no cause to complain, were, for the most part, mere advertising notices, or else contained silly charges against, or gross and uncalled for personal attacks upon, the Editors. Sometimes, worse still, they were written in a tone of jocular approval, or of absurd panegyric. Thus, a leading newspaper in Chicago styled the REVIEW "a copper-head quarterly—Fernando Wood in imperial purple." Another in New York stigmatized it as "an abolition journal, in the interests of New England." The paper of the largest circulation in New Orleans concluded a fatiguingly funny critique, by wishing the Editors "a good time;" another in Boston deemed our tone "Mormonish and heartless;" and one in Philadelphia thought our work "the crowning pinnacle of American science." Out of consideration for their own repute we forbear, for the present, to name these journals, as well as to repeat the disgraceful personal abuse of the authors of certain theories broached in this REVIEW, in which some of them indulged—theories which find their support in the observations and speculations of the profoundest minds in Europe.

It is not business puffs for their REVIEW that the Publishers desire—it is appreciative and critical reviewal. They do not flinch from the keenest sort of examination; the keener the better; because they want to know wherein their publication is faulty; and they cordially invite the press to pass upon it, by the severest canons of scientific and literary criticism. They do not expect it to pass this ordeal unscathed, for they are conscious it must be full of faults, and are daily engaged in repairing such of them as they are able to discover, or as are kindly pointed out to them; but they claim for the work the consideration and respect due to its earnestness and its regard for scientific truth, and, when judgment is passed upon it, that it shall be based upon the scientific character of its contents, and not upon the presumed motives of its Publishers or its Editors.

Aside from these several difficulties the Publishers look back upon the history of the first year of their enterprize with no little satisfaction. The REVIEW was projected by four members of the New York Society for the Advancement of Social

Science, who, one evening, after a meeting of the Society, met around a supper-table at the *Maison Dorée*, and suddenly resolved upon its publication. Started with a limited subscription list, made up in the city of New York alone, the REVIEW has come to be extensively read all over the United States, and Europe; and it may now fairly be classed among the permanently established periodicals of the day. It numbers among its subscribers some of the most gifted of American authors, scientists, and legislators; and has even made its way to Congress, and been instrumental in directing legislative attention to the faults of our internal revenue system.

To disseminate the truths of Social Science—that science which is the sum of all the sciences—was a task not undertaken without misgivings, nor to be performed without difficulty. The soil was very barren—is still very barren—and the fruit we would cultivate will not grow until it is planted in the richest mould.

To expect that our work would become popular, after an existence of a single year, would have been unreasonable ; yet we do not labor without the hope of ultimately making it so ; for our aim will be, while teaching theoretic truths, constantly to apply them to practice.

The student will find in the pages of the REVIEW the most advanced theories of Social Science ; the legislator will find these theories applied to the prevailing state of affairs ; and the commercial classes, bankers, underwriters, shareholders, manufacturers, merchants, jobbers, brokers and shippers, to the every-day operations of business. The statistical department will keep pace with the latest researches ; and the reviews and book notices will receive their full share of attention.

In conclusion, we call upon the scientific and literary talent of the country to aid us in our undertaking. We pay liberally for all accepted contributions to our pages; and give the writer the credit of his work by attaching his name to it. Our object is to draw this talent forth; and we would not have it said that we left any means untried to accomplish this end.

THE PUBLISHERS.

NEW YORK, *October* 1, 1865.

WHAT IS FREE TRADE?

(CONTINUED.)

EQUALIZING OF THE FACILITIES OF PRODUCTION.

THE protectionists often use the following argument:

"It is our belief that protection should correspond to, should be the representation of, the difference which exists between the price of an article of home production and a similar article of foreign production. A protective duty calculated upon such a basis does nothing more than secure free competition; free competition can only exist where there is an equality in the facilities of production. In a horse-race the load which each horse carries is weighed and all advantages equalized; otherwise there could be no competition. In commerce, if one producer can undersell all others, he ceases to be a competitor and becomes a monopolist. Suppress the protection which represents the difference of price according to each, and foreign produce must immediately inundate and obtain the monopoly of our market. Every one ought to wish, for his own sake and for that of the community, that the productions of the country, should be protected against foreign competition, *whenever the latter may be able to undersell the former.*"

This argument is constantly recurring in all writings of the protectionist school. It is my intention to make a careful investigation of its merits, and I must begin by soliciting the attention and the patience of the reader. I will first examine into the inequalities which depend upon natural causes, and afterwards into those which are caused by diversity of taxes.

Here, as elsewhere, we find the theorists who favor protection, taking part with the producer. Let us consider the case of the unfortunate consumer, who seems to have entirely escaped their attention. They compare the field of production to the *turf*. But on the turf, the race is at once a *means and an end*. The public has no interest in the struggle, independent of the struggle itself. When your horses are started in the course with the single object of determining which is the best runner, nothing is more natural than that their burdens should be equalized. But if your object were to send an important and critical piece of intelligence, could you without incongruity place obstacles to the speed of that one whose fleetness would secure you the best means of attaining your end? And yet this is your course in relation to industry. You forget the end aimed at, which is the *well-being* of the community; you set it aside; more, you sacrifice it by a perfect *petitio principii.*

But we cannot lead our opponents to look at things from our point of view; let us now take theirs, let us examine the question as producers.

I will seek to prove:

1. That equalizing the facilities of production is to attack the foundations of mutual exchange.

2. That it is not true that the labor of one country can be crushed by the competition of more favored climates.

3. That, even were this the case, protective duties cannot equalize the facilities of production.

4. That freedom of trade equalizes these conditions as much as possible; and

5. That the countries which are the least favored by nature are those which profit most by mutual exchange.

I. The equalizing of the facilities of production, is not only the shackling of certain articles of commerce, but it is the attacking of the system of mutual exchange in its very foundation principle. For this system is based precisely upon the very diversities, or, if the expression be preferred, upon the inequalities of fertility, climate, temperature, capabilities, which the protectionists seek to render null. If New England sends its manufactures to the West, and the West sends corn to New England, it is because these two sections are, from different circumstances, induced to turn their attention to the production of different articles. Is there any other rule for international exchanges? Again, to bring against such exchanges the very inequalities of condition which excite and explain them, is to attack them in their very cause of being. The protective system, closely followed up, would bring men to live like snails, in a state of complete isolation. In sum, there is not one of its Sophisms, which if carried through by vigorous deductions, would not end in destruction and annihilation.

II. The statement is not true that the unequal facility of production, between two similar branches of industry, should necessarily cause the destruction of the one which is the least fortunate. On the turf, if one horse gains the prize, the other loses it; but when two horses work to produce any useful article, each produces in proportion to his strength; and because the stronger is the more useful, it does not follow that the weaker is good for nothing. Wheat is cultivated in every section of the United States, although there are great differences in the degree of fertility existing among them. If it happens that there be one which does not cultivate it, it is because, even to itself, such cultivation is not useful. Analogy will show us, that under the influences of an unshackled trade, notwithstanding similar differences, wheat would be produced in every portion of the world; and if any nation were induced to abandon entirely the cultivation of it, this would only be, because it would *be her interest* to employ otherwise her lands, her capital, and her labor. And why does not the fertility of one department paralyze the agriculture of a neighboring and less favored one? Because the phenomena of political economy have a suppleness, an elasticity, and, so to speak, *a self-leveling power*, which seems to escape the attention of the school of protectionists. They accuse us of being theoretic, but it is themselves who are so to a supreme degree, if the being theoretic consists in building up systems upon the experience of a single fact, instead of profiting by the experience of a series of facts. In the above example, it is the difference in the value of lands, which compensates for the difference in their fertility. Your field produces three times as much as mine. Yes. But it has cost you ten times as much, and therefore I can still compete with you: this is the sole mystery. And observe how the advantage on one point leads to disadvantage on the other. Precisely because your soil is more fruitful, it is more dear. It is not *accidentally* but *necessarily* that the equilibrium is established, or at least inclines to establish itself: and can it be denied that perfect freedom in exchanges is of all systems the one which favors this tendency?

I have cited an agricultural example; I might as easily have taken one from any trade. There are tailors at Barnegat, but that does not prevent tailors from being in New York also, although the latter have to pay a much higher rent, as well as higher price for furniture, workmen, and food. But their customers are sufficiently numerous not only to re-establish the balance, but also to make it lean on their side.

When therefore the question is about equalizing the advantages of labor, it would be well to consider whether the natural freedom of exchange is not the best umpire.

This self-leveling faculty of political phenomena is so important, and at the same time so well calculated to cause us to admire the providential wisdom which presides over the equalizing government of society, that I must ask permission a little longer, to turn to it the attention of the reader.

The protectionists say, Such a nation has the advantage over us, in being able to procure cheaply, coal, iron, machinery, capital; it is impossible for us to compete with it.

We must examine this proposition under other aspects. For the present, I stop at the question, whether, when an advantage and a disadvantage are placed in juxtaposition, they do not bear in themselves, the former a descending, the latter an ascending power, which must end by placing them in a just equilibrium.

Let us suppose the countries A and B. A has every advantage over B; you thence conclude that labor will be concentrated upon A, while B must be abandoned. A, you say, sells much more than it buys; B buys much more than it sells. I might dispute this, but I will meet you upon your own ground.

In the hypothesis, labor, being in great demand in A, soon rises in value; while labor, iron, coal, lands, food, capital, all being little sought after in B, soon fall in price.

Again: A being always selling and B always buying, cash

passes from B to A. It is abundant in A—very scarce in B.

But where there is abundance of cash, it follows that in all purchases a large proportion of it will be needed. Then in A, *real dearness*, which proceeds from a very active demand, is added to *nominal dearness*, the consequence of a superabundance of the precious metals.

Scarcity of money implies that little is necessary for each purchase. Then in B, a *nominal cheapness* is combined with *real cheapness.*

Under these circumstances, industry will have the strongest possible motives for deserting A, to establish itself in B.

Now, to return to what would be the true course of things. As the progress of such events is always gradual, industry from its nature being opposed to sudden transits, let us suppose that, without waiting the extreme point, it will have gradually divided itself between A and B, according to the laws of supply and demand; that is to say, according to the laws of justice and usefulness.

I do not advance an empty hypothesis when I say, that were it possible that industry should concentrate itself upon a single point, there must, from its nature, arise spontaneously, and in its midst, an irresistible power of decentralization.

We will quote the words of a manufacturer to the Chamber of Commerce at Manchester (the figures brought into his demonstration being suppressed):

"Formerly we exported goods; this exportation gave way to that of thread for the manufacture of goods; later, instead of thread, we exported machinery for the making of thread; then capital for the construction of machinery; and lastly, workmen and talent, which are the source of capital. All these elements of labor have, one after the other, transferred themselves to other points, where their profits were increased, and where the means of subsistence being less difficult to obtain, life is maintained at less cost. There are at present to be seen in Prussia, Austria, Saxony, Switzerland, and Italy, immense manufacturing establisments, founded entirely by

English capital, worked by English labor, and directed by English talent."

We may here perceive, that Nature, or rather Providence, with more wisdom and foresight than the narrow and rigid system of the protectionists can suppose, does not permit the concentration of labor, the monopoly of advantages, from which they draw their arguments as from an absolute and irremediable fact. It has, by means as simple as they are infallible, provided for dispersion, diffusion, mutual dependence, and simultaneous progress; all of which, your restrictive laws paralyze as much as is in their power, by their tendency towards the isolation of nations. By this means they render much more decided the differences existing in the conditions of production; they check the self-leveling power of industry, prevent fusion of interests, neutralize the counterpoise, and fence in each nation within its own peculiar advantages and disadvantages.

III. To say that by a protective law the conditions of production are equalized, is to disguise an error under false terms. It is not true that an import duty equalizes the conditions of production. These remain after the imposition of the duty just as they were before. The most that the law can do is to equalize the *conditions of sale*. If it should be said that I am playing upon words, I retort the accusation upon my adversaries. It is for them to prove that *production* and *sale* are synonymous terms, which if they cannot do, I have a right to accuse them, if not of playing upon words, at least of confounding them.

Let me be permitted to exemplify my idea.

Suppose that several New York speculators should determine to devote themselves to the production of oranges. They know that the oranges of Portugal can be sold in New York at ten cents, whilst on account of the boxes, hot-houses, &c., which are necessary to ward against the severity of our climate, it is impossible to raise them at less than a dollar apiece. They accordingly demand a duty of ninety cents upon Portugal oranges. With the help of this duty, say they, the *conditions of production* will be equalized. Congress, yielding as usual to this argument, imposes a duty of ninety cents on each foreign orange.

Now I say that the *relative conditions of production* are in no wise changed. The law can take nothing from the heat of the sun in Lisbon, nor from the severity of the frosts in New York. Oranges continuing to mature themselves *naturally* on the banks of the Tagus, and artificially upon those of the Hudson, must continue to require for their production much more labor on the latter than the former. The law can only equalize the *conditions of sale.* It is evident that while the Portuguese sell their oranges at a dollar apiece, the ninety cents which go to pay the tax are taken from the American consumer. Now look at the whimsicality of the result. Upon each Portuguese orange, the country loses nothing; for the ninety cents which the consumer pays to satisfy the tax, enter into the treasury. There is improper distribution, but no loss. Upon each American orange consumed, there will be about ninety cents lost; for while the buyer very certainly loses them, the seller just as certainly does not gain them, for even according to the hypothesis, he will receive only the price of production. I will leave it to the protectionists to draw their conclusion.

IV. I have laid some stress upon this distinction between the conditions of production and those of sale, which perhaps the prohibitionists may consider as paradoxical, because it leads me on, to what they will consider as a still stranger paradox. This is: If you really wish to equalize the facilities of production, leave trade free.

This may surprise the protectionists; but let me entreat them to listen, if it be only through curiosity, to the end of my argument. It shall not be long. I will now take it up where we left off.

If we suppose for the moment, that the common and daily profits of each American amount to one dollar, it will indisputably follow that to produce an orange by *direct* labor in America, one day's work, or its equivalent, will be requisite; whilst to produce the cost of a Portuguese orange, only one tenth of this day's labor is required; which means simply this, that the sun does at Lisbon what labor does at New York. Now is it not evident, that if I can produce an orange, or, what is the same thing, the means of buying it, with one tenth of a day's labor, I am placed exactly in the same condition as the Portuguese producer himself, excepting the expense of the transportation? It is then certain that freedom of commerce equalizes the conditions of production direct or indirect, as much as it is possible to equalize them; for it leaves but the one inevitable difference, that of transportation.

I will add that free trade equalizes also the facilities for attaining enjoyments, comforts, and general consumption; the last, an object which is, it would seem, quite forgotten, and which is nevertheless all important; since in fine, consumption is the main object of all our industrial efforts. Thanks to freedom of trade, we would enjoy here the results of the Portuguese sun, as well as Portugal itself; and the inhabitants of New York would have in their reach, as well as those of London, and with the same facilities, the advantages which nature has in a mineralogical point of view conferred upon Cornwall.

The protectionists may suppose me in a paradoxical humor, for I go farther still. I say, and I sincerely believe, that if any two countries are placed in unequal circumstances as to advantages of production, *that one of the two which is the least favored by nature, will gain most by freedom of commerce.* To prove this, I will be obliged to turn somewhat aside from the form of reasoning which belongs to this work. I will do so, however; first, because the question in discussion turns upon this point; and again, because it will give me the opportunity of exhibiting a law of political economy of the highest importance, and which, well understood, seems to me to be destined to lead back to this science all those sects which, in our days, are seeking in the land of chimeras that social harmony which they have been unable to discover in nature. I speak of the law of consumption, which the majority of political economists may well be reproached with having too much neglected.

Consumption is the *end*, the final cause, of all the phenomena of political economy, and, consequently, in it is found their final solution.

No effect, whether favorable or unfavorable, can be arrested permanently upon the producer. The advantages and the disadvantages, which, from his relations to nature and to society, are his, both equally pass gradually from him, with an almost insensible tendency to be absorbed and fused into the community at large; the community considered as consumers. This is an admirable law, alike in its cause and its effects, and he who shall succeed in making it well understood, will have a right to say, "I have not, in my passage through the world, forgotten to pay my tribute to society."

Every circumstance which favors the work of production is of course hailed with joy by the producer, for its *immediate effect* is to enable him to render greater services to the community, and to exact from it a greater remuneration. Every circumstance which injures production, must equally be the source of uneasiness to him; for its *immediate effect* is to diminish his services, and consequently his remuneration. This is a fortunate and necessary law of nature. The immediate good or evil of favorable or unfavorable circumstances must fall upon the producer, in order to influence him invisibly to seek the one and to avoid the other.

Again, when a workman succeeds in his labor, the *immediate* benefit of this success is received by him. This again is necessary, to determine him to devote his attention to it. It is also just; because it is just that an effort crowned with success should bring its own reward.

But these effects, good and bad, although permanent in themselves, are not so as regards the producer. If they had been so, a principle of progressive and consequently infinite inequality would have been introduced among men. This good, and this evil, both therefore pass on, to become absorbed in the general destinies of humanity.

How does this come about? I will try to make it understood by some examples.

Let us go back to the thirteenth century. Men who gave themselves up to the business of copying, received for this service *a remuneration regulated by the general rate of the profits.* Among them is found one, who seeks and finds the means of multiplying rapidly copies of the same work. He invents printing. The first effect of this is, that the individual is enriched, while many more are impoverished. At the first view, wonderful as the discovery is, one hesitates in deciding whether it is not more injurious than useful. It seems to have introduced into the world, as I said above, an element of infinite inequality. Guttemberg makes large profits by this invention, and perfects the invention by the profits, until all other copyists are ruined. As for the public—the consumer—it gains but little, for Guttemberg takes care to lower the price of books only just so much as is necessary to undersell all rivals.

But the great Mind which put harmony into the movements of celestial bodies, could also give it to the internal mechanism of society. We will see the advantages of this invention escaping from the individual, to become for ever the common patrimony of mankind.

The process finally becomes known. Guttemberg is no longer alone in his art; others imitate him. Their profits are at first considerable. They are recompensed for being the first who make the effort to imitate the processes of the newly invented art. This again was necessary, in order that they might be induced to the effort, and thus forward the great and final result to which we approach. They gain much; but they gain less than the inventor, for *competition* has commenced its work. The price of books now continually decreases. The gains of the imitators diminish in proportion as the invention becomes older; and in the same proportion imitation becomes less meritorious. Soon the new object of industry attains its normal condition; in other words, the remuneration of printers is no longer an exception to the general rules of remuneration, and, like that of copyists formerly, it is only regulated *by the general rate of profits.* Here then the producer, as such, holds only the old position. The discovery, however, has been made; the saving of time, labor, effort, for a fixed result, for a certain number of volumes, is realized. But in what is this manifested? In the cheap price of books. For the good of whom? For the good of the consumer—of society—of humanity. Printers, having no longer any peculiar merit, receive no longer a peculiar remuneration. As men—as consumers—they no doubt participate in the advantages which the invention confers upon the community; but that is all. As printers, as producers, they are placed upon the ordinary footing of all other producers. Society pays them for their labor, and not for the usefulness of the invention. *That* has become a gratuitous benefit, a common heritage to mankind.

The wisdom and beauty of these laws strike me with admiration and reverence.

What has been said of printing, can be extended to every agent for the advancement of labor; from the nail and the mallet, up to the locomotive and the electric telegraph. Society enjoys all, by the abundance of its use, its consumption; and it *enjoys all gratuitously*. For as their effect is to diminish prices, it is evident that just so much of the price as is taken off by their intervention, renders the production in so far *gratuitous*. There only remains the actual labor of man to be paid for; and the remainder, which is the result of the invention, is subtracted; at least after the invention has run through the cycle which I have just described as its destined course.—I send for a workman; he brings a saw with him; I pay him two dollars for his day's labor, and he saws me twenty-five boards. If the saw had not been invented, he would perhaps not have been able to make one board, and I would none the less have paid him for his day's labor. The *usefulness* then of the saw, is for me a gratuitous gift of nature, or rather it is a portion of the inheritance which, *in common* with my brother men, I have received from the genius of my ancestors.—I have two workmen in my field; the one directs the handle of a plough, the other that of a spade. The result of their day's labor is very different, but the price is the same, because the remuneration is proportioned, not to the usefulness of the result, but to the effort, the time and labor given to attain it.

I invoke the patience of the reader, and beg him to believe, that I have not lost sight of free trade: I entreat him only to remember the conclusion at which I have arrived: *Remuneration is not proportioned to the usefulness of the articles brought by the producer into the market, but to the time and labor.**

I have so far taken my examples from human inventions, but will now go on to speak of natural advantages.

In every article of production, nature and man must concur. But the portion of nature is always gratuitous. Only so much of the usefulness of an article as is the result of human labor becomes the object of mutual exchange, and consequently of remuneration. The remuneration varies much, no doubt, in proportion to the intensity of the labor, of the skill which it requires, of its being *à propos* to the demand of the day, of the need which exists for it, of the momentary absence of competition, &c. But it is not the less true in principle, that the assistance received from natural laws, which belongs to all, counts for nothing in the price.

We do not pay for the air we breathe, although so useful to us, that we could not live two minutes without it. We do not pay for it, because nature furnishes it without the intervention of man's labor. But if we wish to separate one of the gases which compose it, for instance, to fill a balloon, we must take some time and labor; or if another takes it for us, we must give him an equivalent in something which will have cost us the trouble of production. From which we see that the exchange is between efforts, time, labor. It is certainly not for hydrogen gas that I pay, for this is everywhere at my disposal, but for the work that it has been necessary to accomplish in order to disengage it; work which I have been spared, and which I must refund. If I am told that there are other things to pay for; as expense, materials, apparatus; I answer, that still in these things it is the work that I pay for. The price of the coal employed is only the representation of the time and labor necessary to dig and transport it.

We do not pay for the light of the sun, because nature alone gives it to us. But we pay for the light of gas, tallow,

* It is true that time and labor do not receive a uniform remuneration; because labor is more or less intense, dangerous, skilful, &c., and time more or less valuable. Competition establishes for each category a price current: and it is of this variable price that I speak.

oil, wax, because here is labor to be remunerated;—and remark, that it is so entirely time and labor and not utility to which remuneration is proportioned, that it may well happen that one of these means of lighting, while it may be much more effective than another, may still cost less. To cause this, it is only necessary that less time and human labor should be required to furnish it.

When the water-boat comes to supply my ship, were I to pay in proportion to the *absolute utility* of the water, my whole fortune would not be sufficient. But I pay only for the trouble taken. If more is required, I can get another boat to furnish it, or finally go and get it myself. The water itself is not the subject of the bargain; but the labor taken to get the water. This point of view is so important, and the consequences that I am going to draw from it so clear, as regards the freedom of international exchanges, that I will still elucidate my idea by a few more examples.

The alimentary substance contained in potatoes does not cost us very dear, because a great deal of it is attainable with little work. We pay more for wheat, because, to produce it, nature requires more labor from man. It is evident that if nature did for the latter what she does for the former, their prices would tend to the same level. It is impossible that the producer of wheat should permanently gain more than the producer of potatoes. The law of competition cannot allow it.

If by a happy miracle the fertility of all arable lands were to be increased, it would not be the agriculturist, but the consumer, who would profit by this phenomenon; for the result of it would be, abundance and cheapness. There would be less labor incorporated into an acre of grain, and the agriculturist would be therefore obliged to exchange it for a less labor incorporated into some other article. If on the contrary the fertility of the soil were suddenly to deteriorate, the share of nature in production would be less, that of labor greater, and the result would be higher prices. I am right then in saying that it is in consumption, in mankind, that at length all political phenomena find their solution. As long as we fail to follow their effects to this point, and look only at *immediate* effects, which act but upon individual men or classes of men *as producers,* we know nothing more of political economy than the quack does of medicine, when instead of following the effects of a prescription in its action upon the whole system, he satisfies himself with knowing how it affects the palate and the throat.

The tropical regions are very favorable to the production of sugar and coffee ; that is to say, Nature does most of the business and leaves but little for labor to accomplish. But who reaps the advantage of this liberality of Nature? Not these regions, for they are forced by competition to receive remuneration simply for their labor. It is mankind who is the gainer ; for the result of this liberality is *cheapness,* and cheapness belongs to the world.

Here in the temperate zone, we find coal and iron ore, on the surface of the soil ; we have but to stoop and take them. At first, I grant, the immediate inhabitants profit by this fortunate circumstance. But soon comes competition, and the price of coal and iron falls, until this gift of Nature becomes gratuitous to all, and human labor is only paid according to the general rate of profits.

Thus natural advantages, like improvements in the process of production, are, or have a constant tendency to become, under the law of competition, the common and *gratuitous* patrimony of consumers, of society, of mankind. Countries therefore which do not enjoy these advantages, must gain by commerce with those which do ; because the exchanges of commerce are between *labor and labor;* subtraction being made of all the natural advantages which are combined with these labors ; and it is evidently the most favored countries which can incorporate into a given labor the largest proportion of these *natural advantages.* Their produce representing less labor, receives less recompense ; in other words, is *cheaper.* If then all the liberality of Nature results in cheapness, it is evidently not the producing, but the consuming country, which profits by her benefits.

Hence we may see the enormous absurdity of the consuming country, which rejects produce precisely because it is cheap.

It is as though we should say: "We will have nothing of that which Nature gives you. You ask of us an effort equal to two, in order to furnish ourselves with produce only attainable at home by an effort equal to four. You can do it because with you Nature does half the work. But we will have nothing to do with it; we will wait till your climate becoming more inclement, forces you to ask of us a labor equal to four, and then we can treat with you *upon an equal footing.*"

A is a favored country; B is maltreated by Nature. Mutual traffic then is advantageous to both, but principally to B, because the exchange is not between *utility* and *utility,* but between *value* and *value.* Now A furnishes a greater *utility in a similar value,* because the utility of any article includes at once what Nature and what labor have done; whereas the value of it only corresponds to the portion accomplished by labor. B then makes an entirely advantageous bargain; for by simply paying the producer from A for his labor, it receives in return not only the results of that labor, but in addition there is thrown in whatever may have accrued from the superior bounty of Nature.

We will lay down the general rule.

Traffic is an exchange of *values;* and as value is reduced by competition to the simple representation of labor, traffic is the exchange of equal labors. Whatever Nature has done towards the production of the articles exchanged, is given on both sides *gratuitously;* from whence it necessarily follows, that the most advantageous commerce is transacted with those countries which are the least favored by Nature.

The theory of which I have attempted, in this chapter, to trace the outlines deserves a much greater elaboration. But perhaps the attentive reader will have perceived in it the fruitful seed which is destined in its future growth to smother Protectionism, at once with the various other isms whose object is to exclude the law of COMPETITION from the government of the world. Competition, no doubt, considering man as producer, must often interfere with his individual and *immediate* interests. But if we consider the great object of all labor, the universal good, in a word, *Consumption,* we cannot fail to find that Competition is to the moral world what the law of equilibrium is to the material one. It is the foundation of true Communism, of true Liberty and Equality, of the equality of comforts and condition, so much sought after in our day; and if so many sincere reformers, so many earnest friends to public right, seek to reach their end by commercial *legislation*, it is only because they do not yet understand *commercial freedom.*

Our Productions are overloaded with Taxes.

This is but a new wording of the last Sophism. The demand made is, that the foreign article should be taxed, in order to neutralize the effects of the tax, which weighs down national produce. It is still then but the question of equalizing the facilities of production. We have but to say that the tax is an artificial obstacle, which has exactly the same effect as a natural obstacle, i. e. the increasing of the price. If this increase is so great that there is more loss in producing the article in question than in attracting it from foreign parts by the production of an equivalent value, *laissez faire.* Individual interest will soon learn to choose the lesser of two evils. I might refer the reader to the preceding demonstration for an answer to this Sophism; but it is one which recurs so often, that it deserves a special discussion.

I have said more than once, that I am opposing only the theory of the protectionists, with the hope of discovering the source of their errors. Were I disposed to enter into controversy with them, I would say: Why direct your tariffs principally against England, a country more overloaded with taxes than any in the world? Have I not a right to look upon your argument as a mere pretext?—But I am not of the number of those who believe that prohibitionists are guided by interest, and not by conviction. The doctrine of Protection is too popular not to be sincere. If the majority could believe in freedom, we would be free. Without doubt it is individual interest which weighs us down with tariffs; but it acts upon conviction. "The will (said Pascal) is one of the principal organs of belief." But belief does not the less exist because it is rooted in the will and in the secret inspirations of egotism.

We will return to the Sophism drawn from imposts.

The State may make either a good or a bad use of imposts; it makes a good use of them when it renders to the public services equivalent to the value received from them; it makes a bad use of them when it expends this value, giving nothing in return.

To say in the first case that they place the country which pays them in more disadvantageous conditions for production, than the country which is free from them, is a Sophism.—We pay, it is true, so many millions for the administration of justice, and the maintenance of order, but we have justice and order; we have the security which they give, the time which they save for us; and it is most probable that production is neither more easy nor more active among nations, where (if there be such) each individual takes the administration of justice into his own hands.—We pay, I grant, many millions for roads, bridges, ports, steamships; but we have these steamships, these ports, bridges, and roads; and unless we maintain that it is a losing business to establish them, we cannot say that they place us in a position inferior to that of nations who have, it is true, no budget of public works, but who likewise have no public works. And here we see why (even while we accuse imposts of being a cause of industrial inferiority) we direct our tariffs precisely against those nations which are the most taxed. It is because these taxes, well used, far from injuring, have ameliorated the *conditions of production* to these nations. Thus we again arrive at the conclusion that the protectionist Sophisms not only wander from, but are the contrary—the very antithesis of truth.

As to unproductive imposts, suppress them if you can; but surely it is a most singular idea to suppose, that their evil effect is to be neutralized, by the addition of individual taxes, to public taxes. Many thanks for the compensation! The State, you say, has taxed us too much; surely this is no reason that we should tax each other!

A protective duty is a tax directed against foreign produce, but which returns, let us keep in mind, upon the national consumer. Is it not then a singular argument to say to him, "Because the imposts are heavy, we will raise prices higher for you; and because the State takes a part of your revenue, we will give another portion of it to benefit a monopoly?"

But let us examine more closely this Sophism so accredited among our legislators; although, strange to say, it is precisely those who keep up the unproductive imposts (according to our present hypothesis) who attribute to them afterwards our supposed inferiority, and seek to re-establish the equilibrium by further imposts and new clogs.

It appears to me to be evident that protection, without any change in its nature and effects, might have taken the form of a direct tax, raised by the State, and distributed as a premium to privileged industry.

Let us admit that foreign iron could be sold in our market at $16, but not lower; and American iron at not lower than $24.

In this hypothesis there are two ways in which the State can secure the national market to the home producer.

The first, is to put upon foreign iron a duty of $10. This, it is evident, would exclude it, because it could no longer be sold at less than $26; $16 for the indemnifying price, $10 for the tax; and at this price it must be driven from the market by American iron, which we have supposed to cost $24. In this case the buyer, the consumer, will have paid all the expenses of the protection given.

The second means would be to lay upon the public an Internal Revenue tax of $10, and to give it as a premium to the iron manufacturer. The effect would in either case be equally a protective measure. Foreign iron would, according to both systems, be alike excluded; for our iron manufacturer could sell at $14, what, with the $10 premium, would thus bring him in $24. While the price of sale being $14, foreign iron could not obtain a market at $16.

In these two systems the principle is the same; the effect is the same. There is but this single difference; in the first case the expense of protection is paid by a part, in the second by the whole of the community.

I frankly confess my preference for the second system, which I regard as more just, more economical, and more legal. More just, because, if society wishes to give bounties to some of its members, the whole community ought to contribute; more economical, because it would banish many difficulties, and save the expenses of collection; more legal, lastly, because the public would see clearly into the operation, and know what was required of it.

But if the protective system had taken this form, would it not have been laughable enough to hear it said, "We pay heavy taxes for the army, the navy, the judiciary, the public works, the debt, &c. These amount to more than 200 millions. It would therefore be desirable that the State should take another 200 millions to relieve the poor iron manufacturers."

This, it must most certainly be perceived, by an attentive investigation, is the result of the Sophism in question. In vain, gentlemen, are all your efforts; you cannot *give money* to one without taking it from another. If you are absolutely determined to exhaust the funds of the taxable community, well; but, at least, do not mock them; do not tell them. We take from you again, in order to compensate you for what we have already taken."

It would be a too tedious undertaking to endeavor to point out all the fallacies of this Sophism. I will therefore limit myself to the consideration of it in three points.

You argue that the United States are overburthened with taxes, and deduce thence the conclusion that it is necessary to protect such and such an article of produce. But protection does not relieve us from the payment of these taxes. If, then, individuals devoting themselves to any one object of industry, should advance this demand: "We, from our participation in the payment of taxes, have our expenses of production increased, and therefore ask for a protective duty which shall raise our price of sale;" what is this but a demand on their part to be allowed to free themselves from the burthen of the tax, by laying it on the rest of the community? Their object is to balance, by the increased price of their produce, the amount which they pay in taxes. Now, as the whole amount of these taxes must enter into the Treasury, and the increase of price must be paid by society, it follows that (where this protective duty is imposed) society has to bear, not only the general tax, but also that for the protection of the article in question. But, it is answered, let *every thing* be protected. Firstly, this is impossible; and, again, were it possible, how could such a system give relief? *I* will pay for you, *you* will pay for me; but not the less, still there remains the tax to be paid.

Thus you are the dupes of an illusion. You determine to raise taxes for the support of an army, a navy, judges, roads, &c. Afterwards you seek to disburthen from its portion of the tax, first one article of industry, then another, then a third; always adding to the burthen of the mass of society. You thus only create interminable complications. If you can prove that the increase of price resulting from protection, falls upon the foreign producer, I grant something specious in your argument. But if it be true that the American people paid the tax before the passing of the protective duty, and afterwards that it has paid not only the tax, but the protective duty also, truly I do not perceive wherein it has profited.

But I go much further, and maintain that the more oppressive our taxes are, the more anxiously ought we to open our ports and frontiers to foreign nations, less burthened than ourselves. And why? *In order that we may* SHARE WITH THEM, *as much as possible, the burthen which we bear.* Is it not an incontestable maxim in political economy, that taxes must, in the end, fall upon the consumer? *The greater then our commerce, the greater the portion which will be reimbursed to us, of taxes incorporated in the produce, which we will have sold to foreign consumers; whilst we, on our part, will have made to them only a lesser reimbursement, because (according to our hypothesis) their produce is less taxed than ours.*

Balance of Trade.

Our adversaries have adopted a system of tactics, which embarrasses us not a little. Do we prove our doctrine? They admit the truth of it in the most respectful manner. Do we attack their principles? They abandon them with the best possible grace. They only ask that our doctrine, which they acknowledge to be true, should be confined to books; and that their principles, which they allow to be false, should be established in practice. If we will give up to them the regulation of our tariffs, they will leave us triumphant in the domain of theory.

It is constantly alleged in opposition to our principles, that they are good only in theory. But, gentlemen, do you believe that merchants' books are good in practice? It does appear to me that if there is any thing which can have a practical authority, when the object is to prove profit and loss, that this must be commercial accounts. We cannot suppose that all the merchants of the world, for centuries back, should have so little understood their own affairs, as to have kept their books in such a manner as to represent gains as losses, and losses as gains. Truly it would be easier to believe that our legislators are bad political economists.

A merchant, one of my friends, having had two business transactions, with very different results, I have been curious to compare on this subject the accounts of the counter with those of the custom-house, interpreted by our legislators.

Mr. T. despatched from New Orleans a vessel, freighted, for France, with cotton, valued at $200,000. Such was the amount entered at the custom-house. The cargo, on its arrival at Havre, had paid ten per cent. expenses, and was liable to thirty per cent. duties; which raised its value to $280,000. It was sold at twenty per cent. profit on its original value, which being $40,000, the price of sale was $320,000, which the assignee converted into merchandise, principally Parisian goods. These goods, again, had to pay for expenses of transportation, insurance, commissions, &c., ten per cent.; so that when the return cargo arrived at New Orleans, its value had risen to $352,000, and it was thus entered at the custom-house. Finally, Mr. T. realized again on this return cargo twenty per cent. profits ; amounting to $70,400. The goods thus sold for the sum of $422,400.

If our legislators require it, I will send them an extract from the books of Mr. T. They will there see, *credited* to the account of *profit and loss*, that is to say, set down as gained, two sums ; the one of $40,000, the other of $70,000, and Mr. T. feels perfectly certain that, as regards these, there is no mistake in his accounts.

Now what conclusion do our Congressmen draw from the sums entered into the custom-house, in this operation ? They thence learn that the United States have exported $200,000, and imported $352,000 ; from whence they conclude "*that she has spent, dissipated the profits of her previous savings ; that she is impoverishing herself and progressing to her ruin ; and that she has squandered on a foreign nation* $152,000 *of her capital.*"

Some time after this transaction, Mr. T. despatched another vessel, again freighted with national produce, to the amount of $200,000. But the vessel foundered in leaving the port, and Mr. T. had only farther to inscribe upon his books two little items, thus worded :

"*Sundries due to X*, $200,000, for purchase of divers articles despatched by vessel N.

"*Profit and loss due to sundries*, $200,000, *for final and total loss of cargo.*"

In the meantime the custom-house inscribed $200,000 upon its list of *exportations*, and as there can of course be nothing to balance this entry on the list of *importations*, it hence follows that our enlightened members of Congress must see in this wreck *a clear profit* to the United States of $200,000.

We may draw hence yet another conclusion, viz. : that according to the Balance of Trade theory, the United States has an exceedingly simple manner of constantly doubling her capital. It is only necessary, to accomplish this, that she should, after entering into the custom-house her articles for exportation, cause them to be thrown into the sea. By this course, her exportations can speedily be made to equal her capital; importations will be nothing, and our gain will be, all which the ocean will have swallowed up.

You are joking, the protectionists will reply. You know that it is impossible that we should utter such absurdities. Nevertheless, I answer, you do utter them, and what is more, you give them life, you exercise them practically upon your fellow-citizens, as much at least, as is in your power to do.

The truth is that the theory of the Balance of Trade should be precisely *reversed*. The profits accruing to the nation from any foreign commerce should be calculated by the overplus of the importation above the exportation. This overplus, after the deduction of expenses, is the real gain. Here we have the true theory, and it is one which leads directly to freedom in trade. I now, gentlemen, abandon you this theory, as I have done all those of the preceding chapters. Do with it as you please, exaggerate it as you will; it has nothing to fear. Push it to the farthest extreme; imagine, if it so please you, that foreign nations should inundate us with useful produce of every description, and ask nothing in return; that our importations should be *infinite*, and our exportations *nothing*. Imagine all this, and still I defy you to prove that we will be the poorer in consequence.

Petition from the Manufacturers of Candles, Wax-Lights, Lamps, Chandeliers, Reflectors, Snuffers, Extinguishers; and from the Producers of Tallow, Oil, Rosin, Petroleum, Kerosene, Alcohol, and generally of every thing used for lights.

To the Honorable the Senators and Representatives of the United States in Congress assembled:

"Gentlemen:—You are in the right way: you reject abstract theories; abundance, cheapness concerns you little. You are entirely occupied with the interest of the producer, whom you are anxious to free from foreign competition. In a word, you wish to secure the *national market* to *national labor.*

"We come now to offer you an admirable opportunity for the application of your —— what shall we say? your theory? no, nothing is more deceiving than theory;—your doctrine? your system? your principle? But you do not like doctrines; you hold systems in horror; and, as for principles, you declare that there are no such things in political economy. We will say then, your practice; your practice without theory, and without principle.

"We are subjected to the intolerable competition of a foreign rival, who enjoys, it would seem, such superior facilities for the production of light, that he is enabled to *inundate* our *national market* at so exceedingly reduced a price, that, the moment he makes his appearance, he draws off all custom from us; and thus an important branch of American industry, with all its innumerable ramifications, is suddenly reduced to a state of complete stagnation. This rival, who is no other than the sun, carries on so bitter a war against us, that we have every reason to believe that he has been excited to this course by our perfidious cousins, the English. (Good diplomacy this, for the present time!) In this belief we are confirmed by the fact that in all his transactions with their proud island, he is much more moderate and careful than with us.

"Our petition is, that it would please your honorable body to pass a law whereby shall be directed the shutting up of all windows, dormers, sky-lights, shutters, curtains, in a word, all openings, holes, chinks, and fissures through which the light of the sun is used to penetrate into our dwellings, to the prejudice of the profitable manufactures which we flatter ourselves we have been enabled to bestow upon the country; which country cannot, therefore, without ingratitude, leave us now to struggle unprotected through so unequal a contest.

"We pray your honorable body not to mistake our petition for a satire, nor to repulse us without at least hearing the reasons which we have to advance in its favor.

"And first, if, by shutting out as much as possible all access to natural light, you thus create the necessity for artificial light, is there in the United States an industrial pursuit which will not, through some connection with this important object, be benefited by it?

"If more tallow be consumed, there will arise a necessity for an increase of cattle and sheep. Thus artificial meadows must be in greater demand; and meat, wool, leather, and above all, manure, this basis of agricultural riches, must become more abundant.

"If more oil be consumed, it will effect a great impetus to our Petroleum trade. Pit-Hole, Tack, and Oil Creek stock will go up exceedingly, and an immense revenue will thereby accrue to the numerous possessors of oil lands, who will be able to pay such a large tax that the National Debt can be paid off at once. Besides that, the patent hermetical barrel trade and numerous other industries connected with the oil trade will prosper at an unprecedented rate, to the great benefit and glory of the country.

"Navigation would equally profit. Thousands of vessels would soon be employed in the whale fisheries, and thence would arise a navy capable of sustaining the honor of the United States, and of responding to the patriotic sentiments of the undersigned petitioners, candle-merchants, &c.

"But what words can express the magnificence which New York will then exhibit! Cast an eye upon the future and behold the gildings, the bronzes, the magnificent crystal chandeliers, lamps, lusters, and candelabras, which will glitter in the spacious stores, compared to which the splendor of the present day will appear little and insignificant.

"There is none, not even the poor manufacturer of rosin in the midst of his pine forests, nor the miserable miner in his dark dwelling, but who would enjoy an increase of salary and of comforts.

"Gentlemen, if you will be pleased to reflect, you cannot fail to be convinced that there is perhaps not one American, from the opulent stockholder of Pit-Hole down to the poorest vender of matches, who is not interested in the success of our petition.

"We foresee your objections, gentlemen; but there is not

one that you can oppose to us which you will not be obliged to gather from the works of the partisans of free trade. We dare challenge you to pronounce one word against our petition, which is not equally opposed to your own practice and the principle which guides your policy.

"Do you tell us, that if we gain by this protection, the United States will not gain, because the consumer must pay the price of it?

"We answer you:

"You have no longer any right to cite the interest of the consumer. For whenever this has been found to compete with that of the producer, you have invariably sacrificed the first. You have done this to *encourage labor*, to *increase the demand for labor.* The same reason should now induce you to act in the same manner.

"You have yourselves already answered the objection. When you were told: The consumer is interested in the free introduction of iron, coal, corn, wheat, cloths, &c., your answer was: Yes, but the producer is interested in their exclusion. Thus, also, if the consumer is interested in the admission of light, we, the producers, pray for its interdiction.

"You have also said, the producer and the consumer are one. If the manufacturer gains by protection, he will cause the agriculturist to gain also; if agriculture prospers, it opens a market for manufactured goods. Thus we, if you confer upon us the monopoly of furnishing light during the day, will as a first consequence buy large quantities of tallow, coal, oil, rosin, kerosene, wax, alcohol, silver, iron, bronze, crystal, for the supply of our business; and then we and our numerous contractors having become rich, our consumption will be great, and will become a means of contributing to the comfort and competency of the workers in every branch of national labor.

"Will you say that the light of the sun is a gratuitous gift, and that to repulse gratuitous gifts, is to repulse riches under pretence of encouraging the means of obtaining them?

"Take care—you carry the death-blow to your own policy. Remember that hitherto you have always repulsed foreign produce, *because* it was an approach to a gratuitous gift, and *the more in proportion* as this approach was more close. You have, in obeying the wishes of other monopolists, acted only from a *half-motive;* to grant our petition there is a much *fuller inducement.* To repulse us, precisely for the reason that our case is a more complete one than any which have preceded it, would be to lay down the following equation: $+ \times + = -$; in other words, it would be to accumulate absurdity upon absurdity.

"Labor and Nature concur in different proportions, according to country and climate, in every article of production. The portion of Nature is always gratuitous; that of labor alone regulates the price.

"If a Lisbon orange can be sold at half the price of a New York one, it is because a natural and gratuitous heat does for the one, what the other only obtains from an artificial and consequently expensive one.

"When, therefore, we purchase a Portuguese orange, we may say that we obtain it half gratuitously and half by the right of labor; in other words, at *half price* compared to those of New York.

"Now it is precisely on account of this *demi-gratuity* (excuse the word) that you argue in favor of exclusion. How, you say, could national labor sustain the competition of foreign labor, when the first has every thing to do, and the last is rid of half the trouble, the sun taking the rest of the business upon himself? If then the *demi-gratuity* can determine you to check competition, on what principle can the *entire gratuity* be alleged as a reason for admitting it? You are no logicians if, refusing the demi-gratuity as hurtful to human labor, you do not *à fortiori*, and with double zeal, reject the full gratuity.

"Again, when any article, as coal, iron, cheese, or cloth, comes to us from foreign countries with less labor than if we produced it ourselves, the difference in price is a *gratuitous gift* conferred upon us; and the gift is more or less considerable, according as the difference is greater or less. It is the quarter, the half, or the three-quarters of the value of the produce, in proportion as the foreign merchant requires the three-quarters, the half, or the quarter of the price. It is as complete as possible when the producer offers, as the sun does with light, the whole in free gift. The question is, and we put it formally, whether you wish for the United States the benefit of gratuitous consumption, or the supposed advantages of laborious production. Choose : but be consistent. And does it not argue the greatest inconsistency to check as you do the importation of iron ware, dry goods, and other foreign manufactures, merely because and even in proportion as their price approaches *zero*, while at the same time you freely admit, and without limitation, the light of the sun, whose price is during the whole day at *zero?*"

(TO BE CONTINUED.)

HISTORY OF THE RATE OF INTEREST IN GREAT BRITAIN AND ELSEWHERE.

When California first invited emigration, the scarcity of laborers there, compared with the immense demand which existed for their services, caused the price of labor to rate very high. Besides wealth, which they obtained by digging for gold, men had other wants to supply. Food had to be provided, clothing made, shelter erected, poker packs imported, beards shorn, and even occasionally a little clothes-washing done. All these desiderata had to be compensated for at an immense cost, compared to what was demanded for them in better populated lands. And even in digging for gold, in addition to ready labor, something else was needed. The first lump of gold in California was picked up by a child near Sutter's mill, and for a long time after this, gold was eliminated from the soil by the rude process of handwashing. But when it was known that a much greater yield could be realized from the employment of machinery, a demand sprang up for capital wherewith to buy picks, shovels, pans, rockers, crushers, amalgamators, quicksilver, and a variety of other labor-saving adjuncts. This capital came from the Eastern States and from Europe. Now what was to determine the rate which was to be paid for the loan of it?

Capital is the product of somebody's labor, which has been saved up, and the saver, as the reward of his original labor, requires for its use as much as his labor is worth. If to do a certain piece of work requires the loan of a man's labor for a day, which is worth two dollars, then the use of enough of his capital to perform the same quantity of work without his labor is evidently worth an equal amount. Capital, therefore, stands upon precisely the same ground that labor does, and competes with it in its search for employment, and on the same conditions. When it is plentiful it is cheap; when it is scarce it is dear. And being scarce in California at that time, nay, even more scarce than labor, it earned proportionately large rewards. These rewards were paid in the shape of interest, and interest is therefore seen to be the wages of capital, just as capital itself is the wages of labor.

It is sometimes the case that labor is plentiful, and capital scarce in the same country, or *vice versa*. This would not be the case if all countries were open freely to emigration, and person and capital securely protected from violence or danger; because then both emigration and capital would flow where they found the most profitable employment, and the price of both would find the same level all over the world.

But by the laws of one country emigration is forbidden or discouraged; by the laws of another, capital is restricted in its employment; by the laws or want of laws in a third, both person and property are endangered. And not alone laws, but sometimes ignorance, and sometimes poverty, prevents a free flow of labor and capital from one country to another. If the poorer classes in China knew how much more secure their person would be, and, the richer, how much safer their capital would remain, in this country, than in their own, it would not be long before the United States would be densely populated by the sons of Fu-hi, provided the poorer ones had the means to come.

Ignorant sometimes of the advantages of employing their labor, and sometimes of the advantages of employing their capital in other lands and at other industries; powerless to change their sphere of life at will for want of the necessary means to effect the removal of themselves and their families; and often restricted by arbitrary laws from doing either; it is not surprising should the greatest inequality exist between the wages of labor and the earnings of capital in various countries, and even between the relative value of both in the same country.

In China capital is scarce and labor is plentiful. The former is, therefore, very expensive; the latter very cheap. In this State capital is plentiful, and labor comparatively scarce. The former is, therefore, cheap and the latter, expensive. In England both are plentiful and both are cheap. In California both are scarce and both are expensive. In fine, the poorer a country is in capital, or saved up wealth, as compared with other countries at the same period, the higher are the wages which that capital earns; in other words, the higher is the rate of interest; and the richer it is in capital, or saved up wealth, the lower are the wages which that capital earns; in other words, the lower is the rate of interest. And so it is with labor.

It would, therefore, be highly instructive, if it were possible, to trace the gradual progress of a country towards a state of comparative wealth from one of comparative poverty; but, unfortunately, history, too much occupied with the petty events of war and intrigue, has forgotten to observe the important indications which serve to note the gradual steps of its prosperous growth; and we are left partly to conjecture, and partly to induction, for the solution we would seek. Nevertheless, enough is to be found in the history of some countries to furnish us with a rough guide to the course of their economic progress; and we will now proceed to avail ourselves of these materials in the case of Great Britain.

We give below the market rates of interest which at the present time prevail in Great Britain for paper of various dates:

30 to 60 days	3½ per cent.	6 months—bank bills	4 per cent.
3 months	3½ "	6 " trade bills	4½ to 5 "
4 "	4 "		

The allowance for deposits at the joint stock banks and discount houses is as follows :

Joint Stock Banks	*2½	per cent.
Discount houses at call	*2½	do.
do with seven days' notice	2¾	do.
do fourteen days	3	do.

* At the London and Westminster 1½ per cent. only on sums below £500.

The following are the rates of discount current in the chief Continental cities :

	Bank Rate. p. c.	Open Market. p. c.		Bank Rate. p. c.	Open Market. p. c.
Paris	3	3	Turin	5	4¾
Vienna	5	5½	Brussels	3½	3½
Berlin	4	3½	Madrid	9	..
Frankfort	4	3	Hamburg	...	2¼
Amsterdam	3½	3½	St. Petersburgh	5½	5½

The earliest account which we now possess of the rate of interest in England is from the *Chronicle of Joceline de Brakclond*, and relates to about the year A.D. 1173. From that time forward we have here and there isolated accounts of the prevailing rates of interest at various times ; sometimes the legal rate, which, by the way, is no indication whatever of the market rate—sometimes the rate at which the State borrowed—sometimes that at which the sovereign borrowed, either on his own responsibility, or endorsed by the faith of a city, or the security of a pledge—sometimes the rate at which merchants borrowed—and sometimes that at which land was mortgaged.

From the year A.D. 533, when the law of interest was regulated by the code of Justinian, to the ninth century, nothing occurs in history to indicate what was the rate of interest in any part of Europe. By that law persons of illustrious birth were confined to both borrowing and lending at the moderate rate of 4 per cent., while 6 was pronounced to be the ordinary legal standard. For the convenience of manufacturers and merchants, 8 per cent. was allotted ; to loans on shipping 12 per cent. was granted, but except in such "perilous" business no higher rate than 8 per cent. was permitted (*Gibbon's Hist. Dec. & Fall*, chap. xliv.) These rates afford no indication of the true value of loans of money at that time, for they might have been enacted by the crafty and unscrupulous Justinian, in order that he might take advantage of them for his own benefit. Rome had long since been reduced by repeated invasions from the North, and the insecurity of capital was so great that the true rates of interest were probably much higher; though it is difficult to determine the matter at this remote time. The great code of civil law called the Pandects, framed by Tribonian and other lawyers, which now passes by the emperor's name, and which contains the law of interest just quoted, had just been promulgated; and domestic security must have been the result of its observance.

Nevertheless, this law concerning the rate of interest, appears to have remained unimpaired until the Christian Church began to assume temporal power. In A.D. 800, during the reign of Charlemagne, Emperor of the West, the taking of interest was entirely forbidden by the canon law. (*Macpherson's History of Commerce*, i. 250.) The same influence next extending to the Eastern Empire, a similiar prohibition was inserted in the Basilics, a partial and mutilated version of the Pandects, published by the Emperor Constantine Porphyrogenitus. This was about A. D. 950. (*History Decline and Fall*, chap. liv.) Next, at a great council held at Westminster on the 8th or 9th September, 1126, for the purpose of regulating the dicipline of the Church and the lives of the priesthood, all clergymen were ordered to abstain from interest and "base lucre"—*usuram et turpe lucrum*. (*History of Commerce*, i. p. 318.) From this time to the year 1197 there is no reason to doubt that the taking of interest was interdicted by law, but in that year, again through the influence of the Church, Christians were forbidden to take interest. This was in the reign of Richard I. Of course, this threw the entire business into the hands of the Jews, and this monopoly partly laid the foundation of that extraordinary wealth which these people subsequently possessed; though often and dear were the penalties they were made to pay for the privilege thus conferred upon them unasked.

The reluctance of the early Christians to take interest, arising partly from ignorance of the true nature of capital, and partly from canonical prohibitions, seems to have thrown the business of money lending into the hands of the Jews in other countries besides England. "The Jews," says Mr. Hollam (*Middle Ages*, ii. p. 400,) "were noted for usury in France as early as the sixth century. For several subsequent ages they continued so to employ their capital, with little molestation from the clergy," and "often with some encouragement from princes." In the twelfth century they possessed landed property in Languedoc, and were even appointed there, as well as in Spain, to important civil offices. "If an historian of Philip Augustus may be believed, they possessed (A.D. 1180) almost one-half of Paris." (*Ibid.* i. p. 157.) And all from the enjoyment of an almost priceless monopoly!

The statute of A. D. 1197 (reign of Richard I.) is the earliest enactment upon the subject mentioned in English history; though the labors of a learned association have given to the world some curious and precise information on the subject which relates to a period of over twenty years earlier. This is contained in the *Chronicle of Joceline de Brakclond*, mentioned above, from which it appears that in 1173, William, the sacristan of the monastery of St. Edmundsbury, borrowed from Benedict, a Jew of Norwich, certain sums of money, for which he paid interest at rates varying from 16 to 19 per cent. per annum, giving Benedict his bond therefor, sealed with the convent seal. Subsequently, Benedict had to go to law for the recovery of his loan, and it seems he won the case. After the legal prohibition to Christians in 1197, against taking interest, history is silent on the subject for over half a century.

In *Magna Charta*, granted 15th June, 1215, the clause relating to interest, as interpreted by Blackstone, Hallam, and Hume, clearly recognizes the law as enacted in 1197. After the death of Henry II. the Jews fell into disfavor, and were made the subject of frequent persecutions under King John. In the succeeding reign of Henry III. open war was declared against them, and in A. D. 1253 seven hundred of them were slain in London. (*Stow's Survey of London, p.* 106.) An immediate rise in the rate of interest occurred. Hume says it was 50 per cent. (*History of Eng.*, chap. xii.,) and Matthew Paris asserts that at the same period the debtor paid 110 per cent. every two months, or about 70 per cent. per annum.

In the year 1248 the rate of 43 1-3 per cent. was given for a loan of money, as is evinced by a close-roll of that period. In the year 1272 a bond granted to Bonami, a Jew of York, by Sir Hugo de Nevill, a Lincolnshire knight, bore precisely the same rate of interest. As by ordering that all Jews who lent money on interest should first procure a royal license to do so, and from the evidence adduced by Mr. Bond (*Archæologia* xxvii. 225) and the author of *Anglia Judaica*, there is reason to believe that the English monarchs participated in the gains derived by the Jews from this business—a portion, perhaps a large portion, of this 43 1-3 per cent. went to the crown, while another large portion served to cover the risk which at that time must have been enormous ; so that it is impossible to ascertain what portion of it represented the actual value of loanable money including the ordinary risk. Taking the St. Edmundsbury transaction for a guide, it was probably not much over 15 per cent. All this time the rate of interest in the Republic of Venice was but 4 per cent., (*Macpherson's Hist. Com.*, i. 341,) though in the instance given, the loan was a forced one, and was probably below the rate current on the Rialto. This was in A. D. 1171. In Flanders, A. D. 1201, it was from 20 to 30 per cent. (*Robertson's View of State of Europe*, note xxx.) In Verona, A. D. 1228, it was 12 1-2 per cent. (*Mid. Ages*, ii, 400), though as this was the legal rate, it affords us no definite indication of the state of the market. In Aragon, A. D. 1270, the legal rate was 18 per cent. (*View of State, &c.*, note xxx.) In Modena, A. D. 1270, the legal rate was 20 per cent. (*Mid. Ages*, ii. 400.) In France, about the year A. D. 1272, an edict of Philip Augustus, limited the Jews in France to 48 per cent. (*Hume, Hist. Eng.*, chap. xii.)

Taking a general view of the state of maritime Europe up to the persecution of the Jewish money lenders by Henry III. of England, A. D. 1272, it would seem that the rate of interest for mercantile transactions, varied from 4 to 8 per cent. in Venice, to about 15 per cent. in England, and probably not much over that in France. As to the interior of Europe we have no accounts. But this indicates that capital was much more plentiful in Venice than elsewhere, and that her republican government in affording to the capitalist both security and freedom for his person and for the employment of his capital, was the cause of its flow thither from countries less favored at that period.

From the passage of the Statute of Jewry, A. D. 1290, to the end of the fourteenth century, we have been enabled to gather but two accounts of the rate of interest. In France, A. D. 1311, Philip IV. fixed the interest that might be legally exacted in the fairs of Champagne at 20 per cent (Robertson: *View of the State of Europe*, note xxx) though the general market rate was probably nearer 50 per cent. In Florence (then a Republic) A. D. 1336, the State borrowed money of individuals upon an assignment of the taxes, paying 15 per cent., but, as her neighbor, Tuscany, was agitated at the time by the civil wars between the Bianchi and the Neri, the common rate in Florence was, as Hallam remarks, (*Midd. Ages*, ii. 400,) much lower.

During the fifteenth century we can find but little mention in history of the rate of interest which prevailed in England. In A. D. 1488, the third statute of Henry VII. was passed, totally prohibiting the taking of interest. The statute is entitled "An Act against Usurie and Unlawful Bargaynes;" and recites that "ymportable damages, losses, and empoveryssh-ing of this realme, ys had by dampnable bargaynes, groundyt in usurie, colorde by the name of new chevesaunce, &c.," and enacts that all such contracts shall be void, and the seller, owner, bargainer, or promiser be liable to a penalty of £100 for every such bargain.

The framer of this Act after an attempt to define what constitutes usury—feeling apparently that he had not been very successful—had recourse, by way of example, to this addition: "that is to say, for havyng one hundred pound (c *li.*) in money or in merchandise or otherwise, and therefore to pay or to find suretie to pay six score pounds (vjxx *li.*) or more or less." No time is mentioned; but taking the ordinary mode of measuring interest, by the year, this example would seem to point to 20 per cent. per annum as a common rate at the time. (Hodge on *Interest*, chap. i.) At Piacenza, A. D. 1490, the rate of interest was as high as 40 per cent. (Robertson: *View*, *etc.* note xxx.) But this was after its republican form of government had been destroyed, and when it was convulsed by the bloody and despotic rule of the Sforzas.

This brings us down to the beginning of the sixteenth century and the discovery of America. A new era now opened in the history of the rate of interest in Europe. The Jews had been expelled from England A. D. 1290. From France they had been for the last time banished under Charles VI. A. D. 1395. Spain drove them out A. D. 1492. Sicily banished them A. D. 1493. Portugal followed A. D. 1495. Germany, Switzerland, and the rest of Italy had already banished them. The Republic of Poland was therefore their only refuge, and thither accordingly they flocked from all parts of Europe.

The opening of America was soon to have a powerful effect upon the supply of loanable money. Though after a while new accessions of money in a given quarter cease to have any influence upon the rate of interest, because they adjust themselves to the quantity of exchanges to be made, and, if in excess, simply raise the prices of commodities; yet there is a time when such accessions of money do have a marked effect upon interest, and that time occurs soon after the increase of currency, and before the increase of prices. During this interregnum, while prices are the same as before, there is a redundancy of money in circulation, and it consequently seeks employment at lower rates than usual. And if new supplies of money are constantly added, the rate of interest, unless new employment is found for the money, such as the supplying of a government loan for instance, is constantly kept down; for the redundancy of the circulating medium (unless when a state of war upsets the natural order of things by increasing the ordinary degree of risk) is always first perceived in the fall of the rate of interest before it is lost in the rise in prices.

This is precisely what occurred after the discovery of America; new supplies of the precious metals, which were almost invariably coined and put into circulation, kept constantly coming from the "Indies," and before this increase of the circulating medium produced any effect upon prices, loanable money became common and cheap. In Genoa, one of the earliest places to feel the effects of the new turn which commercial affairs had taken, the rate of interest A. D. 1545 was 10 per cent., (*Macpherson's Hist. Com.* ii., 103,) and this was precisely the rate adopted in the same year by law in England.

The market rate in England must have been higher, however, because Genoa was a republic, and a free port of entry, and possessed at that time the only bank of deposit that existed in Europe, but one. Besides this, there is reason to believe that the ten per cent legal rate adopted in England, A. D. 1545, was so adopted because that was the current market rate at the time in Genoa for mercantile credits, and Genoa, as Macpherson remarks, was then the chief seat of bankers and dealers in money, and regulated, in a great measure the rate of interest throughout Europe. If this was the case, the probability is that in Genoa the rate was lower than elsewhere at the time, and, if that rate was 10 per cent.; in England it must have been higher. On the other side, we read that, in the 37th year of the reign of Henry VIII., land in England was only worth twenty years' purchase! (*Hodge on Interest*, chapter ii.) But this is evidently not all of the story. Some other consideration must have entered into the bargain besides the rent, and this is made more than likely when we learn that the seller of the land was the king himself.

In A. D. 1545 the legal rate fixed by Charles V., in the Low Countries, was 12 per cent. (*Robertson*, note xxx.) Two years later, Edward VI. ascended the throne of England. After getting in debt himself to banks and individuals abroad to the extent of £132,372 10s. at the rate of 14 per cent. interest per annum, (*Sinclair*, *Hist. Public Revenue*, i. 339,) he totally forbade the taking of interest in England, A. D. 1552. (*Statutes of the Realm*, iv. 155.) The ordinary rate of interest in England, after the passage of this act, was 14 per cent. (*Hume Hist. England*, chap. xxxv.) Dr. Wilson, whose book was published at the time, says it was 12 and 14, and sometimes even 20 and 30 per cent. (*Dr. Wilson's Dialogues*, p. 78.) Queen Mary, who succeeded Edward in 1553, continued the same prohibition, but borrowed money herself at 12 per cent. interest on bond and mortgage, the bond being her own, and the mortgage upon her own private estate, while the lender was the City of London. (*Sinclair* i. 342.) About A. D. 1560, the rate of interest charged by the merchants of Antwerp in a loan to Queen Elizabeth, guaranteed by the City of London, though any rate at all was forbidden by law, was 10 to 12 per cent.

(*Stow's Survey of London*, i. 286; *Hume, Appendix, No.* 3; *Sinclair*, i. 187.) At the same period, on the accession of Charles IX. of France, the rate of interest paid upon the public debt of that kingdom, amounting to 43,483,000 livres, was 12 per cent. (*Hist. of the Reformation.* London: 1847; i. 222,) and this was believed at the time to be lower than the current rate in England. (*Hodge on Interest*, chap. iii.) Sinclair, in another place (i. 175—note,) says that the current rate at the time in England was 14 per cent. on State security. It was under this reign, in A. D. 1571, that the prohibitory law of Edward VI. was repealed, and one similar to that of 37th Henry VIII. enacted in its stead, limiting the rate of interest to 10 per cent. Since that time the taking of interest has never been forbidden in England, for, to the honor of Elizabeth, the statute just quoted, and which legalized the taking of interest, was made perpetual. (*Statutes of the Realm*, iv. 917.) In Scotland, from 1586 to 1633, the legal rate was also 10 per cent. (*Macpherson, Hist. of Commerce*, ii. 223, 376, and 382.)

We have hitherto omitted any mention of the effect which the discovery of America had upon the rate of interest in Spain, because the only authority we have been able to find on the subject is hardly entitled to credit. Montesquieu, in his *Esprit des Lois*, liv. xxii. chap. 6, quotes the "Inca" Garcillasso de la Vega (*Commentaries*, translated by Sir Paul Rycaut, Knight—London: 1688,) in support of the assertion that after the discovery of America, the rate of interest in Spain fell from 10 per cent. to 5. This was scarcely probable with interest at 10 per cent. in Genoa, the Low Countries, and France, and England. Besides, the edict of Charles V. A. D. 1545, fixing the rate of interest in the Low Countries at 12 per cent., extended likewise over the kingdom of Spain. This edict, which was re-affirmed in 1560, would have probably fixed the rate lower had the market rate allowed. This sort of evidence is not very conclusive, and were it not supported by the assertion of Macpherson—who says that the market rate in the Low Countries, A. D. 1566, was 12 per cent. (*Hist. Comm.* ii. 463)—we should feel inclined to let it pass unheeded. But this determines the truth of the matter. Finally, Sir Josiah Child (*Discourse Concerning Trade, &c., considered*, p. 6) speaks of the rate of interest in Spain, from a half century to a century later, as being 10 or 12 per cent., adding that "there, notwithstanding they have the only trade in the world for gold and silver, money is nowhere more scarce." Yet, after all, Montesquieu's statement may be true as regards the first forty or fifty years which followed the discovery of America, for Spain was at peace—was filled with foreigners, and it must have taken some time after the Mexican and Peruvian treasures were imported into the country, before they made their way into the commerce of the world. Meanwhile, a heaping up of money and a fall in the rate of interest would have occurred in Spanish trading towns, and have produced the phenomenon quoted from De la Vega.

The rise in the rate of interest from 4 to 8 per cent. in the 12th century to 15 at the close of the 16th (*Colwell's Ways and Means of Payment*, p. 301, note 2) must have excited attention. The cause is the same which, we have seen, influences the rate of interest in all countries—peace and freedom; or war and tyranny. In the 12th century Venice was a republic, and at peace. Towards the close of the 16th, after a series of exhausting wars, she signed a peace at Noyon, which left her stript of her wealth and population and shorn of her power; while the terrible Council of Ten, which governed her domestic affairs, ruled so sternly and secretly, that for over half a century the only acconnt which appeared of its proceedings in the conspiracy of 1618 was to be found in Otway's "Venice Preserved."

At the commencement of the 17th century the rate of interest in the various countries of Europe, so far as we have been enabled to discover, and the prevailing political and social condition which at that time distinguished them, stood as follows:

GREAT BRITAIN: *Political and Social Condition*—Close of Elizabeth's reign and consequent disturbances in Ireland. Custom of endorsing notes not known. Excessive monopolies granted by Queen to political favorites. Bad state of commercial laws. Innocent third parties not absolved from penalty of purchasing goods from insolvents. Laws restricting prices of beer and ale. Laws against speculation. Export duties on coin and bullion, beer, beef, pork, bread, coals, live stock, &c. Apprentice laws of Eliz., and by-laws of trade guilds. Bad poor laws. Foreigners and Jews interdicted from trading. Lack of naturalization laws. Laws limiting number of servants, looms, working tools, &c. Ecclesiastical intoleration. Mercantile classes restricted from participation in national councils. Bad state of crown credit. Exported imports obliged to pay half duties and heavy fees to searchers, waiters, &c. Customs duties, and prohibitions between the three kingdoms. Expense of collection equal to half the amount of taxes collected. Laws requiring all exported produce of colonies to pass through England and there to pay duties. Unequal representation of boroughs. Power of making war and laying taxes divided. Mal-administration of justice. Smuggling. Engrossment of most profitable industries by great trading companies armed with exclusive monopolies. Bad state of roads and turnpikes, and want of navigable rivers and canals. Corporate charters of trades. Election expenses. Insecurity of person, &c. *Rate of interest*—10 per cent., legal limit; 14 per cent., on loans to crown; market rate, higher.

FRANCE: *Political and Social Condition*—Reign of Henry IV. Religious toleration. Edict of Nantes. Administration of Duke of Sully. Grain trade made *free*. Exported imports absolved from paying duties. Financial reform. 332,000,000 livres of public debt paid off. 20,000 of taxes arrearages remitted. Government reserve of 17,000,000 livres deposited in Bastile. Agriculture fostered. Tolls and prohibitions suppressed. Commerce stimulated. Highways and roads built and impaired. Canals constructed. Drainage and mining prosecuted with vigor. Monopolies curtailed, &c. *Rate of interest*:—6¼ per cent., legal limit: 8⅓ to 10 per cent., market rate.

LOW COUNTRIES: *Political and Social Condition.*—Republican Government. Great comparative freedom of commercial affairs. Foreigners and Jews permitted to trade. Good police. Excellent administration of justice. Vast system of canals and roads. Monopolies discountenanced. Mercantile paper passed by endorsement. Bills of exchange in common use.

Great influx of capital. General state of progress and freedom so advanced that had not the war with Spain still lingered, a war which was then but feebly conducted by the latter, the advance which Holland maintained as compared with the rest of Europe would have been if possible still more marked. *Rate of interest:* market rate 6 per cent.

VENICE: *Political and Social Condition.* Desolating wars with Turkey and internal dissensions.

Rate of interest: market rate 15 per cent.*

At this period the Low Countries had become divided into Holland and Belgium, the former having erected itself into a Republic by the confederation of the seven United Provinces, and the latter having remained under the domination of Spain. The political freedom which prevailed in Holland at once attracted to it the most educated, enterprising, and wealthy persons in Europe. Its navy grew to be the largest in the world, and the entire seas were swept between the two Indies. Great trading companies pushed an enormous trade with the East, and numerous canals conducted an immense traffic at home.

The result of this freedom and activity was that a great portion of the entire wealth of Europe emigrated to Holland. This made her the wealthiest of all nations. But the effect of her newly gained freedom was not fully felt yet. Fifty years later we shall find her the chief repository of the garnered wealth of Europe, and capital so abundant in her markets that it went a-begging at 3 per cent.

In A. D. 1600, the rate of interest for mercantile paper in Holland was 6 per cent. (*Hist. Comm.* ii. 463.) In France, in A. D. 1601, it was $8\frac{1}{3}$ to 10 per cent. (*Memoirs, Sully: Paris,* 1814, iii. 6.) The legal limit in the latter country was $6\frac{1}{4}$ per cent. (*Hume, Hist. Eng.: Appendix, No.* 3; and *Macpherson, Hist. Comm.*, ii. 223.) From this time to A. D. 1620, we have no particular accounts. In the last named year, a loan of $200,000 from King Christian of Denmark to his brother-in-

* In China about this time the legal limit was fixed at 30 per cent. and the market rate was about the same. (*Epistles of Pére Daniel: Paris* 1697.)

law, James I. of England bore interest at the rate of 6 per cent.; though this amounts to nothing, since the rate at which the loan was taken and the mutual private considerations which undoubtedly influenced both parties to the negotiation have not been revealed to us. In the following year, a similar loan was effected between the same parties to the extent of $100,000, also at 6 per cent. (*Hist. Comm.* ii. 303, 312.) And yet at the same time, James was borrowing money from one of his own subjects at 8 per cent. This was a noted merchant of that time, named Sir William Courten, who lent James I. and Charles I. together £27,000—which the latter acknowledged as partly his own and partly his predecessor's debt. (*Hist. Comm.* ii. 336.) That 8 per cent. was the common rate, we are positively assured by Sir Josiah Child (*A New Discourse, &c.*, p. 47) who quotos it at 8⅓ per cent. The legal rate at the time was 10 per cent., and it so continued until 1624, when it was enacted by the 25th Jac. I., cap, 17, that from and after the 24th of June of that year, all contracts for the payment of a higher rate of interest than 8 per cent should be void. The law also interdicted brokers from taking more than a quarter of one per cent. commission for negotiating loans, and one-twentieth of one per cent. for making or renewing the bond or bill. During the debate on the passage of this act, it was incidentally stated that the rate of interest in Holland at the time was 6 per cent., and in Spain, and some parts of Italy, much higher than in England, probably 10 to 15 per cent. (*Commons' Journal*, i.) In Scotland, meanwhile, the legal limit since 1586 had been 10 per cent., and it so continued until 1633, when the example of England was followed and the limit reduced to 8 per cent. (*Hist. Comm.* ii. 182, and 376.)

In June 1641, although the legal limit still remaining 8 per cent. and although a bill for reducing the same to 6 per cent. had recently been read a second time in the House of Commons, (*Commons' Journal*, ii. 108,) such were the pressing wants of the Parliament that it was proposed to allow 10 per cent. discount on all moneys brought in. (*Ibid.* ii., 178.) In the month of December following, the Company of Merchant Adventurers was induced by dint of severe pressure to loan the government £50,000 upon the security of Parliament, at 8 per cent.* The common rate, however, was much higher, for the kingdom was disturbed by those agitations which preceded the eventful period of the Revolution. In 1641, the Star Chamber still existed, though that was its last year. In 1642, the civil war between Charles and the Parliament commenced. In 1649, the king was beheaded.

This brings us to the end of the first half of the seventeenth century. The state of Northern Europe at the time can be briefly described. England had just emerged from civil war, the most important result of which was the triumph of constitutional government. France was disturbed by the wars of the *Fronde*, occasioned by the opposition of a powerful nobility to the complete centralization of power in the sovereign (Louis XIV.) which was then being consummated. Holland had just exacted from Spain the treaty of Westphalia, by which her independence was acknowledged; and she was at peace. The legal limits of interest in these countries were: in England, 8 per cent.; in France, 6¼ per cent.; and in Holland, by a law passed A. D. 1640, 5 per cent. (*Sir J. Child, New Discourse, p.* 64.) But there existed this difference between them: in England and France, the market rate had always been above the legal limit, while in Holland it was always below it. Thus, when the market rate in Holland was 6 per cent., the limit was 8 per cent.; when it was 5 per cent., the limit was 6 per cent.; and now that it had fallen to 4 per cent., the limit was 5 per cent.

From this time forward, however, a great change took place in the relative claims of these three nations to wealth and commercial supremacy. Having finally and effectually curbed the power of the crown and established religious toleration, England was enabled to institute such reforms in her social and political legislation that, compared with the rest of Europe,

---

* It was in this year that the expression, debt of the kingdom, or public debt, first appeared in British history. Previous to that time it was the king who borrowed, and the king who owed. But royalty had become dwarfed, and it was now the kingdom that borrowed and owed. Following this example, it has now become the practice of all modern governments to establish public debts; but we apprehend that in time this privilege, like its forerunner, will succumb to some other one—one less fraught with danger to the honor and credit of the people.

except Holland and some parts of Italy, she offered the most complete security for person and property; as a consequence, large amounts of capital made their way to her shores from all parts of the world, even from America and the Indies; and, though Holland and the Italian commonwealths led the van of commercial freedom, yet England was making every attempt to overtake them. A short maritime war with Holland only served to illustrate how closely this rivalry was maintained between the two northern republics—for their combined fleets numbered hundreds of vessels; and when Admiral Von Tromp was defeated, in 1653, 10,000 men were slain in the contest. It was at this period that the Dutch, under De Ruyter, sailed up the Thames and blockaded the port of London—that is to say, in 1666.

From A. D. 1650 to A. D. 1700, we meet with the following accounts of the rate of interest in Great Britain and elsewhere. For the sake of convenience those relating to Great Britain have been placed in tabular form.

Rate of Interest in Great Britain A.D. 1650 to 1700.

[The legal limit previous to the 29th September, 1651 was 8 per cent. It was then fixed at 6 per cent by an act which was passed on the 8th August previously. This limit was continued until near the 19th century.]

Year.	*Political and Social Chronology.*	*Rate of Interest.*	*Authority.*
1650	Cromwell subdues Irish rebellion, returns to England and wins the victories of Dunbar and Worcester.	Land worth 14 to 16 years' purchase.	*Child's Discourse*, p. 15 *Davenant*, i. 359.
1660	Death of Cromwell and prevalence of anarchy. Longing after peace and order. Fall of Richard Cromwell's government. Negociation with Monk. The Restoration. Accession of Charles II. Reign of Licenciousness.	Forfeited estates, worth "not more than 15 years' purchase."	*Sinclair*, i. 267.
1665	Great plague in London. New York taken from the Dutch.	8, 10, and 12 per ct. on exchequer bills	*Child*, p. 20.
1666	Defeat of the Dutch at sea. Great fire in London.	Land 14 to 20 years' purchase.	*Davenant*, i. 359.
1670	Peace of Aix la Chapelle 1668. Infamous treaty of Dover, by which Charles II. sold himself to Louis XIV.	7 per cent.	*Macauley's Hist. Eng.* i. 308. *Locke's Works*, v. 9.
1670		8 to 10 per cent.	*Sinclair*, i. 346.
1670		Goldsmiths allowed 4 to 4½ per cent. on deposits.	*Child*, p. 65.
1672	Charles II. openly plunders the goldsmiths. War declared against Holland.	Loans almost impossible to negociate at any price.	*Somer's coll. of Tracts*, vol. iv, p. 67. *Sinclair*, i. 349.
1674	Peace with Holland.	8 to 10 per cent.	*Hume*, chap. lxxi.
1680	Habeas Corpus Act passed 1679.	Land 18 to 23 years' purchase.	*Locke*, v. 39.

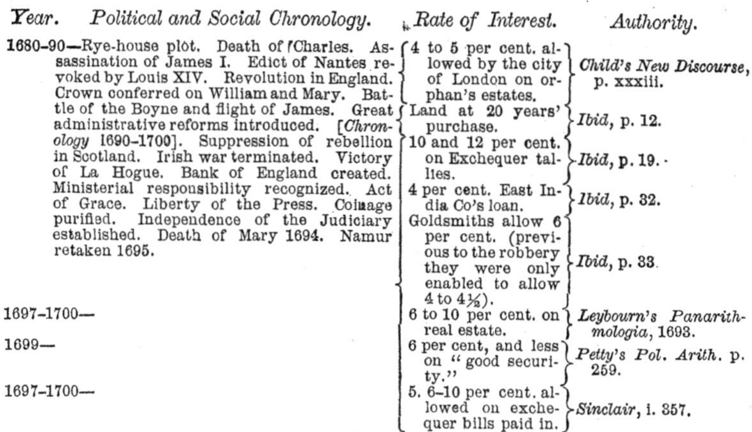

Year.	*Political and Social Chronology.*	*Rate of Interest.*	*Authority.*
1680-90—	Rye-house plot. Death of Charles. Assassination of James I. Edict of Nantes revoked by Louis XIV. Revolution in England. Crown conferred on William and Mary. Battle of the Boyne and flight of James. Great administrative reforms introduced. [*Chronology* 1690-1700]. Suppression of rebellion in Scotland. Irish war terminated. Victory of La Hogue. Bank of England created. Ministerial responsibility recognized. Act of Grace. Liberty of the Press. Coinage purified. Independence of the Judiciary established. Death of Mary 1694. Namur retaken 1695.	4 to 5 per cent. allowed by the city of London on orphan's estates.	*Child's New Discourse*, p. xxxiii.
		Land at 20 years' purchase.	*Ibid*, p. 12.
		10 and 12 per cent. on Exchequer tallies.	*Ibid*, p. 19.
		4 per cent. East India Co's loan.	*Ibid*, p. 32.
		Goldsmiths allow 6 per cent. (previous to the robbery they were only enabled to allow 4 to $4\frac{1}{2}$).	*Ibid*, p. 33.
1697-1700—		6 to 10 per cent. on real estate.	*Leybourn's Panarithmologia*, 1693.
1699—		6 per cent, and less on "good security."	*Petty's Pol. Arith.* p. 259.
1697-1700—		5. 6-10 per cent. allowed on exchequer bills paid in.	*Sinclair*, i. 357.

During the same period the rates of interest prevailing in other parts of Europe were as follows:

In Holland, A. D. 1650 and for some years previously the public debt bore an interest of 5 per cent. In 1655 the government was enabled to reduce it to 4 per cent. (*Hist. Com.* ii. 463.) In Scotland and Ireland A. D. 1661 the rate was 10 to 12 per cent. and it so continued up to A. D. 1690. (*Child's New Dis.*, p. 13.) At the latter period the legal limit in France was 7 per cent., (*Ibid.*, p. iii. and *Petty* p. 168,) and land was worth eighteen year's purchase (*Child*, p. 13.)

In Sweden the rate was 10 per cent., though the legal limit was 6 per cent. (*Ibid. p.* 85.) In Spain it was 10 and 12 per cent. (*Ibid.* p. 13.) In the Island of Barbadoes it was 15 per cent., (*Ibid.* p. 85) and in Turkey 20 per cent. (*Ibid.* p. 40.) The lowest rates of interest prevailed in Holland and some parts of Italy; and in both of these countries the legal limit was higher than the market rates. In the former country, about A. D. 1690 the market rate was 3 to 4 per cent.; (*Ibid.* p. 31) the higher rate only in times of tight money markets (*Ibid.* p. 32.) In the latter country about A. D. 1685 the debts of the Pontifical government amounted to about $50,000,000, and the Pope, Innocent XI., finding that they were selling at 22 per cent. premium, though they bore interest at the rate of 4 per cent., offered the holders the alternative of taking back their capital, or of lowering the interest upon it to 3 per cent. The reduction to 3 per cent. was not only assented to, but the 3 per cent. stock shortly afterwards rose to 112 in the market; (*Hist. Com.* ii. 622 ;) which shows that the Pope's bond was at that time the best in the world, for this was equal to 2. 67-100 per cent. at par, a lower rate, even, than that which prevailed in Holland. Usury was forbidden by the Pontifical law, (*Child's New Dis.* p. 66,) but the law was evidently a nullity. The rate upon real security was 3 per cent. and land stood at 35 to 40 years' purchase (*Ibid.* p. 13.) This is confirmed by Manley in the preface to his *Usury at 6 per cent. Examined*, who wishes his readers to notice that all Europe exceeded England in the rates of "usury"—Holland and *some Commonwealths* of Italy only excepted.

This brings us down to the 18th century, from which time forward the rates of interest which prevailed in Great Britain and elsewhere are tolerably familiar to modern readers of political economy. From the cursory review we have been enabled to make, the following deductions appear to enforce themselves upon our attention :

First. The rate of interest depends upon three things : 1. That social state and average progress of the community which governs the relation between what it produces and consumes —in other words that which influences the rate of the accumulation of capital in each particular locality. 2. The rate of wages. 3. Those political and social conditions which govern the security to person and property in various countries as compared one with another. The latter is the most important of all, since it is that which invites or repels the emigration of capital from or to countries more or less favored.

Second. The rate of interest is therefore mainly the result of international comparisons.

Third. The rate of interest cannot be lowered by mandatory legislation, nor indeed could it be raised by the same means, were no penalties attached to the infraction of usury laws. Such penalties, however, in common with all modes of commercial restraint, tend, by impairing the freedom and security of capital, to raise the rate upon which it is loaned.

Fourth. The most effectual means of lowering the rate of

interest is through a just and firm administration of justice, particularly in relation to the rights and obligations of contracts; entire religious and political freedom and equality; and complete commercial freedom. Beyond this, nothing can be effected but by the inculcation of a high and noble standard of public morality.

EMILE WALTER.

DRAPER'S CIVIL POLICY OF AMERICA.

Thougths on the Future Civil Policy of America. By JOHN WILLIAM DRAPER, M. D. LL. D., New York: Harpers & Brothers, 1865.

IF anything were required to prove to us that our National institutions are ahead of our National wisdom, and our organic National theories ahead of our National practice, that proof must have been furnished by the experience of the past four years. Inside and outside of the legislative halls of the country there seemed to be an almost total ignorance of the more abstract principles of Finance, Public Economy and Civil Policy. If the patient had not possessed a constitution sufficiently robust—a robustness imparted by the strength of our original theory of government—to have withstood all the quack nostrums which he was compelled to take, he would, most assuredly, have succumbed to the thousand and one malpractices which were tried upon him by those who had the care of the body. That we have successfully passed through the rebellion without subverting our civil liberty has been rather in spite of than by reason of our government and leaders of public opinion. We are so *practical* a people that all social theories were hitherto looked upon with disfavor and distrust; a distrust evidenced by the fact that our National Councils do not contain a man guilty of a knowledge of Political Economy or Social Science. The time, however, has arrived when empiricism will no longer accomplish our ends. With a debt upon our shoulders of three thousand millions; with a large population in our midst more or less disaffected; with three millions, or more. of brutalized freed slaves upon our hands—men who, without that preparatory training and discipline, which can only be acquired by working out their own enfranchisement and effecting their own elevation in the social status, but who, on the contrary, without any active movement on their own part, have been suddenly, and in many cases against their own will, delivered from the state of most abject and complete bondage to one of liberty,—we are called upon to solve questions of greater importance and higher meaning than has fallen to the lot of any Nation upon the face of the earth. We agree with Mr. DRAPER in saying that no "topics are more worthy of public attention than those with which American statesmanship will now necessarily be called upon to deal. With what else can the American reader who has faith in the destiny of his Nation, more profitably occupy himself? There are political problems of surpassing importance for which solutions must now be found." The much decried and little understood scientist whose general principles can alone aid us in solving these riddles has risen somewhat in the estimate of the American Nation, and ere long a change must and will take place in the character of the men who shall be called upon to represent us in Congress and the State Legislatures. The transition period is at hand, and any one who has any suggestions to offer upon the future Civil Policy of America can depend upon a patient and impartial hearing. In so far as we are concerned, we are certainly not disposed to quarrel readily with any one, who, with the slightest pretensions to scientific accuracy and research, shall attempt to teach us to apply the universal truths of sociology to the practical life of a Nation to which, for weal or woe, the destiny of ourselves and children are linked. We shall always hail with sincere satisfaction any co-laborer in the sciences which occupy our attention and engross our thoughts. The field is so wide, the land so rich, and the soil as yet so little tilled, that ages will in all probability elapse before we can crowd each other or be otherwise than benefitted by co-operation. We do not therefore exaggerate, when we say that the announcement of Professor DRAPER'S work, on the Civil Policy of America delighted us. We confess to a few misgivings before we took the book in hand. The author's work on the Intellectual Development of Europe appeared to us, in many respects, an undigested mass of historical facts. In its scope and objects far too wide for the then intellectual grasp of Mr. DRAPER, and in its execution less then we had a right to expect from the author's promises. Yet, many things may be said in mitigation of any severe sentence upon Mr. DRAPER'S first performance in the domain of Social Science. He had spent the best part of his life in analytical processes in the physiological and chemical sciences. Synthetical operations of the intellect, operations which alone can yield fruitful results in Social Science, must necessarily have been somewhat foreign to him. Four years, however, had elapsed between the publication of "The Intellectual Development of Europe" and the announcement of the "Thoughts on the Future Civil Policy of America;" years within which Mr. DRAPER could have made great progress in acquiring those forms of thought, and habits of mind, which might have made his reflections upon our social status of equal value with his thoroughly scientific and exceedingly able researches into our physiological organization. We have, however, been more than disappointed. We read the book again and again, in the hope that it was our own obtuseness and not the author's lack of philosophy which had led us to the sad conclusion that Mr. DRAPER'S "Thoughts on the Future Civil Policy of America," are about of the same value as guides to the formation of any intelligent opinion upon the questions which it is our task to meet and resolve, as a work on the Conic Sections or Virgil's Euclid would prove to answer the same purpose. We do not deny that the work under review is replete with many interesting historical facts, and scientific truths, but so is "Goldsmith's England" and "Mitchell's Astronomy," and yet neither one nor the other of these school books would throw much light upon the advantages or disadvantages of giving the Southern negro a vote, or whether free trade or protection will best subserve the interests of the American people.

Mr. DRAPER'S work is divided into four chapters. The first is devoted to an examination of the influence of climate in the formation of character. In that chapter Mr. DRAPER very elaborately proves that which every man of intelligence—if he has read anything of universal history—knows, that Nations, like individuals, are "transitory"—that climatic and physical differences produce different forms of thought, different habits, and, consequently, heterogeneousness in governments. Not to do Mr. DRAPER injustice, we shall quote his own words.

"Turning from these special cases, to which many others might be added, if there were occasion. I shall now endeavor to bring plainly into relief the facts that have been considered in the preceding pages. What is it that they amount to? This—that the body of man cannot resist external influences. It is helplessly modified by heat and cold, dryness, moisture—that is, by climate. The complexion of the skin changes, as also does the construction of the brain. In a restricted locality there may, therefore, be a sameness in the population; but in a vast continent where there are all kinds of climate, there will, *inevitably*, be all kinds of modified men. Their thoughts and their actions must necessarily be diverse (?) To unite them under one government becomes then, proportionately, more and more difficult. *But now, if there be a point on which America as a Nation has come to an irrevocable resolve, it is that one government alone shall hold sway on this Continent!*"

If the author's premises are correct; if climatic differences produce differences in men, and differences in men produce differentiations in government, we certainly do not see what the resolution of the majority of the American people arrived at in the year 1865, can possibly have to do with, or in the slightest degree affect or alter the eventual result. Mr. DRAPER himself says, on page 34: "We gather, therefore, a most important lesson from inquiries respecting the origin, maintenance, distribution and extinction of animals and plants; their balancing against one another from the variations of aspect and form of an individual man, as determined by climate—from his social state, whether in repose or motion—from his secular opinions, and the gradual dominion of reason. This lesson is, that the government of the world is accomplished by immutable law. Then, again, at page 240, the author says: "There is a course through which we *must* go. Let us cast from ourselves the untrue, the unworthy belief that the *will* of man determines the events of this world. National life is shaped by something far higher than that; it is shaped by a stern logic of events."

Formulated into a syllogism the author's reasoning seems to be as follows: The government of the world is accomplished by immutable natural laws. Natural laws cannot be altered nor their effects counteracted by human interference—therefore, the resolution of the American people that there shall be but one government on this continent will prevail over natural laws. We do not quarrel with the author's premises. We too believe that the progress of society should not and does not depend upon human caprice, but his deductions are absurd. That the American people firmly resolve that America shall never be divided is perfectly natural, but that, in the estimate of one who believes in the government of natural laws, such a resolution should assume any importance whatever is to us incomprehensible. If a vote had been taken, at any time of the period of Rome's greatness and power, Romans would have, and doubtless had resolved, that Rome shall ever remain the empress of the world. Notwithstanding this resolution, however, Rome had to make way for a better and higher civilization. To this position, Mr. Draper may reply, that American resolutions are more enduring than Roman resolves. But if man is governed by his intellect, if his intellect depends upon the character of his brain, and if the structure of his brain depends upon climate and soil, then with the modifications constantly going on in man adapting him to the climate and soil in and on which he is born or to which he emigrates, his brain structure changes and either himself or his descendants will not be bouud nor influenced by any such resolution as our fellow-citizens appear to have arrived at at the present day. Mr. Draper seems to have seen the difficulty of reconciling his philosophical convictions with his "patriotism," for he continues by saying:

"Look at the zone of American population inhabiting the countries in which the cotton plant can grow. Does not the luxuriance of that delicate product, that so quickly suffers on the approach of cold, imply a homogenous climate? Is it surprising that there should be a mental sameness, a concordance among the inhabitants in their manner of thinking? We have seen that a common climate makes men think alike and act alike."

"Turn now to that other zone stretching from the Atlantic westwardly, in the direction of the great lakes. Here there is none of that climate homogeneousness occuring in the other case. Even before the region of the lakes is fairly reached, four distinct strands of different temperature have been passed through. Follow that zone with a prophetic eye, as it becomes peopled to the shores of the Atlantic, and tell me, as those busy hordes extend over the vast sandy desert, climb up the threatening ridges of the mountain chains, descend through the moaning forests of enormous pines beyond, how many are the vicissitudes through which life must be maintained, and I will tell you how many different families of men there must be."

"We must steadily bear in mind the principal that has forced itself so strongly on our attention. Scientific physiology has no better ascertained fact than that man possesses no innate resistance to change. The moment he leaves his accustomed place of abode to encounter new physical conditions and altered modes of life, that moment his structure commences slowly to change. It may take several generations before an equilibrium is reached. Then his countenance, his complexion, his hair, testify to what has been going on."

"Public policy should therefore hold these great facts steadily in view, and shape its course accordingly. It should not only discern herein the hidden causes of those dreadful events through which, as a Nation, we are passing, it should also foresee that this is the rugged path through which, in the future destiny leads us. To the innate sympathies and antipathies thus engendered the demagogue will in all future time appeal."

"As they have done in our day, so will they ever hereafter constitute an instrument apt for his purpose. We have been called upon to deal with the variations as they now exist, our descendants will have to deal with the greater variations coming. No European country can serve us as an examplar, for none has encountered a problem so complicated and vast. The nearest approach to its solution was made by the Roman Empire, but that lay, for the most part, in an easterly and westerly direction, in which the wants and intentions of men were very much the same. That imperial system was intrinsically unable to extend itself north and south. Had it made such an extension, the difficulty of its government would have been far greater than it was. Whoever will study its disintegration and disruption will see how true these principals are."

"And here I cannot help making the remark, that whoever accepts these principals as true, and bears in mind how physical circumstances control the deeds of men, as it may be said in spite of themselves, will have a disposition to look with generosity on the acts of political enemies. Even when in madness they have rushed to the dread arbitrament of civil war —a crime in the face of which all other crimes are as nothing —and brought upon the country unmeasureable woes, he will distinguish the instrument from the cause, and, when he has overpowered, will forgive."

If we were disposed to be very critical we might press home the question, why, from the author's stand-point, civil war is " a crime in the face of which all other crimes are as nothing ?" We will, however, let that pass. The wounds inflicted upon the nation by our recent strife are as yet too recent to expect that even philosophers shall think of it and its authors dispasionately. But the following rhapsodical and sophomorical sentence, coming, as it does, immediately after our preceeding extract, cannot pass unchallenged.

" Philosophy alone can raise man to that grand elevation which enables him to perform acts that centuries will admire. Philosophers alone can place him :

> " Above all pain, all passion, and all pride,
> Above the reach of flattery's baleful breath
> The lust of lucre, and the dread of death."

These are the things that no human legislation can accomplish. Perhaps he who considers the supreme difficulties incident to our political position may look in the picture almost in despair, and come to the conclusion that in such a case no human statemanship can avail."

And why should human statemanship avail? If the laws of nature, ordained, as Mr. Draper believes, by divine wisdom, will eventually divide the domain of the United States into separate nationalities then they will do so because according to the divine ordination of things such a course of events will best subserve human happiness and human progress. If decentralisation results in dismemberment, then dismemberment is best for us, however strongly our pride, patriotism, or sentiment may protest.

Mr. Draper, however, thinks differently, and he therefore bids us to take courage. "Once, in the history of the world, has a parallel attempt at the Union of a continent been made. In the eleventh century was born a great man, who resolved to convert all Europe into one federation, with the Sovereign Pontiff at its head, and Emperors and Kings his pro-consuls —that Europe which, as we have seen, presents all sorts of climates and all kinds of modified men. A religious foundation was, under the circumstances, the only one that could be given to the contemplated structure; but Gregory VII., saw not only its capabilities, but its defects, as any one may find who will consider his relations with the heretic Beranger. Those effects he would have remedied if he could, and brought that foundation in more complete accordance with human reason."

"What was the practical instrument on which Gregory VII. relied in carrying out his intention? His legates could pass from Scotland to Spain, from the Atlantic to the confines of Asia, and meet in every monastery and at every church men speaking the same tongue. The Latin language gave him intelligent allies all over Christendom, but allies only among the men of education; with us, how much is the prospect—one language from Ocean to Ocean—and that among the lowly as well as the high. That bond of union is for us a bond of strength. It aids in compensating for diversities of climate. It gives us a common history of the past, a common hope for the future. Conterminous groups of men are far more effectually isolated by different forms of speech, than by intervening rivers and mountains, but groups that may be far apart may be in communion through a common tongue. They may learn to have faith in the greatness and permanence of their political creations, and in unbroken unity discern unconquerable power."

"With such an inappreciable advantage in our favor, we are encouraged to look again at the great problem before us, and to ask, can we not neutralize those climate differences, which, if unchecked, must transmute us into different nations?"

The remedy, according to Mr. Draper, against this threatened disruption is to be found in "Education and Intercommunication." "Nor is this the suggestion of mere theorists. Under that formula four hundred millions of men—one-third of the human race—have found stability for their institutions in China. By their public school system they have organized their national intellect; by their canal system they have made themselves, though living in a climate as diversified as ours, essentially one people. The principal on which their political system is thus founded has for many thousand years confronted successfully all human variations, and has outlived all revolutions. But what is their public education compared with what ours might be? What is their canal system compared with what our railroads will become?"

It is rather unfortunate for Mr. Draper that, the only illustrations he can find to encourage us in the hope that by the means he indicates, the promptings of our patriotic aspirations, as to the future greatness and unity of the Republic, may be realized, are woeful failures to achieve the same end. Gregory, by Mr. Draper's own admission, did not succeed in his attempt to unite Europe under the banner of the Church of Rome, and China exchanged progress, individuality, and energy, for stagnation, immobility and despotism in the effectuation of a strongly centralized unity—a unity not even then sufficiently strong to prevent constantly recurring rebellions, and civil strife. Even if peace and tranquility could be purchased at the price of liberty and individuality the bargain would be a bad one.

"Intellectual development necessarily implies centralization," says Mr. Draper. This we most emphatically deny. The converse of this proposition is the truth. Intellectual developement causes and implies greater and greater decentralization. History proves, and universal experience confirms, the fact that in the proportion as nations are centralized and strong in that proportion, are the individual particles of which it is composed weak. Mr. Draper seems to be conscious of the fact that the progress made of late years, by the western powers of Europe, would tend to militate against the validity of his argument in favor of a perpetual unity of the American States under one government—a government which shall not only stretch its protecting arms from the St. Lawrence to the Gulf of Mexico, and from the Atlantic to the Pacific Oceans, but which, according to the resolution before referred to, shall overshadow the whole American continent—he therefore boldly denies European civilization to be based upon any solid foundations. We fear to do the author of the Intellectual developement of Europe injustice if we should attempt to do aught else than to give his startling propositions in his own words.

"In Europe the attempt has been made to govern communities through their morals alone. The present state of that continent, at the close of so many centuries, shows how great the failure has been. In America, on the contrary, the attempt is to govern through intelligence. It will succeed."

"From the American principle it follows, that whoever seeks the improvement of his fellow men, the ennobling of the community among whom he lives, or the true glory of the Nation, can best accomplish his purpose by spreading forth the light of knowledge, and strengthening and developing the public understanding. For more than a thousand years the moral system has been tried in Europe. Its agent, the *Ecclesiastic*, was animated by intentions that were good, by perseverance unwearied, by a vigorous energy. The failure is attributable, not to shortcomings in him, but to intrinsic defects in his method; though on that continent, in a very imperfect manner, in later times, the other method has spontaneously, and with much resistance, made itself felt; a wonderful result is beginning to be apparent. The apprehension entertained by many good men in former times, that if the mind be instructed, the morals may be injured, has proved to be unfounded. Men are better in proportion as they are wiser. In whatever direction we look we see the improvement. The physical man is more powerful—the intellectual man more perfect—the moral man more pure. For the poor, in the midst of all this social activity, this business energy, charity is none the less overflowing; for him who wishes to improve his life, there is certain to be encouragement."

And again, on a subsequent page—

"The American political system is founded on the principle of public intellectual culture. Recognizing the truth of the maxim that ideas govern the world, it rests its hopes on universal education. In this respect it differs essentially from its contemporaries. They furnish enlightenment to certain classes only, not to the lower social strata. Such a repressive policy can, however, never impart intrinsic strength to a community as those who devised, and those who adopted it, supposed. *The insecurity of Europe, whose civilization hangs over an awful gulf*, and the strength of America, whose development is proceeding with so much energy, are each due to the course that has been followed in this respect. In Europe, men grope about in political darkness, not knowing whither they are going, and afraid to look into the future. In America, the sentiment of a manifest destiny to imperial greatness gives to every one a determinate direction and an energetic life."

It would be difficult to crowd into the same number of lines a greater number of historical inaccuracies and perversions of facts, than Mr. Draper has succeeded in doing in the foregoing. It must certainly prove news indeed to every student of history that "in Europe the attempt has been made to govern communities through their morals alone." The people of Europe, like the people everywhere else, have been and still are, to greater or less degree, governed by force. After repeated revolutions and struggles, the people of Western Europe have wrung from their governing classes some slight recognition of their rights. This fact is so patent, lies so much on the surface in every page of history, that unless Mr. Draper use language in a different sense than it has ever been used by any one who has written intelligible English, we are justified in saying that this sentence is arrant nonsense. No less untrue and absurd is the phrase that "in America, on the contrary, the attempt is to govern through intelligence." Every act of government is an act of constraint, and every act of constraint is a denial on the part of those who impose it, of the intelligence of those upon whom it is imposed. It is, doubtless true, that we place more faith in the intelligence of the masses than they do in any part of Europe, Switzerland excepted ; but to say that our government is a government of intelligence is as wide of the truth as to say that our system of government is one of an absolute tyranny. The Government of the United States, as we have experienced, admits of, and practices, numberless tyrannies of all kinds. Monopolies and restrictions still abound ; the rights of minorities are still unrecognized, and though better off than some less favored nations, we are not by any means in so happy a position that no further concessions need be demanded from government, nor further rights secured from encroachment by the governing power. What Mr. DRAPER means by saying that the civilization of Europe hangs over an awful gulf, we shall not take the trouble to inquire. It is, we presume, a mere flourish of trumpets to introduce the exceedingly flattering and consoling reflection, that while the stupid and barbarous Europeans are groping about in political darkness, we, happy Americans, are possessed of a determinate direction and an energetic life by reason of our faith in the "manifest destiny" to imperial greatness.

When Fourth of July orators indulge in flights such as these the more sensible portions of the community regard them as the fulminations of empty-headed demagogues. Mr. DRAPER, however, has proven that a man may be a very correct physiologist and yet not be preserved from parading sentences such as we have quoted.

In denying to Mr. DRAPER, as we have done, at the outset of our review, the power of generalization, we by no means desire to be understood to say that Mr. DRAPER cannot make very sweeping assertions. He offers abundant proof of his capacity in that particular in the book before us. For instance, on page 52 of the work we meet with the startling statement: "The absence of Summer is the absence of taste and genius; where there is no Winter loyalty is unknown." This proposition lacks but one element to make it a very profound, philosophical axiom; that element, however, unfortunately for Mr. DRAPER, is an essential one—truth, equally well-founded, seems to us to be the assertion that, "to convince the man who lives under a roof, an appeal must be made to his understanding; to convince him who lives under the sky, the appeal must be to his feelings."

The chapter on emigration contains some sensible remarks upon a subject in reference to which, we believe, that our countrymen require less light than upon any other. The advantages we have derived from the accretions to our population, by the influx of the laboring classes of Europe, have been so manifold and so obvious that it is rather puerile to devote much space to prove that which everybody knows. But even upon this subject we find Mr. DRAPER's desire for novelty leading him into most manifest errors. At the outset of his remarks upon the subject, he says: "In considering the effect of such emigration, we must bear in mind the statement of Machiavel, that in every great society there are necessarily three orders of men—a superior order, who understand things through their own unassisted mental powers; an intermediate order, who understand things when they are explained to them; a lower order, who do not understand at all. * * * Now, the political effect of emigrations depend upon this condition: from which of these three orders has the emigrating mass issued? We detect the guiding principle at a glance. If the drain has been from the lower or laboring class, the consequent result may not amount to much, for the diminution of that class is capable of quick repair. On the other hand, should the emigrating body have diminished seriously the number of the higher class, the result is a far more important, a far more permanent affair. A loss of the direct influence of these men is no inconsiderable thing; for no matter what may be the form of government the affected community may live under, they will and do control public thought."

Without wasting any criticism upon the question whether the assumption is philosophically correct that there ever existed a class of men "who understand things through their own *unassisted* mental powers," or a class "who do not understand at all," we judge that the influence, upon the wealth and prosperity of any country, of emigration from any one of these classes, depends very much, if not entirely, upon the abundance of that class from which there is a drain. For a few philosophers to emigrate from America to Germany, would be a serious drain upon us and but little gain to that thoroughly intellectual Nation—whereas, a large number of thinkers could be readily spared by the Germans, and their influx might prove of inestimable benefit to the United States.

In this chapter Mr. DRAPER takes a very decided stand against blood admixture of races, and warns us most emphatically against intermarrying with negroes. As Mr. DRAPER feels very warmly upon the subject, and seems upon this point to be throughly in earnest, we extract his peroration for the benefit of those degraded and unwise mortals who " thirst for the body of the stranger."

" It is not consistent with the prosperity of a nation," says our author, " to permit heterogeneous mixture of races that are physiologically far apart. Their inferior product becomes a dead weight on the body politic. If Italy was for a thousand years after the extinction of the true Roman race a scene of anarchy, its hybrid inhabitants being unable to raise it from its degradation, how indiscribably deplorable must the condition be where there has been a mortal adulteration with African blood."

The third chapter in Mr. DRAPER'S work " on the political force of ideas" has about the same relation to the subject matter of the book as a chapter from Mr. DRAPER'S work on Physology on the function of the Liver would have. We therefore refrain from any criticisms of its statements as foreign to the objects of our review. In concluding, we would state, and that in fairness to the Doctor, that there are some detached sentences in his work with which we can most heartily concur. Who, for instance, can refuse his assent to the following propositions ?

" The body-politic, like the body personal, must be ruled by the intellect. It is of no use to affirm that the foot, or the hand, or the stomach, can guide as well as the head. The social machine is composed of parts, each of which has its own appropriate duty to do." Or, say aught but aye to the following sample of profundity: "A dozen rich gentlemen may meet together and proceed to build a railroad across the continent, or lay a telegraphic wire under the Atlantic Ocean. They may do whatever is possible to the omnipotence of wealth. But, though all Americans should constitute themselves a joint stock company, *they never, by any votes, or any resolves, could call into existence a great soldier, a great law-giver, a great philosopher*. They could never create a Newton, a Milton, an Alexander. Talent is a God-given gift." After citing Macauley's History to prove the miserable condition of England a few centuries ago, Mr. DRAPER triumphantly asks, "Why is it that such things are impossible now?" He answers himself with a proposition which no one has the hardihood to dispute, by saying: "The answer promptly given to such an enquiry is, that men are more enlightened. Exactly so; and does not that confession concede the principle I am endeavoring to enforce, that the improvement of society can only be accomplished through the intellect?" We do not believe that any very great credit is due for dogmatically stating and elaborately proving a series of truisms which nobody has ever been sufficiently wrongheaded to deny, but after having mentioned many points of difference between Mr. DRAPER and ourselves, it was but fair to give samples of the character of the propositions in which we agreed.

Our readers may, with some degree of justice, say to us: You have severely criticised detached parts of Mr. DRAPER'S work, now examine it in its entirety and pass judgment upon its *general* scope and tendency. To this demand we reply, that that is an impossible task. Mr. DRAPER displays such a sovereign contempt for all the primary rules of logic, he gives such an unbridled rein to his imagination—an imagination which resembles the purble-brained, but healthy, imagery of early youth as much as the ghastly simper and twaddle of second childhood may be likened unto the joyousness and innocent prattling of infancy—that it is impossible to discover either the aim, purpose, or thread of the book. To this our readers may interpose—"Why break a butterfly upon the wheel?" Because, as social science is in its process of formation and crystallization, would-be social scientists will in all probability abound, and this work of Dr. DRAPER is but the precursor of a number of books which the American press will strike off, written by men who desire to make social science, or their limited understanding of it, bend, become subservient to, or be in harmony with their patriotic dreams and aspirations.

Analogous to the desire to make our conceptions of patriotism and the teaching of social science agree is the desire to harmonise our conceptions of religion with the physical sciences. Every student of science knows and very greatly deplores the attempts which have been made to achieve the latter. To them may be attributed the numberless books that we possess, professedly treating of scientific subjects, yet written with a theological bearing and in a theological spirit. Works such as those are neither scientific nor theological. Science, as such, stands in no relation whatever with either religious fervor or patriotic zeal. It is truth, simply and nakedly. A celebrated French philosopher was once asked whether science was atheistical or deistical, he replied: "You might as well ask whether a triangle is yellow or blue." This witty reply contains a great deal of philosophy. A triangle, as such, has no color—if you desire to see colored triangles, you must return to the picture books of your early infancy. Mr. DRAPER does not like the cold harsh abstractions of social science; he therefore colors his triangles with patriotic fancies, and he has created a book for children. M. Taine, in his preface to one of his earliest books, (an Essay on La Fontaine's Fables,) says, "Life is no longer a saloon wherein one converses, but a laboratory wherein one works." Dillitanteism is at a discount. When a man writes a book, the world has some right to say, We are too busy to have our time taken up with anything except solid information or amusement—you must instruct or delight, otherwise we will none of you; we cannot afford to let you practise at our expense—know something, at least, of the subjects upon which you treat; if you enter the arena of science, you should not only be fully armed, but also understand the use of your weapons. Fencing lessons should not be taken on the field of battle. Our only apprehension is that there are some persons so ill-informed upon the subject of Social Science that they will regard Mr. DRAPER's book the result of study in that department of human knowledge, and that such will hereafter regard with a just and wholesome fear any work relating to the topics purporting to be treated of in this one.

S. S.

DEBT AND RESOURCES OF THE PEOPLE OF THE UNITED STATES.*

We have not yet seen a single written argument which demonstrates, upon any rational grounds whatever, our ability to yield revenue and pay debt. The compositions of Messrs. Elder, Cooke and Walker are a type of all that have yet been written on the subject; as statements of fact they are totally unreliable, and as synthetical compositions, they are totally illogical. They base all their computations of our present financial strength and future resources upon the supposed facts set forth in the census of 1860, and build one error upon another by taking it for granted that the rate of progression which is therein stated to have occurred from 1850 to 1860, will continue the same to the end of time. All this is unscientific; and though this fact may not be recognized at home, for our patriotism makes us blind, it cannot fail to be detected abroad. To make matters even worse, Mr. Cooke in his circular, and a certain Mr. Lanier, who recently addressed a meeting of American stockholders in Frankfort, both promise that the resources of the country shall be speedily increased by the imposition of export duties on cotton and tobacco. The deplora-

---

* Les Finances Américaines apres la Guerre Civile—Par M. George Walker: *Revue des Deux Mondes*, 15 Juillet, 1865. The National Debt—Mr. Jay Cooke's Circular: New-York *Times*, May 6, 1865. How our National Debt can be Paid—By Dr. William Elder: Philadelphia; Sherman & Co., 1865. Our Burden and Our Strength—By David A. Wells: New-York; 1864. The Commercial and Financial Strength of the United States—By Lorin Blodget: Philadelphia; King & Baird, 1864.

ble ignorance which is exhibited in the confidence with which these announcements were made, not confidence that they would be fulfilled, but confidence that the mere announcement of them would increase European investments in our bonds, is truly pitiable. Our financially victimized countrymen here, have become so used of late to accept anything as oracular which emanates from official or semi-official quarters, that they do not take the trouble to turn to the Constitution and learn that export duties are forbidden by that compact; Europeans, however, either oblivious or careless about this point, only look at the effect which such measures would have upon the prosperity of the country; and it is curious to note how resolutely they shook their heads when Mr. Lanier incidentally mentioned them, and how they told him that they had tried such measures themselves, but found that they didn't work well. What stupid people Mr. Lanier must have thought these Germans were, who couldn't see the advantages of export duties!

The common method adopted by the writers who have hitherto undertaken to exhibit "the inexhaustible resources of our country" is this: the total wealth of the country in 1850 and in 1860 as determined by the census is contrasted. The rate of gain is shown to have been 126 per cent. during the decade. Therefore, it is argued, the rate of gain will be the same during the next decade, and the next, and the next—in short, forever. So much for our "resources." Now for our debt. This amounts to 3,000 millions. The government will fund it at 6 per cent; this will amount to a yearly charge on the country of say 180 millions. Add 120 millions more for other expenditures and we shall have 300 millions a year to pay. To a country which doubles its capital stock every eight years or so this is a mere bagatelle. And here they rest their arguments, which, for simplicity of method, are truly admirable and unrivalled. In order to throw an air of attractiveness over the subject, glowing pictures of the hidden treasures of California and the bubbling wealth of Pit Hole Creek, are dashed in here and there. The composition is then complete.

Oh, how sensible men must jeer and scoff at these ridiculous exhibitions! Oh, how all that is truly great of this country is hidden under a bushel; and its weakenesses paraded with conceited triumph!

Not a single boast is made of our noble laws of personal freedom and equality; not a single allusion is made to social reform, to the expected restoration of the civic authority and the act of *Habeas Corpus*; not a promise is vouchsafed of a better Administration of Justice than that which commonly prevails here. These things are evidently not deemed to have any relation whatever to our public credit. It is supposed to be enough to rely upon the census figures and the vague balderdash about inexhaustibility which has grown so common of late.

What is the result of this wretched tinkering, this vain and conceited haranguing? United States 6 per cent. bonds which ought to be at par to-day stand at the humiliating figure of 68; lower than Chilian 6 per cents which sell at 101, lower even than Dutch 4's which command 96. Truly a humiliating comparison for this proud people to contemplate!

Let us once for all demolish this absurd system of showing off the peoples's resources; and place the demonstration upon a sound basis. Then will foreigners, for the first time, learn how truly ample these resources are, and our countrymen cease to fear that the public debt may be repudiated. And then, also will it be seen, that our resources are to be found in the Constitution and the laws; and that the palladium of our credit is not our mineral wealth, but our civil freedom.

We select Mr. Walker's demonstration of our resources for the purposes of refutation.

His essay contains the following tabular statement:

Proportion de la Dette a la Richesse Nationale.

Années	Population.	Richesse Publique. fr.	Richesse Moyenne. Par tête. fr.	Dette Moyenne. Par tête. fr. c.	Intérêt Annual. Par tête fr. c.	Proportion de la dette à la richesse.
1860	—31,445,080	87,258,600,000	2,754			
1865	—34,000,000	116,499,600,000	3,426	444 69	28 89	13.90 per ct.
1870	—40,950,000	174,517,200,000	4,261	395 60	23 65	9.28 "
1880	—53,235,000	349,034,400,000	6,556	304 29	18 25	4.64 "
1890	—69,205,500	698,068,800,000	10,141	234 52	14 04	2.32 "
1900	—89,964,150	1,396,137,600,000	15,514	180 04	10 80	1.16 "

From which he logically reasons that our resources are more than fully equal to our debt.

To ascertain the value of these premises, it is only necessary to open the census at p. 195 of the Preliminary Report. We shall there find a table numbered 35 which furnishes "the true value of real estate and personal property according to the seventh census (1860) respectively; also the increase, and the increase per cent.* In fact this is the very table upon which Mr. Walker's argument is based, only he has not taken the trouble to read it through attentively. This table we shall acknowledge to be correctly compiled, as, indeed, we believe it is. But it is as well to know what it contains. By referring to p. 79 of the same work we learn that the table embraces the value of all individual property in the States and Territories in the year 1860, and none that belonged to the States or to the United States. A good deal of domestic furniture and personal ornament and dress was also omitted. With these exceptions, the table is believed to fully include everything of value in the country which belonged to individuals, and; moreover, that it was made up on the same principle and in the same manner as the corresponding table of 1850. Therefore, the table itself, is not only correct, but all comparisons made in it between the valuation of 1850 and that of 1860, are considered correct also. The two valuations comprise the same classes of things; and omit the same classes of things.

Opposite the name of the State of Vermont is placed the rates of increase which the capital stock of that State underwent from 1850 to 1860. This increase is seen to have been but 32 per cent.—a rate only one-fourth as much as that of the entire country together. Taking it for granted that this rate will not alter in the future, it would not be a difficult matter to show that Vermont, if called upon to duly discharge her fair share of the debt, would, in a very few years, become hopelessly insolvent; and, to a certain degree, this would be the fate of most of the Eastern and Middle States. To say nothing

* For a copy of this table see *The New York Social Science Review*, vol 1, p. 207.

of the great State of New-York being brought to this condition, it would go hard with Mr. Walker's thrifty and busy State of Massachusetts, if she too were reduced to it.

On the contrary, Iowa increased her capital stock at the rate of 943 per cent. If Mr. Walker's method of calculation is correct, this thrice happy State will, therefore, have increased her capital stock in 1870, to 2,470 millions; in 1880, to 24,700 millions; in 1890, to 247,000 millions; and in 1900, to 2,470,000 millions! This, of course, must at once dispel any doubt concerning the payment of the public debt, for it apparently would not inconvenience Iowa if she took the whole charge of it herself, and relieved her sister States from that which, while it is, it seems, a mere trifle to her, is quite a sensible burthen to them.

If Mr. Walker says that this is absurd; that the capital stock of Iowa will not increase at this stupendous rate; that it will *not* amount to 2,470,000 in the year 1900, nor to anything like it, and that, therefore, she cannot pay the whole debt herself, we would ask him then, upon what kind of authority is it that he bases his own argument. The United States, he says, will pay her public debt, because she increased her capital stock 126 per cent. from 1850 to 1860; for if she increased it at that rate during the past decade, she must continue to increase it at the same rate during the present and all future decades; and as this increase left her in 1860 with an absolute capital of $16,000,000, therefore, will she be amply able not only to meet the interest on her debt, but also to maintain a sinking fund for its speedy extinction. We shall be told that his argument is based on the irrefragable authority of the census. In return, we reply, so is ours. Precisely the same authority which proves that the United States will be worth 30,000 millions in 1870, 60,000 millions in 1880, 120,000 millions in 1890, and 240,000 millions in the year 1900, proves that the single State of Iowa will be worth 2,470,000 millions; for every time the United States doubles her capital, Iowa increases hers tenfold. If this position is deemed untenable, so must the other be, for they both rest upon the same foundation. And as upon this foundation rests every one of the arguments on this topic which has yet appeared in print, we offer the absurd deduction which we have logically arrived at, as a complete refutation of them all.

Before proceeding to establish the plain facts and principles upon which the solvency of this country now rests, and upon which it must ever rest, let us indulge in a parting passage at arms with Mr. Walker.

He says that the entire wealth of the country increased from 1850 to 1860 one hundred and twenty-six per cent. Is this true?

In 1850, the Census returned $7,135,780,228 as the total capital stock of the country. In 1860, it returned $16,159,616,068—*ergo*, an increase of 126 per cent. But, in 1850 there were 3,204,313 slaves in the country, and their market value was included in this estimate. This, at $500 per head, amounted to $1,602,156,500. So in 1860, there were 3,953,760 of these persons here, which, at the same rate, were worth $1,976,880,000. This sum was included in the estimate of 1860. Mr. Walker, therefore, in assuming the rate of increase in wealth to have been 126 per cent., cannot deny having included the negroes in his calculation. It follows that if negroes are an element of financial strength, it were a pity ever to have liberated them. If the increase of slaves in the South from 3,204,313, in 1850, to 3,953,760, in 1860, affords this gentleman ever so small a plank with which to build his platform of "inexhaustible resources," it seems to have been an act of questionable policy to have ever liberated the negroes from their former condition of bondage.

But how does our author propose to get over the damning fact that these slaves are now free, and that their market value no longer helps to form a portion of the capital stock of the country? Perhaps, we shall be asked to continue to reckon their increase among our resources of wealth. Be it so; but why not capitalize every white man as well. If it be held that slaves are not chattels, and that a man's complexion does not reduce him to the rank of a bale of goods, and yet that three or four millions of blacks shall be valued and reckoned up when the people take their decennial "account of stock," then there remains no reason why the 27,000,000 of whites should not be valued and included in the estimate. But, we presume, in the profound deliberations which preceded the composition of the article we have chosen for reviewal, that the author did not waste his time on such frivolous considerations as those which determine whether the market value of a fellow-creature shall make part of the census result or not.

We will now proceed to clear away the rubbish with which this question of debt and resources has been surrounded. In the first place, then,

THE DEBT IS ALREADY PAID.

Yes; it is no longer a question of whether the government can pay the debt or not. *That* question was settled when the war terminated. Indeed, there never was a day when it was not settled. The true question is, can one class of individuals among our people pay to another class of individuals among our people an annual amount in taxes equal to the interest on the debt added to its cost of collection and the other current expenses of government. That is the question, and the whole of it. For governments do not borrow from each other now-a-days. They borrow from individuals, principally from their own people, and they cannot borrow more than their people can conveniently spare—because, even if they wished to do so they could not get the capital, as no civilized people would be willing to risk their all; and as the wherewithal to pay these loans must also come from the people, a government debt in modern times is simply the creation of an obligation between one portion of a people and another. To determine whether this obligation will be fulfilled or not, it is necessary to know who these classes are, and what resources they respectively possess.

Before proceeding to make these inquiries, let us once more show how it is that the government really owes nothing, and that the debt is already paid. In the late war 24 millions of people were arrayed against 7 millions. To conduct it successfully on the part of the former, it was necessary to sink, we will say, 3,000 millions of dollars. This was equal to $125 per head of population during a period of four years; or, say $31\frac{25}{100}$ per year. This, for every able-bodied man in the North would have been $150 a year, and had the government been able to exact just this amount from each male adult there would have been no debt at all, for this was due by each one of them as his quota towards the cost of preserving a Union which was deemed invaluable, and for which every one is supposed to have been willing to pay. Every one, however, was not willing to pay, while many who were willing were not ready. Some held back from fear—others had no means—others again refused to contribute, and fled to foreign countries. In this strait the government borrowed from the rich, and pledged the poor to pay the loan, and to be sure that this pledge should not cause the lending class to pay the same taxes as the borrowing class, it exempted the bonds, and the income derived from them, so far as it could from any taxation whatever. That is the whole story. The debt is one owing by the poor and the timid to the prosperous and the confident—and the "government," except in name, has nothing whatever to do with the matter. The debtors may or may not pay the debt, and the government remain as powerful and undivided as ever, so that the expression which has of late gained so much currencey that, "if the government paper isn't good, nothing is," is absolutely destitute of any force whatever.

But, as we shall presently see the debt itself is so comparatively small an amount, that it would not be worth while to repudiate it. Nor would it be just; and when justice, which means ultimate interest, and expediency, which means immediate interest, unite, they can be no doubt of the result. We, therefore, believe REPUDIATION TO BE A PURELY VISIONARY IDEA, having no foundation whatever, and destined never to have any, except, when maddened by governmental errors and abuses, (which may, perchance, grow to be unendurable,) the people of this country should rise up and shake off all federal obligations. We apprehend that such a time will never come, for whatever grievances may exist, will doubtless be quickly removed by a Congress, which, from the nature of our institutions, must always be elected by the very class who will have the most cause to complain. So that in the broadness of our suffrage, which some mistaken people bewail as the only weak part of our Constitution, is to be found the palliative that shall always render repudiation an idle question.

In proceeding to determine whether this obligation of debt from one class of our people to the other will be duly fulfilled or not, we have, therefore, only to consider the question of ability, not that of desire, since the latter we regard as thoroughly and effectually disposed of already. There lurks no thought of repudiation in this people's mind. It is beneath them—they scout it with honest indignation. The question is simply one of ways and means, and this is the one which we shall discuss.

We have said that it is necessary to know who the classes are that respectively own and owe this debt, and what resources they possess. This requires some explanation; for why should it be necessary to know any thing about the resources of the creditor class, seeing that it is not it which pays, but the debtor class? For this reason: that, owing to the many processes of equalization which are constantly occurring between individuals and classes, the creditor class are compelled to contribute towards the payment of the debt as well as the debtor class, although it is impossible to determine precisely how much is paid by each. Taxes are first unequally laid, then they diffuse and equalize themselves or form part of some other temporary level of equalization. Monopolies first heap up resources in one direction, then fall by their own weight and form a new level, or gravitate into one already established. So with every other source of social inequality. Constant movements are going on towards new levels, and a constant tendency towards equalization is disturbed by constant interruptions. Hence, to determine the resources of the debtor class, it is necessary to study with equal attention the resources of the creditor class—we mean, the combined resources of the whole people.

Mark the distinction between our method and that of the writers who have gone before us. They set out to inquire into the resources of the country called the United States, and are naturally led to lay great stress upon the gold imbedded in the rocks of California and the oil deposits buried beneath the soil of Pennsylvania. On the contrary, while not ignoring these advantages, we set out mainly to inquire into the resources of the People, and we shall find ourselves led to the contemplation of their comparative political and social condition, their institutions, their laws, and their customs.*

This, if we mistake not, is what United States bondholders want to know; and this is what we shall, though with a sincere consciousness of our inability to do the subject justice, endeavor to point out to them.

As the political and social status of a people depends, to some extent, upon the sort of country they inhabit, its climate, situation, &c., we shall first briefly touch upon these topics so far as they concern the United States, before proceeding to treat those which, like comparative freedom, education, wealth, &c., more immediately affect the resources of a community like ours.

Geography of the United States.

The United States is 2,400 miles long and 1,300 miles wide, and contains about 3,000,000 square miles; so that it could accommodate the whole population of the earth with as much room for each inhabitant as the people of Belgium now enjoy; namely, a square mile of land to every 400 persons. More than three-fourths of this immense area is habitable.

There are 21,354 miles of sea coast and bay boundary line; and over 3,000 miles of lake and river boundary line. The country is intersected in every direction by navigable rivers which flow either into the Gulf, the Atlantic, or the Pacific.

With scarcely any artificial communications at all, the natural facilities for penetrating the country in every direction are therefore most abundant. A vessel laden at Liverpool can discharge her cargo at a port in the State of Minnesota on Lake Superior; another can sail direct from Louisiana to Dakotah by way of the Mississippi and Missouri Rivers, and a third can load in Pennsylvania, sail down the Ohio and Mis-

* Formerly, the richest countries were those in which Nature was most bountiful; now, the richest countries are those in which man is most active. —*Buckle, Hist. Civ. in England*, vol. i. p. 112.

sissippi, and then up the Red river, and finally discharge her, freight in upper Texas.

Added to these natural facilities the country has 32,000 miles of railways in operation, and 5000 miles of working canals, besides endless common roads. These roads and canals are mainly carried through the valleys of rivers not large enough for navigable purposes, and as the navigable rivers on the Atlantic and Gulf run for the most part north and south these artificial means of transit run principally east and west. There are many exceptions to this rule, however. Even the largest rivers have proved inadequate to the immense demands of commerce, and railways have been built along their banks to compete with the steam vessels which float upon their bosoms. Instances in point are the railways from New Orleans, La., to Columbus, Ky., and from New York to Albany and Troy.

The whole system of natural and artificial highways form a vast net-work which cuts up the entire face of the country; and brings the whole of it within reach of the markets of the world.

CLIMATE.

The climate is temperate ; and Saxon, Latin, Oriental, Indian, Mongolian, Aztec, and Negro, each find locations adapted to their wants and habits. With the exception of a few well-defined localities, such as the rice swamps of South Carolina, the Gulf cities in summer, the low lands at the confluence of some of the western rivers, and the arid plains in the Far West, the country is quite healthy. The average temperature throughout the year is 50 degrees Fahrenheit. The following table gives the particulars in regard to certain localities :

Place of Observation.	Latitude.	Spring.	Summer.	Autumn.	Winter.	Year.
Fort Monroe,	37.00	56.87	76.57	61.68	40.45	58.89
New-York,	40.42	48.74	72.10	54.55	31.38	51.69
Eastport, Me.,	44.15	40.15	60.50	47.52	23.90	43.02
St. Louis, Mo.,	38.40	54.15	76.19	55.44	32.27	54.51
Chicago, Ill.,	41.52	44.19	67.33	48.85	25.90	46.75
Fort Ripley, Minn.,	46.19	39.33	64.94	42.91	10.01	39.30
Monterey, Cal.,	36.36	53.99	58.64	57.29	51.22	55.29
San Francisco,	37.48	54.41	57.33	56.83	50.86	54.88
Astoria, Oregon,	46.11	51.16	61.58	53.76	42.43	52.23

NATURAL RESOURCES.

This is the feature upon which, after the Census tables, our authors rest their arguments. Now the natural resources of this country are unquestionably very great, but so are those of Spain and Hungary, and so, we are told, are those of some parts of Central Africa and South America. But why don't people invest their capital in those countries? Because natural resources, unless developed by means which spring up wherever JUST LAWS and FREEDOM are planted, go for nothing. That is the reason; and much comfort may our evil prophets of coming export tariffs find in it. Still, as with freedom and justice, good natural resources are better than bad ones (at least, so long as the population of the whole earth is not completely *mobilized*,) we shall proceed to briefly enumerate those which chiefly contribute to the wealth of this country. We commence with those of least value, and proceed towards those of most value.

HUNTING AND FISHING.

These are of little account. The former occupation is still pursued by the trappers and the few Indians who still exist in the Far West; and the latter by the Massachusetts fishermen and New-York and Virginia oystermen. A man can have all the game and all the fish he wants, if he chooses to hunt and angle; but comparatively few persons make a living by these occupations in the United States.

AGRICULTURAL.

Hill and dale, terrace and meadow, table and bottom lands abound all over the country; and almost every thing that it is possible to grow anywhere, can be grown here. Orange and lemon groves can be seen in the South, and vineyards in the North; but the most profitable crops are cereals, sugar, cotton, and tobacco. The land is also well fitted for grazing; while timber is plentiful nearly everywhere except near the populous districts, and on the plains.

MINING.

The extent of these resources is unknown—they are so vast and illimitable. We can tell how many bushels of corn or wheat the country would raise if put to its limit; but it is utterly impossible to measure the extent of the unmined wealth which lies beneath its surface. Gold and silver, copper, coal, iron, and other valuable ores exist in quantities sufficient for the use of all mankind, for ages to come—all that is needed is, that the ores shall be dug out and prepared for use.

Manufacturing.

Our resources in this respect are very extensive. We have an abundance of water-power; (though steam-power is more to be depended upon during the summer months, and is being extensively substituted for the former motor wherever circumstances have enabled manufacturers to afford the expensive substitution;) and through the unfairness of our patent laws towards foreigners we can appropriate as many foreign labor-saving inventions as we please, and call them our own, if we only take care to improve them a little before applying for patents upon them—but this remark only applies to those rich monopolists who can influence the Patent Office, when "interferences" are decided, and "extensions" are asked for. There are many classes of manufactures which would flourish in this country independently of protective tariffs, and do now flourish—not by reason of the tariff, but through the great natural advantages which the country and the climate afford them.

Commercial.

These are the most important of our natural resources. We have already adverted to our vast sea-coast line, our enormous rivers and lakes, and the artificial roads and canals which cover the country in every direction. Besides these natural facilities for commerce, the position of the country itself is most advantageous. It lies directly between Europe and China, Europe and India, Europe and Polynesia—in fine, between Europe and the Pacific Ocean. The shortest route to the Indies lies across it; and, in five years time, a line of telegraph already completed and in operation between Halifax and San Francisco will unite the hemispheres across the Asiatic continent. The United States lies also between Europe and Mexico. Continuous lines of railways exist between Maine and Texas, and goods and passengers can be transferred from London to the capital of the Montezumas in the short space of twenty days.

The trade-winds blow towards, while the Gulf stream flows away from, the continent—thus affording ready means of locomotion in opposite directions for vessels bound to and from its shores. But commerce depends not alone upon superior natural resources. The higher we ascend in the scale of human occupations, the more do we find them depending for their success upon Liberty. Agriculture may flourish in spite of the most arbitrary laws and regulations; Commerce only blooms in an atmosphere of almost perfect freedom.

SUMMARY.

These, then, are the natural resources of this country:—Plenty of arable land, rich mineral deposits, a wholesome climate, and the means of intercommunication in every direction, —the whole lying directly in the path of commerce and empire.

We now proceed to speak of its people.

POPULATION ACCORDING TO THE LAST CENSUS.

Whites,	26,975,831
Indians,	294,431
Free Colored,	488,374
Slaves,	3,961,129
Total,	31,719,765

The greater portion, nearly seven-eighths, being whites.

DENSITY OF POPULATION.

The United States contained, in 1860, but ten persons to the square mile. This indicates an exceedingly sparse population —one of inferior density to that of almost every civilized country in the world, and superior only to that of the thinly settled regions to the north and the south of us. This fact indicates the great need in which we stand of immigration; and it imperatively calls upon our legislators to afford every inducement for immigrants to settle in this country, by conferring upon them entire freedom of person and a free soil; and by sparing them the infliction of any enactments that may tend to set up class privileges, monopolies, or industrial restraints.

The following table affords a comparative view of the density of population in the various countries of the world:—

Population of Various Countries to the Square Mile.

Belgium,	400	India (British,)	145
China (Proper,)	362	Denmark,	110
Netherlands,	309	Portugal,	98
Great Britain & Ireland,	244	Spain,	89
Italy,	220	Turkey (in Europe,)	76
German States,	189	Greece,	68
France,	176	Russia (in Europe,)	32
Prussia,	171	Sweden & Norway,	18
Switzerland,	166	Turkey (in Asia & Africa)	12
Japan,	160	Central America,	12
Austria,	148	United States,	10

But, as the United States is a new country and some very considerable portions of it are but lately inhabited at all, the comparison is hardly fair. If the Northern region west of the Mississippi be excluded, the density of population to the square mile would be very largely increased; and this, we think, is a much fairer comparison, since the North-west, at the date of the previous census, was nearly all Territorial, (there having been but two States already founded in that region, and those, too, within the previous thirty years,) while it will be remembered that by far the largest portion of our territory lies in this very region.

Ages and Sexes.

The average age of the population was 23 $\frac{28}{100}$ years, or from three to eight years younger than the average age of European populations. Of the whole population about half were females. The working population consisted of about one-third of the whole number of both sexes and all ages.

Religion and Education.

The religion of the country is mainly Protestant Christian—the greatest number of churches belonging to the Methodist and Baptist sects. Next in order come those of the Presbyterian, Congregational, Episcopal, Roman Catholic, and Lutheran—the Methodist churches outnumbering them all combined. The Baptists, however, possess the largest church accommodation, and the Presbyterians own the most valuable church property. These facts and the scanty statistics on comparative education which are to be found in official reports, united with the personal observation of the writer (who has travelled throughout the entire country, as well as through the principal countries in Europe) justify the commonly received conclusion that while education in the United States has not developed itself in the formation of leading minds, it is better diffused among the whole people than it is in any other country. Public schools are plentiful, newspapers common and cheap, and books within the reach of the most indigent. The latter facts are due to the fortuitous circumstance of our language being the same as that of the leading empire of the world. Accordingly, we "appropriate" many of the ideas of her foremost statesmen, authors, newspaper writers, and inventors, without having to pay for them; and, in this way, the people may be said to be educated principally at Great Britain's expense. We are largely indebted in this respect also to France and Germany; nor should it be concealed that we occasionally repay Europe for these borrowed thoughts in kind. In the main, however, the people of this country are educated at the expense of Europe; and this education extends superficially all through the country. This brief religious and educational summary indicates a people more amenable to law than to reason; and more to reason than to passion.

Occupation.

We have no means of determining what portions of the population are engaged in the several divisions of human industry—commerce, manufactures, mining, agriculture, fishing and hunting; but we shall presently see to what extent these various branches of industry respectively contributed, in value, at the date of the last census, towards the yearly product of the people, and from this and the changes which have occurred since, we may arrive at an estimate which will, probably, be not far removed from the truth.*

* In the Population volume of the Census report there is a Table, on p. 652, which purports to give the "Occupations" of the people of the United States; but, as the whole number of persons embraced in the Table form scarcely more than a fourth of the population, its completeness is very much impaired. Nevertheless, as this number includes all the working males (the number given is 8,287,043), the Table might be epitomized and classified in such a manner as to prove a very valuable addition to the statistics of our people. This, however, has never yet been done; and, until it is done, very little use can be made of the mass of undigested figures which the table presents.

In 1850, as we learn from the census of that date, the male population of the country over fifteen years of age was employed as follows:

In Commerce, trade, manufactures, mechanic arts, and mining,..........	1,596,265
Agriculture,..........	2,400,583
Labor (not agricultural,)..........	993,620
Army,..........	5,370
Sea and river navigation,..........	116,341
Law, medicine and divinity,..........	94,515
Other pursuits requiring education,..........	95,814
Government civil service,..........	24,966
Domestic servants,..........	22,243
Other occupations,..........	22,159
Total,..........	5,371,876

But the enumeration is deficient and the classifications arbitrary. Yet, out of the 2,400,583 classified under the head of "agriculture," 2,363,958 were taken by the census marshals as "farmers," and, as in the census of 1860, where no general classifications at all are made, the number of "farmers" given is 2,423,895, some approximation may be made towards ascertaining at least what proportion of the population was engaged in agriculture. To this end we shall add to each enumeration of "farmers" 33⅓ per cent. for "farm hands" and deficiencies, as well as the entire slave population of the country between the ages of 15 and 60—it being well known that these persons were nearly wholly employed in that occupation.* The free colored and Indians are left out of the computation, their numbers being too small to merit notice. For the purposes of comparison, we shall also introduce the few results of the census of 1840, which bear upon the point:

* Since writing the above, Mr. De Bow (the Superintendent of the Census of 1850) has very kindly furnished us with an estimate which he had made of the number of slaves employed in rural occupations. These he placed at 2,304,313 —the total slave population, at that date, having been 3,204,313—allowing 304,313 for house-servants, etc. Mr. De Bow estimates that 2,500,000 were employed in agriculture, as follows:
Hemp, 60,000 Rice, 125,000 Sugar, 150,000 Tobacco, 350,000 Cotton, 1,815,000. But he makes no allowance for *children, &c.*, so that the figures we have assumed —viz., 1,630,673—we believe to be more correct.—*See De Bow's Compend. Census.* 1850, p. 99.

Census of 1840.—Total population 17,069,453; total laboring population, 5,689,817. Of these there were employed in agriculture 3,717,756 white males and negroes of both sexes, or 65 per cent. of the entire laboring population of the country.

Census of 1850.—Total population 23,191,876; white male population over 15 years* of age, 5,926,336; total slave population between 15 and 60 years of age, 1,630,673; aggregate of active laborers, 7,557,009. Of these there were employed in agriculture, 3,151,944 white males, and 1,630,673 negroes, making in all 4,782,617 persons, or 63 per cent. of the entire laboring population of the country.

Census of 1860.—Total population 31,747,514; white male population over 15 years of age, 8,373,538; total slave population between 15 and 60 years of age, 2,021,248; aggregate of active laborers, 10,394,786. Of these there were employed in agriculture, 3,231,860 white males, and 2,021,248 negroes, making in all 5,253,108 persons, or 50 per cent. of the entire laboring population of the country.

SUMMARY.

Year.	Total Pop.	Laboring Pop.	Agriculturalists.	Agricultural proportion of Laboring Pop.
1840	17,069,453	5,689,817	3,717,756	65 per cent.
1850	23,191,876	7,557,009	4,782,617	63 " "
1860	31,747,514	10,394,786	5,253,108	50 " "

From this summary it will be seen that the number of persons engaged in Agriculture, relative to the number of the laboring population, has continued to grow less every decade. Though in 1860, this number was still one-half of the whole of the laboring population, we shall presently find that they produced but one-fourth in value of the entire yearly product of the country—proving the inferior productive powers of the class engaged in this pursuit. In depending every year less and less upon agriculture, and more and more upon pursuits requiring greater skill and demanding increased social free-

* It may be proper here to remark that, after this age, but comparatively few males in the United States are unemployed. Boys leave school in this country and enter upon some vocation at a much earlier age than is common in other countries. Old men, too, remain active laborers in our country until a more advanced age than elsewhere, generally until sickness or death removes them from their useful and honorable labors.

dom and equalization, the people of this country are not only increasing the fruitfulness of their sources of income, but furnishing the best evidence that they are steadily gaining in intelligence and refinement; though this gain, we are bound to say, has occurred in opposition to, and not in conformity with, the laws which have been made to "regulate" this subject.

Wealth and Increase of Wealth.

The estimated value of all the real and personal estate in the United States belonging to individuals, in 1850, was $7,135,780,228. This included the value of $3,204,313 slaves, which, at $500 each, amounted to $1,602,156,500. This, deducted from $7,135,880,228, would leave $5,533,623,728.*

The estimated value of all the real and personal estate belonging to individuals, in 1860, was $16,159,616,068—this included the value of 3,953,587 slaves, which, at $500 each, amounted to $1,876,793,500. This, deducted from $16,159,616,068, would leave $14,282,822,568. Thus, the total capital stock of the country increased, from 1850 to 1860, at the rate of 158 per cent. Of this amount of increase it is estimated that over 100 per cent. was due to the labor of new immigrant settlers and to accessions of capital from abroad—either brought hither by immigrants or invested in the United States by foreigners residing in other countries—and the balance to natural increase.

In other words, that the 5,500 millions of capital stock, in 1850, increased by savings and accessions, to about 14,000 millions, in 1860; of which 5,860 millions, more or less, were brought hither by immigrants, or invested in securities, commercial credits, or otherwise, by foreigners residing either here or abroad. This exhibits a yearly increase, from savings alone, of about 6 per cent. per annum compounded.

Production.

The yearly product of the entire people is shown by the following Table:—

* It is hardly necessary to explain to the intelligent reader that, to include the market value of human beings in a sum which represents the value of the capital stock of the community, is a gross absurdity. As well might a valuation be put upon the white laborers as the black, and the same included in the total wealth of the country. One cannot have his cake, and eat it; and, as a nation, we cannot include in the estimate of our total wealth both the product of the slave's labor and the slave himself—and yet this very thing has been done in some of the Essays which we have under review.

Total Gross Product of the United States, for the Year 1860.

Products.	Value in Millions of Dollars.
Agricultural products: including animal products, increase of live stock during the year, and products of the forest....................................	1,700
Manufactures: including $24,358,222 worth of home-made goods—including house and ship-building, and excluding the value of raw materials consumed......	897
Mineral Products—including coal, salt, and the precious metals, and excluding bar and rolled iron and castings—the latter being included in manufactures....	100
Fisheries..	13
Domestic Commerce: transporting commodities and passengers in every direction within the country, and distributing commodities to consumers, and all incidental labor devoted thereto.................	1,500
Foreign commerce: *i. e.*—gross increase of value derived from foreign exchanges, $180,000,000; and from the carrying to and fro of passengers, $10,000,000..............................	190
Total gross product,	4,400

That is to say, on a capital of 14,000 millions, the whole people earned about 4,400 millions during the year 1860—and would have continued to earn more and more every year, had the war which occurred in 1861 not put a stop to the rate at which wealth was being accumulated in the country. Of this 4,400 millions, 3,224 millions were consumed within the year, and 176 millions saved. Several hundred millions per year must also be allowed for the annual *net* increase in the value of lands. This increased value was due either to the cultivation of new lands or to improvements put upon lands previously cultivated. This savings of 176 millions for the year, added to the gain derived from the yearly increased value of real estate already alluded to, amounted to about 4 per cent. on the capital stock.

At this rate, eighteen years would suffice to double the entire wealth of the country, since this would be the numerical power of 4 per cent. gain per annum compounded yearly with the principal. But, between 1850 and 1860, this rate of gain was doubled by the constant immigration of persons and capital, both of which poured into the country at a gradually accelerating rate of increase until interrupted by the commercial crisis of 1857 and finally stopped by the war.

The figures given above are rude calculations intended to show the sources to which the country is mainly indebted for its wealth and prosperity, and are not by any means to be regarded as critical data.

GOVERNMENT AND LAWS.

In a scientific enquiry, views, prompted by what are termed patriotic feelings, should find no place. Patriotism, like love, is simply a passion, and science has nothing to do with passion. We shall, therefore, instead of passing over this part of the subject with the usual settled conviction that our government is " the best on earth," proceed to enquire how it compares with other governments in the advantages which it confers upon the people. That in many respects our government and laws are not so good for the people as those which prevail in other countries is abundantly evident. For instance, in regard to that part of our system of government which does not permit the ministers of the executive to confer personally and officially with the representatives of the people in Congress, assembled, it may fairly be questioned if the practice which prevails in Great Britain is not better. Then as to our laws, we have no such beneficial legislation in regard to the Liability of Stockholders and Partners as is embodied in the laws which prevail upon the subject in most of the advanced countries in Europe. Neither are litigated contracts so equitably enforced here, as they are there, nor fraud so promptly punished.

In many other respects our government and laws are better, and in one respect we are far in advance of all the rest of the world. We have already adverted to our laws of personal freedom. In this country all men are legally equals; we have no laws of entail, of primogeniture, of villienage; the rights of women are better respected; the road to honor, preferment, and wealth, is open to all alike. These are unquestionable advantages. Whatever our shortcomings are, this is enough to cover them all; for here, upon this broad belt of earth, exists no spot where one man may say to another, as he may say almost any where else in the world: "I am better than thou." The effect which this equality of person has upon social progress and the accumulation of wealth can hardly be estimated. Take our two last Presidents, for example: both of them were once rude and friendless lads, who were born in frontier settlements, and lived lives of early penury and toil; and yet both of them afterwards rose to distinction and to affluence. Such advancement would have been impossible in Europe; and the state of affairs which throws open the fields of competition so wide as this, affords the best assurance that, come what will, the resources and wealth of this people will never diminish; and what better guarantee than this can a public creditor desire? But, as to our shortcomings, we believe they are only in common with those of other peoples. Our late governmental interferences with currency, commerce, and manufactures, are not only (as we hope) merely temporary, and incidental to a time of war and passion; but they find precedents in both English and French practice. The suspension of the *Habeas Corpus* Act (also a temporary expedient) is a not uncommon practice in such parts of Europe as possess any *Habeas Corpus* at all. Our elections are no more disorderly than their's are; nor do our candidates have to expend any more money in order to be elected to office. Not that we need no reform—on the contrary, we need a great deal. We need a final renouncement on the part of government of its assumed right to interfere in currency, banking, and other commercial affairs; we need a total repeal of the usury laws which prevail in most of the States; we need a repeal of every law which degrades a woman below the rank of a man—but so does almost every other country to which we may be compared, and they need quite as much reform (though in other respects) as we do. Above all, we need more attention to be paid to the Administration of Justice in our country. This is the real business of the General government, and we could wish that it devoted itself more to it than it does. For a people intelligent enough to require a republican form of government, the special function of that government should be—Justice. The equalization of natural rights is supposed to have been effected by the very form of government which had been adopted; it is, therefore, only the equalization of Legal Rights which the government should busy itself with afterwards. Having effected this, our government may then (and not until then) have just reason to call itself the "best on earth."

CUSTOMS.

But whatever evils have arisen from the need of the reforms we have suggested have been greatly modified by the customs into which our people have grown. The social privileges which our proverbial gallantry to the other sex has conferred upon women has partly supplied the place of those equal laws which have been denied them. Our industrial habits have made the country prosper in spite of adverse legislation. Our trading customs have nullified the absurd usury laws which still disgrace our statute books. Our quick movements and our habit of economising time have made up for the slow growth to which our intermeddling laws have consigned the development of the natural resources of the country. Our inventive knack and genius for ready adaptation have compensated for the repeated legislative triumphs of centralization. Our disposition to compromise has largely made up for the notorious inefficiency of our civil courts of justice—by far the largest portion of all differences which occur between Americans being settled by this means, or by stipulated reference to a third party; * and it is this difference between customs—and government, and laws, which has so much puzzled foreigners to determine our real status compared with the various communities of the civilized world. Those who judge us by our government and laws hold back both talent and capital from emigrating to our shores. Let them see to our customs; let them learn to appreciate the real good sense, the fairness, the activity, the genius, the industrial aptitude, the effective desire for wealth, and the solidity of character which distinguish our people, and this want of confidence will disappear. They will find here an active and a frugal

* The extent to which arbitration is carried in this country is little known; but, we are assured by competent judges, that the statement made in the text is quite reliable.

population, in whose path towards the highest state of wealth and civilization lies no obstacle but a true appreciation of their merits by the people of other lands.

Changes since 1860.

The changes which have occurred in the resources of this people, since 1860, are worthy of note. The geography of the country, its climate and natural resources, and the number, age, sex, religion, and education of the population have not changed; but their aggregate wealth and its rate of increase, their occupations and their laws have experienced considerable alterations. Some of those which have occurred in their laws, we have already included in our review. The alterations made, mainly comprise the enforcement of such temporary expedients as naturally grew out of a state of war. In the course of a few years, it is believed, they will all disappear. In the other respects, the changes, since 1860, will probably remain more permanent. The war has taken not less than 5,000 millions out of our capital stock; the rate of our former increase in wealth has been diminished, and the occupations of the people have been changed. Concerning the altered rate of increase in wealth, we shall have more to say further on. In regard to occupation, it will be remembered that, during the early part of our career as an independent political community, we were a commercial people. It was during this period that we made relatively the greatest strides* towards education, affluence, and power. This was due to the fact that commerce, to a country like this—embracing, as it does, so large an area, so many climates, and such an enormous coast line and such long channels of water communication—is the most profitable of all occupations for the people at large. In the face of this fact, however, successive high tariffs were forced upon the people by mistaken legislators zealous for the public good, but ignorant of how to promote it. These tariffs little by little tended to discourage commerce and promote other and less profitable occupations. Still, up to 1860, fully

* This opinion conflicts with the tables of progressive wealth furnished by Dr. Elder, and incorporated in Mr. Walker's Essay. But we cannot regard these tables as being reliable. Those who are familiar with the progress of this country can testify to the unequalled development of its resources and that of its people from the close of the war of 1812 to the commercial panic of 1837.

half of our annual gains continued to be derived from this source. But the war which commenced in 1861 gave another opportunity to the advocates of high tariffs; and they were not slow to seize it. The injudicious Act of 1862 was the result; and the consequence has been that the foreign branch of our commerce is seriously crippled; much of the capital formerly engaged in it having been transferred to manufactures—an occupation for which our people have less aptitude than for the other. Besides that, our manufacturing facilities are not so great as those of countries which have hitherto competed with us in this branch of industry; and this inequality, contrary to the opinion of some persons, can never be altered by means of legislation. We trust, however, that in the course of a few years this state of affairs will right itself; for, once let our people understand their true interests, and it will not be long before they will be followed out. The country is fortunate in having, at the present time, a Citizen at the head of affairs who not only truly understands what ought to be done and how to do it, but also possesses the desire to do it, and the capacity and energy necessary to do it well. As a statesman of the *laissez faire* school, Mr. JOHNSON, in succeeding to the Executive chair, was the one needful instrument to bring the country out of a state of war and destruction to one of peace and economy—for no man better understands than he that the affairs of a republican government never prosper so well as when they are left to shape themselves in obedience to the natural laws of crystalization and harmony which pervade the social as well as the material world.

But the changes noticed do not vitiate any of our premises. We are essentially the same people that we were in 1860—we are as numerous, as industrious, and as hopeful as ever. Whatever incongruous legislation the war has called forth, the customs of the people—deeply engraved in their natures—have already partially effaced and will, eventually, totally efface. The debt will not be without its social effects, it is true; but neither will the war; and, we believe, that in so far as regards the bearing which these changes will have upon the ability of the people to pay taxes, they will about balance one another. The debt will have a strong tendency to distribute wealth unequally, and so to form classes of our population with observable lines of demarcation between each other—a state of affairs which has hitherto not occurred. The war will have a tendency to make our country and our people better known to Europe; and, as we shall presently see, the beneficial effect of this will be sufficient to outweigh the prejudicial effect of the other.

Recapitulation.

We have insisted that the proper way to estimate the value of United States bonds was to examine into the resources of the people instead of those of the country; since without an industrious people and wise laws the others are valueless. This examination we have gone into: the result has been that, without hiding any of our faults nor any of our disadvantages, we can fairly claim (taking us all in all) that we do not, at least, stand below any other people. As regards our institutions—we are, in some respects, ahead of the world; in many respects, behind it; but the few respects in which we are ahead, fully balance, by their superior weight, the many respects in which we are behind. As regards our laws, we could not say so much; although we regarded the most objectionable of them as merely due to a temporary state of war but lately brought to a close; and believed that they would soon be reformed. As regards our customs, we looked upon these as the most admirable feature of our civilization. The American people are generally regarded as essentially money-seeking and practical: this is true; and, whatever our changing laws may for the moment be, the practice will be that which, (without violating them,) will conduce the most to profit and economy. The loss of effort occasioned in this manner is common in all countries; and will eventually attract public attention here as soon as elsewhere.

If, therefore, we not only do not suffer in comparison with other communities, but in many respects outdo them—why is it that capital is comparatively so scarce in this country? why is it that it does not flow hither from Europe to seek its best market? and why is it that the price of our bonds stands as low as we have mentioned?

These phenomena are to be attributed to nothing else but

a want of knowledge concerning the true state of affairs here. Americans are too apt to exaggerate; foreigners too prone to depreciate: the result is, that the world to-day holds an opinion of our institutions which is incorrect. European capitalists prefer 3 per cent. investments in London to 6 per cent. investments in New-York; just as capitalists here prefer 6 per cent. investments in New-York to 12 per cent. investments in Chicago; and, for the same reason: neither of them are aware of the exact comparative value of the security which is afforded to capital in either place. We are willing to admit that English security is better than American, if the English will admit that Dutch security is better than English. Money is lent at lower rates in Holland than in England, and at lower rates in England than in the United States; but from this it does not follow that money is safer in Holland than in England, nor safer in England than in the United States. Yet, so strongly does the impression prevail among capitalists that a high rate of interest is always synonimous with bad security, that they prefer to keep their funds in England at a low rate of interest, when they could obtain just as good security here with much higher rates of interest. The difference between absolute security and a mercantile risk may be greater here than in England, (and we are free to acknowledge that it is—for this is the natural result of the inferiority of our commercial legislation as compared with that of England,) but we contend that this difference is largely over-rated. One can obtain absolute security here with guarantees against all risks but those which arise from political disturbances, and yet earn 4 per cent. on money at call. In England, with similar security, no greater rate than 2 per cent. is procurable; yet, will it be contended that political risks in this country amount to 2 per cent. per annum?

The whole truth is: we are not known—the security of our concern is under-rated. We may show our account books—Mr. Walker and his colleagues may exhibit our past dividends and issue attractive prospectuses for the future, in vain; nothing of this sort will do. To equalize the rates of interest between here and Europe—to increase the capital of the country by promoting a flow of it from other countries—to make our government paper bear a high price in the markets of the world—the true status of this people must be preached louder than it ever has been yet. And it must be preached understandingly, for the mere vauntings of sanguine patriots will do us more harm than good. Political economists must take up the theme and illustrate it, and the people must constantly bear in mind that the necessity of keeping up their good name is too important to be entrusted to incompetent agents.

Nor must they stop with merely publishing the state of their credit to-day—they must constantly seek to improve it; for other communities are not standing still, and good credit is merely a term of comparison. Compared with that of other peoples, our status to-day may be much superior; to-morrow, it may be much inferior—for, if even we do not fall away ourselves, others may surpass us.

The readiest way in which the credit of this country could be strengthened, we have already hinted at: this is, to improve our Administration of Justice—a function which should entirely engross the consideration of republican governments; for, when people are intelligent enough to support this form of government, it is to be supposed that natural rights are familiar to them, and that only legal rights can be subjects of contention among them. Next to this, is demanded the repeal of all those laws which tend to interfere with the freedom of commerce and other industrial occupations. Left to themselves, the people would not fail to engage in those occupations which would prove most profitable to them. Influenced by tariff and tax laws (having for their object something besides the raising of revenue) many of them have been driven into occupations which, however lucrative to a few individuals, have been strikingly unprofitable to the multitude; and, consequently, a source of loss to the State. All this legislation should be carefully undone: the result would be, that the income of the government from taxes would not only largely augment, but the general happiness and wealth of the people would increase. Foreign capitalists would not fail to notice these changes, nor to improve their opinions of our institutions; and the result of this improved opinion would be an immense flow of European capital to the United States. We have insisted upon inviting investments of foreign capital, more than perhaps the reader may deem justifiable; but we are prepared to establish its importance. The positive savings of a community,* when not increased by accessions of foreign capital, are extremely small. In the United States, they are not much above 4 per cent. per annum (or 48 per cent. in ten years); so that, if no foreign capital flowed into the country and no capital went out of it, the capital stock of the whole country would, by the year 1900, amount to about $43,000 millions, as follows :—

Year.	Wealth.	Year.	Wealth.
1860.	$14,000,000,000	1880.	$19,713,600,000
1860–65.	5,000,000,000 (sunk by war)	1890.	29,176,128,000
1870.	13,320,000,000	1900.	43,190,669,440

* The writer has elsewhere (see *New-York Social Science Review* for July, 1865,) endeavored to show that the rate of these savings in all countries is indicated by the average rate of interest prevailing in them—indeed, that it would be identical with it, were the elements of Risk and Labor which are commonly embraced in the rate of "interest" subtracted from it. For instance, a loan of money is made in New-York, with "interest" at seven per cent. Of this seven per cent., perhaps one-half of one per cent. is a compensation for labor performed or time lost, either in waiting for the borrower or upon him, or in drawing the notes, or other evidence of the debt; or in collecting it when due; or in some other way. Then for the risk of war or civil commotion, and the risk of not being able to compel a due observance of the contract through the agency of the law, or the risk of any *ex post facto* laws, which shall impair the contract, let us say that one per cent. is a fair compensation. Then for the risk that the borrower may fail to pay the debt when due, either from temporary inability or permanent insolvency, let us allow one per cent. Finally, for the risk that some accident may occur to the lender through which the debt may not be paid —such as neglect, legal dereliction, absence, sickness, or death—let us allow one-half of one per cent. Placed in tabular form, the transaction assumes the following shape :—

Rate of "interest" at which the loan is negotiated,		7
Less compensation for superintending wages,	½	
" " political risk,	1	
" " business, "	1	
" " personal, "	½	
Total, Labor and Risk,	—	3
Residuum, or Pure Interest,		4

It is this residuum or Pure Interest (as we have ventured to term it—though we think that *Capital Gain* is a better word) that we mean when we speak of the rate of interest being identical with the rate of net savings. If, with interest at 3½ per cent. in London—1½ per cent. of which is Labor and Risk—and interest at 7 per cent. in New-York—3 per cent. of which is Labor and Risk—then the real rate of Pure Interest is higher in New-York than in London; *and this we believe to be the case.* This distinction between interest and pure interest (or Capital Gain) explains the parodox—that "capital always runs towards a low rate of interest." True; it does run toward a low rate of "interest;" but this means *a high rate* of Capital Gain.

In England, these yearly savings do not exceed 2 per cent.; but, if we compare the total amount of wealth in each country at various periods, we shall find that they both increased in wealth to a much greater degree than would result from a natural increase from savings. The difference was due to accessions of foreign capital; hence the importance of inviting capital towards this country. We do not disdain to invite foreign immigrants—why not foreign capital? The immigrant, when he lands here, becomes an American; the capital, when it finds its way here, becomes naturalized just the same. It will stay here just as long as American capital will, and will do as much good to us.

Capital is constantly flowing from one country to another. In past years, it has flowed hither from Europe in large sums, and has been the making of the country. It has also flowed freely between the States, and its exodus from the Eastern to the Western States has caused just such phenomena as we noticed in relation to the State of Iowa—a large decennial increase to the wealth of the Western States and a corresponding diminution of the wealth of the Eastern States—the latter, nevertheless, retaining in many instances enough to constitute a positive gain above their natural rate of increase—phenomena, which, if solved through the aid of the assumptions made by our authors, would lead us into the most extravagant conclusions.

There exists opportunities here for the employment of capital which, if known to Europeans, could not fail to invite their capital to this country. Not five, not ten—but twenty, thirty, and forty per cent. per annum can be realized on large investments of capital, without going out of this city. As for security, let the most ample allowance be made for risk, and the rate would still remain highly attractive. All that is wanted is that these facts should be known : once known, the wildest dreams of our most sanguine patriots concerning the future wealth of this country would be exceeded by the plain facts. Above all, let us have our commerce again, for it is commerce which most effectually diffuses public credit—carrying, as it always does, substantial proofs of the comparative freedom, security, and wealth which prevails in distant countries.

To sum up: our ability to yield revenue and to pay debt, though sufficient even to cope with the difficulties incidental to an entirely new posture of affairs, and with the additional aggravation of an unnecessary high rate of interest, could be largely increased by a few simple legislative enactments having in view the attraction hither of a steady stream of foreign capital. These should not go beyond repealing, by gradual steps, a number of obnoxious laws which are now in vogue, some of which we have already pointed out. In addition to this, the Treasury would find it to its interest to take proper steps towards disseminating among Europeans a true knowledge of the state of affairs which exists here. We have hitherto done much to invite population towards this country; let us now do something to invite capital.

But, if even these reforms are not established, we contend that a fair comparison between the People of this country—their government, laws, and customs, and the People of any other country—their government, laws, and customs—establishes beyond all doubt our superior claims to credit. And, no matter how plentifully capital makes its way towards this country, the country is so vast that it can absorb it all, without materially lowering its rate of earnings for many years to come; while our institutions are so truly admirable that they will not only leave this capital more free to employ itself than in other countries, but in the long run afford it more ample security.

A. D.

FAWCETT'S POLITICAL ECONOMY.

Manual of Political Economy. By HENRY FAWCETT, M. A. Second Edition. Cambridge and London: Macmillan & Co.; 1865.

Mr. FAWCETT has given us a volume which is destined to become popular, because written in easy language and with not too fine a point upon definitions. For this very reason, however, do we feel prejudiced against it; for nothing is more pernicious in its tendencies than a scientific work which neglects precision, for the sake of attractiveness. But, without any preconceived opinions, let us glance through the work and form our judgment of it as we go along.

In his preface, the author says:

> "The end I hope to attain, I may briefly state to be this: I think that all who take an interest in political and social questions must desire to possess some knowledge of Political Economy. Mr. Mill's treatise is so complete and so exhaustive that many are afraid to encounter the labor and thought which are requisite to master it; perhaps, therefore, these may be induced to read an easier and much shorter work. I so well remember the great advantages which I derived from reading Mr. Mill's book that I would not publish my own work if I thought that it would withdraw students from the perusal of a more complete treatise. I am, however, convinced that those who become acquainted with the first principles of Political Economy will be so much struck with the attractiveness and importance of the science that they will not relinquish its study."

This is well; and it leads us to hope that we shall discover something new in Mr. Fawcett's book. But, as we shall find, this is not the case. In the several instances wherein he differs from Mr. Mill, though his points are generally well taken, they are not of much consequence. Definition is his bane—a bane that he swallows too often, and, when he does not swallow, analyses too closely to comport with the general arrangement of the work.

For instance, (p. 20,) capital is defined as being, "all that wealth, in whatever shape or form it may exist, which is set aside to assist future production;" yet, the whole of the chapter (which is a very long one) is filled with illustrations of this general definition, which are more or less at variance with it. For instance, it is admitted (p. 31) that tobacco may be Capital, because the part it performs in animal economy may conduce to assist future production—

> "The relations between chemistry and physiology are as yet by no means settled. The theory of food is most imperfectly understood: a chemical analysis may very possibly show that such an article as tea contains none of those ingredients which are commonly considered to nourish the human frame; and, hence a rash and ignorant assertion is often made that tea is not a necessary of life, and that therefore a heavy tax upon tea is no hardship to the laborer: the tax is simply a salutary sumptuary law, because the consumption of tea ought rather to be discouraged than encouraged. But, although tea may not nourish the body, yet it undoubtedly soothes the mind—and this is equally important; for, without some soothing influence, life would be almost intolerable—and, even the body itself would be wasted by the weariness of the mind."

But, though tobacco may be Capital—and so may the fund devoted to the maintenance of courts of justice and a police force—yet, materials of war, forts, the pay of soldiers, etc., are not Capital:

"Cannon-balls, gunpowder, and mortars are commodities which cannot be appropriated to assist the future production of wealth; laborers cannot be fed by them; and, therefore, when the loan is converted into such commodities, it cannot form a portion of the capital of the country."

But, is this not the case also with Mechlin laces, hoop skirts, waterfalls, gold-headed canes, gilt bindings for books, and in short, ninety-nine hundredths of all that men and women covet and consume?

These nice distinctions are not new to us. Political Economy has always been loaded with them, and always will be, so long as its teachers confine themselves to the examination of its statical phase and neglect its dynamical aspects; then will it doubtless be perceived that all wealth is capital—for man produces nothing which he does not want; his wants depend upon his character, education, circumstances, etc.; these last are elements of further progress, of future production, etc.; consequently, whatever he produces assists to produce something else—and is therefore, even within the definition quoted,—Capital. Distinctions such as our author enters into ultimately lead to rank nonsense; as, for instance, (on p. 21,) where he suggests that one portion of the wheat crop of a country may be Capital, and the other portion not Capital but merely wealth. The utility of the distinction between circulating capital and fixed capital does not appear obvious to us either; nevertheless, these hair-splittings are not Mr. FAWCETT'S. He has simply taken them from the authors who have gone before him—and we never should have remarked the fact had his preface not prepared us for some improvement in this respect.

Before finishing with this chapter on Capital, we cannot resist questioning the practical soundness of the oft-repeated tenet, that—

"If government spends the loan at home, the loan has not diminished the capital of the country—it has merely caused a portion of it to be diverted to other purposes. * * * * The National Debt, considered in this aspect, is a mortgage upon the industry of the nation; and the creation of a mortgage cannot diminish the wealth of a nation, *unless the persons who own the mortgage should be foreigners, etc.*"

Should a wall be built about every country, so that all nations would be completely isolated from each other, then this proposition would be correct; but, as the case stands, it is totally untrue. Wealth is continually flowing from one country to another, seeking better security or better profits ; and this movement, as regards the extent to which it enrichens the gaining country and impoverishes the losing country, is affected in no manner by any counter-movements of Interest on public debts. Take the movement of populations, as an illustration precisely in point. Let it be assumed that an addition to the number of its inhabitants is an advantage to any country. Applying our author's proposition to emigration, it would follow that, if a man went abroad instead of from one local point to another, the country which he left would lose by it, But this is not the case ; the moment that that man left his country, (England, for example,) provided no movement of population either into or out of it was going on, there would be one man less in it than before. Assuming that the same state of affairs existed in the country to which he emigrated, (France, for example,) there would be one more man in France than before. Further assuming that perfect freedom of emigration existed between the two countries, (which we have a right to assume, in order to reduce the conditions of our hypothesis to that statical phase which our author deals with,) then it is plain that France would be over-crowded, and England less thickly settled. The obvious result of this state of affairs would be the counter-emigration of some other man from France to England to restore the equilibrium. Another illustration : There are twenty-four persons seated in two omnibusses—twelve in each ; a man from one omnibus gets out, jumps into the other and squeezes himself into a seat—so that now there are thirteen men seated in one, and but eleven in the other. If both vehicles are going the same way, and no questions of fare, relative speed, etc., arise—is it not likely that somebody will leave the over-loaded omnibus and secure the vacant seat in the other? Of course. Now apply this principle to emigration and to the movements of capital ; load it with every possible complexity of condition concerning differences in language or rates of interest, tolls on travellers, or duties on bullion, and the result will be that, as a practical matter, it makes no possible difference to any nation whether its debt is held abroad or at home.

It is time that this old error of the Mercantile System was

banished from works having any pretensions to a scientific character, It admits a principle which would impede the free movements of men, of money, and of goods from one country to another. It is, therefore, uneconomical in its tendencies, and should find no place in economical treatises.

We have now gone through with the chapter on Capital. Before looking through Mr. FAWCETT's work any further, let us revert to his opening chapter—he, there, very aptly remarks, that—

"The vagueness of popular conception has generated a vast amount of prejudice towards Political Economy. Hard-hearted and selfish are the stereotyped epithets applied to this science. Ill-defined antipathy is sure not to rest long suspended upon a mere abstract idea—it seeks some concrete object; and, therefore, the epithets applied to the science are speedily transferred to those who study it; and a Political Economist exists vaguely in the haze of popular ignorance as a hard-hearted, selfish being who wishes to see every one rich, but who has no sympathy with those higher qualities which ennoble the character of man. The error of this ignorant prejudice shall be abundantly exposed in these pages; but we will make a few preliminary remarks upon it in order to convince the student that the Political Economist is not the harsh being generally portrayed, but that he possesses that information which tells him how to improve the lot of his fellow-men. He may therefore be the most useful of all philanthropists; because a mere desire to do good, without any principles of guidance, is ever liable to be a futile and misdirected effort."

Chapter II. of the First Book is devoted to the *Requisites of Production*. These are deemed to be three in number; labor, appropriate natural agents upon which this labor may work, and capital.

Here is another radical error: if this definition be correct, a valuable gem, which may be exchanged for vast quantities of wheat, cloth, or money, is not to be deemed a product. A similar conclusion must be arrived at concerning the interest paid for the use of capital—this cannot be deemed a product. Neither labor, capital, nor appropriate natural agents may have been involved in the production of either the gem or the sum of interest. Consequently, they are not products. What will Hobnob say to this, who bartered his cargo of grain for an annual income derived from the profits of a discount bank; and what says Madame Petroleumini, who swapped off her lamented husband's oil stock for a diamond pin and a pair of pearl bracelets?

The truth is, that, fortunately for Hobnob, he bothered not his head with the absurd definitions of Political Economists, and the equally absurd conclusions to which they ordinarily lead. And, as for Madame, she declared very sensibly that no work on the subject should find a place in her library. Both of these persons probably (if they reflected at all upon the subject) would have considered that the *time* of the pearl-diver and the diamond-finder, and the *time* of the capitalist, during which the borrower obtained the use of his money—was an element in the production in that form of wealth which each of them preferred. Hence, *human time* is also an element in the production of wealth ; and this is one of the statics of the science of which our author seems not to have been aware.

Chapter III. is devoted to *Labor as an Agent of Production;* chapter IV. to *Capital,* and the remainder of the Book to the other subjects which properly pertain to *Production.*

Of chapter VIII. on the *Increase of Capital,* we cannot speak too highly. It gives a very clear insight into the causes which generate wealth. Capital is the result of saving. Saving is attributed to two motives—foresight and desire for profit:

"Nothing more distinctly marks the superiority of man over the brute creation than the prudent foresight which causes an adequate provision to be made for the future. To provide against the contingencies of the future engrosses perhaps the too anxious care of the nation. The precept that the morrow will take care of itself is disobeyed with scrupulous anxiety by civilized men, and implicitly followed by those tribes who still grovel in wretched barbarism. The Jesuit missionaries who, a century since, formed a settlement in Paraguay, found the great difficulty they had to contend with was the utter recklessness of the people. The missionaries gave them seed : they knew that this seed would, if sown, in a few months yield them a plentiful supply of food, yet they could not be restrained from eating the seed, instead of sowing it—the smallest present enjoyment was by them preferred to the greatest prospective advantage. People in such a condition can be little superior to the more intelligent animals whose hereditary instincts induce them to provide against danger which they may have to encounter. Birds build nests which are most perfectly adapted to protect their young ; beavers construct their habitations on a plan so admirable that it seems almost to rival the skill of man ; and even dogs collect a store of food to which they will resort when pressed by hunger."

In illustrating this principle, however, our author again falls into an error—this time a very common one :

"Any circumstance, therefore, which tends to augment the wealth of the nation will induce increased saving."

This he deduces from the fact that men by force of habit become used to a certain style of living which they continue after their income has increased. The most superficial examination of this sophism must lead to its detection. Like those already noticed, it belongs to the Mercantile School. The wealth of a nation cannot be augmented except by savings, at the rate denoted by the prevailing rate of interest; (less risks, superintending labor, etc.;) by net increase of population from births over deaths, at a rate which may be approximately determined by the life tables used by insurance companies; or by accessions of capital and immigrants from other nations; *unless* a wall is built around the country to completely isolate it from all others; and even in the latter case the augmentation which may take place can be of no possible advantage to the nation itself until it shall be again opened to intercourse with some other nation, when a comparison between the estimation in which certain elements of wealth have meanwhile been respectively held by the two nations may furnish that sole criterion by which wealth can be recognized—exchangeable value. The discovery of petroleum deposits in Pennsylvania, for instance, brought no additional wealth to this country. The competition of labor and capital soon brought down the profits of extracting the oil from the earth to a level with the profits in other enterprises, because the labor and capital profitably employed in the business must have first been taken from some other business. Wealth, according to our author, (p. 7) consists of every commodity which has an exchangeable value. But as he himself very correctly says on the same page, water, air, natural agents have no exchangeable value. Consequently petroleum oil has not. It is therefore not wealth. Neither is the gold of California to be classed as wealth. Only to the extent that labor and capital (and, as we contend, *human time*, also) enter into the value of petroleum, or gold, or wheat, or diamonds, or any other commodity, are they to be deemed wealth.* Leaving out augmentation of wealth from natural increase of population, and accessions from other countries of population or wealth, a nation therefore cannot increase its wealth except by savings. The rate of these savings is denoted by the average rate of interest, and is determined by education, national character, etc. Savings being the only "circumstance which tends to augment the wealth of a nation"—Mr. FAWCETT's proposition therefore stands thus:

* See Bastiat—Harmonics of Polit. Econ., chap. V., Of Value.

"Savings will induce increased saving," which we take the liberty to pronounce as somewhat too mystical for general comprehension. If the immigration from abroad, either of capital or persons, or the natural increase of population, are held to be inducements to "increased saving," we confess we are unable to comprehend why, and would much desire to know.

Of the two motives to which our author attributes national savings—foresight and desire for profit—we have a word to say. That savings is the result of foresight we admit; but to say that it results from "the desire for profit" is to say that it results from desire, because profit and savings in the sense used are synonyms. That savings is the result of desire is an expression which explains nothing. The desire of a Spaniard for profit is certainly equal to that of an Englishman; yet the people of England, composed nearly wholly of Englishmen, contrive to save and grow rich; while the people of Spain remain poor. Therefore we deny that desire has any thing to do with the matter, it being readily conceivable that an Englishman's desire for profit is fully equal to that of a Spaniard's, or a Yankee's to that of a Turk's, and *vice versa*. The author in another part of his book uses a more correct formula:

"It, therefore, appears that the amount of capital accumulated, *or in other words, the current rate of interest which prevails through an average of years*, may partly depend on national character."

He herein not only discards any mention of "desire for profit" but also incidentally establishes a proposition which we found occasion to use above, viz: that the rate of the accumulation of capital (or from an elevated point of view, all kinds of wealth) is denoted by the average rate of interest prevailing.

The Second Book of the volume is devoted to *Distribution*. The introductory chapters contain a brief survey of the various laws and customs which regulate the tenure of land in various countries and the schemes of philanthropists to render these tenures less irksome Then follows a chapter on the law of Ricardo, which determines the rent of land. These chapters are well written, and display an amount of forethought, care, and judicious selection of language and illustration, which not only give a high character to the work but relieve it of that monotonous and weary tone which is almost inseparable from scientific treaties on statical economy. The chapter on Wages is not so well conceived. Looking from an entirely too English point of view, and ignoring the effect of that freedom and that education which follows freedom, which is still withheld from the poorer classes in England, the author arrives at the dismal conclusion of Malthus, that England's population grows too fast, and if not thinned by emigration must be checked in its growth by preventitive legislation!

Let our author reject Malthus, and take up the works of another of his countrymen—a writer eminently more profound than Malthus—and he will learn in theory that which the history of the American people has verified in practice, viz.: that Liberty is the sole cure for all social disorders*—not Liberty absolutely, but the Utmost Liberty which the capacity of a people enables them to appreciate and enjoy.†

To give our readers an opportunity of comparing the condition of the free laborer of the United States, with no land tenures or local customs to tie him down to the soil or restrain him from doing what he pleases and going where he pleases, with that of the laborer of other countries, we shall quote a few stray paragraphs from the work before us:

"In England, land can be entailed and devised by will to an unborn child." (P. 117.)

"In France, the owner of land has no power to prevent his children sharing it equally upon his death." (P. 117.)

"In Europe, the land is chiefly the property of private individuals; whereas, in India, the bulk of the land is owned by the government." (P. 117.)

"In many parts of Italy, according to an invariable custom, metayee rents are paid—or, in other words, one-half the produce is given for the use of the land." (P. 118.)

"A great portion of the land of India is occupied, not by peasant proprietors, but by peasant cultivators. The land is generally owned by the government. The peasant cultivators often rent from the government a small portion of land, which they can cultivate with their own labor and capital. Sometimes the government grants the land at a fixed rental to individuals, who occupy the position of middlemen and who re-let the land to peasant cultivators. Land which is cultivated by slaves is in an anomalous position, for in this case it would appear that the whole produce is shared between rent and capital; since the slaves must be regarded as a portion of the slave-owners capital, just in the same manner as horses which plow our own soil are a portion of an English farmer's capital.

* Herbert Spencer. † Ibid.

The slaves do not receive any wages; they cannot accumulate wealth; they have none of the rights of property. The slaves are fed, it is true; but so are the horses fed.

It has been already stated that, in parts of the continent, the landlord uniformly receives as rent one-half the produce of the land—he never thinks of asking more or less, although his land might very likely yield him a larger income than if it was let to the tenant who might consent to pay the highest rent for it. In many professions the charges made are absolutely fixed by custom—lawyers and physicians do not adjust their charges like ordinary traders—the charges are regulated by the custom of the profession. Equally rigid customs affect many classes of laborers—artisans, in particular trades, must serve a fixed term of apprenticeship, and the wages received are often determined by customs which though, perhaps, not so rigidly observed as some others, yet are frequently not easily modified."

"A Dorsetshire laborer can seldom either read or write; he, therefore, has little or no information with regard to the wages paid in other districts. His ignorance magnifies the difficulties of removing to a distant part of the country and makes him disinclined to leave the locality to which he has been accustomed. Again: if he has a family, he is far too poor to pay the expense of conveying them to a comparatively distant place; for we have carefully ascertained the fact that an agricultural laborer has saved even a few shillings. Moreover, there is associated with our system of poor-relief a law of settlement which has often bound and fettered the laborer to the district in which he was born. No law has perhaps ever more grieveously oppressed a class. A man, by resorting to a place not far distant, may much improve his position—employment there might be much better, and he would therefore get higher wages; but the law of settlement often prevents him from availing himself of these advantages—he is not allowed to settle in another district, because it is feared that he or his family may some day become chargeable on the poor rate.

The combined influence of the causes just enumerated prevents laborers readily migrating from one district to another in order to avail themselves of the advantages which they will secure from a greater demand for their labor.

"The most intelligent of our workmen would freely leave the place in which they were employed, if they thought that by so doing their prospects would be improved: and as our agricultural laborers gradually become more intelligent, they will show an equal readiness to avail themselves of any advantage which might be offered to them by a more favorable state of the labor market in some other locality. The strong opposition which has been expressed to the law of the settlement has already caused it to be somewhat modified. The law is no doubt destined to be abolished: this will remove a restriction which has seriously impeded the laborer from offering his labor where he might consider it would meet with the best reward."

And see, generally, chaps. VI. and VII.

The chapter on Profits is exceedingly good. We, however, strenuously dissent from the following proposition:

"But, independently of any effects produced upon the accumulation of capital by these differences in the character and condition of various nations, it may be observed that the accumulation of capital is always influenced by the rate of profit. *If, for instance, the current rate of interest should be greatly increased in England*, an additional inducement would be offered to every one to save, and *the result would be strikingly exhibited by a greatly increased accumulation of capital.*"

According to our views, (the same which have always been held forth in this Journal,) the contrary effect would ensue. And so, indeed, admits our author in the paragraph which immediately follows the above, and which we cannot for the life of us succeed in reconciling with it; so that we must take it for what it appears to be—and that is, a flat contradiction of its predecessor—

"For, if in any particular year there should be some irregularity *which should cause a much larger capital to be saved than is customary*, the laborers would in consequence of this augmentation of capital receive higher wages, and the cost of their labor would thus be increased, *and the current rate of interest would fall*."

This comes on examining dynamical phenomena by statical laws; and, for a long time yet, the student of Political Economy must expect to remain the victim of this false method of treating the science.

The chapter on *Trades Unions and Strikes* is very interesting; so is the one that follows on *Co-operative Institutions*. The author ably traces the causes and effects of strikes—shows wherein they are injurious and wherein beneficial; when they have failed, and why and when they have succeeded, and why. He favors co-operative institutions, and traces their origin, history, and instances of success and failure, together with the cause which in each case produced the result that happened. With a few remarks on Slavery, this chapter closes the book, which, taking it for all in all, we may fairly term a valuable addition to Economical literature.

The Third and last Book of the volume is devoted to the subject of *Exchange*.

The opening chapters on Value and Price are cleverly written, but are much inferior to Bastiat's exposition of the same subject. A new element of value is introduced by Mr. FAWCETT, which he terms, "Difficulty of attainment"—as instanced in the case of the price for which a rare work of art will sell. The introduction of this element into Value we regard as superficial.

In treating of the function of Money, the writer very properly insists that "Money must possess an intrinsic value of its own." While not ignoring the advantages of credit and paper, when left free to establish themselves in public estimation, he nevertheless demands that the basis of all transactions wherein price is concerned should be the precious metals, which he deems to be the most suitable materials for money. His views on Foreign Commerce are happily summed up in these words, and we commend them to the attention of the reader—

"Man, we conceive, has an indefeasible right that the wealth which ministers to his wants and provides his enjoyments should be produced with as little labour as possible. This can only be secured by perfectly free commercial intercourse between all nations. The benefits conferred by foreign commerce are truly cosmopolitan: it brings men of every nation in contact, and thus becomes the most powerful agent of civilization. Foreign commerce removes the barriers between nations, and makes them one as far as their industrial economy is concerned. A rancarous enmity, combined with an ignorance of the true principles of trade, has for centuries opposed every possible obstacle to a trade between France and England. Many of our manufactured commodities were far superior to those possessed by the French; and they, on the other hand, had products which could not be grown on our own soil and under our climate. If the Straits of Dover were bridged over by a narrow strip of land, and the two countries formed one nation, it would seem inexpressibly absurd that those who lived in the north of the country should scarcely be permitted to taste the products which are grown in the south; and it would seem equally absurd that people in one part of the country should be compelled to manufacture certain commodities under the most unfavorable conditions, because they were not permitted to purchase these commodities in another part of the country, although there the quality would be better and the price cheaper. A restrictive policy which seems so unreasonable if two nations become one is not more defensible when the two nations are separated by a boundary, which is often merely artificial."

On the Rate of Interest, the author is singularly felicitous. The following paragraph, however, we consider unsound:

"If five per cent. was the current rate, instead of three per cent., there would be a greater inducement offered to every individual to save, and consequently a greater amount of capital saved. But, on the other hand, the demand to borrow capital varies inversely with the rate of interest; for there will be a greater demand to borrow when money can be obtained at three per cent. than when it is necessary to give five per cent."

The author herein appears to forget that the rate of interest in any country is the result of a certain condition of affairs, and that, therefore, were the rate of interest five per cent. instead of three per cent. in any particular country, the state of affairs in that country would also necessarily be different. With a different state of affairs the "inducements" for borrowing, lending, saving, etc., would vary in degree; consequently, any measurement between the state of affairs which exists at any particular time and a rate of interest which may exist at some other time is totally inadmissible.

Further on, the author very truly and aptly remarks concerning the obstacles which "patriotism" foolishly interposes between various countries to hinder the free flow of persons and capital between them—

"Patriotism has achieved many blessings for the human race, but it has isolated nations from each other and placed a barrier of prejudice between them."

The Fourth Book is devoted to the subject of *Taxation*. Some of the author's observations on this point are very good;

others seem to us to be written from too English a point of view. We, therefore, pass it over, and close the volume.

On the whole, we regard Mr. FAWCETT'S work as a valuable addition to the literature of Political Economy. Yet, works of this character should aim to be cosmopolitan rather than national, scientific rather than political ; and this is a desideratum which our author has not always kept in view. For instance, at the very beginning of the work, he says in the true John Bull tone :

"If any nation should ever threaten England with invasion, England ought to speak in unmistakeable language that *her vengeance* should not be confined to a retributive slaughter of soldiers, but that she would destroy all the public works upon which the wealth of the nation mainly depended. This will give a practical check to vaunting ambition, and might rouse a nation to restrain the military designs of the most despotic ruler."

Now, we submit, in all kindness for the author, that this fling at France—this cheap boasting of England's power—is entirely out of place in a work on Political Economy. It is enough to outweigh all the good qualities of the work, and condemn it at the outset. The increasing interest now generally displayed in Economical researches appeared to us a harbinger of that day when the barriers between nations would be dissolved ; for this is the inevitable tendency of a science which teaches that the interests of all mankind are harmonious. But, if a Professor of Political Economy in the University of Cambridge, and the author of a professedly scientific treatise on the subject, allows himself to display in print at this late day, the petty passions of a patriot—passions which alone have hitherto kept international interests from assimilating, the friends of progress, might well despair of any early realization of their dreams.

But, as Liebig has very truly observed. "He, who makes no mistakes, produces no masterpiece ;" we, therefore, pass over the blemishes in Mr. FAWCETT'S work in the contemplation of its many excellencies—and these, we think, are sufficient to render it a desirable addition to any scientific library.

* * * *

BOOK NOTICES.

Eight Years in Congress, from 1857 *to* 1865. By SAMUEL S. COX, of Ohio. New York: Appleton & Co., 1865.

This is a volume of 432 pp., filled with the best speeches of this keen and watchful statesman. The chief events of the late war, the current public measures which were planned while it lasted, the finances and tariff, the demands and threats of factions, are here presented to the reader in a graphic style which is all the author's. Mr. Cox is both trenchant and witty, genial and severe, quick and farseeing. During his career in Congress his lance was thrust at every man's breast, and every man's at his;—but none of these weapons were ever barbed with malice, nor, indeed, any ill-feeling at all. This never failing good humor and readiness of repartee, made him not only generally loved, but not a little feared. All this we find in his speeches—which we regard as an indispensable part of the history of these times.

General Statute Laws of the State of New-York concerning Insurance. By WILLIAM BARNES. Albany: Weed, Parsons, & Co.; 1865.

Mr. BARNES, the well known and much respected Superintendent of the Insurance Department for the State of New-York, has issued a new volume from the press concerning his department. This volume contains all the laws of the State relating to Insurance matters and is therefore a most useful one to a very large class of persons. Mr. BARNES' industry in publishing insurance data is worthy of note; for few public officers in these degenerate days care to exert themselves to serve the public farther than is required by the letter of the law. In addition to his annual reports, which are marvels of industry and research, Mr. BARNES has issued circulars containing the requirements of the law upon the subject of insurance, which cannot but prove very useful to the public. His bureau at Albany possesses an excellent library, which he is constantly enrichening. He omits to take no newspaper or periodical which devotes itself to the subject of insurance. In short his bureau is kept up as it ought to be.

Reverting to the volume before us, we only perceive one passage worthy of particular mention, and that occurs in the Laws of 1865, chap. 328, § 1. It runs as follows:

> "Any number of persons, not less than thirteen, may associate and form an incorporation or company for the purposes specified in either of the following departments: * * * * * * To make insurance upon * * * * * * *and also against any loss, damage, or liability arising from any unknown or contingent event whatever* which may be the subject of legal insurance, etc."

This noble provision of the law, rescuing as it does the entire subject of insurance from the toils of special legislation, and placing it in the list of General Acts, for which our State has become so justly distinguished, is due to the Superintendent's individual efforts ; and to him should be accorded the credit which flows from it.

Under this beneficent provision, an Insurance Company can be instituted for any lawful purpose without being obliged to go to the legislature for a special charter, and every one familiar with the slow progress of law in the direction of justice and wisdom, must acknowledge that this is a vast step in the right direction.

Lyrics of Life. By ROBERT BROWNING. Price 50 cents. Boston: Ticknor & Fields ; 1865.

This is one of a series of Companion Poets for the people, beautifully printed by the publishers, and expressly illustrated by Eytinge. It is scarcely necessary to say anything of ROBERT BROWNING'S genius ; so, without more ado, we at once commend this pretty volume to the reader.

De Bow's National Review.—The Editor of this Review, J. D. B. DE BOW, has acquired a national reputation as a Statistician and Public Economist, having been elected Professor of Political Economy and Statistics in the University of Louisiana, compiled the United States' Census of 1850, and edited several elaborate works upon American commerce and industry. He has also been at the head of his well-known Review for over twenty years, and has been elected an Honorary Member of the New-York, New-Orleans, Charleston, and Cincinnati Mercantile Societies.

Mr. DE BOW'S work, in the past, identified itself with the fortunes and career of the South, but, since the close of hostilities, he has accepted the amnesty of the President, announcing his purpose to make his Review entirely a NATIONAL WORK : and has located himself in New-York for that purpose. In his Circular, he says :—

"My purpose in the future is to give the REVIEW a NATIONAL CHARACTER, and to devote all of my energies and resources to the development of the great material interests of the Union—its Commerce, Agriculture, Manufectures, Internal Improvements, and General Industry.

"In addition to those important topics, the work will embrace discussions upon such great questions of legislation as affect the relation of the States, the permanency of the Union, and the HONOR AND PROSPERITY OF THE COUNTRY.

"Regarding the issues of the past as dead, about which a practical philosophy will not dispute, and those of the present as living and potential, it is the part of the REVIEW to accept in good faith the situation, and deduce from it all that can be promotive of the best interests of the whole Country."

Offices of the REVIEW are located in New-York, Washington City, Charleston, Nashville, and New-Orleans. The principal Office is at 40 Broadway, N. Y.

www.ingramcontent.com/pod-product-compliance
Lightning Source LLC
LaVergne TN
LVHW021139110826
845150LV00005B/1074

* 9 7 8 1 4 2 5 5 4 8 8 5 8 *